Play Direction

Play Direction

JOHN E. DIETRICH

Director of Theatre
Department of Speech
The Ohio State University

PRENTICE-HALL, INC.

Englewood Cliffs, N. J.

L.C. CAT. CARD NO.: 52-14043

First Printing .... March, 1953
Second Printing .... June, 1954
Third Printing .... May, 1955
Fourth Printing ...... April, 1957
Fifth Printing .... July, 1958
Sixth Printing .... June, 1959

PRINTED IN THE UNITED STATES OF AMERICA

68334

To
Lois and Lisa

Preface

This book is written for directors at all levels of attainment. For the beginner, it should open a fairly straight and reasonably clear path through the maze of controversies and contradictions that have grown up around the dramatic production process during its long history. For the advanced director, it should provide a basis for comparison, a method of evaluating his own procedures, and a clear-cut organizational pattern which may be helpful in teaching directing.

Predicated upon a point of view somewhat different from many of its predecessors, the book applies psychological as well as aesthetic principles to directing. The two never come into conflict. Psychology and aesthetics go hand in hand in producing the play. Psychology is brought into the foreground because it provides a definite basis and starting point for play production. Later, aesthetic principles are used to implement and evaluate the expression of the psychological forces.

A concern for the simple, concrete, and systematic should not appear dogmatic. No doubt valid questions and objections may be raised to certain of the principles discussed, for the possibility of error must be recognized by those whose thinking penetrates the surface. On the other hand, if each statement were to be qualified to include every conceivable exception, the trail would be sadly obscured. In hewing down the brush, I may well have cut some flowers. In areas where moot questions clearly exist, both sides of the argument have been weighed carefully.

The book is divided into four parts. The beginning director who wishes to study in a logical order from the philosophy to the execution should begin with Part One, "The Bases of Play Direction." The director who has sufficient background to understand what he is trying to do may decide to begin with a study of the technical principles that confuse him. They are found in Part Two, "The

Principles of Play Direction." The director who finds that he must direct a play tomorrow may begin with the practical procedures of production referring to the principles and bases as they are needed. He should begin with Part Three, "The Procedures of Play Direction." Part Four, "The Problems of Play Directing," deals with many of the basic problems to be solved by every director and offers some special help for the director who is producing a play of a particular type. Thus, some directors may even begin at the back and work forward.

It is impossible to give specific credit to all who have helped make this book possible. First, there are the professional and non-professional directors from whom I had an opportunity to learn while posing as an actor; second, there are the teachers and colleagues who have stimulated my thinking throughout the years; finally and most important of all, there are the students who, in their eagerness to learn, helped me learn. For those who can be singled out, I am particularly indebted to Mr. Max Lyon, without whose initial push this book might never have been started; to Professor Samuel M. Marks of Purdue University, who not only did the drawings for the book but also offered many helpful criticisms; to Professors Gladys L. Borchers, H. L. Ewbank, and A. T. Weaver, whose friendly consultations made the task seem easier; and finally, to Lois Dietrich, my wife, without whose editorial assistance this book would never have been completed.

JOHN E. DIETRICH

Contents

PART ONE

THE BASES OF PLAY DIRECTION 1

1. INTRODUCTION 3

What Is Drama? • The Bases of Play Direction • The Principles of
Play Direction • The Procedures of Play Direction • The Problems
of Play Direction

2. DRAMA AND HUMAN CONFLICT 6

The Law of the Drama • Human Conduct: The Source Book of
Drama • Action: The Framework of Drama • Motivation: The
Basis of Action • The Motivational Complex • Summary of Mo-
tivation

3. DRAMA AND THE PLAYWRIGHT 23

The Illusion of Reality or Unreality • The Materials of the Playwright • The Tools of the Playwright • The Process of the Playwright • Play Structure • The Five Parts of a Play • The Director
and Play Structure

4. DRAMA AND THE AUDIENCE 37

Why Do People Go to the Theatre? • What Is a Theatre Audience?
• Psychological Factors Influencing the Theatre Patron • Building
a Theatre Audience • Desirable Responses in the Theatre

5. DRAMA AND THE DIRECTOR 54

The Rise of the Director • The Place of the Director • The Responsibilities of the Director • How Much Direction? • The Qualifications of the Superior Director

ix

PART TWO

THE PRINCIPLES OF PLAY DIRECTION   69

6. THE MOTIVATIONAL UNIT   71

The Characteristics of the Motivational Unit • Types of Motivational Units • Analysis of the Motivational Unit • Directing the Motivational Unit • Dangers in the Unit Method • Sample Analysis of Motivational Units in Henrik Ibsen's A DOLL'S HOUSE

7. STAGE COMPOSITION   91

Motivational Aspects of Composition • Technical Aspects of Composition • The Playing Area • Pictorial Aspects of Composition • Control of Attention • Geometric Arrangements • Other Factors of Dominance • The Relative Strength of Compositional Factors

8. STAGE MOVEMENT   119

The Principles of Movement • Should There Be Movement? • The Characteristics of Movement • Summary of General Principles of Stage Movement • Specific Techniques in Stage Movement • Summary of the Technical Principles of Stage Movement

9. STAGE BUSINESS   143

Types of Stage Business • Creating and Projecting Stage Business • Technical Problems in Handling Business

10. EMOTION AND KEY   158

Definition of Conventionalized Emotion • Sources of Emotional Key • The Characteristics of Emotional Tension • Principles for Controlling Key

11. TEMPO   173

The Stage Use of Tempo • Characteristics of Good and Fast Tempo • General Considerations in Determining Tempo • Techniques for Gaining Variety

PART THREE

THE PROCEDURES OF PLAY DIRECTION 187

12. PLAY SELECTION 189

Determining Theatrical Worth • Practical Problems in Play Selection • Choosing a Season of Plays • Sources of Plays

13. INTERPRETING THE SCRIPT 200

The Purpose of the Play • The Five Readings • Planning the Production • The Prompt Book

14. TRYOUTS 214

Criteria of the Tryout • Pre-Tryout Organization • Tryout Procedures • Special Tryout Techniques • Seasonal Auditions Versus Individual Play Tryouts

15. CASTING 227

The Range of the Role • Judging the Actor • Determining the Actor's Range • Casting the Individual Actor • Casting the Ensemble • Special Casting Problems

16. REHEARSAL 242

Planning Rehearsals • Rehearsal Schedule • A Rehearsal Plan • The Interpretation Rehearsals • The Blocking Rehearsals • The Polishing Rehearsals • The Mounting Rehearsals

17. PERFORMANCE 264

The Responsibilities of the Director • Evaluating the Performance • Making Changes in Succeeding Performances • Special Performance Problems

PART FOUR

PROBLEMS IN PLAY DIRECTION 285

18. HANDLING THE ACTOR 287

The Relationship of the Director and the Actor • Kinds of Actors • Common Faults in Acting • Criticizing the Actor

19. FLOOR PLANS AND SETTINGS   305

The Stage • General Requirements of a Good Setting • Planning the Setting • Planning the Parts of the Setting • Planning the Furniture Arrangement • The Floor or Ground Plan

20. CROWD AND GROUP SCENES   329

The Make-up of the Crowd • General Problems in Crowd Scenes • Technical Problems in Staging the Crowd • The Group Unit System • Special Types of Crowd or Group Scenes

21. THE MUSICAL SHOW   347

Tryouts and Casting • Planning the Musical • Rehearsing the Musical • Organizing the Musical Cast • Technical Aspects of Musical Production • Dialogue in the Musical • Composition and Movement

22. CENTRAL STAGING   372

The Advantages of Central Staging • Problems of Central Staging • Play Selection for the Central Stage • Principles of Direction • Technical Problems in Central Staging

23. STYLES OF PRODUCTION   394

Presentation and Representation • Realistic Styles • Departures from Realism • Non-real Styles of Production

24. PERIOD DRAMA   408

Selecting the Period Play • Adapting and Producing the Period Play • Modern Dress

25. COMEDY   420

What Provokes Laughter? • The Comic Attitude • Criteria for Classifying Comedy • Types of Comedy • Mixtures of Comic Styles • Technique in Comedy

APPENDIX   443

Selected Bibliography • Director's Glossary

INDEX   469

Part One

The Bases
of Play Direction

I

Introduction

PLAY DIRECTION is an art and a craft. Ideally, the art and the craft should be blended so thoroughly that the result is a finely molded thing of beauty—a dramatic production. However, before the director can practice his art or his craft, he must understand the medium in which he works. He must have assimilated the principles that control the manner of his artistic expression. He must know the procedures to be followed from conception to completion. These are the subjects with which this volume deals.

WHAT IS DRAMA?

One of the simplest definitions of drama is Aristotle's, "an imitation of an action," which goes one step beyond "a doing," the meaning of the Greek word from which our term, drama, is derived. A definition that includes all of the main points of agreement may be synthesized from the classical and contemporary elaborations of these first definitions. Such a definition might read: DRAMA IS A STORY, IN DIALOGUE FORM, OF HUMAN CONFLICT, PROJECTED BY MEANS OF SPEECH AND ACTION FROM A STAGE TO AN AUDIENCE. The core elements in the definition define and delimit the director's medium. They prescribe the bases, the principles, the procedures, and even the problems of play direction.

3

THE BASES OF PLAY DIRECTION

Drama is, first of all, the story of *human conflict;* therefore, for the director to understand his medium and project its meanings, he must delve beneath the surface values of the play and study the human being. The director cannot perceive the depth and vibrance of the drama until he understands the when, why, and how of human response.

Drama is also a *story in dialogue form.* Drama is more than a representation of life. It is an art form. The playwright limits and controls his imaginative flight within a well-defined dramatic structure. He molds and shapes human action into an artistic pattern. The director, therefore, must go beyond the study of human conduct and examine and understand not only the playwright's meaning but also his tools, principles, and procedures.

Drama is *projected to an audience.* Drama depends upon communication. The production that does not communicate the playwright's meaning and, in turn, arouse emotional responses in the audience is a meaningless exercise. Therefore, the director must understand why the audience gathers, what the audience is, and how the audience responds.

Drama is interpreted by the *director.* Who is he? What are his qualifications and responsibilities? He is the creative and interpretative artist who coordinates and directs the *story of human conflict for the audience.* Every director must understand the scope and limitations of his job.

THE PRINCIPLES OF PLAY DIRECTION

Only after the director understands his medium and his job may he turn to the principles that determine the manner in which his art can be communicated. His task is to project the story of human conflict to the audience *by means of speech and action from a stage.*

The director must understand the strengths and weaknesses of the platform on which he works. Whether the stage is a lighted box or a free and open playing circle, projection of dramatic values depends upon a thorough technical knowledge of what can or cannot be done. The director must choose the visual and vocal means of projecting the story to the audience. After he finds the working unit, he may apply the principles of communication. He arranges his characters, moves them about, provides them with things to do, selects and intensifies the emotional expression, and determines the time relationships. In more technical terminology, he applies the principles of *composition, movement, business, emotion and key,* and *tempo.* Used wisely, these principles can communicate the meaning of the play.

THE PROCEDURES OF PLAY DIRECTION

The procedures of directing define the path that the director follows. Without a clear understanding of the bases and principles, procedure is largely meaningless. But even with this knowledge, unless he understands and applies a systematic process, the director may tumble into any one of the pitfalls of procedure. He must *select the play, interpret the script, conduct the tryouts, cast the production, rehearse the play* and finally *evaluate the performances.* Each step in the procedure must be handled efficiently.

THE PROBLEMS OF PLAY DIRECTION

Assuming a thorough knowledge of the bases, principles, and procedures of play directing, one might infer that the task is complete; however, there are many kinds and styles of plays and productions. In addition, there are problems that, although general in nature, may ruin a production if they are not handled effectively. Every director must understand the actor. The floor plans and settings can help or hinder a production. Crowds, when the playwright includes them, create special problems for the director.

Either because of changes in the style or complexity of the production or a change in the stage itself, the director has other problems to solve. He should know how to produce the musical show, how to work on the central stage. He should appreciate the advantages of different production styles. He should recognize the specific problems of period drama. Above all, he must be prepared to cope with the special problems imposed by comedy.

Directing is an art and a craft. Craftsmanship can be taught. Artistic sensitivity and awareness can be stimulated. It is hoped that this book may serve both masters.

2

Drama and Human Conflict

EXAMINE THE HEADLINES of your morning paper. The subjects: birth and death, marriage and divorce, crime and punishment, war and peace. The themes: courage and cowardice, faith and treachery, greed and generosity. The emotions: anger, love, hate, joy, grief, and fear. Each is the story of the beginning, the progress, or the conclusion of some act of human struggle. This is the stuff of which drama is made.

Even without the assurance of the psychologists, every human knows that conflict is dramatic and compelling. In ancient Rome, thousands of spectators poured into the Colosseum to witness the combat of the gladiators. During the French Revolution, thousands fought for a point of vantage near the guillotine. In merry England, thousands clamored for the chance to observe the burning of the witches. In modern America, hundreds jam the courtroom of a murder trial, thousands brave the elements to pack the football stadiums, millions sit glued to radio loudspeakers, squint at television screens, pack the legitimate and motion picture theatres. Why? The answer is always the same. That which depicts human conflict will command attention and interest.

THE LAW OF THE DRAMA

This interest in conflict is the basis of drama. During the last half of the nineteenth century, Ferdinand Brunetière, the great French dramatic critic, evolved this concept into a "law of the drama." In essence, Brunetière maintained that the play must em-

6

body the assertion of a human will against strenuous opposition of one kind or another. In other words, drama is based upon the clash of contending human desires.

In the play as in the newspaper, the subject, theme, locale, characters, and emotions may change, but the conflict of opposing human forces is almost always present. The play may depict the conflict of man against man, as in *Macbeth,* or man against himself, as in *Death of a Salesman,* or man against his environment, as in *Awake and Sing,* or man against society, as in *An Enemy of the People,* or man against nature, as in *Yellow Jack.* In most cases the environment, the society, nature, even man's opposing self is embodied in the form of other men who stand as obstacles in the path of accomplishment.

Plays are rooted in human struggle. They concern the wants, needs, desires, wishes of human beings. Even more important, the play is the story of conflicting wants, conflicting needs, conflicting desires, conflicting wishes. In its barest form, the play is the story of a protagonist who *wants* something and an antagonist who opposes the fulfillment of the want. The clash of these opposing forces results in dramatic action.

HUMAN CONDUCT: THE SOURCE BOOK OF DRAMA

Since the human being and his actions lie at the core of drama, the ideal starting point for the playwright, the actor, and the director is the study of human conduct. The playwright must understand the why and the wherefore of man's response if he is to create a credible and meaningful picture of human action. Similarly, the actor cannot create a living character without a knowledge of the forces that cause man to react as he does. And above all, the director must be a student of human conduct, for he is responsible for interpreting the dramatic action of the playwright through his agent the living actor, for and before a reacting human audience.

The form of the play matters little. Be it realism, fantasy, naturalism, expressionism, the core of drama is still the human being. Exaggeration or distortion of the natural human response found in plays of a non-real nature can be communicated to an audience only to the extent that the exaggerations and distortions can be compared with logical, normal, real, anticipated conduct. The only criterion by which the spectator can judge the distortion is the real or normal activity which he has experienced. Therefore, regardless of the style or form used in the production, the foundation must be human conduct, for human conduct is the base from which all drama real or unreal must arise.

ACTION: THE FRAMEWORK OF DRAMA

Conflict is expressed in action. It may be covert or unobservable action, such as the inner struggle which may engross a man when he is weighing the possible results of a particular deed, or it may be overt action, action which can be seen, as when one man strikes another man.

Drama needs overt action. After all, the audience can judge and assign meaning only to actions that can be seen and heard. Inner struggle has no meaning until it is translated into some sort of observable action. For example, a man waiting anxiously in a railroad station may, in life, give no sign of the turbulence of the emotion within him. On the stage, this emotion must be translated into overt action. The man must release his inner tensions through outward activity. He may glance at his watch, fidget in his seat, pace before the gate.

The playwright is aware of the importance of action in drama. He knows that action holds attention and creates excitement. For this reason, rather than having his characters tell the audience about the action, he has the players act out the struggle on the stage. Many weak plays have a lack of dramatic action as their basic fault. In these plays the characters tell the story of conflict and crisis which has occurred at some point far distant from the stage. Such plays will lack the excitement engendered when the spectator can see and hear and participate in the struggles of the characters. Fighting a duel, waiting for a lover's return, crushing an offending letter, retreating before an overpowering force, dying in the throes of agony can be seen and experienced by the spectator. Such actions supplant hundreds of words, for action is the framework of drama.

MOTIVATION: THE BASIS OF ACTION

Even more important than the action itself is the reason for the action. The action is the end product of human conduct. The forces that cause the action excite the audience and make the action believable.

The newspaper headline that proclaims, WOMAN COMMITS SUICIDE, tells of an exciting action. It is compelling in and of itself, but the reader wants to know more. Why did the woman take her own life? How did it happen? What are the results of the action? The drama is the tale of the background of the climactic action stated in the headline. It traces in an exciting fashion the interplay of the forces that ultimately drove the woman to suicide.

The headline above might stand as the final statement of many different plays. For example, *Hedda Gabler* and *The Second Mrs. Tanqueray* both end in suicide. The final action is identical, yet the plays are radically different. Why? Because a play is the story of the struggle and conflict that caused the final action. In other words, the play is the story of the reasons for a climactic action. These reasons or forces are the springs of action and are called *the motivation*.

The playwright, the director, and the actor must understand the motivating forces in human life that cause man to act. Every action has an underlying motivation. The motivation to act lies in the wishes, needs, desires of the human. When these wishes are opposed by other wishes, needs, and desires, when obstacles stand in the path of the normal resolution of the wish, a disequilibrium, resulting in conflict, occurs.

When we see a youngster running down the street, the action means little until we ascertain the reason for the action. Is he running because he wants to get rid of excess energy? Is he running because he sees his father is home from work? Is he running because he has been frightened by a vicious dog? Is he running because his sister is drowning in the river? In every case, the spectator must know WHY? The reason or motivation behind the action is the factor that makes the action dramatic. In the first two instances, there is no conflict and, thus, little that is dramatic. In the third and fourth instances, conflict is involved, and the explanation will transfix the attention of the spectator.

Motivation Defined

Motivation may be explained as *the sum total of the dynamic forces that cause a human to respond.* These forces govern every action of the human being at any given moment.

Motivation is frequently called "the springs of action," for the motivating factors have a distinctly dynamic quality. In this sense, they are not only the reasons for but also the causes of all action. Man acts only when the reasons for action are greater than the reasons for inaction. Whenever a man reacts, it is because the forces in the motivating pattern are great enough to bring about a response.

Motivation can arise from several sources. First, it may stem from the basic human drives. Second, it may arise from the situation in which a man finds himself. Third, it may be derived from social interaction, that is, the stimulus provided by contact with other men. Fourth and finally, the action may be motivated by the character pattern of the person involved.

Let us define motivation by examining some simple human actions and determining the reasons for and the causes of the action. All of the motivational factors need not be present in equal force, as will be seen in the following illustration. Suppose the dramatic action is described as follows:

"A young man cowers against the wall of a
building. It is a windy winter night."

The dramatic action: cowering against a building. What motivational factors determine the action?

1. *The basic drive:* desire for security and self-protection from the cold
2. *The physical situation:* the cold of the winter night
3. *The character complex:* a frightened, sickly, stupid, young man

Note how each of these factors not only determines the action as a whole but also prescribes the specific characteristics of the action. If the spectator is to appreciate the action, he must be made aware of all of the forces that dictate it. To appreciate the full significance of the "cowering," we must know that the man is protecting himself from the wintry blasts. We must know what kind of a young man he is. All of this can be read from the action itself only if the action reflects the motivational pattern causing it.

Now let us change the motivational pattern. Though the action will, in a total sense, remain the same, the specific characteristics of the action will change with the change in the motivational pattern:

> "A young man cowers against the wall of a build-
> ing. It is a windy winter night. A man with a
> gun approaches stealthily."

The dramatic action: cowering against a building. What are the motivational forces that determine the action?

1. *The basic drive:* desire for security and self-protection from the man with the gun
2. *The physical situation:* the darkness providing security
3. *The character pattern:* a frightened, sickly, stupid, young man

The dramatic action in each case is "cowering." However, the specific action in the two situations should be quite different. A man does not "cower from wintry blasts" in the same way that he "cowers from a gunman." In each case, the action is determined in every detail by the motivational pattern. If the audience is to recognize the action and assign the correct meaning to it, the audience must be made aware of the characteristics of the motivational complex.

Each of the preceding illustrations has involved human conflict. n one case, the young man is in conflict with the elements. In the ther, he is in conflict with another man. In each case the situation is dramatic because of the conflict involved.

A simple formula may help to illustrate the relationship of the key elements in drama: *motivation, action* and *conflict.*

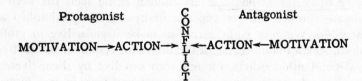

Since drama is the story of opposing forces, we may assume that the protagonist is motivated to a particular action. The antagonist is motivated to an opposing action. When these actions clash, there is conflict. In each case the specific determinants of the action are discovered in the motivation. Therefore, the key to drama lies in the knowledge of human motivation.

THE MOTIVATIONAL COMPLEX

In the preceding section, the four basic motivational forces were mentioned. If the director is to understand the role of motivation in drama, these key factors must be considered in some detail.

The Basic Drives

Psychologists have long recognized that much of man's activity can be directly related to his attempt to satisfy his fundamental needs. These basic urges have been labelled instincts, motives, drives, forces, wishes, prepotent reflexes, sentiments. Controversies have raged concerning whether they are inherited or acquired. Fortunately, there is little significance in the name or their origin. The important point is that man's action is controlled by these basic wants. For the purposes of this discussion we will call these forces basic drives; *basic* because they are fundamental to most of our life action, *drives* because they are dynamic and thereby tend to control and direct our actions.

The different lists of the basic drives are as numerous as the names applied to them. Some psychologists maintain that man has as many as twenty-five to thirty basic drives; others have simplified the list to three or four. Fortunately, there is a great deal of uniformity in the lists of drives. One of the most widely accepted classifications is that set down by W. I. Thomas in *The Unadjusted Girl*. This list includes the human drives for response, recognition, adventure, and security.

The drive for response. Every human being feels the need for intimate contact with others, the desire for companionship and fellowship. We join clubs, strive to make friends, live in groups, indeed, seek a mate because of the desire for response. In our living we depend upon others, for few men can live by themselves. Although the desire for response is an important force in each human's daily existence, it is usually limited to romance and love in the drama. The classic comic playwriting formula of boy meets girl, boy loses girl, boy gets girl is largely based upon the protagonist's fight for response. Conflict arises when the human need for response is denied.

2. *The drive for recognition.* The urge to gain fame, influence, authority, renown, indeed any action that gains deference from others and expands our own egos may be traced to the desire for recognition. This drive is frequently used by the playwright, for the exploitation of the drive is laden with the potentials of conflict. In play after play the hero is driven by a desire to increase his reputation or his power or his fame. Frequently, this drive is exemplified in the contests in business and politics for a more powerful position, in the social struggles to be more cultured, more affluent, more highly respected than our neighbors.

3. *The drive for adventure.* We have the urge for new and thrilling experiences, the force that urges us to try the dangerous thing. It is the adventurous spirit that causes us to take trips, climb mountains, race automobiles, stunt airplanes. Anything new and different or with the thrill of danger will satisfy the urge for adventure.

This drive is basic to much drama, for drama frequents the realm of the thrills and excitement found in adventure. The hero in many romantic plays is driven to engage in exciting activities by a compulsion for new experiences.

4. *The drive for security.* The desire to cling to the safe way, the fight for the preservation of life and limb, of home and family, of state and nation are all results of the drive for security. The desire for security is in a sense antithetic to the drive for adventure. We desire the thrill of the new, but at the same time we will fight to preserve the old. In most men there is an uneasy equilibruim between the two wants. Many great dramas are built upon the conflict of the two urges. In one case, the new ideas and new forces are in action. In the other, the old ideas and old ways rebel against the possibility of change. The playwright embodies these opposing drives in the actions of men. Violent conflict is the result.

As a matter of fact, the basic drives are much more clear in drama than they are in life. The characters of the play are for the most part prototypes. They have been simplified. Their drives stand out in sharp relief as reasons for their acts.

The Situation

The second source of motivation is found in the situation. The situation may be defined as the pattern of circumstances affecting behavior at a given moment. Two aspects of situation may cause action and direct its course: the physical situation and the social situation.

The physical situation. Locale is an obvious determinant of action. A soldier writing a nightly letter to his wife from a foxhole will, by virtue of his physical surroundings, approach the process in a way different from that of a businessman writing to his wife from a hotel room. In the case of the soldier, the foxhole, perhaps rain and mud, poor light, inadequate writing instruments, no table or chair will "set the stage" and motivate specific kinds of action. Similarly, the businessman writing home from his hotel room will be motivated by a different set of physical factors.

The playwright, who is aware of the significance of the motivation arising from the physical situation, places his characters in surroundings that logically motivate activity most helpful in expressing the desired ideas and emotions.

The social situation. Societal factors, as differentiated from the physical surroundings, also have a direct bearing upon the course of action. Societal pressure is a powerful force in determining how the individual will respond. Most men are extremely sensitive to "what is expected of them." The traditions, customs, and mores of society make up a strongly motivated code of action. For example, a man conducts himself differently in church than he does at a carnival. The difference in activity is the result of the different social pressures which dictate conduct in the two places.

If the spectator is to accept the actions of the play, the characters must reflect the motivation in the social situation. Frequently, audiences are confused because the characters do not seem to respond in terms of the societal code represented in the play.

Many times the basic conflict of a play may be derived from a character's deliberate refusal to abide by the rules of the social situation. Antisocial action in life and on the stage has the same result. It brings to bear the full power of an aroused community. The man who desecrates a sacred object brings down upon his head the wrath of those who revere the object. Complete evaluation of all the elements in the social situation will reveal the cause of much of the action in drama.

Social Interaction

Whenever two persons come into direct social contact, that is, become aware of and respond to each other, social interaction begins. The characteristics of interaction are extremely simple. The first person motivates the action of the second person, who, by responding in a particular way, in turn motivates the reaction of the first person, and so on.

Expressed in psychological terms, a circular response is developed. The stimulus provided by the first person causes a reaction. That reaction, in turn, acts as a stimulus to the original speaker. This concept may be expressed graphically in two different ways. In A, Figure 1, the circular process is indicated. In B, the chain effect of continued interaction may be seen. This chain reaction is called a serial response.

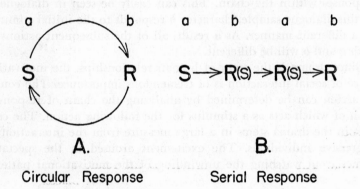

A.	**B.**
Circular Response	Serial Response

FIG. 1. SOCIAL INTERACTION

The key to the understanding of the circular response and subsequent interaction is the realization that the *response* has the power to act as a *stimulus*.

To illustrate: Two boys meet on the street corner. (They are symbolized in Figure 1 by the small letters at the top of the drawing.)

CHARACTER *a:* Go Home!	*Stimulus*	S
1.) CHARACTER *b:* I won't!	*Response (stimulus)*	*R(S)*

　　CHARACTER *a:* Oh, yes you will!　　*Response (stimulus)*　R(S)
　　CHARACTER *b:* Make me!　　　　　*Response*　　　　　　R

The same boys on the same street corner.

　　CHARACTER *a:* Go Home!
2.)　CHARACTER *b:* Sure, let's go!
　　CHARACTER *a:* O.K.
　　CHARACTER *b:* I'll race you.

Examine each of the dialogue units with care. The characters and situations are identical. In dialogue 1, character *a* has stimulated character *b*. *Character b's response acts as a stimulus which motivates the next action of character a.* Such a chain or series can continue indefinitely with each new response acting as a stimulus until the chain is broken or a balance is regained or the aggressor gains his end.

The course of the interaction will be determined by the specific responses within the chain. This can easily be seen in dialogue 2. In this dialogue sample, character *b* responds to the initial stimulus in a different manner. As a result, all of the subsequent actions of both *a* and *b* will be different.

Since drama is the story of human relationships, the motivating force of social interaction is of tremendous importance. The course of action can be determined by analyzing the chain of responses, each of which acts as a stimulus for the following action. The conflict in the drama stems in a large measure from the interaction of aggressive individuals. The excitement aroused in the spectator comes from watching the unwinding of the motivational pattern.

The Character Complex

The specific reaction of any human being to motivation arising from the basic drives, the situation, and social interaction will be determined by the particular characteristics of the individual. This complex of characteristics, known as the character or personality, is evidenced by a specific pattern of reactions. Some of these qualities are native, some acquired. Regardless of their origin, the individual tends to respond in a so-called characteristic manner because of a specific blend of these physiological, psychological, and cultural attributes.

These characteristics act as motivating forces in some situations and, in others, as limiting factors that determine the type of action in which the individual will engage.

Let us assume that a large and brawny man says, "COME HERE!" and points to a spot directly in front of him. The response of each individual will differ, depending upon the factors involved in his personal character complex. A young, courageous, physically dynamic chap may respond to such a command with immediate physical aggressiveness. The stimulus of the command may motivate him to display his own physical prowess. In such a case, the young fellow's physical characteristics may motivate the action. Another temperamentally less courageous person may spring into flight at the command. A third may comply. A fourth may stand his ground and argue. But in every case the action or response to the stimulus will be determined by the characteristic traits of the individual. Thus, a knowledge of the factors in each man's character complex is essential in the determination of the reason for his actions.

The following list of human attributes will help the director, the actor, and the playwright define human personality. The divisions of the following list are not all inclusive and mutually exclusive. Some characteristics can be traced to more than one category.

The traits and characteristics may have a dynamic quality. They are frequently predispositions to specific action, the quality and amount of which will depend upon the nature of the stimulus and the characteristic.

The constitutional attributes. Such qualities as health or sickness, strength or weakness, youth or age, beauty or ugliness, largeness or smallness, determine the type and quality of reaction. In a like manner, the acuity of the senses, such as the ability to see and hear and, in a lesser degree, the ability to taste, smell, and feel, affect reaction. Even the ability to move and speak determines the response of an individual to a stimulus.

The individual is not usually aware of the operation of these constitutional attributes unless the responses are extreme variations from the normal. A little analysis will show that almost every action in everyday living is at least in part the result of our physical make-up.

In the drama, the physical characteristics take on added value and meaning. The characters in a play are set up before an audience to be examined, judged, and responded to. The playwright uses constitutional differences to help differentiate his characters. Since stage characters are simplifications, they tend to respond clearly in the manner dictated by their physical attributes. The aged, the crippled, the ugly, the deformed reflect their physical make-up in thought and deed to a far greater extent than will their real-life counterparts. Almost every stage character will have distinctive physical attributes, idiosyncrasies, or peculiarities that forcibly limit or control his reactions to stimuli. Thus, the constitutional aspects of character must be considered a part of the over-all motivational pattern.

The intellectual attributes. These attributes also qualify, direct, or limit the potentialities of reaction. The dull and stupid respond to varying stimuli in a manner far different from that of the quick and bright. The man with imagination, efficient capabilities of perceiving, a good memory, and maturity of judgment responds differently from the man with lesser intellectual qualifications.

In the drama, the intellectual factors in character are less frequently used by the playwright because these qualities are harder to reduce to visible and audible action. However, the extremes of intellectual differences are used upon the stage. The comedies of the world are laden with fools and oafs whose poor judgment, lack of imagination, and inability to perceive cause them to respond in a manner judged as comic by the spectator not afflicted with these intellectual defects.

In an occasional play, extreme intellectual deficiency may be used as an almost complete motivational base for response. Lenny, in Steinbeck's *Of Mice and Men,* is such a character. His lack of intellect is the base upon which this powerful play is built.

The emotional attributes. One of the prime attributes of character may be defined as the emotional stability, the moods, the attitudes evidenced by the character in his response to stimuli. The emotionally excitable person's reaction differs from that of the phlegmatic. The moods and emotionalized attitudes of a person reflect differences in emotional stability. We speak of our next door neighbor as being a taciturn, irascible man or a happy-go-lucky, hail-fellow-well-met sort of person. These are generalized definitions of his temperament, his emotional attributes.

Obviously, the emotional characteristics of each person will shape his reaction in almost any situation. These qualities have special importance in the drama, for the play is primarily an expression of emotional conflict. The playwright frequently differentiates his characters on an emotional basis. These differences manifest themselves in the character's mode of reaction to both external and internal motivation. Indeed, in most dramatic characters, the emotional potentialities of the character are used by the playwright as powerful motivating factors controlling his actions.

Crimes of passion, for example, would be impossible without a particular emotional make-up that facilitates rather than limits the action. Much of the conflict in drama would be nonexistent if the characters who peopled the plays were phlegmatic or emotionally stable individuals.

The expressive attributes. These attributes represent the amount and kind of expression that result from the basic drives. In many ways they are a reflection of the physical, intellectual, and emotional qualities of character combined in an expression of the basic drive. The terms *loyal, ambitious, proud, creative, curious, acquisitive, destructive,* and the like describe the individual reaction caused by the basic drives. It is true that these reactions to the basic drives may differ because of other human characteristics, but, at the same time, they stand by themselves as a particular type of responsiveness which limits and directs the action caused by the drives.

In drama, the expressive attributes cause or control much of the action. The characters in a play manifest particular qualities because of the drives urging them on. The way the individual responds to the drive is controlled in part by the expressive qualities of the individual. Two men may be driven by a desire for security. One may be considered an ambitious man, the other a greedy man. The particular manner in which the drive is made manifest not only affects the reaction of others but is a directive force in the man's own actions.

In a less dynamic sense, certain other expressive attributes are present. The terms *slovenly, punctilious, callous, serene,* and the like describe individual character traits. While these traits also indicate the response or the lack of response to the basic drives, they suggest a less energetic state than the preceding group. At the same time, it is obvious that they are determinants of the kind and quality of action that results from stimulation.

The expressive attributes are frequently called character traits. They are actually society's judgments of the individual's responses. Since society approves of certain traits and disapproves of others, the expressive attributes act as powerful causes of and limitations to specific conduct.

The cultural attributes. Individual characteristics that result from the background of the individual are called cultural attributes. Customs, traditions, mores, more specifically social class, educational advantage, social refinement, occupation, or profession—all act as powerful factors in limiting or controlling the actions of the individual. The response of a young man who has been trained from birth to accept a particular code of action will be different from that of the young man who has had no such training. In the life situation the cultural attributes of character stemming from our backgrounds affect our daily lives. This is particularly true if we find ourselves in a social situation depending upon cultural training which has been denied us.

This difference in social background and the attendant differences in reaction are often used by the playwright to provide major interest and conflict. For example, George Bernard Shaw comments upon the superficialities of the cultural differences in *Pygmalion*.

In actuality, the number of different character complexes is as great as the number of individual human beings. No two character complexes can be alike, for no two people have identical attributes. This statement may be easily confirmed by tracing the individual elements that make up your own character and comparing them with the character complex of any other person. To carry the idea further, imagine a stimulus and consider the specific way that you would respond to it on the basis of your own character traits. Imagine or watch a friend's response to the same stimulus. Because of the particular characteristics of the person in each case, the response will be peculiar to the individual who is responding.

SUMMARY OF MOTIVATION

In life and in drama, the study of the human being resolves itself into an evaluation of the motivation that provokes action. Whenever there is an equilibrium or a balance of forces in man's life, he does not act. When the motivational forces are strong enough to overcome the basic inertia, action results.

For example, I sit at ease in my comfortable living room, presumably without a trouble or wish in the world. Such a state of complete equilibrium can last only a short period unless I go to sleep. Let us suppose that I notice a package of cigarettes on the opposite side of the room. They act as a stimulus. I begin to want a cigarette. Soon my equilibrium has been upset by the motivating desire. I reach into my pocket. This is my first action. No cigarettes. I lapse back into inertia, as the desire is not great enough to force me to cross the room. Soon the desire for a cigarette increases, and the motivational forces become powerful enough to get me to rise, cross the room, get the cigarette, look for a match, recross the room, sit down, and light it. The desire has been fulfilled. The motivational forces have been satisfied. For the moment, an equilibrium has again been reached.

In the preceding simple example, all of the sources of motivation have been working. First, I felt the need for a cigarette. Psychologically or physiologically a disequilibrium arose and set off the basic drive of security. I moved in order to regain my physical sense of well being. The physical situation motivated the action in that the cigarette was not at hand. The social situation, though not very important in this instance, helped direct the action. My character complex will determine the manner of my performing the action. In other words, by tracing the action to its motivational base, every aspect of the action can be understood.

Exactly the same process will be in operation, whether I am in conflict with myself over the exertion of getting up to get a cigarette, or whether I am in conflict with another person. The only difference lies in the pattern of the motivation. In the one case, the desire for a cigarette motivated the action; in another, the social interaction with another person may cause the action.

Regardless of the action, its reason for being is found in the motivation. The drives, the situation, interaction, and the individual complex will cause it, determine its form, and dictate its resolution. Man's smallest or most complex action can be understood by tracing the motivation.

In the drama, the director has an easier task than does the psychologist in tracing the pattern of conduct. The playwright provides clues to the individual character complex. He establishes the basic drives with simple clarity. He describes the situation in great detail. And finally, he provides the dialogue which traces the exact course of the interaction between the characters. From this complete picture, the director who understands the how and why of motivation should be able to transform the inanimate script into a living play, for the motivational forces provide the complete background of the action at each instant. If the direction starts at the beginning of the play, the initial curtain will expose a scene in which all of the motivating forces are present. Once these forces are found, the succeeding action is merely an unwinding of the natural reaction pattern that must result from the character complexes, the drives, the situation, the interaction found in the script. As the motivational pattern is changed, so will the resulting action change.

It has been said that every good play has the quality of inevitability. Every action is the inevitable result of the preceding actions. The course of the conflict should appear to be the perfectly natural result of bringing a particular pattern of motivational forces together.

In conclusion, the play, whether it be an imitation of life, a suggestion or illusion of life, or a distortion of life is controlled by the processes of human conduct. At the same time, it should be realized that however hard the playwright may try, he cannot make the play an exact duplication of life. The play has a specific form, which, despite passing innovations, has persisted over hundreds of years. The human conduct pattern is developed within the framework of a particular structure or dramatic form. The study of this structure is the next step in understanding the bases of drama.

3
Drama and the Playwright

DRAMA IS LIFE, it has been said. Strangely enough, though there is
considerable truth in the idea, it would be hard to find a statement
more misleading. Drama is based on life, but it is by no means a
mere representation of life. An analogy may be drawn between the
play and the painting. Each is an art form. As such each involves
discipline and interpretation. The painter who reproduces a segment of life upon his canvas without interpreting it in any way
does not succeed in producing a work of art. So it is with the playwright. Even the most zealous naturalists failed in producing worthy
plays when they attempted to reproduce human life in its entirety
upon the stage.

In the preceding chapter, considerable space was devoted to the
study of human conduct. The purpose of this discussion was not to
lead the playwright or the director into believing that he should
merely try to lift out bits of life and set them on a stage. Human
conduct is the base from which the art of the drama springs. The
play is an art form. It is an interpretation of life created by the
artist to communicate particular ideas, emotions, or moods. The
dramatist perfects life, gives it order and purpose. Drama can never
be life.

THE ILLUSION OF REALITY OR UNREALITY

The great proportion of drama written through the ages has
been concerned with the illusion of reality. A much smaller proportion has aimed at creating an illusion of unreality, and a tiny

23

fragment of drama has deliberately tried to destroy illusion. Whether the purpose of the playwright has been to create the real or the unreal is of little importance, for the unreal can be nothing more than distortion of the real. The truly significant factor in each case is that the playwright-artist is dealing in *illusion*. (For non-illusory dramatic style, see Chapter 23.)

The modern stage and setting with its highly conventionalized picture frame and single open side, its artificial lighting and sound effects, its canvas and wooden scenery can never be real. At best, the spectator suspends his critical judgment and accepts the illusion of the real or the unreal.

The characters of the play portrayed by human actors in grease paint, crepe hair, wigs and costumes, cannot be real. They simulate reality, create an illusion. The actors strive to appear natural, though by virtue of the specialized conventions and mechanical limitations of the stage they obviously cannot merely act naturally. Mere naturalness will appear artificial on the stage.

Above all, the play, which runs from two to three hours, follows an artificial dramaturgical pattern and is tailored to communicate particular meaning and emotion, mood and message, must be more than life itself. Even the "slice of life" plays can never be actual reproductions of life.

The purpose of the preceding paragraphs is to emphasize that the playwright and director, as artists, must *adapt* human conflict to the stage, by means of the actors, for the audience. Their success is judged not in terms of whether they reproduce life upon the stage but rather in terms of whether they are successful in creating a highly dramatic illusion that moves the audience.

THE MATERIALS OF THE PLAYWRIGHT

The art of the drama is a combination of many arts. It involves the graphic visual effects of the painter, the plasticity and depth of the sculptor, the rhythm and movement of the dancer, the tonal changes of the composer, the language of the poet. Perhaps to a greater extent than the other artists' materials, the playwright's are those of life. The real or imagined characters, situations, themes and subjects of life are the basic materials from which drama is wrought.

Character

The dramatist, in developing conflict, has the human character as his basic material. As was shown in Chapter 2, drama is the story of characters in conflict. The dramatist must draw upon life for his characters. They may be real men who have led exciting lives or they may be wholly imagined persons synthesized from the attributes of many people.

The playwright seldom merely lifts characters from life and transports them to the stage. He modifies, interprets, and perfects them in terms of his specific dramatic purpose. He carries his characters through a series of crises that are manifested in action. The purpose, development, and even characteristics of the characters will vary from play to play, depending upon the intent of the playwright. But however they may be treated, human character is the base material of the playwright.

Situation

Just as situation is basic to action in life, so it is in drama. A play is a series of situations. The situations may, as in the case of the characters, be real or imagined. They are drawn from life. The art of the playwright is found in his handling of the situation. The development of situation, like the development of character, seldom merely duplicates circumstances in life. The life situation is interpreted and perfected in order to express the special meaning of the playwright.

Every play begins with a situation that is altered and developed during the course of the action. The source material will be found in life; the art of the drama lies in the treatment of the material.

Subject

The subject or theme is the central thought of the play. The theme may be a particular story which the playwright wishes to tell, perhaps the story of a real happening; or it may be a highly imaginative combination of topics based upon the background and experience of the playwright. In social drama, the playwright may desire to propound a distinct social thesis. Some plays may be nothing more than the forceful statement of a simple proposition, such as "jealousy sows bitter seeds" or "murder will out."

The purpose in listing the materials of the playwright is simply to suggest that all of the bases of drama lie about the playwright in life itself. Drama differs from life in its method of handling the material. In creating a work of art, the playwright like other artists works his materials with a special set of tools and follows a universal artistic process.

THE TOOLS OF THE PLAYWRIGHT

The tools of the playwright are dialogue and action. Whether the playwright writes on a scratch pad with a blunt pencil or on the finest bond with a typewriter, his mind is elsewhere. Unlike the novelist or poet, the printed page of the playscript is merely a step in the ultimate production of the play. The mind of the playwright is concentrated upon the sight and sound emanating from a stage. He is creating living drama.

Dialogue

Plays are written in the form of conversation, conversations of characters with others and occasionally with themselves. While the dialogue must give the illusion of reality, of having actually occurred, of being spoken for the first time, it is actually highly artificial in form. The playwright uses vivid, colorful, expressive conversation to project his story, his situations, and his characters. Through dialogue, the playwright integrates the background necessary to the understanding of the characters. He gives the characters speeches to help project their characteristics. He develops the story in a clear and logical manner. Above all, he shows the mounting of the conflict with its resultant climax and resolution. All of these things must be done in what appears to be simple, logical, colorful conversation. Little wonder that a playwright who can use the tool of dialogue effectively is considered a master.

Action

In some ways action is more important than dialogue. The statements, "action speaks louder than words" and "to see is to believe," have real meaning. The superior play is one in which the characters, situations, and conflict are visibly expressed for the audience. As we mentioned in Chapter 2, action is the core element in drama.

THE PROCESS OF THE PLAYWRIGHT

Assuming that the artist goes beyond the mere indulgence of his own creative desire for self-expression and wishes to communicate his ideas to a viewer or listener, he must follow an artistic process which gives poignant meaning to his work. The need for clear communication is more intense in drama than in the other arts. The dancer may be satisfied with creating an impression upon the viewer, without insisting that a particular meaning be communicated. In music, the most abstract of all the arts, the composer may be totally unconcerned with the effect that his music has upon a listener. In drama, with certain notable exceptions, the author writes for the audience. His prime purpose is to project his interpretation of life clearly and forcefully, so that the experiences of the characters in the play may be shared by the spectator. To do this successfully, the playwright must follow the universal artistic process in adapting life to the stage. Selection, rearrangement and intensification are key steps in the creation of a work of art.

Selection

After the initial imaginative concept, the first major step the playwright takes in the creation of a play is selection. The conflict, the characters, the situations, all must be selected with the greatest of care.

Conflict in life is usually protracted and confused. The conflict leading a man to suicide may have developed over a number of years. In between crises there may have been long periods of quiescence. There are only a few truly dramatic moments in most lives. The tensions and crises of which drama is made must be carefully selected by the playwright from the welter of life. In many cases the events of a single play are a mixture of dramatic conflicts and crises selected from many lives. In some plays the playwright imaginatively selects those elements from his own background and experience, either overt or vicarious, which can best project his message to an audience, regardless of whether the events have actually occurred. The playwright's artistic license allows him to draw upon the entire breadth of human experience.

Just as the playwright selects his basic conflict with great care, so he develops his characters to embody the individual characteristics that cause them to react dramatically to the motivational forces. If you look about, you will realize that most human beings do not make very good dramatic material. Occasionally it is said, "That man acts like a person in a play." Such a statement implies that the speaker is describing an exciting or humorous individual. Dramatic characters are not run-of-the-mill humans. Occasionally, they are startling individuals. More frequently, they are synthetic beings made up of numerous carefully selected dramatic characteristics.

The playwright also selects his situations carefully. The situation must make a specific contribution to the dramatic whole. In most plays, situation is a key to action. Highly selected dramatic characters are placed in highly selected dramatic situations. The result is exciting drama or hilarious comedy.

Theme must be selected with equal care. The number of plots in drama are limited because relatively few themes are sufficiently dramatic to hold an audience. Most of the chosen themes concern conflicts that provoke high tension or hilarity.

Rearrangement

It has been said that nature has a way of arranging things to perfection. The petals of a flower need no rearrangement; they are perfect in their natural state. Unfortunately, the same cannot be said for the actions and characteristics of man in his society. Man's activities seldom show the order and simplicity of which beauty is made. His life is usually confused and disordered. If it has a nicely arranged tranquility, it is seldom dramatic.

The playwright must bring order out of the chaos. The characters of a play respond in a vital, logical, carefully ordered way, always showing their individual characteristics and the controlling motivation. In other words, the dramatist organizes the confusions of life into a meaningful pattern of cause and effect. He eliminates the chance relationships which dog man's existence. The story is developed in a straightforward way. Any twists or turns or retardation in the story line are made to appear perfectly logical. In the same way, the subject or theme is argued to an apparently logical conclusion. Situations are placed side by side with the semblance of naturalness.

In actuality, the arrangement of characters and events in the play is more rigidly determined than is ever apparent. The artistic form of the play has developed over several thousand years. The specifics of play structure will be considered in a later section.

Intensification

The playwright has a story to tell, a message to project, a mood to create. He is interested in communicating all of these elements to an audience. He is, therefore, vitally concerned with intensification. In a sense, all of the preceding elements in the artistic process are designed to increase or intensify communication.

By careful selection, the playwright chooses the conflict, theme, characters, and situation that communicate his meaning. By rearrangement, he creates a dramatic and exciting sequence.

In addition, the playwright may intensify by highlighting certain characters and subordinating others. He may emphasize particular ideas to the exclusion of others. He may develop some situations fully and trace others only lightly. Through the tools of speech and action, the playwright may stress any aspect of the drama he desires. In one play, he may stress a social concept such as man's inhumanity toward man; in another he may project the ecstasy of a great love; in still another he may powerfully depict the cleansing surge of grief. In each of the dramas, the characters, the plot, the situation may be similar. The meaning and the power of the play will depend upon the elements the playwright intensifies.

PLAY STRUCTURE

For over two thousand years, dramatic structure has remained essentially unchanged. Aristotle, in his analysis of the best plays of his day, defined a play as having two parts, the complication and the unraveling. Interpretation of Aristotle's writings have led to a definition of play structure including five parts: the exposition, the complication, the climax, the resolution or denouement, and the conclusion or catastrophe.

In 1863, Gustav Freytag, the noted German dramatist, diagrammed the action of a play in his *The Technique of the Drama.* His pyramid of action employed the five Aristotelian divisions to indicate a rise in the dramatic action to the climax and a falling away of the action to a conclusion. Note that this definition is based upon the two major divisions set up by Aristotle, the complication and the unraveling. In Figure 2, Freytag's pyramid is reproduced with minor substitutions in the interest of uniform terminology.

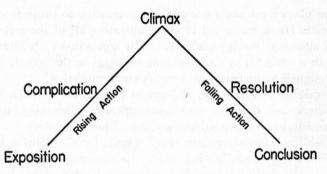

FIG. 2. PYRAMID OF DRAMATIC ACTION (AFTER FREYTAG)

Brander Matthews in his *A Study of the Drama,* criticizes Freytag's picture of dramatic action as being misleading. He observes that falling action implies a dropping away of the interest and excitement, which is not, or certainly should not be, the case. Matthews would diagram the dramatic action with a single rising line, indicating that the tensions of the play increase from beginning to end.

Adapting this concept of dramatic action to the conventional contemporary three-act division of a play, the diagram shown in Figure 3 may help the student to visualize the course of dramatic excitement in a play. In this diagram the five Aristotelian divisions are still present, with the addition of a turning point in the action, the inciting action, which will be discussed in detail in a later paragraph.

Do not misunderstand. The lines of action indicated in Figure 3 project a generalized picture of the action of most plays. The action in any specific play seldom, if ever, coincides with that shown in the drawing. The inciting action which sets off the complication need not appear at the end of the first act. Indeed, it occasionally opens the play. Similarly, the climax or turning point of the play

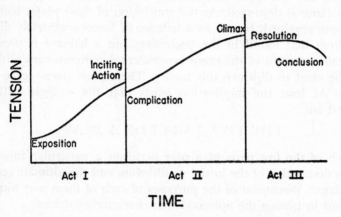

FIG. 3. LINE OF ACTION SHOWING TENSION (AFTER MATTHEWS)

does not always occur at the end of the second act. Though the sequence of the parts is maintained in most plays, the length or degree of tension may vary greatly.

In general, the increase in tension approximates a straight line rather than a pyramid. The second act and the third act begin at a tension somewhat lower than the end of the preceding act because the playwright realizes that the audience must have time to regain its orientation to the play. The decrease in tension shown at the end of the third act indicates the usual lessening of tension as the play reaches its conclusion, though even this change is eliminated in some plays which reach their highest point with the final curtain.

In the discussion of human conduct it was noted that man strives to maintain an equilibrium. In much the same sense, the play may be considered a study in equilibrium. The Aristotelian complication and unraveling is in reality nothing more than destruction and restoration of the balance of forces. More simply, it is the process of getting into trouble and getting out again. Stated in terms of Freytag's rising and falling action, the play depicts a rising disequilibrium of the forces which, at the climax, can go no further and therefore gradually return to a balance through the resolution and conclusion. Examine any play and you will find that at the outset an equilibrium exists; the potentials of struggle may be present, but the apple cart has not been upset. During the play, the balance is destroyed. At the conclusion of most plays, balance has been regained. It may be a balance of forces completely different from that found in the beginning, but a balance is present. Of course, certain of the more experimental contemporary authors can be cited to disprove this theory. Their plays never come full circle. At least the implication exists that the struggle will go on and on.

THE FIVE PARTS OF A PLAY

Each of the five parts of a play performs a particular function in the destruction of the initial equilibrium and the ultimate return to balance. Discussion of the purposes of each of them may aid the director in tracing the upheaval that characterizes drama.

Exposition

The exposition is the beginning, the introduction. It is that part of the play in which the initial situation is described. The time, the place, the social and psychological aspects of situation are set forth for the information of the audience. The characters are introduced, and the audience is given all data necessary to understanding their reasons for being. And finally, the theme is introduced with the background information sketched in so that the spectator is aware of all the forces leading to the conflict, though during the exposition they are still essentially in balance. Above all, the exposition, as is true of all introductions, must catch the interest of the audience.

The inciting action. The inciting action is really a point during the play rather than a division of the play. It is the destruction of the balance of forces, the upsetting of the apple cart. Sometimes it is called the *overt act,* meaning that it is the visible action which incites the struggle.

Complication

Once the balance of forces has been disturbed by the inciting action, the playwright may go about the business of getting his characters into trouble. The complication is the body of the drama. It is the bringing together of the protagonistic and antagonistic forces. The disequilibrium caused by the inciting action begins a series of more and more important crises in the struggle. The development of the conflict continues with increasing fury until it can go no further without resolution. As exposition is the beginning of the play, complication is the middle or heart of the drama.

Climax

The climax is the high tide of the drama. The complication can go no further without resolution of some kind. Compare the play with a case of pneumonia. The complication is the process of getting sicker and sicker until a point is reached at which one must either die or begin to get well. The high point of the fever is the climax. So it is with the drama. The climax is the point from which the complication can go no further.

In reality, the climax is a point in a play rather than a true division. In most plays it is a short scene in which the final die is cast. From the spectator's standpoint, it is the high point in the excitement of the drama. From the standpoint of conflict, it is that point at which the protagonist and antagonist become so embroiled that there can be no solution but to resolve their difficulties. In the modern play, the climax usually appears near the end of the second act, though occasionally it may appear well into the third act. In the older five-act play the climax usually appeared in the third act.

Resolution

After the turning point of the climax passes, the resolution must set in. It is the inevitable unwinding of the conflict and is governed by the turn the conflict takes at the climax. Freytag maintained that the resolution shows falling action, that is, a gradual lessening of tension. In one sense, this is true. After the climax of the conflict has been reached, it is impossible to regain such a height again. On the other hand, Matthews, with just as much logic, has observed that the tension dare not drop materially or the audience will lose interest. This is equally true. Therefore, it may be said that during the resolution the tension does drop somewhat, in that the audience is able to forecast the final result though not the method of reaching it, but the unwinding of the conflict must be handled without any loss of interest.

Conclusion

The conclusion—called the catastrophe by Aristotle, who was observing classic tragedy with the end of the play literally involving a catastrophe—serves to return the play to a semblance of equilibrium. It is the section in the play that logically and finally answers all of the questions of the audience.

THE DIRECTOR AND PLAY STRUCTURE

A knowledge of play structure is essential to the director for at least three reasons. First, it should help him to realize how life is modified into the art form of the play. It should not only illustrate that the play is a selection, a reorganization, and an intensification of life's conflicts, but it should also explain how these principles are used.

Second, the director who understands play structure will be better equipped to produce the play. He will be able to understand the basic pattern within which the playwright is working. He can better define the balanced relationship between characters at the outset; he can isolate the inciting moment; he can trace the development of the minor crises into major crises resulting in the climax; he can lead the audience through the diminishing crises to the end. In other words, by a knowledge of play structure, he can more effectively project the meaning and emotion of the dramatist to the audience. This is the prime job of the director.

And finally, the most significant thing the director can gain from a knowledge of play structure is the recognition of the playwright's and indeed the director's working unit. Although, in a general sense, the playwright constructs the play so that it follows the five major structural divisions and is divided into acts and scenes, the playwright actually labors with a much smaller unit.

The concept of action as a line, diagrammed in Figures 2 and 3, although meaningful in a general way, may be misleading. No play actually develops in a straight line of mounting tension from exposition to climax to conclusion. In fact, if a segment of the straight line shown in Figure 3 were enlarged, it would undoubtedly look like the jagged line illustrated in Figure 4. The play is, after all, a series of minor crises and climaxes with intervening moments of lessened tension.

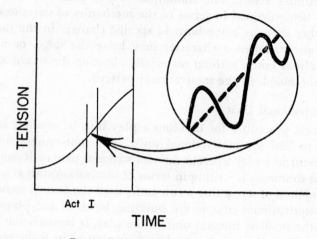

Act I

TIME

FIG. 4. ENLARGED SEGMENT OF A PLAY

The playwright introduces this constantly changing stimulus by creating a sequence of small scenes which develop various elements of the play. The story is seldom unfolded in a simple straightforward way. The conflict is never joined and constantly increased until the climax is reached. The characters are seldom developed in a single, long, involved sequence. Instead, the playwright introduces many twists and turns and obstacles. He introduces circumstances or characters who cause detours in the story or changes in the course of the conflict. This is accomplished by writing in a series of small scenes. There are several methods for finding these little units. The French dramatists deliberately divided their plays into numerous small units. These units take their name from their proponents and are called French scenes.

The French Scene

In classical French drama, the play was divided into as many as twenty to forty scenes. Each of these scenes was defined by a change in the characters. Any major character's entrance or exit represented the limits of the French scene. There is considerable logic in the definition of the French scene. When a character enters the action, there is usually a change in the motivational pattern of the scene. The same is true when a character leaves the stage to the remaining actors. The limitation of the French scene arises from its being defined in terms of the mechanics of entrances and exits rather than its being born of specific changes in the motivational pattern. Often a character may leave the stage, or a new character may enter, without materially affecting the situation, the theme, the mood, or the motivational pattern.

The Motivational Unit

A second procedure for dividing a play into its smallest logical parts is to find the motivational units. The motivational unit is *any* segment in a play wherein the motivational pattern is constant. Since the dramatist is writing in terms of motivation, this is a more logical method of separating scenic units than the French scene.

The motivational unit is the building block of the playwright and, as the smallest integral unit in the play, it becomes the working unit of the director. A complete discussion of its form, recognition, and application is contained in Chapter 6.

Thus far in the study of the bases of directing we have shown that the director's source material is life, which undergoes change as it is transferred to the stage. The resulting drama may be more or less than life, but it is always an interpretation of life because the play is an art form. The director who understands the source materials, the tools, the procedures, and the form the playwright uses should be ready to study the group for whom the play is to be produced—the audience.

4

Drama and the Audience

DRAMA IS FOR THE AUDIENCE. As such, the audience is an integral part of dramatic production. Without an audience, the performed play is meaningless. The specific response desired by the playwright and the director may vary from play to play, but, in every case, the true measure of the success of the production is its effect upon the audience.

The audience participates in the production, overtly with laughter in comedy and covertly with inner tension in serious drama. Response is not a one-way street. The response of the audience to the play affects the cast, which in turn affects the audience, and so on. The circular response is less apparent than in the public speaking situation, but it is a part of the dramatic process.

Many directors who know little about the audience rationalize their failures by blaming the audience. This is foolish. If a production does not move the audience, the fault lies in the production rather than in the audience. In some way, the director has miscalculated. It is true that audiences differ. Some are, as a whole, more sophisticated than others. Some have better theatre backgrounds and training. However, if the play is dramatic, if it has been selected with an eye to the limitations of response in a particular audience, if it is good theatre, if it fulfills the needs of the human beings who go to the theatre, it cannot fail.

Too many directors think of the audience as a vast, inanimate mass. They produce their plays without the slightest knowledge of or regard for the spectator. This unreasoning attitude dictates the failure of hundreds of productions. The audience is not an inanimate mass. It is a highly sensitive and susceptible organism composed of human beings who go to the theatre to satisfy their own needs and desires. If the audience is to respond as the director wishes, he must understand its composition, its reaction tendencies, its reasons for attending, its strengths and weaknesses, its limiting factors.

WHY DO PEOPLE GO TO THE THEATRE?

George M. Cohan, actor, playwright, producer par excellence of the American theatre, once said that people go to the theatre for one of three reasons—to laugh, to cry, to be thrilled. He was right. These are the reactions we hope to experience when we attend the theatre.

Why do we drop our daily tasks, drive miles and miles, fret over parking problems, and pay money, often to sit on thoroughly uncomfortable chairs in a high school auditorium, to see an amateur college or community group produce a play? Last year, several million people did that. The answer lies in the laughter, the tears, the thrills.

The theatre is the land of illusion and imagination. It provides a break in the humdrum pattern of our lives. More important, it can satisfy some of our basic needs that cannot be satisfied in any other way. In the theatre, we can vicariously find an outlet for our own desires. To be sure, there are other reasons for going to the theatre. Some go because it is the thing to do. Some search for a temple of culture or art. And some attend, I am sure, because they can't think of anything better to do with their time. But most of us go because the theatre can provide a satisfactory outlet for our personal needs, wants, and desires.

The Basic Drives

In Chapter 2 the basic drives that motivate human conduct were discussed. These drives were: desire for response, recognition, adventure, and security. They were found to be the motivating forces that control the actions of all humans, including the characters of the drama. An analysis of the basic drives will help to explain why the theatre knows no limits in its appeal to men, women, and children.

The desire for response. The need every human being feels for intimate contacts with others—the desire for companionship and fellowship—can be fulfilled by the theatre in at least two different ways. First of all, it is a social institution. People seldom go to the theatre by themselves. The theatre production is a social activity which groups of people may enjoy together. In fact, this is the basis for much theatre attendance. It is a social outing. Some members of the audience use the theatre as a meeting ground, regardless of the power or meaning of the production.

In a more universal sense, the theatre can satisfy the desire for response by providing the spectator with a chance to participate in the production. The spectator who is caught up in the imaginative whirl of the theatre feels a fellowship and an intimate personal contact with the characters in the play. When the spectator projects himself onto the stage and joins the action, he is able personally to enjoy the responses evoked by the character with whom he has identified himself. In other words, the spectator is able to broaden his social sphere in the theatre.

The desire for recognition. In the theatre, the spectator is able to enjoy vicariously all of the recognition denied him in life: fame, influence, authority, reputation, and renown. The drama is peopled with fabulous characters. The spectator can enjoy the homage given kings and princesses. He can receive the plaudits of a grateful society for bringing arch villains to task. He may make clever piercing comments upon life, which will be heartily approved by all. He may become a romantic hero with the world applauding at his feet. He may live for a few hours in an opulence that real life will never permit. All of his desire to be what he is not, to aggrandize his own ego, to be recognized as important, is granted in the theatre.

But if this be true, how can the spectator enjoy plays in which destitution, depravity, and madness are the keys? It is a simple reversal. The magic of the theatre with its partial detachment allows the spectator to feel the power that is his own. When the spectator views the stupid and the foolish, he is able to feel superior to those weaklings who make mistakes which he knows he could never make. Standing somewhat apart as he does, the spectator is able to pick and choose the qualities and characteristics with which he will identify himself.

The desire for adventure. No man's life is so complete that he doesn't desire vital new experiences beyond the possibility of attainment. The theatre is the land of action and adventure. The spectator is able to enjoy the thrills of romance and conflict so frequently denied him in life. He may grapple with the problems of a falling dynasty. He may stand casually, gun in hand, and thwart the mob. He may, like Robin Hood, protect the weak and destroy the wicked. Not only does he gain recognition in the theatre, but all of the adventure of an exciting new world are his for the price of a gallery seat.

The desire for security. Every man, despite his great desire for the new and adventurous, clings desperately to the safety and security of what he already has. The true magic of the theatre lies in its safety; for response, recognition, and adventure are his without any of the attendant dangers involved if he were to chase them in actuality.

In most plays, the hero emerges triumphant. The spectator who identifies himself with the hero can pass through the trials, the struggles, the crises, and be reasonably sure that virtue will win out. This accounts for the popularity of plays with happy endings. Some will say, "How immature! Life isn't like that." Of course, it is immature, and, obviously, life isn't like that. But most people do not go to the theatre to prove their maturity or to see life as it is. They go to indulge their emotional and imaginative sensitivity, to be stimulated and diverted, and to see life as it "ought" to be.

Note what the playwright does in a tragedy to protect the spectator. He provides a fatal weakness in the protagonist or a set of insurmountable circumstances, allowing the audience to rationalize the defeat of its hero. After Macbeth has met his doom, every spectator can say, "Why, of course, it had to be so!" This does not mean that the audience will actually enjoy, in the sense of being pleased, the death of the young lovers in *Winterset* or the love of Ethan and Mattie turned to hate in *Ethan Frome,* but a basis for acceptance has been established.

The Similarity of Drives

Much of the emotional power of the theatre lies in the fact that the characters in the play and the playgoer are driven by the same motivational forces. A mutual understanding between the character and the spectator is possible because the spectator can readily identify himself and his desires with those of the characters. He recognizes certain facets of himself on the stage and is able to participate in the action. The director who can recognize this similarity of emotional need on the part of the character and the spectator and work to create his characters in the image of life cannot fail to strike a sympathetic note in the breast of the playgoer. It is true that many characters are more than a mere representation of the real. It is equally true that the emotional core of the character must be such that the spectator can identify, appreciate, and understand the forces that control the character. The theatre depends in a large measure upon emotional identification. Without emotional participation on the part of the audience, most of the magnetic power of the theatre is lost.

Other Reasons for Playgoing

The director should not assume, on the basis of the preceding discussion, that the emotional drives are the only valid reason for theatre attendance. Many plays have great intellectual as well as emotional values. They comment upon life and its problems, many times posing specific argumentative propositions. The intellectual pleasure derived from these theatrical discussions can be great. In fact, a limited, critical few may enjoy dramatic productions without experiencing any emotional identification. The theatre can also provide deep aesthetic and artistic experiences, different from response to the basic drives. The higher the level of appreciation, the greater will be the depth of the appeal of the theatre. However, when all is said and done, the great attraction of the theatre lies in the opportunity to participate imaginatively in the dramatic action. A play can survive without art or intellect; it cannot survive without emotion.

WHAT IS A THEATRE AUDIENCE?

At first glance, one might think of the theatre patrons as a heterogeneous collection of people of all ages and backgrounds from all walks of life. Judging them as they enter the theatre, this impression would be correct. After the play has begun however, and the spectators have joined the characters in their struggles, the composition of the spectator group changes. The playgoers cease to be Mr. and Mrs. Brown and Miss Smith and become a part of a more homogeneous grouping known as the theatre audience. The theatre audience has many of the characteristics of the psychological crowd. A battery of psychological factors present in any crowd modifies the individual characteristics of the isolated spectator. If he is to control an audience successfully, every director must understand the reactions of the crowd, the psychological factors that encourage crowd activity, and the specific process of building a theatre audience or crowd.

Reactions of a Psychological Crowd

As early as 1898, Gustave Lebon, a French psychologist, discovered, in studying the mob activities of the French Revolution, that crowds did not respond in a manner characteristic of the individuals who made up the crowd. He assumed that the difference in response was the result of a "group mind" which took over when people responded in a group. Though in later years his theory of the group mind was discredited, his analysis of crowd reactions has stood the test of time. Lebon maintained that the individuals, when they became members of a crowd, regressed, became more animal, less human.

The members of a psychological crowd show a distinct lessening of intellectual activity. They tend to become more subjective and less objective. Crowd response involves a suspension of judgment. As critical intellectual activity decreases, emotional excitability increases. Basic emotions come into free play. The individual loses many of the identifying elements of his own personality and takes on the more uniform characteristics of a crowd member.

Note how the responses desirable in the theatre are similar to the responses resulting from crowd participation. In the theatre, the spectator is asked to suspend his critical judgment and imaginatively accept the illusion of the play. Since the theatre is more concerned with feeling than with thinking, the increase of emotional excitability of crowd response is ideal. The theatre deals in basic emotions. The increased suggestibility of the crowd response is also important in the theatre. In many ways, the standard for conduct in the theatre is like the conduct expected from a crowd.

As individuals in everyday life, we hesitate to laugh heartily or weep copiously. In the theatre, such behavior is expected and encouraged. In everyday life, the emphasis is upon intellectual control; in the theatre, it is upon emotional release. To the extent that the director can turn his theatre audience into a psychological crowd, he will evoke desirable theatre responses.

PSYCHOLOGICAL FACTORS INFLUENCING THE THEATRE PATRON

Examination of the theatre audience indicates that it is subject to the same psychological pressures that unify any group of individuals into an audience or crowd. The five contributing elements are defined below.

Polarization

Whenever a group of people assemble and a stimulus claims their attention, some degree of polarization is present. Polarization is a term borrowed by the psychologists from the physicists to indicate the tendency of a given mass to orient itself in relationship to a particular stimulus. The iron filings in the simplest experiment in magnetism line up in a specific pattern about the poles of the magnet. In a similar way, the individuals in the theatre audience "line up" in both a physical and a psychological sense in relationship to the stimulus from the stage. The greater the fixation upon the stimulus, the greater the polarization. When a high degree of polarization is present, the individual responds as a member of the audience or crowd. This group response is basic to real enjoyment in the theatre. The factors that induce polarization are the power of the stimulus, social facilitation, social anonymity, and regimentation.

The Stimulus

The process of concentrating attention upon a particular stimulus, in and of itself, tends to bring about a favorable reaction to the stimulus. Complete attention results in hypnosis, with its attendant reduction of rationality and increase in emotionality and suggestibility. Thus, one factor that will determine polarization is the power of the stimulus. The logical concern of the director who has carefully selected, ordered, and intensified the meaning and emotion he desires to project will be to create such a powerful stimulus within the picture frame that the attention of the spectator will be transfixed upon the stage.

Social Facilitation

Whenever a group of people are together, they tend to react with each other. If one person is part of a crowd, the actions of others in the crowd affect his actions. He will be "facilitated" to respond as they do. When a powerful stimulus is provided, the group reaction to the stimulus will affect the individual's reaction to the stimulus. For example, if everyone in a crowd is attending to a side show barker, and you join the crowd, you will be facilitated to respond to the speaker because others are doing so. When you see or hear the others in the group respond, you will respond. The laughter of others in the audience will facilitate your tendency to laugh; a sharp tension in the audience will stimulate you to be tense.

Many times when the studio audience for a radio show laughs uproariously at a not very funny comedy line, we at home wonder if they are very intelligent. The studio audience has been turned into a psychological crowd and is responding on a level different from that of the single, objective listener at home. Social facilitation is of tremendous importance to the director, for he must get his spectators to respond as a group, thereby facilitating each other to even greater response.

Social Anonymity

Crowd response is more intense than individual response because of social anonymity. When the individual is submerged in the group, he tends to lose his personal identity, for he feels himself to be anonymous. Such is the case in the theatre audience. A playgoer will laugh with greater abandon, cry without shame, shriek when thrilled when he is lost in the crowd and unconsciously realizes that no one else is aware of his reactions. His inhibitions are decreased because of this anonymous quality. Obviously, this factor which contributes to more intense polarization will be important in the theatre, for it helps facilitate response, the prime aim of the director.

Regimentation

The loss of individuality is further increased by regimentation, the act of bringing the group into either physical or psychological conformity. Any group forced into a pattern of similar activities will tend to become polarized to a stimulus more easily than a group that is not systematized.

In the army, for example, almost all life is group life. Individuality is de-emphasized; collective or team responses are urged. This collective response is brought about by conformity or regimentation in everything from dress to responses to commands. In a similar sense, though to a much lesser degree, the theatre audience is carefully regimented to ensure a greater uniformity of response.

The uninformed may not realize that theatrical tradition has produced a series of conventions based upon crowd psychology. Each of the five elements necessary to the creation of a psychological crowd is employed with deliberate care in the theatre. Perhaps the best way to make this clear to the beginning director is to trace the process of turning individual spectators into a psychologically homogeneous theatre audience.

BUILDING A THEATRE AUDIENCE

When Mr. and Mrs. Brown and Miss Smith and her date enter the theatre, they and all of the other patrons are concerned with their own personal activities. The Browns may be discussing the problem of putting the children to bed. Miss Smith and her date may be planning a picnic for the next day. There is no uniformity of response among the patrons. The moment they enter the theatre, the process of building the uniform crowd response begins. First, their tickets are taken, and they are ushered to a seat. Theatre seats are usually set in rows facing a stage. The patron is regimented by the seating pattern. In the theatre seat, it is comparatively difficult to carry on a conversation with the other members of the party because one has to lean forward and labor to be seen and heard. The theatre is usually dimly lit, making it more troublesome to continue normal individual activity. In addition, the patron is given a program which tends to occupy and direct his attention toward the idea of the play and the performers. If the director watches the convening audience, he can see that they gradually give up the attempt to maintain the small group activity in which they were engaged when they entered the theatre and slowly tend to become isolated from surrounding stimuli.

When the patron is seated in the theatre, he may wonder why he is placed next to other people, regardless of the number of empty seats at the edges or the back of the auditorium. The usher has been instructed to fill the center of the house first for two reasons. It makes the placing of latecomers an easier and less distracting job; but, more important, the physical closeness of the spectators increases the amount of social facilitation they experience from their neighbors.

As an experiment, the director should go to a hit comedy at a motion picture house early in the afternoon when there are few patrons scattered about the auditorium. Note the response to the humor in the show. There will be frighteningly little laughter. Come back in the evening when there is a full house and again note the response. The increase in laughter will be tremendous. In the evening the closely packed spectators have facilitated each other to laughter. For this reason, producers "paper" poor houses; that is, give out complimentary tickets to fill up the empty seats.

A few minutes before the play is to begin, an orchestra may play several selections. The music may be related to the play to be produced and usually carries something of the mood of the play to follow. Note that the first stimulus drawing attention to the front of the auditorium has been applied. During the music it becomes even more difficult to continue a conversation with one's neighbors. Unless the patron is a rugged individualist, he begins to succumb to group pressures. When he notes that others about him are listening to the music, he is facilitated to do likewise.

As the orchestra leaves the pit, the asbestos or fire curtain is raised. The expectations of the spectator are increased, and his attention is more sharply directed to the stage. After the asbestos has been raised, the footlights come on, and the house lights are lowered. There is an old adage in the theatre, "Never leave the audience in the dark." Why? Simply because in the darkness all stimuli are eliminated. All attention must be controlled. As the footlights come up, the stimulus from the stage is increased still further. Then the house lights are lowered. This carries out three additional steps in the process of polarizing the audience. First, by contrast to the darkness of the auditorium, the stimulus of the footlights is increased; second, the lowering of the house lights blots out any stimuli that might distract the spectator from the stage; and third, the darkened house makes the spectator much more anonymous, since he can no longer be a center of attention in his little group.

When should the curtain be raised? For the director who will listen to the gradual orientation of the audience, there can be no question. As the house goes black, the murmur of the audience slowly subsides to complete silence. Every eye is focused expectantly upon the stage. Then, and only then, may the curtain be raised to disclose the brilliantly lighted stage.

In most plays, nothing of any importance happens in the first few moments of the play. The playwright allows the audience to look at the setting, determine the time and place, and adjust his eyes to the powerful stimulus of the lighted stage. After this adjustment, the playwright slowly begins to supply the expositional material necessary to the audience if it is to understand and respond to the conflict and crises of the production. During the first moments of the play, the audience has not been fully polarized by any means. All of the preparatory activity has probably done no more than decrease the individuality of the playgoer. He is more susceptible to the illusion of the theatre than he was when he entered the theatre. The actual process of getting the audience to respond as a crowd lies ahead. In a comedy, the early laughter will be scattered and tentative; in a serious drama, concentration without emotional tension will be present. In each case, the director must have rehearsed his play so that a gradual accumulation of impact tends to increase the body or scope and the depth of the crowd response.

This may be done by increasing and varying the power of the stimulus, by providing a clearly defined visual and auditory focal point at all times, by eliminating any distraction that might cause the spectator's attention to wander from the stage focal point, by striving early in the performance for a uniform response such as laughter which will facilitate later responses, and by carefully avoiding any action that might disturb the anonymity which has been so carefully built.

Paying attention is an extremely fatiguing process. If the director does not vary the stimulus from the stage, the spectator will be unable to attend for any extended period. Static plays with little visual or auditory variety will quickly tire an audience. If the playwright has not provided the necessary variety, the director must do so.

If the audience is to respond as a whole, a clear-cut, well-defined focal point must be provided at all times. The spectators must know where to look and listen, or they will become confused and be unable to follow the action with increasing excitement.

Above all, the audience must be given meaningful cues for response. The frame of reference for a comedy and a serious drama is completely different. Comedy or drama must be labelled for the audience not only on the program but also in the actions of the characters early in the play.

The commercial theatre at times goes even further in instructing and facilitating its audience. The producer hires "claques," paid responders, to provoke laughter and applause. In line with the observations made concerning social facilitation, the claque can aid the audience's enjoyment by providing the facilitation to hearty laughter or applause. Usually the non-professional theatre does not use claques, allowing the play to stand on its own merits. This is probably wise, but the principle of the claque is valid. The audience is led to respond because the claque responds. Any director may easily test this phenomenon of audience response. In a musical show, for example, select a point at which the audience might applaud but never has. At that point applaud boldly and strongly in the back of the house. The audience will follow in kind.

DESIRABLE RESPONSES IN THE THEATRE

Assuming that the spectators have been polarized with the attendant increase in emotional excitability and decrease in intellectual judgment, just what types of response are desirable in the theatre?

Throughout this book it has been stated that the theatre is concerned with *illusion* rather than reality. (See Chapters 2 and 3.) Illusion is defined in a strict sense as *a perception of a sound, appearance, or object which does not correspond with reality.* To continue with a strict psychological definition, illusion is a misinterpretation of sensory experience. Defined in the sense that the term is used in the theatre, illusion is *a willing acceptance as real of a perception that does not correspond with reality.* Or, again, it involves a suspension of critical judgment, permitting acceptance of the misinterpretation of sensory experiences.

The spectator in the theatre audience knows that the walls of the room are made of canvas; he knows that the light streaming in the window does not come from the sun; he knows that the villain who stabs the hero doesn't really harm him. Yet he is willing to accept all of this falseness as real. And more significant, he is apparently willing to respond, in part, as though it were real. Why? Because he has come to the theatre to play imaginatively. Because he wants to *participate* in the illusion of the drama. Because, by being able to recognize that the illusion exists, he is able to maintain a *detachment* which permits him to enjoy the illusion without any of the consequences which might accrue if the situation were real.

The ideal theatrical production encourages the spectator to participate in the illusion and at the same time permits the spectator to maintain a detachment because it is an illusion. Both the participation and the detachment must be subjective responses; that is, responses based on one's own feelings, for illusion is subjective. The moment that the spectator becomes objective, or critically evaluates the actual artificialities in the dramatic performance, the illusion is gone. The greatest performance creates a balance between the enjoyment derived from participating in the illusion and the enjoyment derived from being able, simultaneously, to preserve an artistic detachment. Analysis of these responses will indicate how the balance can be maintained.

Participation in the Illusion

In an earlier section it was noted that people attend the theatre primarily to satisfy their own individual basic needs and desires. The playgoer satisfies his needs by participating in the illusion of the play. This may be done in at least two ways. The spectator may respond to the actions and sounds of the play with imitative motor responses, sometimes called *empathic responses,* and he may participate in the play by *emotionally identifying* himself with certain of the characters.

The empathic response. Empathy is discussed with clarity and detail in Langfeld's book, *The Aesthetic Attitude*. Every student of play directing will do well to read it with care. The empathic response may be considered an imitative motor response. It is the process of "feeling into" the object or action being viewed. In other words, the spectator assumes certain motor attitudes—positions or postures—corresponding to the characteristics of the actions or objects to which he attends. For example, the sport's fan vicariously enters the field event and lifts his leg to help the pole vaulter over the bar. The spectator at the ballet vicariously dances with the ballerina by following the rhythm and actions with small imitative motions of his own. The playgoer assumes the muscular set of the hero as he prepares to vanquish the villain.

The enjoyment arises in part from the actual motor participation in the scene. The play director must create a stimulus sufficiently powerful to motivate the playgoer into an active motor participation in the production.

Emotional identification. A second desirable participatory response is emotional identification. When a spectator identifies himself with a character in the play, he experiences, vicariously, the emotions of the stage character. In most cases men tend to identify themselves with the hero, while women participate with the heroine. For example, if the hero is aroused to righteous indignation at the calumny of the villain, the sympathetic spectator finds himself similarly aroused.

The imitative motor response and the emotional identification are complementary. The spectator takes on both the physical attitudes and the emotional state of the character in the play. The preceding comments may seem to imply that the greater the participation, the greater will be the enjoyment in the play. This is true only as long as the response on the part of the spectator is a subjective one. If, for example, the spectator becomes so tense in imitation of the action on stage that he becomes aware of the fact that his muscles actually ache, he has objectified the situation, and the illusion of the play is destroyed.

In other cases, the stimulus from the stage may become so powerful that the spectator loses his role of spectator and becomes an *actual* participant in the action. He charges onto the stage screaming, "Hold, villain, hold!" Obviously, such a response is not desirable in the theatre, for the illusion has been annihilated not only for the reacting spectator, who will be embarrassed when he becomes aware of his plight, but also for the rest of the audience, who see a spectator charge onto the stage. In each of the preceding cases the participation has become so complete that the illusion has been broken. Objectivity has replaced subjectivity, and the spectator's artistic detachment has been destroyed. The subject of artistic detachment is of such importance in the theatrical performance that it deserves treatment by itself.

Artistic Detachment

In contemplating any work of art, the viewer must be able to maintain a subjective detachment, which Langfeld labelled *aesthetic distance*. He implied by the term a physical and psychical separation of the spectator from the object to be enjoyed. His classic example involves a man standing on the deck of a ship enjoying the roll and sweep of the waves. The man's appreciation of the beauty of the waves is dependent upon his subjective detachment. If one wave larger than the others breaks across the bow of the ship and deluges the man with water, his artistic contemplation is destroyed. His point of view changes. He objectifies the situation. He runs for safety. The illusion of the beautiful waves is gone. The physical proximity of cold, wet water, and the psychological concern for his own self-preservation break down his artistic detachment.

Since the theatre succeeds or fails upon the basis of the illusion created, artistic detachment—a basic component of illusion—must be maintained. This separation of the audience and the play is brought about in many different ways. The arrangement of the contemporary auditorium with a space between the audience and the stage, a proscenium frame surrounding the stage picture, a lighted stage and darkened house—these help to remove the spectator physically and psychologically so that contemplation is possible.

Contemporary traditions of acting and directing also maintain the artistic illusion. The actor plays without violating the "fourth wall"; that is, without breaking into direct contact with the audience. Every technical aspect of the production is handled so that it will contribute to the illusion. The director's concern for the imaginative whole of the production, his elimination of spectacular stage tricks, which might call attention to themselves, all help to maintain the attitude of subjective contemplation.

Perhaps a theatrical illustration of aesthetic distance, with an example of how the detachment may be broken, will clarify the concept. At one point in the sentimental melodrama, *Seventh Heaven,* two sisters are called upon to tussle at the head of some steps. Diane is the heroine; Nana, her sister, is a villainess. During the struggle, Nana pushes Diane so that she falls down the flight of stairs. In the production in mind, the fall was rehearsed with great care. Each movement—Diane's hand placement, body turns while falling—was planned. The impression of a bad fall was perfectly maintained, yet the fall was so gracefully accomplished that the audience was subconsciously aware that it belonged as a part of the play. The spectator was able to maintain his contemplative attitude. The illusion was present. He saw (and this is important) Diane, the *character* in the play, fall; and he hated Nana, also a *character,* for her cruelty. At one performance the actress who was playing Nana pushed too hard, and Diane missed the first handhold on the bannister. The actress playing Diane took a terrific tumble down the stairs, hitting her head sharply on the bottom step. Instantaneously, the illusion of the fall was broken. The spectators were no longer able to contemplate the action of the play. They lost their subjective attitude and became objectively analytical. They saw the *actress* rather than the *character* tumble down the stairs. They turned to their neighbors with concern as to whether the actress had been hurt. The aesthetic distance usually present during the scene was gone.

The Balance of Participation and Detachment

Participation and detachment appear to be desirable responses working in opposition. If there is too much participation, the detachment is destroyed. If there is too much detachment, little participation will result. Assuming the extremes, this will be true. In the ideal relationship, each response will complement the other in creating pleasure for the theatregoer. The director's task is to encourage the highly sensitized crowd spectator to participate in the production as completely as possible without losing his security and detachment as a spectator. Expressed in reverse, the director must select, order, and intensify every bit of dialogue and action, every technical device, so that the spectator may be caught up in the illusion of the whole without ever becoming objectively aware of the artificial elements of production.

Any discussion within the narrow limits of a book can survey the characteristics of the audience in only a cursory manner. If it is now clear that the audience is more than a static mass seated in the void of an auditorium, that it is a vibrant, animate organism that can be created, molded, excited, and controlled at the discretion of the director, this chapter has served its purpose. Much of the remainder of this book is concerned with the principles and techniques by which the director and the actors, as agents of the playwright, may gain the desired responses from the audience.

5

Drama and the Director

IN THE PRECEDING sections of Part One, the elements that make up drama have been defined. Little has been said about the cooperative group of artists and craftsmen who make play production possible. The actor, the technician, the dancer, and the musician, all play an integral part in the production process. They are the living forces who infuse with life the static, paper-bound manuscript.

One of the most important of these artists is the director, who must creatively blend all of the dynamic elements of production into a single, meaningful whole. This chapter deals with the qualities and responsibilities of the director.

THE RISE OF THE DIRECTOR

One hundred and fifty years ago, there were no directors. There were managers and producers and stars, all of whom assumed the responsibilities of production in varying degrees. To all intents and purposes there was little need for the integrating force of the director. The drama of realism, with its ensemble playing, was yet to make itself felt. Plays were acted in a formalized style. The arrangement of characters was largely predetermined by the importance and prominence of the star. The portrayal of the characters had little to do with creating an impression of reality. The stage was a platform from which the star displayed his virtuosity, with the minor characters mere foils to these histrionics.

With the rise of the new theatre movement, beginning with the

Duke of Saxe-Meiningen, Antoine, *et al,* a new concept of drama developed. A transfer in interest from the player to the play created new problems in the theatre. A need arose for someone to stand apart from the production and maintain a perspective of the whole.

For a time, this person had little authority. This so-called director handled the necessary details of the production without bringing to bear any particular knowledge of drama as a whole. The force in the play was still the star. Indeed, this practice still exists today. In frequent commercial productions, the star directs the play (often to his own rather than the play's advantage) while the director stands by to supply his ready agreement with each new move.

Probably the greatest force that facilitated the rise of the director was the Moscow Art Theatre. Constantin Stanislavski and the Moscow Art Players intensified the interest in the ensemble. They disregarded the star system and placed the emphasis upon the group. Many times Stanislavski, himself, played small roles, allowing others the major ones. No detail was too small, no role too menial, to escape attention. The unity of the whole was of paramount importance. In this situation, the director became a necessary addition to the dramatic scene.

The new system soon reached America, first in the art theatres of the early 1920's, such as the Provincetown Players, and later the Group Theatre. From there it spread to Broadway. The director became an important force in the professional theatre. This beginning led to a fine tradition in professional direction. In fact, today, some professional plays are better known for the director than for the star or even the author.

Another factor contributing to the rise of the director was the death of the road and stock company and the growth of the community theatre movement. These amateur groups entered the play production field for the enjoyment and the social experience rather than for the profit involved, and they usually lacked experienced personnel. An experienced director was necessary to guide their experiments in playmaking.

The colleges and high schools also have had a constantly expanding dramatic program in the last quarter century. They have needed and still need directors who can guide and teach the players and directors of succeeding years. Today, the colleges rather than the commercial theatre act as the training ground for directors.

THE PLACE OF THE DIRECTOR

Drama may be considered as a triangle composed of the author who has created the script, the actors and technicians who express the author's ideas in action upon the stage, and the audience for whom the play is produced and without whom the play is meaningless.

FIG. 5. PLACE OF THE DIRECTOR

Standing in the center of the triangle is the director. He acts as the unifying force. Not only must the director coordinate the creative efforts of the actors and technicians, but he must be an artist in his own right.

Many arguments have been raised about whether the director is a creative artist or an interpretative artist. Little is to be gained by taking sides, for the director at different stages of the production is something of each. It is true that the author is probably the prime creative artist in that he is completely free to select, arrange, and intensify the materials in life from which he makes the play. Considering the author as the creative artist, the director is an interpreter, for he begins with the manuscript and interprets its meanings for an audience. On the other hand, each production of a play is new and different. The director, having as his materials the inanimate script, the living actors, and craftsmen creates a new drama for the audience. His imaginative sensitivity is responsible for the creation of a new aural and visual experience for the audience. The playwright has worked with imaginary sounds and pictures expressed in cold print upon a page; the play director creates the three dimensional, living picture.

THE RESPONSIBILITIES OF THE DIRECTOR

Be he creator or interpreter, the director has well-defined responsibilities to each of the individuals or groups with whom he works. Since the director stands at the center of the triangle, it is important to determine his relationship to each of its points.

Responsibility to the Playwright

The director's first responsibility is to the playwright. He must project with integrity the moods, meanings, and emotions set down by the dramatist. The playwright has written, published, and copyrighted a specific story with distinct characters and situations. He has labored long and arduously to create the balance of forces, the crises and climaxes, the meaning and messages he believes important. The director must respect the playwright's desires.

Sometimes the director feels that the playwright is wrong in his character or plot development. The director believes that his own ideas of the play's meaning are more significant. In that case, the director should select another play, one with which he can concur. No director has the right to distort the playwright's meanings.

This problem was clearly illustrated by a semi-professional production of Shaw's *Arms and the Man*, presented during the early days of the war in Korea. Shaw's play is a witty satire on military life. Perhaps the director did not feel that the military should be ridiculed during a war. Whatever were his reasons, the director presented the play as a farce bordering in style upon burlesque. Shaw's meanings were lost in the buffoonery. The average spectator, unfamiliar with the play, undoubtedly could not detect the difference and believed that he was witnessing Shaw's *Arms and the Man*, but he was not. The spectator was treated to a play that might as well have been written by the director. The rights of the playwright had been violated. If, as suggested above, the director did not wish to ridicule military life, he should have selected a different play.

In some plays, the author's intent is difficult to divine. For ex-

ample, a centuries old argument has raged among scholars debating whether Shakespeare's Hamlet is sane or insane, strong in
character or weak. In such cases the director, after considering all
of the possibilities of interpretation in the light of the available
scholarly research, must decide upon a particular interpretation
and develop it with consistency.

The director's opportunity for creative effort lies in his interpretation of the playwright's intent and his production methods.
As we have stated, no two productions can ever be the same.
Different directors will have different interpretations. Different
actors will project different aspects of the characters. Different designers will create settings varied in style and design.

Responsibility to the Actor

The actor is the greatest creative force in the theatre. The actors,
more than any other group, lift the printed page into living drama.
Plays can be produced without settings, without lights, without
properties, without music, without a stage, and without a director,
but they cannot be produced without actors. The responsibilities
of the director to the actor and the problems of the actor are of
such importance than an entire chapter is devoted to a discussion
of handling the actor. (See Chapter 18.)

Responsibility to the Designer and Technician

The relationship between the director and the designer is similar
to that between the director and the actor. The director, acting as
the interpreter of the author's intent, must encourage the designer
to make a dynamic contribution to the whole. Many directors are
prone to dictate setting, lighting, costumes, and other properties
to the last detail. This is usually a mistake; for if a designer deserves the title, he knows more about form, mass, color, and line
than does the director.

As with the actor, the scenic background should be the result
of cooperative effort. The director is vitally concerned with the
floor plan, the entrances and exits, the acting areas, the furniture
arrangement, the general tonal quality of the settings, lighting,
costumes, and make-up, the style of the production. (See Chapters
19 and 23.) But if the designer is to make a creative contribution,

he must be encouraged to think independently and submit his ideas. Together they will arrive at the best possible visual means of projecting the ideas of the author to the audience.

Responsibility to the Audience

The preceding discussion should have made clear that the director is working with the other members of the producing group to create vibrant drama that will have an impact upon the audience. But what are the director's specific responsibilities to the audience?

In the preceding chapter it was shown that the audience is an active participant in the play. If the play is successful, the audience joins the conflict presented upon the stage. The director, throughout the creation of the production, has taken the place of the audience. He has judged every aspect of the production from the standpoint of the audience. Thus, his first responsibility to the audience is a complete understanding of the way it responds. He must be an audience psychologist.

Many directors feel that success depends upon pleasing the audience, and this is largely true. The audience goes to the theatre to laugh, cry, or be thrilled. They go to the theatre to participate in the production. The director has the responsibility of creating a production that will excite the audience to full participation.

On the other hand, the director must control and challenge the spectator, not merely cater to the playgoer's desire for self-indulgence. Any play, presumably, has meaning and purpose. The director must see to it that these elements are communicated to the audience. Some productions, although extremely effective theatrically, are failures. They thrill or amuse the audience through the use of clever stage devices so exciting that the tricks are remembered rather than the meaning of the play. This type of production can never be condoned, for the director has not fulfilled his responsibility to either the playwright or the audience.

This discussion of the responsibilities of the director emphasizes his central position in the scheme of things. It stresses the importance of the director as a coordinator of many diverse creative elements. Even more, it suggests how the impact of the director's personality and skill will influence the production of a play. The director's place has been established. This discussion has not solved the problem of degree. The extent to which the director may justifiably influence the production is discussed below.

HOW MUCH DIRECTION?

The director, particularly in the non-professional theatre, is in a peculiar position. He has rather complete autonomy in the production of the play. He is apparently the final authority on all matters of production. When the play is produced, his personal prestige as a director hangs in the balance. He receives modest applause in comparison to the actor if the play succeeds, and he is sharply criticized if the play fails. He is frequently judged on the same basis as the painter, the sculptor, or the vocal or instrumental soloist.

The solo artist is a final authority with complete control of his media; the play director is not. The painter can apply his color and texture in any way that his imagination dictates and his technique permits. He may be logically judged on the results.

The play director, like the symphony conductor, is a group artist. He may guide but never completely dominate his materials. His assembled artists must contribute of their abilities. The director's success or failure, therefore, is not always a measure of his own ability.

It is little wonder that some directors, aware of this critical pressure, become dictators and that others, confused by the dynamic personalities of these collected artists, lose their grip on the directorial reins. The results are overdirected and underdirected plays. The ideal middle course may be best explained by citing the extremes.

The Overdirected Play

Director X is a mild mannered, heavy set man whom we shall call Jones. In everyday life he is studious, thorough, conscientious, pleasant. In the rehearsal room his personality undergoes a violent change. He becomes the complete dictator. With no tolerance for ideas other than his own, he forces his predigested concept of the production upon his frightened players.

The interpretation for each role has been determined before-

hand in the cloister of the director's study. The actor's only purpose in the production is to create a replica of the role that Mr.
Jones has undoubtedly acted out as he conceives it to be. As to
the mechanics of direction, Mr. Jones tells each actor the meaning
of every line. He dictates the point at which the actor should
breathe. He counts out the dramatic pauses in every speech, regardless of whether or not they fit the actor's style. The actor who
hesitates is lost. Jones reads and rereads each line for the actor,
not by way of suggesting a point of view, but as a model to be
copied. Jones determines the vocal quality. This vocal quality
must be maintained even though the actor's vocal mechanism is
not fitted to produce it.

In the matter of composition, movement, and business Jones
either laboriously copies every direction from the publisher's script
or demands exact adherence to the patterns he has studiously
lettered in his prompt book. No actor is allowed an original idea
on any of these counts. Jones's decisions are final. Jones is probably a disappointed actor, for at the slightest provocation he
hurries to the stage to act out the role with gestures, which, of
course, the actor must imitate.

The settings have been decided in advance by Mr. Jones. He
hands the technical director complete floor plans, elevations, property plots, costume plots, light plots, sound plots, and make-up
plots. His organization is to be applauded, but his determination
that every item shall be exactly as he has conceived it is to be
abhorred.

The preceding description is indeed extreme, but far less so
than one might imagine. There are dozens of Joneses directing in
the non-professional and commercial theatres—and successfully.
Since Jones is a perfectionist, his plays carry the stamp of audience
approval. They may be somewhat stilted, but they are clear-cut
and precise.

The tragedy of the overdirected production lies in the stifling
of general creative effort. In this production there is only one
artist, Mr. Jones. The production will reflect the strengths and
weaknesses of the director. Every production will carry the same
stamp. We shall see a bit of Mr. Jones in each of the characters.
The creative ability of each of the production workers has been
eliminated so that Mr. Jones's effort might shine. The basic pur-

pose of the play production process, which should be to give every
talented person a chance to contribute the best that is in him, has
been defeated.

The Underdirected Play

The difficulties of the underdirected play are greater for all concerned than are those of the overdirected production. In the overdirected play, an automatic if non-creative precision has been the
result; in the underdirected play, chaos reigns.

Director Y is an extremely charming, casual, happy-go-lucky,
bald-headed fellow whom we shall call Brown. He is very well liked
by everyone, but little respected for his directing ability. All who
know him are aware of his laissez-faire attitude toward life in general and toward directing in particular. His rehearsals are social
gatherings in which everyone has a good time, but little is accomplished. His ability to organize the manifold segments of a
production is nil. When he goes into rehearsal, he has few general
notions of how the play should be produced. He has not worried
about anything beforehand. "It will all work out all right," he says.

During rehearsals Mr. Brown sits back and lets the production
take care of itself. In this situation the experienced actors become
a battery of directors, while the inexperienced players are completely lost. For example, each actor is allowed to move where he
wishes and pretty much when he wishes. The experienced actors
have definite ideas about this and dominate the stage accordingly.
The newcomers shuffle uncertainly in the background. The game
is played with every man for himself. The result is a meaningless,
purposeless production without any semblance of unity. It is impossible for the actor to direct the play from onstage because he
conceives the play in terms of himself. He is unable to project himself bodily into the audience and, therefore, is unable to gain any
feeling of the whole.

The technical aspects of production are handled in the same non-
purposive manner. The floor plans are never clearly set. The
costumes, lights, sets, and props may or may not be right for the
production, depending upon the initiative and responsibility of
the workers in charge. Each part of the production is developed
in isolation from the others, with no central control.

The ultimate production is usually as disorganized as the methods for creating it. The characters have little relationship to each other or to the whole play. The movement is haphazard. The compositions do not reflect the meaning and purpose of the scene. In other words, there has been no guiding force to stimulate the many creative artists and, at the same time, to forcefully integrate and modulate all of the elements into a production.

It is obvious that Mr. Brown has not fulfilled any of the responsibilities of the director. He has been a pleasant bystander lost in the swirl of eager, energetic enthusiasm of his cast and crews. Mr. Brown has not interpreted the play. He has not motivated and guided the actor. He has not developed a tight producing unit. He usually has not either pleased or challenged the audience. Indeed, he has failed as a director.

Mr. Brown, of course, rationalizes his behavior by stating that everyone has been given an opportunity to express himself. There have been no inhibiting factors. In fact, Brown feels that his is the truly creative procedure. Examine any piece of art, and the impossibility of this concept is immediately discernible. Every work of art has form as well as imaginative flight. It must have balance, rhythm, emphasis, unity, coherence, and harmony, to name a few of the bases of art. Note that each and every one of these items implies an order, impossible with Mr. Brown's method of directing.

Unfortunately, there are hundreds of Mr. Browns directing. The underdirected plays far outnumber the overdirected ones. In the case we have cited, Mr. Brown's lackadaisical attitude has been a dominant factor. There are several other reasons for underdirection. Lack of knowledge and experience makes many directors hesitant to take a firm hold of a production. Fear of personalities involved is frequently the reason for underdirected or poorly directed plays in the community theatre. In the high schools, where directors are often selected at random, a simple lack of interest and appreciation of the dramatic form often leads to mere supervision where real direction is necessary.

The ideal director has certain qualities, characteristics, and knowledge which delineate him as the leader of a group art. These characteristics are examined below.

THE QUALIFICATIONS OF THE SUPERIOR DIRECTOR

The process of play directing requires a number of strangely assorted and, in some ways, widely separated abilities. The director must be artist, critic, student, and teacher. Normally, these attributes are not found in full complement in any one person. Very few, if any, directors will perform superiorly all the tasks required of the director. In other words, the following list is not set down to frighten the beginning director but rather to suggest the ideal qualifications toward which he may strive.

The Director as Artist

The director creates a work of art. The play must have the elements of beauty and inspiration present in any art. As such, the director must have the personality attributes associated with the artist.

Imagination. The director must be imaginative. The playwright has provided a cold printed page for the director to bring to life. Every situation, every character, indeed, every line may be treated in many different ways. The director must use his imagination to select the new and different, the varied and colorful, the inspired and powerful means of transforming the dead page into radiant life.

Sensitivity. The director must be sensitive to the meanings and beauties of life. He must be able to respond easily and deeply to the joy and sorrow, the good and the evil, the beautiful and the ugly in human life. If he is to be an interpreter of life, he must be deeply sensitive to life. One of the standard jokes in the theatre suggests that suffering is necessary to great art. In a sense, this is true. The depth of the awareness and responsiveness of the director will be enhanced by his having experienced profoundly.

Visualization. The director must be able to visualize. When the director reads a play, it springs into action before his eyes. He sees the conflict acted out before him. If he cannot picture the action as he reads, he will have trouble transforming the two dimensions of the printed page into the three dimensions of the stage in action. The lack of the ability to visualize is one of the great problems of the beginning director.

Vitality. Since play direction is a group endeavor, the director must have a vitality and energy not always required of other artists. He must be able to stimulate others. Play production demands a great expenditure of energy on the part of the director, the actors, and the craftsmen. The director, in particular, must have the vitality to direct and control the energies of his group of artists.

The Director as Critic

Most artists are poor critics. They become so engrossed in their personal imaginative flight that they are unable to restrict it within carefully defined boundaries. The director must have the qualities of the critic. The technical aspects of direction require keen analysis and calculating evaluation. Every action, every sound must be carefully weighed in terms of the effect that it is to have upon the spectator. The director must create, then step back from the creation, and apply cold critical judgment. It is not enough that he be pleased with his work. It must stand the test of the spectator. Since it is a group art, dozens of co-workers will be unhappily affected if the director's judgment proves to be wrong.

The Director as a Student of Life

Since drama is derived from human conduct, the director must be a student of life. He must be a keen observer. Every experience, whether overt or vicarious, must be carefully stored for future reference. The wealth of his knowledge of the human being in any and all situations can be used again and again to bring the playwright's meanings to the audience.

The Director as a Student of Human Relations

Several studies have shown that actors are more imaginative, more sensitive, have less emotional stability than the average person. All of these qualities are important to the actor who portrays human conflict upon a stage. At the same time, these qualities make the task of cooperative work more complex. The director must be able to handle his players so that the best rather than the worst is stimulated. He must handle each actor and technician as an individual, understanding the personality differences of each. (See Chapter 18.) He must be a master of human relations.

The Director as a Student of Audience Psychology

The audience is an integral part of any production. The director must have complete knowledge of audience characteristics. He must be able to calculate audience response to varying types of stimuli. General knowledge of audience behavior has been discussed in the preceding chapter, and additional information can be obtained in any book on social psychology.[1] The specifics of audience behavior in the theatre can be gained only by careful observation. The audience is a dynamic force, and every director must learn how to deal with it.

The Director as a Student of Drama

Obviously, the director must be a student of drama and dramaturgy. His background of plays must be broad. He must know the history of drama and its development; moreover, a knowledge of play structure is imperative. Only by intensive study of all types of plays from every period can this knowledge be acquired. Thorough understanding of why the playwright did as he did and how he went about it will make direction of the play more meaningful.

To make an intelligent selection of plays for production, the director must be well read in the drama of every period. The director's ability to evaluate the drama he produces will increase as his background in drama increases. (See Chapter 12.)

The Director as a Student of Acting

The director need not be a superior actor, though some acting experience is very helpful. The director who has been a successful actor will understand and have greater sympathy for the problems of the actor. On the other hand, success as an actor does not in any way guarantee the ability to direct successfully.

A complete knowledge of the theory and technique of acting is essential to good directing. Since most directors must train their actors, they should have a knowledge of all facets of acting. (See Chapter 18.)

The Director as a Student of Design

The director must be skillful in the handling of line, mass, color, movement, and even time. His materials are living players, and he

1 See S. E. Asch, *Social Psychology* (New York: Prentice-Hall, Inc., 1952).

must be able to paint beautiful and meaningful pictures. In order to accomplish his purpose he must have a complete knowledge of the denotative and connotative meanings of all of the factors that make up design.

The Director as Teacher

Above and beyond all of the other requirements of the director in the non-commercial theatre is the necessity that the director be a superior teacher. The high school, college or community theatre director works with young, eager, inexperienced people. Their enthusiasm and desire to learn about the drama and the theatre are their greatest assets. Some want to make the theatre their livelihood; others merely seek the social and artistic experience. In either case the director, as the most experienced and proficient member of the group, is responsible for teaching his art and craft to others. The surprising growth and efficiency (all things considered) of the school and community theatres attest the fact that directors are successfully imparting their knowledge to enthusiastic and talented young people.

The purpose of this chapter has been to show the importance of the director and the complexities of his responsibility and authority. Far too many directors plunge into the play production process without a clear view of what is expected of them.

The ideal director is able to maintain a balance between his responsibilities to co-workers and to himself. He recognizes the true meaning of the term, *director.* He realizes that he must be a dynamic force, operating for the good of the whole production, and that he dare not whimsically distort the values contributed by the other artists. He is a leader but not a dictator. He stands at the center of the play production process. It is his job to imbue the play with warmth and truth, with clarity and energy, with beauty and meaning.

Part Two

The Principles
of Play Direction

6

The Motivational Unit

THE MOTIVATIONAL UNIT has been defined as the smallest integral scene in the play. These units are the building blocks of the playwright. By tracing their sequence in the play, the director can easily reconstruct the pattern employed by the playwright.

The five major conventional units of play structure—exposition, complication or development, climax, resolution, and conclusion—trace, in a general way, the over-all pattern of construction. The sequence of motivational units exposes the exact method of development employed by the playwright.

It was emphasized earlier that no play represents a straight-line development. (See Figure 4, p. 35.) Since a growing tension and excitement is basic to good drama, none of the elements of the drama can be developed completely in a single sequence. For example, it is impossible to keep the story or plot line in the foreground throughout the play. Likewise, the conflict cannot be joined and consistently increased in intensity from complication to resolution. Even the characters cannot be created and drawn completely in a single sequence. And finally, the situations have to be changed frequently before they have been fully developed.

Drama must have the elements of surprise and suspense if it is to have maximum impact upon the viewer. These qualities are brought about by deliberately interrupting the action, by introducing new obstacles, characters, and situations. The playwright may heighten the excitement by planting twists and turns in the story line. He usually introduces characters who create new obstacles and problems and thereby change the course of the conflict.

71

By changing different aspects of the physical and social situations, detours in the action are created. All of these changes increase the dramatic values of the play and are possible because the playwright builds his drama out of small integral scenic units.

At the risk of oversimplification, let us outline the playwright's problem. Let us assume that in a given play the dramatist wishes to project four different things: (1) a love story, (2) a struggle between good and bad, (3) character portraits of several interesting people, (4) a particular social message. It is obvious that a play will not give equal emphasis to each element. On the other hand, a great many plays do treat all four.

How is the playwright able to handle these four elements? Though they may be closely related—and if it is a good play, they will seem to belong together—it is impossible to develop them simultaneously. For example, the love story cannot be developed at the same time as the conflict between good and bad. At the opposite extreme, none of the elements can be developed singly without interruption. If the love story is developed fully in one section of the play, then the conflict is developed, and so on, there can be no crescendo of action from the exposition, through the climax, to the conclusion.

The playwright solves this problem by introducing a sequence of little scenes. The scenes are played consecutively, but they may be quite disconnected in their contribution to the advancement of the dramatic action. For example, one scene may project the love story. Before its completion, this scene will be interrupted by the next scene, which may involve violent conflict. The scene of conflict may be stopped to make way for a scene that projects the social message. This scene may, in turn, be dissolved into still another scene with the love story again prominent.

In poor plays, the sequence of scenes is obvious. One of the great skills of the good playwright is his ability to disguise from the audience his technical use of small units with different purposes. In good plays, the units apparently evolve so logically one from the other that the spectator receives the impression of a single crescendo of dramatic action.

Do not misunderstand. The spectator may feel that the play develops with a continually increasing excitement. This does not in any way imply that each little scene is necessarily more intense than the one preceding it or less intense than the one that follows. One scene may end in tension; the next may be extremely tranquil; the third may show another sharp rise in tension. In such an arrangement there will be a cumulative impression of tension. The quiet second scene will, because of the contrast in tension, strengthen the power of the third scene. As indicated in Figure 4, not even excitement continues to increase throughout the play. The total impression may be one of rising action, but the individual units will not follow a consistent pattern.

At the end of this chapter, the first act of Ibsen's *A Doll's House* has been broken down into motivational units. Examination of this unit analysis should clearly indicate the segmental quality of the dramatic sequence.

The clues to the playwright's technique and purpose can always be found in an analysis of the motivational units. These little scenes, therefore, are the starting point and basis of play directing. If the director is to interpret and project the playwright's messages, he must be able to define the units, determine their purpose, and fit them together into a meaningful whole.

THE CHARACTERISTICS OF THE MOTIVATIONAL UNIT

The motivational unit derives its name from the complex of motivational forces that control human conduct. (See Chapter 2.) The motivational unit may be defined as *an integral scenic unit in which the motivational pattern remains unchanged.* Usually the basic scenic components of character, situation, and theme are unchanged throughout the unit. Note that this does not in any way imply that the unit need be static. We are concerned only with total changes in the entire motivational pattern.

For example, if we assume a single pattern of motivating forces established in the characters, the situation and the theme, there may be sharp changes in tension and conflict during the natural unwinding of the cause and effect relationships in the scene. If two antagonistic characters are brought together, the natural result of their meeting may be a struggle of ever mounting intensity.

In this case, the entire struggle with all of its changes in tension still composes a single unit. The unit remains unchanged because it depicts the relationship created by a single set of motivational forces.

Remember that the characters in a play are brought together by the playwright for a purpose. There is always a reason for their meeting. Once they have come together they respond in a particular manner because of (1) the situation in which they meet, (2) the theme or topic about which they are meeting, (3) their individual wants and desires as reflected in their individual character complexes. The interaction between the characters will follow a logical course, prescribed by the playwright, until the action is completed or interrupted by a change in one of the three elements. (For a more complete discussion of the motivational elements, the reader is referred to Chapter 2.) When a change in characters, situation, or theme occurs, a new scene begins. Perhaps the problem of isolating the motivational units may be made clear by examining the results of a change in any of the three major factors.

A Change in Characters

Usually the addition or deletion of one of the characters in a scene will change the motivational pattern and thus the unit. In this sense the motivational unit is identical to the French Scene defined in Chapter 3.

Let us examine a simple scene in order to determine how a change in character changes the motivational pattern. John and Mary are in love. They are seated on a swing in the garden. The characters: John and Mary. The theme: love. The situation: a tryst on a garden swing. One may assume that, depending upon the individual character complexes of John and Mary, a logical sequence of activity will follow.

Now, let us suppose that the scene is interrupted by the introduction of another character, Mary's mother. Immediately, the motivational pattern changes. No matter how the young people were responding, their activity will change. This change is accompanied by a corresponding change in the mood and meaning of the scene. If Mary's mother is angry at finding the young people alone in the garden, the scene may change from one of love to one of conflict. Obviously, the motivational forces have shifted. Thus, a new scene has begun.

To carry the illustration a step further, let us assume that after a conflict unit in which Mary's mother sharply berates her for romancing, Mary leaves the garden in tears. Once again the motivational pattern changes. Mother probably will not respond to John alone as she did to Mary and John. Thus, with the deletion of a character, another unit begins.

In each of these cases, the addition or deletion of a character has changed the motivational pattern. Occasionally characters may be introduced or removed without any motivational change. If two characters are plotting the downfall of a kingdom, the addition of a third conspirator may not change the motivational pattern. In such a case, the unit continues unabated until some change in the motivation does occur.

A Change in Situation

The most obvious changes in situation are shifts in either local. or time. Usually if the curtain has been lowered to signify a passage of time, the motivational forces will be changed when the new scene begins. Changes in place also create new circumstances with a different pattern of motivational forces.

Apart from these obvious changes in situation, numerous other factors may influence the situation thereby changing the motivational forces. Suppose, for example, a telephone call interrupts a scene. The message received may modify the meaning, mood, and theme of the action. In such a case, a new motivational unit will be started even though the characters remain constant.

To go back to the illustration of John and Mary, the author may alter the circumstances in numerous ways, causing a change in the motivational unit. Suppose that Mary is wearing a flower given to her by another admirer. If John finds out, the love scene may become a quarrel. Or the dramatist may create a storm, which would put an end to the romance in the garden. In a farce, the swing might collapse, changing the mood and meaning of the scene. In each case as the situation is altered, the scene is interrupted, and the motivational unit is ended.

A Change in Theme

In most cases the theme will remain constant throughout a motivational unit. There are times, however, when the theme may change without any change in the characters or situation.

Let us suppose that John and Mary, in their love-making, decide to get married. With the change in topic, a change in mood and meaning will result. The old scene will be completed and a new scene begun.

Sometimes the entire motivational pattern may be changed by the introduction of a new topic of conversation. If, for example, a group of characters suspected of murder are carrying on a desultory conversation involving social amenities and, suddenly, one of the characters introduces the subject of the murder, a complete change in the motivational factors will result. Such a change in theme will end one unit and begin another.

A word of warning. A new motivational unit does not begin each time a character shifts the topic of conversation. The new topic or theme must be one that changes the motivational forces. Such alterations can usually be readily recognized because there will be corresponding changes in the mood and emotion in the scene.

The Importance of Recognition

For several reasons, the director must be able to recognize change in the motivational unit, the logical working unit of the director. (1) The constancy of the motivational pattern throughout each unit with a corresponding unity of character, situation, and theme, provides the director with the information necessary for direction. (2) Since the motivational unit is the structural unit of the playwright, the director can ascertain the purpose and intent of the author by tracing the sequence of the units. (3) The director must be able to recognize the motivational units so that he can determine the relationship between each unit and the play as a whole. The method of direction, the intensity of the playing, are dictated by the contribution the unit makes to the whole play.

After isolating the motivational unit, the director's next task is to determine its purpose. Some of the major functions of units are discussed below.

TYPES OF MOTIVATIONAL UNITS

Many motivational units combine more than one purpose and may be of more than one type. In general, however, the motivational units are related to the major concerns of the playwright: story, character, conflict, and mood.

Storytelling Units

The most common type of storytelling unit is the purely expository unit usually found in the early sections of the play. The purpose of this type of unit is to give the spectator information concerning the antecedent action, the locale, the time, the relationships of the characters. In superior plays, the expository materials are frequently subtly woven into the fabric of the action so that there are few, if any, units with storytelling as their sole purpose. In weak plays, and especially older plays, obvious storytelling units are found. They are frequently scenes involving servants or an old friend and confidante of the household.

A second kind of story unit advances the plot. This type of unit may be found at any point in the play. In these scenes the action is brought up to date or summarized and explained to the spectator. Ideally, the entire plot should be acted out, but this is not always possible. Many events cannot be staged. These events are frequently related to the audience in a storytelling sequence.

Character Units

Despite the fact that some character information is forthcoming in almost every scene in the play, many units primarily develop or elucidate character. In the second act of *The Second Mrs. Tanqueray,* the feline chat between Paula and Mrs. Cortelyon serves the sole purpose of showing the spiteful qualities of Paula Tanqueray.

Clifford Odet's *Golden Boy* studies Joe Bonaparte's struggle with himself and his society. His character is developed throughout the play, but certain of the units are more clearly devoted to this purpose. Act I, scene 4, a motivational unit by itself, is a striking example of a character unit. Joe Bonaparte and Lorna Moon are seated on a park bench. Bonaparte tells Lorna of his hopes and fears, his needs and desires. At the close of the unit, the spectator is more fully aware of the facets of Joe's character.

Conflict Units

Since conflict is the basis of drama, little need be said about units of this kind, for they are readily recognizable. It should be noted, however, that a conflict unit need not involve physical combat. A conflict unit may depict a character's struggle with himself, with an idea, or with his environment. In *Hamlet*, Shakespeare has used every conceivable type of conflict unit ranging from Hamlet's inner struggles so forcibly exemplified in the soliloquies to the violent overt struggles at the end of the play

Mood or Emotional Effect Units

Frequently, a motivational unit has no tangible purpose other than the creation of a particular mood or emotion in the audience. These units do not delineate character, tell a story, or advance the conflict. The author inserts the units to heighten the dramatic effect.

Many times, units of this kind are found at the beginning of a scene or an act. They set the mood or emotional quality of the scene. In other cases, they may be deliberately inserted to provide a mood in contrast to the preceding or subsequent units.

A typical example of an emotional effect unit is found in the second act of *Night Must Fall,* when Mrs. Bramson finds herself alone in the house. This unit precedes the climax of the play, a scene in which Danny murders Mrs. Bramson. The gradually increasing hysteria of the scene in which Mrs. Bramson waits for Danny serves to heighten the suspense and make Danny's entrance more exciting.

Units of Combined Purpose

Many motivational units serve more than one purpose. Even in the illustrations above, diversified purposes can be found. In Mrs. Bramson's fear, the audience is given a greater insight into her character and her struggle to control herself. In Hamlet's soliloquies, character and plot are advanced at the same time that conflict is shown. Even seemingly expository units will frequently delineate character and suggest the coming conflict.

The reason for defining the purpose of the motivational units is that each unit will usually have a dominant characteristic or purpose, even though other elements are present. Successful interpretation of the play will depend upon the director's ability to recognize the primary contribution of the unit to the play and to direct the unit so that it serves this primary purpose.

Having defined the motivational unit and considered the major types and purposes, the director should be ready to analyze the individual unit.

ANALYSIS OF THE MOTIVATIONAL UNIT

The number of motivational units in different plays varies greatly, depending upon the structure of the plays. Some full-length plays may have as few as twenty to thirty units; others may have as many as fifty to sixty. Static plays may have long, involved units. Plays that are episodic or depend upon violent action may have very short units. The number of units is determined by the type of play and is not a valid sign of the play's worth.

In isolating the units, the director may find short sequences that do not seem to belong to a unit and, at the same time, do not appear to have any real meaning by themselves. These are usually transitional sequences between units. In music they are bridges, used to get from one key to another or from one spirit to another. They serve the same purpose in the play. They act as transitions or modulations from one motivational pattern to another and maintain the flow of the action.

After the director has isolated the units, he should analyze the purpose and meaning of each. This may be accomplished in eight steps: (1) discovering the relationship of the unit to surrounding units; (2) judging the relationship of the individual unit to the whole play; (3) assessing the significance of the theme or subject; (4) tracing the motivational forces arising from the situation; (5) analyzing the drives motivating the individual characters; (6) tracing the interaction between characters; (7) discovering the individual characteristics of the characters; and (8) determining the mood of the unit and the effect the unit should have upon the audience.

Relationship to Surrounding Units

Although the motivational unit is an entity, it seldom stands by itself. The unit is affected by the units coming before and after it. The director must study this relationship between units. In the sample analysis of the first act of Ibsen's *A Doll's House,* the unit in which Krogstad threatens Nora with exposure stands between a scene depicting Nora's joyous play with the children and one in which Torvald's attitude toward forgery crystallizes the conflict. The directing of the Krogstad scene is affected by this relationship. We may assume that the gay scene with the children is placed before the Krogstad scene to increase the emotional impact of the threat. The interpretation of these emotional extremes is the task of the director. Note that in terms of emotional impact upon the audience, the relationship between the two units is fully as important as the purpose and meaning of either unit by itself.

In a similar manner, Torvald, in the scene following Krogstad's threat, is adamant in his refusal to rehire Krogstad and expresses his abhorrence of crime. The director must decide which of these two scenes is of the greater importance to the total meaning of the play: Krogstad's threat or Torvald's attitude. They cannot be directed with equal emphasis. The director's decision concerning the ideal balance between the two units will affect the meaning of the play as a whole.

Relationship of Unit to the Play

The preceding example indicates how emphasis upon one unit and subordination of another will affect the meaning of a play as a whole. Similarly, the interpretation of a single unit may affect the entire meaning of a play. For example, in many plays the personality of one or more of the characters undergoes change during the play. If an early character unit is interpreted in a particular manner, the results of this interpretation will be felt throughout the play.

An excellent illustration of this is found in *The Second Mrs. Tanqueray.* The first entrance of Paula Tanqueray is primarily a character sequence. It is essential that the audience approve of Paula at the outset. If the director handles this first unit so that Paula Tanqueray is a sympathetic character, later sequences showing the disintegration of her personality can be understood and appreciated by the audience. If, on the other hand, the audience dislikes and disapproves of Paula in the beginning, her downfall will evoke little or no sympathy. Without sympathy for Paula's position, the play loses much of its meaning.

The Significance of the Theme or Subject

In evaluating the motivational unit, the director must determine the amount of emphasis to be given the theme or subject. It should be noted that the theme and subject of a play are not necessarily identical. In Sidney Howard's *The Silver Cord,* the theme is possessive mother love; the subject is the marriage of David and the question of whether or not he and Christina will leave the home of David's mother. In Lillian Hellman's *The Children's Hour,* the theme is children's gossip and its effect upon the community; the topic is abnormal sexual activities.

In some units, neither the theme nor the subject are of particular significance. For example, in a conflict unit the subject may be unimportant, since the characters could probably struggle just as well over some other topic. Frequently, theme or subject is unimportant in character units. On the other hand, in some units the theme or subject is far more important than the characters or the situation. Or in some cases the theme is more significant than the subject and vise versa. Any lack of balance in the interpretation of these factors may destroy the play.

An excellent example of such a lack of balance is found in *The Children's Hour,* though in this case the difficulty probably lies in the writing rather than in the directing. As stated above, the theme is gossip; the subject is abnormal sexual relations. Throughout the play, the subject dominates the theme. No matter how the director tries to lift the theme to its rightful dominance, it is lost because of the startling quality of the subject. In most other plays, the director has a choice. He may choose to emphasize theme, subject, character, conflict, or situation.

Subject may in some plays be more important than theme. This is particularly true in social problem plays. The social philosophy of the playwright as expressed in the subject or discussion of the character may demand dominance.

The point of this discussion is to stress the importance of careful selection of the particular quality to be given emphasis in each unit. The choice is the director's. Misplaced emphasis in a single unit may spoil the play.

The Importance of Situation

Situation has been defined as the set of physical, social, and psychological circumstances. These circumstances may directly or indirectly influence the playing and meaning of a motivational unit. Situation also may act as a motivating force. Usually the physical surroundings are the least important aspect of situation. The entire action of a play will frequently take place in a single room. The physical surroundings will influence the playing, to be sure, but the circumstances that bring the characters together, the previous associations of the characters, their stations in life, the societal pressures motivating the characters—all are a part of the situation.

In the opening unit of Arthur Miller's *All My Sons*, the physical circumstances are unimportant. The drowsy Sunday morning in the backyard is merely a background against which the powerful forces arising from past actions and earlier relationships begin to make themselves felt. In order to interpret this simple expositional unit effectively, the director has to take into account all of the situational forces acting at the time. Change the social situation, and the scene must be handled differently. For example, many plays might begin on a drowsy Sunday morning. The initial unit in each might have identical physical surroundings, identical characters, and an identical theme; but the playing of each will differ if the circumstances affecting the action are different.

The Influence of the Basic Drives

Fundamental to the interpretation of the motivational unit are the basic drives that influence the actions of the characters. In a general sense, the basic drives will be reasonably constant throughout the play. However, the playwright frequently brings new desires and wishes into play diverting the energies of the character into new channels. As a result, the desires that drive the characters will undergo modification from one motivational unit to the next. The recognition and portrayal of these changes in the character drives give meaning and force to the production. In *All My Sons*,

Joe, the father, is driven to action at different times in the play by a great variety of needs. The desire for a secure home life, the wish for recognition as a father, the driving wish for the well-being of his family, the fear of being discovered for what he is, and many other specific wants affect the development of the play. The development of these forces is found in the motivational units. They do not explode simultaneously but, rather, are felt at different times. Analysis of the motivational units will readily show the director how basic drives are developed as one of the facets of the total motivational pattern, which, in *All My Sons,* drives Joe to a desire for death as the solution to all problems.

The Importance of Interaction

The forces that arise from the interaction between characters can be found and interpreted in the motivational units. In *Macbeth,* the powerful drives that control Lady Macbeth in turn influence the thoughts and actions of Macbeth. Without the influence of Lady Macbeth, the dramatic action could never reach the climax that it does. In *A Doll's House,* the interaction of the personalities of Torvald and Nora is more important as a driving force in the play than the individual drives of either character. The interplay and development of these forces can be determined only by examining the motivational units, for the interaction is found in the relationships between the lines of dialogue. The development of the play is dependent on the step by step application of new and changing forces that modify or intensify drives already in operation.

The Search for Individual Characteristics

In the study of human conflict (Chapter 2), the character complex was established as a major determinant of how each individual will act in a given situation. The playwright gives each of his characters a set of individual characteristics. The impact of these divergent characteristics is depicted in the motivational units. In many plays the playwright does not alter the individual characteristics; that is, the characters do not grow or change. In plays of this type the director may determine the individual pattern in the early motivational units and then maintain the pattern throughout succeeding units. In other plays, and these are frequently the greater plays, the individual character pattern changes as new forces are brought to bear. The personalities of the characters are re-formed as the play progresses.

In a play such as Steinbeck's *Of Mice and Men,* the characters are relatively static in their individual patterns; the drama arises from the interaction of these divergent personalities. During the course of the play, the personalities are not modified to any material degree. In O'Neill's *Emperor Jones,* the disintegration of the personality of Jones emphatically illustrates the way the individual characteristics may be modified. Study of the motivational units is the best way to determine the changes in the personality of the characters. The changes are usually wrought as an evolutionary rather than a revolutionary process. Throughout the sequence of little scenes new characteristics are added and subtracted from the character.

The Mood of the Unit

Finally, the director must consider the mood or atmosphere of the unit. Mood will depend upon the preceding analyses. Just as scenes are often interrupted at their climax, as units with different purposes are adjacent to one another, so the playwright will vary the mood or atmosphere in the sequence of motivational units. Many plays lack variety because the director has not made use of changes in mood. Most playwrights realize that attention is a fatiguing process. To avoid fatigue, the playwright presents a series of units with changing atmospheres. The director must recognize these changes in mood and develop the scenes in a manner that will clearly depict them.

After the director has analyzed the units, he is ready to proceed to the technical task of projecting the results of his analysis and interpretation to the audience. If he has followed with care the eight steps for each of the units, he should be able to begin directing at any point in the play. Normally, because of the sequential arrangement of the units, the director starts at the beginning. However, some directors prefer to vary this procedure.

DIRECTING THE MOTIVATIONAL UNIT

Since the motivational unit is an integer, it is really a tiny play by itself. At the beginning of the unit a set of circumstances, characters, a theme and subject, and a pattern of basic drives will be "discovered onstage." The director must employ the visual and vocal means for communicating this "scene" or motivational pattern to the audience.

In starting the unit, the director will arrange his characters to communicate the meaning and emotion of the motivational pattern. For example, in the opening of *A Doll's House,* we see a comfortable, well-furnished room and find Nora and the porter with the Christmas tree. At the very outset we must sense that here is an attractive woman in her comfortable home preparing for Christmas. Any director who understands this simple scene should be able to recreate the meanings and emotions established by the motivational pattern.

Remember that the spectator can understand and respond only to the things he can see and hear. In watching Nora and her Christmas bundles, the spectator immediately begins to assess her character from her speech, her appearance, her movement, and her attitude. The director's job is to make sure that the playgoer draws the right conclusions.

The moment Torvald speaks, the pattern of interaction is set in motion. When, after a few lines, he enters, the spectator makes further decisions. Again, sight and sound are the only tools the audience has. From this point forward the motivational forces begin to make themselves felt with ever greater intensity. As with any motivational unit, the interaction between Torvald and Nora could continue to a natural conclusion were the pattern not interrupted. The audience might view a quiet Christmas Eve in the home of the Helmers. But drama involves selection and arrangement of life in a dramatic sequence, so the playwright ends the unit after it has served its manifold purposes of setting the locale and time of the action, telling us something of the financial position of the Helmers, suggesting the strange parent-child relationship between Nora and Torvald, drawing a fragmentary picture of the characters of husband and wife and creating a simple, pleasant atmosphere, underlaid with a feeling of strain that foreshadows the conflict to come.

Since this opening unit in *A Doll's House* is primarily an expository unit with overtones of character, there will be little rise and fall in emotional tension throughout the unit. It starts simply, runs with little change in tension, and ends with the introduction of a visitor.

Actually, the director has five basic means for communicating the purpose of this unit. They are: the compositional arrangement of the characters, the kind and quality of the movement, the adequacy of the business, the visible and vocal projection of emotional tension, and, finally, the use of time. Read the preceding five items again. You will find that they are the principle means of implementing communication of the meaning of any scene. The following five chapters consider these principles in detail.

Using composition, movement, business, emotion, and tempo, the director will select, order, and intensify the visual and vocal elements that best project the particular meaning of the motivational process. No two directors or casts will conceive identical interpretations of the motivational units. No two groups will select the same visual and auditory means for projecting the pattern. Dramatic production is a creative process.

DANGERS IN THE UNIT METHOD

Some directors will object strenuously to the time spent in this volume on the motivational unit. They will maintain that analysis and interpretation of the units is an approach from the part to the whole rather than from the whole to the part. This criticism may be valid if the director begins his interpretation at the level of the motivational unit. Certainly, a feeling for the entire production must be developed. It has been stressed that the unit is meaningful only to the extent that it is considered in relationship to the whole play.

If used wisely, the motivational unit can be of tremendous value to the director. It is the core and starting point at which the specific techniques of direction may be applied. In interpreting a piece of music, the musician must start with a single note and continue, note by note, to the end. In painting a picture, the artist must draw the first line and continue, line by line, until the picture is completed. No musical number or painting is attacked vaguely as a whole. The motivational unit is the working segment of the director. By working from unit to unit, with an ever present concern for the total concept, he may create a play.

SAMPLE ANALYSIS OF MOTIVATIONAL UNITS
Henrik Ibsen's *A DOLL'S HOUSE*

ACT ONE

Scene: The tastefully furnished living room of the Helmers

Unit One

CHARACTERS: Nora Helmer, a porter, and a housemaid
TYPE: Exposition and Mood
THE ACTION: Scene defines locale and time of action. Sets a mood of
quiet, good cheer with the arrival and hiding of the Christmas
tree
MOOD: Quiet, pleasant, and cheerful
CAUSE OF CHANGE: Introduction of a new character, Torvald Helmer

Unit Two

CHARACTERS: Nora and Torvald
TYPE: Exposition and character
THE ACTION: Describes the financial position of family, Torvald's position at the bank, etc. Delineates Nora's character as extravagant
and child-like. Depicts Torvald as precise, somewhat pompous,
more father than husband. Takes the form of a domestic conversation between Nora and Torvald. Brings to light pressures created
by differences in the characters of Nora and Torvald
MOOD: Similar to Unit One, with slight undertones of dissatisfaction
and tension on Nora's part
CAUSE OF CHANGE: Introduction of a new character, Mrs. Linde

Transition

ACTION: Doorbell rings. Maid enters announcing two visitors. Dr. Rank
to see Torvald. Mrs. Linde to see Nora. Torvald goes to his room
to meet Dr. Rank.
PURPOSE: Removes Torvald from the scene and introduces Mrs. Linde

Unit Three

CHARACTERS: Nora and Mrs. Linde
TYPE: Exposition and character
THE ACTION: Mrs. Linde's background is explained: Mrs. Linde's
loneliness and need for a job. In contrast, we discover Nora's
happiness. She is a worker as well as a lark. A typical expository
conversation between the heroine and the family friend and
confidante
MOOD: Essentially serene and optimistic
CAUSE OF CHANGE: Introduction of a vital change in subject

Unit Four

CHARACTERS: Nora and Mrs. Linde

TYPE: Exposition and Character

THE ACTION: The basis for conflict is laid when Nora tells her secret. We are informed that a woman cannot borrow money without her husband's consent. Nora has borrowed money to save Torvald's life.

MOOD: Tension and excitement of the secret. Unit ends on note of happiness.

CAUSE OF CHANGE: Introduction of a new character, Nils Krogstad

Unit Five

CHARACTERS: Nora, Krogstad and Mrs. Linde

TYPE: Conflict and exposition

THE ACTION: Unit plants Krogstad as the person Nora fears. Foreshadows the conflict to come. We learn that Krogstad works at Torvald's bank and Mrs. Linde knows Krogstad.

MOOD: Tense and uneasy

CAUSE OF CHANGE: Introduction of a new character, Dr. Rank

Unit Six

CHARACTERS: Nora, Dr. Rank, and Mrs. Linde

TYPE: Exposition and character

THE ACTION: A domestic social conversation in which two facts are revealed. Krogstad is morally ill. Nora desires power and independence.

MOOD: Pleasant and convivial

CAUSE OF CHANGE: Introduction of a character, Torvald

Unit Seven

CHARACTERS: Nora, Mrs. Linde, Torvald, and Dr. Rank

TYPE: Plot Advancement and Transitional

THE ACTION: Nora assures a job for Mrs. Linde at Torvald's bank. This is important to later action. Torvald, Mrs. Linde, and Dr. Rank exit

MOOD: Pleasant and convivial

CAUSE OF CHANGE: Exit of the three and the entrance of the children

Unit Eight

CHARACTERS: Nora, the children, and the nurse

TYPE: Emotional effect

THE ACTION: Play with the children

MOOD: Extreme gaiety and happiness

CAUSE OF CHANGE: The entrance of Krogstad

Transition

THE ACTION: Fearful recognition of Krogstad and exit of the children

Unit Nine

CHARACTERS: Nora and Krogstad
TYPE: Exposition and conflict involving the inciting moment
THE ACTION: Krogstad asks that he be retained at the bank. He believes Mrs. Linde has cost him his job. Krogstad is the money lender. He proves that Nora has forged her father's name when borrowing the money. He threatens Nora with exposure if he loses his job.
MOOD: Growing violence and fear
CAUSE OF CHANGE: Krogstad's exit after the threat

Transition

ACTION: Nora's rejection of the children. The setting up of the Christmas tree
PURPOSE: Indicates Nora's concern and anxiety. Shifts to emphasis upon her desire to make Torvald happy. Provides time lapse for Torvald's entrance

Unit Ten

CHARACTERS: Nora and Torvald
TYPE: Emotional effect
THE ACTION: After the skirmish about lying, the scene settles down into a pleasant picture of family excitement before Christmas
MOOD: Gradual relaxation into happy and serene feeling, with underlying tension on part of Nora
CAUSE OF CHANGE: Introduction of change in subject

Unit Eleven

CHARACTERS: Nora and Torvald
TYPE: Conflict and Storytelling
THE ACTION: Torvald explains that Krogstad's crime was forgery to which he would not confess. He expresses complete intolerance for such an action. Asserts that it shows a moral illness that can affect the minds of Krogstad's children
MOOD: Gradually increasing concern and anxiety
CAUSE OF CHANGE: Torvald's exit

Unit Twelve

CHARACTERS: Nora
TYPE: Conflict and emotional effect
THE ACTION: Nora struggles with her fear. The nurse asks to be allowed to bring in the children. Nora refuses. Fears possibility of depraving them

MOOD: Anxiety and fear
CAUSE OF CHANGE: End of the act

The motivational units are clearly observable in *A Doll's House*. By analyzing them in much greater detail than in the preceding sketchy analysis, the director can discover all of the keys to direction. It is particularly interesting to find the units in *A Doll's House*, for it is a completely realistic play in which, according to H. L. Mencken, "[Ibsen] left the dramatic machinery out."

7

Stage Composition

EXAMINE THE PICTURES in any of the national magazines. The camera has recorded small segments of life. Each picture, particularly those that are apparently unposed, has meaning. It may tell the story of a family's reaction to the death of one of its members, or it may show the intensity of a high level policy conference, or the tranquility of a congregation at worship, or the gaiety of a costume ball. In every case, if it is a good picture, it communicates the tale of a life experience to the viewer.

In addition to telling a story, the picture always has form. The cameraman at the scene, or the printer in the darkroom will have arranged the picture so that it fits within a frame, so that it is pleasing to the eye, so that it directs the attention of the viewer to the most significant point. In other words, the picture represents a composition.

So it is with the play on the stage. In a visual sense, a play is a series of meaningful pictures all of which tell a story and all of which have a form which fits within the picture frame. One of the primary purposes of movement, which will be discussed in the following chapter, is to dissolve one picture in order to form another. In a rudimentary sense, the visual dramatic process is: picture—dissolve and re-form—picture—dissolve and re-form—picture. These pictures are called compositions. The process of dissolving and re-forming is called movement. Substituting terms the process will read: composition—movement—composition—movement—composition. The length of time that a picture may be maintained depends upon which motivational forces are operating.

Sometimes it will last less than a second, or occasionally more than a minute. Whenever the movement ceases and the characters of the play hold their positions, there must be a meaningful picture; a composition. This chapter is concerned with the principles of creating stage compositions.

Definition of Composition

Composition in the graphic arts may be defined as the make-up of the picture; that is, the artistic placement of line and mass within the picture frame. The stage director should assume that the scenic background will represent good composition. If the stage is poorly arranged, the director will be at a constant disadvantage in arranging his actors. The student is referred to Chapter 19, in which the requirements of a good setting are discussed.

Assuming a well-composed background, stage composition may be defined as *the artistic and meaningful arrangement of characters upon a stage.* As in the case of the setting, it is essentially the process of arranging human figures so that the assembled line and mass creates an artistic and meaningful picture. In other words, it is the make-up of the human picture.

Principles of Composition

In each of the definitions given above, the terms "meaningful" and "artistic" have appeared. Many critics may maintain, and rightly, that meaning is a part of art. The two have been separated here because all too frequently stage directors concern themselves with arranging "pretty pictures" without giving sufficient thought to the question of whether or not the picture fulfills a dramatic purpose. As we have said again and again, the prime function of play production is to communicate the meanings of the playwright to the audience. To be sure, these meanings should be projected in an artistic and beautiful manner. But meaning must be the first consideration.

In composing a meaningful and at the same time a beautiful picture both the motivational pattern found in the scene and the technical limitations of the conventional stage must be considered. The principles of composition will be discussed under these two major headings.

MOTIVATIONAL ASPECTS OF COMPOSITION

Creation of a stage picture that reflects the motivational forces operating in the scene depends upon the director's knowledge of human conduct; his sensitivity to the possibilities of imaginative expression; his knowledge of play structure; and, finally, his awareness of the possibilities of audience response.

The specific procedure for determining whether or not a picture reflects the motivation in a scene is difficult to discuss in a concrete way. The compositional requirements will differ with each new situation, conflict, and set of individual character complexes. The starting point and the desired result can be pointed out. The success with which the director is able to create a meaningful picture will depend upon his skill and imagination.

Compositions Should Appear Natural

In setting the initial aspects of the picture the director should try to create an illusion of reality. If the question is asked, "How should I arrange the people on the stage?" the answer must be, "Arrange them as you feel they would naturally arrange themselves in life." If it is a group of people in a drawing room enjoying a summer afternoon's desultory chit-chat, the characters should be arranged so that they give that impression. Although there are innumerable possibilities of arrangement, the naturalness of the composition depends upon the motivational characteristics. For example, people arrange themselves differently in a drawing room than they do in a park (situation). Tense people sit differently than do relaxed people (basic drives). People who dislike each other arrange themselves differently than do people who are fond of each other (social interaction). Old people take different positions than do young people (character complex).

After the "natural" arrangement has been determined the director will have to modify this grouping until it conforms with the technical limitations of the stage. However, the illusion of reality is the first consideration.

Compositions Should Tell a Story

Deprived of sound and context, does the composition make a point? Most paintings and photographs don't need dialogue to make them clear. They tell a story by themselves. So it should be with a stage composition. In addition to appearing real, it should also tell the viewer about the situation and the people. Storytelling value is dependent upon arrangement, as different compositional arrangements connote different things.

Pupils at the feet of the master, a family at prayer, a king addressing his subjects, a lady serving tea, two cronies exchanging anecdotes; or any story involving human beings can be made more clear if the composition of the characters provides a clear insight into the meaning of the scene.

Compositions Should Depict Emotion

Emotion is projected visually by bodily tension. The eye of the spectator must perceive the emotional meaning from the bodily tension of the characters. Emotional tension may be shown by muscular tension, posture, and position. Thus the arrangement or position of the characters will help provide the audience with clues as to the emotional meaning of the scene.

Examine the list of actions in the preceding illustration and visualize how the addition of emotional implications will dictate changes in the muscular tensions, postures and positions of the characters. Suppose the list were changed to read: cringing pupils at the feet of a hated master, a terrified family at prayer, a grief-stricken king addressing his angry subjects, an anxious lady serving tea, two excited cronies exchanging an anecdote. In each example the storytelling value of the composition takes on added emotional meaning as the tension of the characters reflects the motivational pattern.

Compositions Should Indicate Character Relationships

In most groups some person holds a dominant position. Such a person is the leader, the aggressor, or at least the key member. In the situations listed above, the master, the king, the lady are the dominant characters. At a particular moment one member of the family at prayer and one of the two cronies is probably more important than the others. This dominance must be indicated in the composition.

In the dramatic situation, the person who speaks is usually the dominant character. This dominance should be reinforced by the arrangement. In addition, the relationship of every other character to this central point of interest must be indicated.

At the same time, the physical arrangement of the characters in the composition must connote their emotional or social relationships. The natural groupings of friends, families, and lovers, as opposed to the separations of enemies and strangers, will help to define each character's attitude toward and relationship to the others.

In summary, stage compositions, coupled with movement and business which will be discussed in succeeding chapters, can help to express meanings. They should give the appearance of reality though they cannot actually be arranged in a real fashion because of the specific limitations of the stage. The peculiar requirements of the stage necessitate technical modifications. These technical considerations of stage composition are discussed in the following sections.

TECHNICAL ASPECTS OF COMPOSITION

The technical aspects of composition can never be completely divorced from the motivational requirements. On the other hand, the technical aspects may be discussed separately. A perfectly motivated composition may fail to communicate meaning or seriously disturb an audience because the director has not been able to adapt the arrangement to the characteristics of the stage. For a detailed discussion of the stage, floor plans, and settings as they affect the play direction, the student is referred to Chapter 19.

The technical process of (1) fitting the composition to the playing area, (2) creating compositions which are pictorially superior, and (3) arranging compositions which control and direct attention, must be learned if the desired response is to be obtained from the audience.

THE PLAYING AREA

Assuming a picture frame stage, that is, a stage in which the playing area lies wholly behind the proscenium arch, the playing area will be enclosed on three sides by a setting and open on the fourth. The exact dimensions of the playing area will be determined by the sight lines and the "fourth wall."

The Sight Lines

The sight lines of a typical auditorium are shown in Figure 30 p. 317. These lines of vision are just as important in the arrangement of a composition as they are in the creation of a setting. Probably the first rule of composition should be that *the composition must be seen*. No major action may take place in areas which cannot be seen by all members of the audience. This means that although the walls of the setting are apparently the confines of the playing area, in actuality the usable playing space will be reduced by the line of vision of the spectator.

The Fourth Wall

The "fourth wall" is a somewhat artificial concept. The early naturalists tried to place the actor within the setting rather than merely in front of a decorative background. Carrying the idea to an extreme they assumed that since three walls of the stage room could be seen, the fourth wall literally had been removed. Therefore the spectator sat outside the room and looked through the fourth wall.

In modern drama this literal concept of the fourth wall has been abandoned except in some rather dubious experiments in which baseboards, fireplaces, windows, and doors are placed along the curtain line to define the wall. The modern director is more concerned with maintaining a picture within the frame established by the proscenium arch.

The Framed Picture

Just as the sides of the playing area are defined by the sight lines, the front edge of the playing area is marked by an imaginary "playing line" which runs between the front edges of the setting. Any action which violates this line will appear to burst out of the frame and destroy the illusion of the framed picture. Using the older term, this process is described as "breaking the fourth wall," since the actor does apparently walk through the wall of the room.

The illusion of the framed picture may also be broken in another way. Just as the actor may walk out of the frame, he may destroy the illusion of a picture by establishing eye-to-eye contact with members of the audience. The artistic detachment of the spectator is based in part on his physical removal from the scene. When an actor "breaks the wall" and looks directly at him the spectator feels as though he has been drawn through the frame into the action. The illusion of a picture is broken.

Note that the concept of the framed picture belongs in a discussion of the representational style of play. In presentational style the concept of the framed picture is eliminated entirely. The specifics of these styles are discussed in Chapter 23.

The Nomenclature of the Playing Area

The playing area, bounded at the front by a playing line, on the sides by the walls of the setting or the sight lines, and at the rear by a back wall or drop, is shown in Figure 6.

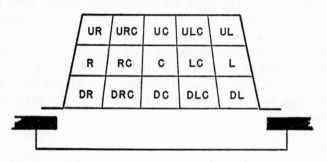

FIG. 6. DIVISIONS OF THE PLAYING AREA

To simplify the process of directing the actor, the stage area is roughly divided into fifteen small areas. These smaller divisions are labelled in combinations of the terms left (L), center (C), right (R), up (U), and down (D). In theatrical terminology, left and right always refer to the actor's left and right. Up or upstage means away from the footlights or toward the back of the stage; down or downstage is toward the footlights or the audience. The terms up and down may be more meaningful if the director will remember that older stages were built with an actual incline, so that the back portion of the stage was raised slightly above the front of the stage. The stage was constructed in this way so that the actors at the back could be seen easily. In these old theatres to go upstage meant literally to walk up a little incline toward the back of the stage.

PICTORIAL ASPECTS OF COMPOSITION

Since the spectator views the stage setting and the arrangement of characters in the compositions in much the same way that he looks at a picture, the artistic principles which control the painting of a picture will also determine the arrangement of a composition. The only real difference between the technique of the painter and that of the play director is a difference in depth. The painter is working in a two dimensional form, the stage director is working with three dimensions. Even this difference is largely nullified by the use of perspective through which the painter gains an impression of depth.

In examining any composition, whether it be in a photograph, on a canvas, or on the stage, the pleasure the picture gives is in a large measure determined by the presence of unity, variety, coherence, contrast, balance, and emphasis. In addition to the beauty of the individual composition the stage director has an additional problem, in that he must construct dozens of compositions that will appear in rapid succession. Therefore the relationship of each composition to the preceding and following ones takes on significance.

Unity

Unity may be defined as a quality of singleness or wholeness. Each composition must appear as an integral unit. Unity in composition depends largely on the singleness of purpose in the picture and the successful application of the mechanics of selection, arrangement, and intensification.

No composition can appear unified if it doesn't have apparent and logical justification for all of its parts. Thus every aspect of a unified composition must contribute to the motivational meaning of the picture. Pictorially the director must arrange his characters in such a way that each of the characters has a definite relationship to the whole picture. If the spectator is able, consciously or unconsciously, to pick out individual elements in the picture that distract from the whole, the composition lacks unity.

In one sense unity is the ultimate value for which the director strives. The impression of unity depends largely on the fortunate combination of variety, coherence, balance and emphasis.

Variety

Psychologically and aesthetically, variety is a key to making a powerful impression upon the spectator. Unity without concurrent variety quickly loses its power to move the spectator. One of the most common compositional pitfalls is the tendency to drop into a repetitive pattern of arrangement. If the possibilities of arrangement on a stage are exploited to the full, there are literally an infinite number of possible combinations. The imaginative director can provide a variety in arrangement that makes each new picture a refreshing one. Nothing will fatigue an audience more quickly or impair the pictorial stimulation more effectively than a constant repetition of the visual pattern.

Coherence

Coherence is one of the major factors in gaining the impression of unity. Coherence means to "stick together." Compositions must stick together. If the characters are arranged so that the composition gives a feeling of being scattered over the stage the unity of the impression will be lost.

In a pictorial sense, coherence is frequently a space relationship. If a composition is arranged into two separate groupings, the composition will appear to split in half. If the characters are placed with equal distances between them, a scattered feeling will result. In each of these situations the spatial relationship must be corrected so that there is a correlation of all of the parts.

There is one major exception to the preceding principle. When only two, or at most three, characters are on the stage, coherence decreases in importance, for the spectator no longer views the characters in terms of the entire scene. The eye of the spectator acts in much the same manner as the lens of a motion picture camera when the camera moves in for a close-up. The viewer focuses on a small area surrounding the two people. Likewise, the spectator's eye frames this smaller segment of the entire picture.

Balance

Any discussion of stage composition must deal at some length with the problem of balance. Since the stage picture is framed, the spectator is provided a basis for judging balance. If the picture had no frame, balance would be less significant, for the viewer could adjust his view so that there would be an equilibrium of contending forces.

Man natively tries to establish a balance or equilibrium in everything he encounters. In discussing the forces of motivation it was noted that man's reaction to disorganizing forces is an attempt to regain an equilibrium. Anything that is not in equilibrium is displeasing. When a man sees a house which appears ready to topple over, he empathically adjusts his own musculature in an attempt to right it. So it is in looking at the stage picture. If a disequilibrium exists within the picture frame the spectator finds it dissatisfying and tries to correct the balance.

Balance may be defined as the equilibrium between contending forces. These forces may be physical, as in an actual distribution of mass and weight, or they may be psychological forces which give the impression of mass; for example, a dynamic personality as opposed to a pallid one. In any case, if a picture is to be pleasing it must be in balance.

Physical Balance. Physical balance involves an equilibrium in the distributions of physical mass about the stage. If the stage picture frame is placed on a fulcrum set on the center line, the contending

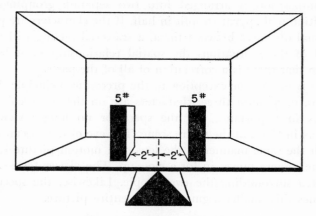

FIG. 7. SYMMETRICAL BALANCE

physical forces on either side of the mid point must be in equilibrium. In the simplest sense it is comparable to one of the first problems posed in mechanics. In this experiment, it is found that the mass times the distance from the fulcrum on one side of the scale equals the distance times the mass on the opposite side of the fulcrum point when the scale is in balance. This is illustrated in Figures 7 and 8.

This balance may be stated in a mathematical formula:

$$M \times D = D \times M$$

In Figure 7 it can readily be seen that an exact balance exists on the scale because:

$$5\# \times 2' = 2' \times 5\#$$

This kind of balance is called symmetrical balance. It has an exact repetition of forces and distances on either side of the center axis. Symmetrical balance is seldom used in the theatre because the formality and regularity of symmetrical balance appears artificial.

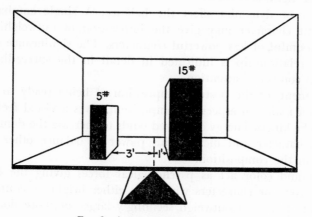

FIG. 8. ASYMMETRICAL BALANCE

Asymmetrical balance is illustrated in Figure 8. Note that physical balance as indicated by the formula $M \times D = D \times M$ still holds. The principle is that of the teeter-totter: a heavy mass placed near the fulcrum point will be balanced by a lighter mass placed farther from the axis. Substituting in the formula as before, we find that:

$$5\# \times 3' = 1' \times 15\#$$

Asymmetrical balance is an important tool for the stage director. Assuming a setting which is in balance, an arrangement in which heavy masses like furniture, fireplaces, or staircases (see Chapter 19) are so placed in relationship to the center axis that an equilibrium is obtained, the director can group his characters in a myriad of asymmetric combinations which will maintain a pleasing equilibrium within the picture frame.

Psychological Balance. Balance has been defined as an equilibrium of contending forces. In physical balance the forces have been actual weights or masses placed specific distances from an axis. Even more important to the director than physical balance is the more nebulous psychological balance.

The forces involved in psychological balance are those which give the *impression* of weight or mass. Many of these factors are intangibles that the director should learn to recognize. Some of them can be readily identified. They are energy, movement, speech or sound, light, and color.

Energy or dynamics affect the balance. A single emphatic or dominant character may give the impression of outweighing an entire roomful of less powerful characters. The significance of this type of relationship is indicated in detail in the succeeding sections on control of attention.

Movement, or the postural impression of being ready to move, while not really an aspect of composition, gives a visual feeling of force. The kinetic energy displayed tends to increase the dominance of the character and increase his power to balance other larger masses in the composition.

Light and color act as psychological forces giving the heavily lighted areas or characters who wear either bright or contrasting colors the power to outweigh seemingly larger or more dominant masses.

The effective use of psychological balance depends largely on the director's imagination and experience. These factors may be manipulated in a truly amazing variety of combinations. The particular application will depend upon the specifics of each new situation. As the director's experience increases he will find that he can sense quickly the relative "weights" of energy, movement, light, and color. To conclude, the basic factor in balance is physical in nature, that is, the bodies of the players. The modifications and variations in compositional arrangement stem from the psychological effects of these elements.

Other Aesthetic Factors

In addition to unity, variety, coherence, and balance, several other aesthetic values should be found in the composition. They are rhythm, grace, harmony, contrast, and emphasis and subordination.

Rhythm may be defined as *regular recurrence*. Within the limits of the picture there should be recurring elements that help to maintain the unity of the composition. Grace is the ease and attractiveness found in the form of the composition. The grace of a composition may at times be in direct conflict with the motivational forces operating. In such cases motivation must control the arrangement. If the situation is one that demands harsh unpleasant arrangement of line and mass, grace must be subordinated. Harmony refers to the adjustment of the various parts to form a whole. The use of line and mass must be aesthetically integrated whether the purpose be to picture passion or poise. Contrast is concerned with the indication of differences. The meaning and force of compositions can be increased by showing sharp differences within the framework of the arrangement. Procedures for using contrast are discussed in a later section. Mere repetition or continued uniformity numbs the senses; contrast is used to sharpen the meanings.

A final aesthetic value is emphasis, with its logical corollary, subordination. This value is of such significance in theatrical composition that it is discussed as a major division under the heading, "control of attention."

CONTROL OF ATTENTION

Attention is a concentrating or focusing process. There is little to be gained by a detailed definition. It will suffice to say that when one stimulus is more powerful than the others which are impinging upon our systems, we attend or concentrate upon that stronger stimulus. The process of focusing may be voluntary or it may be involuntary. Since paying attention is at best a fatiguing process, the theatre director desires voluntary attention. Every director hopes that his audience will be caught in the magic of the production and held transfixed by the dramatic action.

In reality, "being transfixed by the dramatic action" implies a specific control of attention. The director wishes to stimulate the spectator to attend or focus upon a particular line, character, movement, sound, object, or idea at every moment throughout the play. Thus the problem of controlling attention is one of making some elements in the production emphatic and subordinating others.

The Focal Point. Every well-composed picture has a high point of interest. This high point is called a focal point. Examine any advertisement, graphic print, photograph, motion picture scene, or stage composition, and you will find that some element in the picture is more dominant than the others. In the advertisement it is usually the product; in a portrait it is the face of the character; in a group scene a key character or group of characters is more emphatic than the others. Considered visually, the focal point is the spot in the picture to which the eye travels first.

A stage composition is like a picture except that it involves living human characters. The focal point of the composition is dictated by the motivational relationships of the characters. Characters who have lines which must be heard and understood by the spectator are usually at the focal point. Occasionally an object or action must be seen, as when the villain draws his dagger. The dagger then becomes the focal point. In every case the focal point is that single line, movement, action, or object which must be perceived to the exclusion of everything else.

It should be noted that in the stage composition, the focal point is always determined by the motivational relationship rather than the social status of the characters. In the Attic play, for example, a lowly messenger who comes bearing news may be the dominant person in the scene despite the fact that he is surrounded by kings and queens.

In the stage composition, as in other forms of graphic art, attention may be directed by manipulating a series of variables which are usually present in a picture. Since each of these variables, used properly, helps define the focal point, they are discussed and illustrated in some detail.

These factors are: (1) body position, (2) area, (3) level, (4) space, and (5) focus. Since all five factors appear simultaneously, it is difficult to isolate a single factor. Thus, values assigned to a single factor assume that all of the others are held constant. Therefore, each of the five compositional factors will be considered as if the other four were not functioning. This singleness of operation is of course not possible in any literal sense.

Body Position

Body position may be defined as the physical relationship of the actor to the audience. More specifically, it is the degree to which the actor faces the audience. There are eight basic body positions, illustrated in Figure 9.

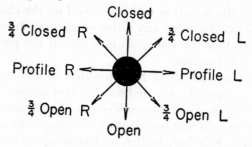

FIG. 9. EIGHT BASIC BODY POSITIONS

The actor who is standing or sitting so that he faces the audience squarely is in a *full open* body position; open in the sense that his face can be clearly seen. At the opposite extreme, the actor who turns his back to the audience assumes a *full closed* body position. The actor who turns his profile to the audience while facing stage left is said to be *profile left*. The actor in profile to stage right is in *profile right*. By dividing the possible body positions again we have the ¾ positions. These positions are labelled by combining left or right, open or closed in the proper combinations.

The director who trains his actors to recognize the body positions can, by combining them with the names of the stage areas, describe the exact position and placement of the actor on the stage in an instant. For example, an actor who has been directed to stand down left (DL), ¾ closed right (¾CR) should be able to find his place immediately. The need for the actor to understand this simple terminology cannot be over-emphasized, for the placement of the actor on the stage is fundamental to arranging a composition.

Body position is a powerful factor in creating emphasis. When we wish to determine what a man is feeling or thinking we try to maneuver ourselves into a position from which we can see his face and hands, since they are the most expressive parts of the body. The principle governing the use of body position to increase dominance is based upon this premise. The principle, assuming that other factors giving emphasis are constant, may be stated: *The more open the body position, the greater the emphasis.*

For example, if three characters are placed on the stage with one in an open position, a second in profile, and the third in a closed position, the attention will be focused on the character with the open position. Examine any series of pictures showing groups of people. Note how the eye tends to settle on the person who is in the most open position.

Before analyzing the use of body position in a composition, let us add another principle. It may be stated very simply. *People face each other when in direct communication.* There are exceptional situations, but usually the positions of two people in conversation are face to face, their feet, bodies, and faces squarely facing each other.

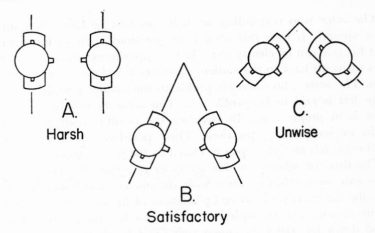

A.
Harsh

B.
Satisfactory

C.
Unwise

FIG. 10. SHARED EMPHASIS BY BODY POSITION

Applying the two principles simultaneously, the possibilities of emphasizing and subordinating characters should be clear. If two characters have equal dominance they should be placed in profile positions. This relationship, illustrated in *A*, Figure 10 is called *shared emphasis.* With both in profile position the spectator can see each of the characters equally well. Thus they appear to have equal dominance. In order to improve the sight lines and soften the effect of the relationship, the downstage foot of each of the characters is usually pulled back slightly, which opens the body positions accordingly, as shown in *B.*

Note, however, that the body positions are more nearly profile than the ¾ positions shown in *C.* The ¾ positions create an artificial effect which will confuse the audience. People just don't talk to each other while maintaining a ninety-degree angle.

In most dramatic conversations, the characters are not equally emphatic. One of the characters is more important than the other. He may be more aggressive, have the more meaningful lines, or emotionally dominate the other character. In such a case a single emphasis is desirable. Again applying the two principles of body position, the relationship will be that shown in A, Figure 11. The dominant character is placed slightly upstage of the subordinate character. Accordingly, the dominant character's body position is opened slightly, and the subordinate character is somewhat closed. The spectator can see the open character more clearly; therefore, he will have the greater emphasis.

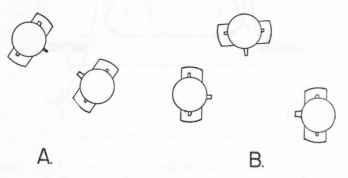

A.   B.

FIG. 11. SINGLE EMPHASIS BY BODY POSITION

In B, the same principles of single emphasis through body position are applied to three characters. The number of characters in the scene may be increased at will. The principle is the same.

In a composition involving several people, the director must employ considerable variety in body position. Actors are prone to assume the body position of a neighboring player. Undue repetition in body position results in a dull and artificial composition. A good rule to follow: *Avoid identical body positions in the same composition.* A clear-cut exception to this rule will be found in those situations wherein repetition in body position is necessary to create a highly regular or stylized effect.

Playing Areas

The stage areas were defined in a preceding section. The strength or emphatic value of the playing areas is largely related to the audience sight lines. It may be said that *the more prominent the area, the stronger the emphasis placed on the character within the area.*

Since the downstage areas are more clearly within the sight lines than the upstage areas, they are the stronger. Similarly, since the central areas are more easily seen than the side areas, they tend

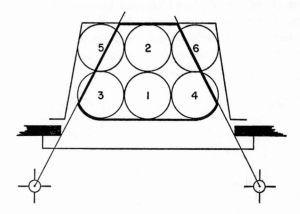

FIG. 12. DOMINANCE OF THE PLAYING AREAS

to be dominant. In Figure 12, the playing areas of the stage are ranked from the strongest to the weakest.

The two central areas are the strongest in emphatic value. If a doorway or arch is placed in the center of the back wall of the setting, the upstage center area will equal or surpass the downstage area in dominance because the arch will frame anyone standing in front of it. Since the left and right downstage areas are well within the audience sight lines, they follow the central areas in strength. The down stage right area is somewhat stronger than its counterpart on stage left because the spectator is accustomed to reading from left to right. Areas 5 and 6 are weak, for they are removed from the audience by distance and poor sight lines.

Another factor that strengthens the emphatic value of the central areas is the fact that the spectator expects to find the focal point of a picture near the center rather than at the periphery.

The strength of the various areas is reflected in the arrangement of the setting. The furniture that motivates composition is usually placed in areas 3 and 4. This leaves areas 1 and 2 open for playing.

The varying strengths of the different areas can be used to establish emphasis and subordination in composition because a character in a strong area tends to be more dominant than a character in a weak area.

If two or more characters are placed in a single area, area ceases to be a factor affecting dominance. This does not imply that scenes may not be limited to a single area. As a matter of fact, most dual and trio scenes do involve only one area. In such cases area should be disregarded as a factor of dominance regardless of whether the area is strong or weak.

The emphatic power of the areas may be used in another way. The dramatic value of a scene can be heightened by playing it in a strong area or softened by playing it in a weak area. The director must choose his area of play partly on the basis of the degree of dominance the scene deserves. Occasionally scenes have such terrific dramatic impact that it is wise to play them in a weaker area in order to soften the effect upon the audience. To illustrate: The scene in which Othello smothers Desdemona is so powerful in its display of agony and terror that it is usually played in a weak area. If it were played in the strongest area, the artistic detachment might be destroyed and the empathy could become too intense and result in a loss of illusion.

Level

Level may be defined as the height relationship to the stage floor. A character may be prone, sitting, standing, or raised to a still greater height by steps or platforms. The principle governing the use of height or level is similar to that in life. In general it may be said that *the higher the level, the greater the emphatic value.*

The power of level is actually derived from two factors. First, we associate height with dominance in life. The giant towering over the puny man, the victor standing above his victim, and the king upon his raised dais are all typical examples of the motivational significance of level. Secondly, the power of level is in part the result of the stage sight lines. A character in a raised position is more easily seen. As in the case of body position and area, level that increases visibility will increase dominance.

Space

The use of spacial relationships is inherent in the arrangement of compositions. Despite the depth that is present in the stage picture, the audience sitting on the main floor of an auditorium receives, for the most part, a two dimensional impression. For this reason, the upstage-downstage space relationships are far less significant than those occurring between characters from stage left to right.

If a group of characters is arranged on the stage so that there is an equal lateral spacing between them, a repetitious monotony will result, regardless of whether they are placed in different depths

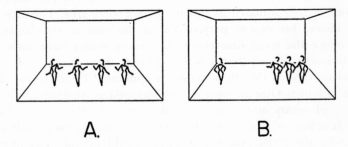

A.   B.

FIG. 13. DOMINANCE THROUGH SPACE

on the stage. If, on the other hand, one character is placed somewhat apart from the others, that character will receive emphasis based upon space. In A, Figure 13, the characters are equally spaced. Note in B the sudden dominance placed on one character by opening a greater space between him and the others. The principle may be stated: *The greater the space separating one character from two or more other characters, the greater the dominance.*

Visibility and motivation are also the bases for the emphatic value of space. Any character who is set apart from the others can be seen easily, while the rest of the characters blend together. As to motivation, the separation of one from others has a connotative value. If a group of children are playing and one sits apart, we become interested in the lonely one. In times of stress people huddle together; only the aggressive dare to step forth. Most people will join a crowd rather than run the risk of becoming conspicuous. Interest is aroused when a separation occurs.

Focus

Attention has been defined as a focusing process. One of the characteristics of the process is a physical arrangement in which the receptors are turned toward the stimulus. We turn to face a sharp sound; a quick movement causes us to turn to see it better; a delicious aroma leads us to turn or even move toward it. In other words, we pay attention by orienting our bodies toward the exciting force.

This process of physical orientation can be used to influence other persons. When we see a group of people staring at the sky, we are curious and do likewise. A very old trick is based upon this principle. Hunt some non-existent object with great energy; soon everyone within range will have joined the search. This process is called *focus* and may be stated in a simple principle: *We look where others look.*

The focusing process is of great importance in defining the focal point for the audience. If three characters on the stage look at a fourth, the man who is watched will become dominant. If a group of characters all look at an object, for example, a vase, the audience will look at the vase.

Direct focus. In general it may be said that when several characters on a stage look at an object or person the object of their attention becomes the focal point for the audience. This process is called direct focus.

A powerful means of directing the audience's attention, this device must be used with care. If too many characters direct their attention toward a particular person or object, the composition will appear unreal and artificial. To avoid this crude direction of attention, the picture is softened and made more real by the use of delayed focus.

Delayed focus. The process of delaying focus is achieved by carrying the spectator's eye through one or more steps before it reaches the focal point. The two types of focus are illustrated in Figure 14. In A, characters *b, c, d, e* are all looking directly at *a,*

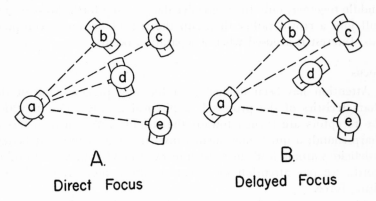

A.

Direct Focus

B.

Delayed Focus

FIG. 14. DOMINANCE THROUGH FOCUS

who is the focal point. In B, this obvious focus is softened by having characters *b, c,* and *e* look at *a,* while character *d* looks at *e.* The spectator's eye will be carried to the focal point immediately if he looks at characters *a, b,* or *e.* If, however, the spectator looks at character *d,* his eye will be led to character *e,* and then in turn to the focal point, character *a.* This delay in arriving at the focal point will soften the reaction to it.

The use of focus is a primary means for establishing the dominance of a stage character. It is completely logical in terms of motivation. We do look where others look. This power of focus is further enhanced in the stage composition, for the players are on a raised stage before an audience.

Contrast

Contrast is not an element in the control of attention in the same sense as the preceding five factors. It is rather the process of indicating differences. The emphatic characteristics of body position, level and space may be reversed through the use of contrast.

If several characters have open body positions, a player in a closed body position will be dominant because his position is different. If several characters are standing, a character who sits will gain dominance. If many characters are arranged with liberal spacing about the stage, a small knot of characters will become emphatic by contrast.

The reversal of the general principles governing the technical factors of composition should be used sparingly. Contrast is an appetizer, not an entrée. In establishing a reversal of the general principles, both the psychological and visual values are lost. For example, level gives dominance because the character in a high place is more easily seen and heard and because height connotes strength. With a reversal emphasis arises from contrast alone.

Many directors take great delight in reversing the principles of composition to prove that it can be done. Of course it can be done! Used with discretion it provides a valuable variety to composition. Overused, contrast can lose its power because the only way one can sense a contrast is by seeing the normal procedure from which the contrast is derived.

GEOMETRIC ARRANGEMENTS

Lay out a number of paper clips, match folders, or any other handy item of uniform size on a piece of paper. Unless the objects are deliberately scattered at random, some geometric pattern will result. The arrangement will usually form a rough line, circle, square, or triangle. The same possibilities exist in the placement of characters upon the stage. Each of these patterns has specific emphatic characteristics. Some are extremely useful in stage composition; others should be avoided.

The Line

A line, because of its uniformity, does not stop the eye at any particular point along it. If we look at a line the eye will usually drift to the end. Thus the ends of a line will be the emphatic points. This peculiarity can be of considerable use in arranging compositions. For example, a line of characters reaching from a weak area to a strong area will emphasize the end of the line in the strong area. Or a line of characters with closed body positions pointing toward a character with an open body position strengthens the character with the open body position.

The situations suggested above are exceptional. Normally, people do not group themselves in lines. For this reason a line of characters on the stage will appear formal and artificial unless there is some sound motivational reason for it. Soldiers are expected to march in lines. People waiting to pass through the customs may line up. Subjects waiting for an audience with a king may form a line, but these are the exceptions in drama.

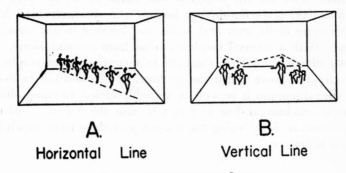

A.
Horizontal Line

B.
Vertical Line

Fig. 15. Arrangement in Lines

The discussion thus far has dealt with a horizontal line, formed by placing characters with comparatively even spacing across the stage. A second type of line of which the director must be aware is the vertical line.

A vertical line may be formed by an evenness in the height of the characters' heads. Similar vertical lines should be avoided, for they look artificial. Also, any repetition of vertical line characteristics should be changed. For example, if the characters are arranged so that their head heights are repeated one high, one low, one high, one low, the effect will seem artificial. Horizontal and vertical lines are illustrated in Figure 15.

The Square

In life, the normal arrangement for four characters who are conversing is a square. Each person stands so that he may see and hear the others. This arrangement will not work on a stage because one side of the composition must be kept open so that the audience may see and hear. No matter how you turn a square, at least one and usually two of the characters will be covered, screened from the audience by another player. In addition, it will be difficult to establish a focal point by compositional means.

The Circle or Semi-circle

For obvious reasons the circle is never used on the stage. There is no emphatic point in a circle and the characters forming the downstage section of the circle will always cover those in the upstage positions.

The semi-circle or arc, called in theatrical terminology a chorus circle because of its similarity to a chorus or quartet arrangement, should also be avoided. The even order of the characters makes it extremely difficult to establish a dominant point.

Unfortunately, this arrangement is frequently used by inexperienced actors and directors. Whenever three or four actors assemble in a group to converse, they tend to cluster in a little chorus circle with the open side to the audience. In such an arrangement, the body positions are usually repetitious, resulting in an artificial composition. The chorus circle is illustrated in A, Figure 16.

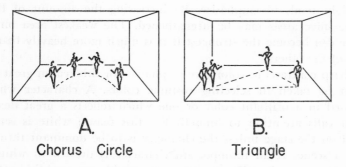

A.
Chorus Circle

B.
Triangle

FIG. 16. GEOMETRIC ARRANGEMENTS

The Triangle

The triangle is the most satisfactory geometric arrangement. (See B, Figure 16.) The spectator's eye goes either to the upstage point of the triangle or to its apex. In addition, the triangle can complement the effective use of body position and focus. The apex of the triangle can be emphasized by an open body position with more closed body positions at the points. (See B, Fig. 11.) In the same manner focus can be used. Finally, the triangle is ideally adapted to the stage because it roughly conforms to the playing areas of the stage.

In large group or crowd compositions a single major triangle may be formed with several smaller triangles placed within it. A complete discussion of directing the crowd with specific suggestions for crowd composition is found in Chapter 20.

OTHER FACTORS OF DOMINANCE

The same factors which contributed to psychological balance will affect emphasis and subordination on the stage. They are speech, movement, light, color, and energy. Although speech is not a visual quality, it is one of the most important methods of establishing dominance. The attention of the audience is attracted to the speaking character. Thus it is important that the speaking character be placed at the focal point of the composition.

Movement also attracts attention and must, therefore, be constantly associated with the focal point in the scene. Chapter 8 is devoted to this subject.

Light tends to emphasize. By increasing the amount of light, some stage areas may be strengthened. The weakest area on the stage can become the strongest if it is much more heavily lit than any of the others.

Sharp contrasts in color give emphasis. For this reason great care must be taken in selecting costume colors. A character who is dressed in a brilliant color or one which reflects a great deal of light calls attention to himself. For this reason white is seldom used on the stage unless the character is to be dominant throughout a scene. If an unimportant character is dressed in white, it will be extremely difficult, if not impossible, to establish a focal point elsewhere on the stage.

Personality, size, energy, tension, or aggressiveness of any kind attracts attention. The young giant in the crowd scene is difficult to de-emphasize. The highly dynamic individual calls attention to himself. Any quality that suggests excitement creates dominance.

If any of these qualities are present in excess, it is hard to shift the focal point through composition.

THE RELATIVE STRENGTH OF COMPOSITIONAL FACTORS

One of the questions asked by every beginning director is, "What are the relative dominance values of the compositional factors?" This is an extremely difficult question to answer because it depends in each case upon the specific application. On the other hand, it is an important question because usually some of the factors will be in conflict with others. Indeed, the director seldom uses all of the elements simultaneously, for that will make the focal point too obvious.

No objective measure of emphatic value has been established, but experience would suggest that the factors may be ranked in somewhat the following manner. (1) Body position will probably hold first place, assuming that the open body position of the key character is contrasted with the partly closed body positions of the subordinate characters. Body position is definitely stronger than area. An open body position in a weak area will command more attention than a closed body position in a strong area. (2) Focus should probably be ranked second. The dominance achieved through focus is, of course, definitely related to the number of characters who are doing the focusing. Direct focus of a large number of characters may, in fact, outweigh body position. (3) Level, provided that the superiority in height is clear-cut, may be placed in the third position. (4) Space would come next. (5) Area probably makes the least important contribution to dominance.

The student should realize that the validity of the preceding ranking is doubtful. In each case it depends upon how the element is used. For example, space may become a tremendously powerful element if a single character is sharply separated from a large, tightly knit group. Experience is the only real teacher. After the director has combined and re-combined the elements hundreds and hundreds of times in the production of several plays, the relative strengths of the elements will become apparent.

In conclusion, it must be re-emphasized that all of the technical devices discussed throughout the chapter are without value unless they serve to make the meaning and emotion of the scene more clear. A pretty, well-balanced, beautifully focused, harmonious picture is not enough. Composition must be used as one of the visual means of communicating an idea.

By combining the elements of body position, area, level, space, and focus in various ways, literally thousands of different compositions can be created with three or four characters. There is, therefore, little excuse for a monotonous repetition of visual pictures in any production. Too many directors are satisfied with finding and repeating a minimal number of satisfactory groupings.

The techniques discussed in this chapter are the tools of the artist. A knowledge of their use in no way guarantees an artistic result. Great composition is the result of great imagination and sensitivity on the part of the director. The nuances of meaning, the ultimate beauty of the visual effect will depend upon the superiority of the artist. On the other hand, it may be asserted emphatically that without a knowledge and control of the techniques of composition, even the most inspired director will fail to produce a meaningful visual picture.

8

Stage Movement

MOVEMENT IS ONE of the most important aspects of dramatic production because it is dynamic. Movement has meaning. Whether it be the tortuous plodding of the defeated soldier or the gay and awkward romping of a child, movement can tell a story without the use of sound. Movement has the power to catch and hold the eye. It can create suspense, point up conflict, express emotion. Movement has excitement. Whether it be the frenzied bustle of the subway crowd or the solemn procession of a bridal party, it can intrigue and grip us.

Drama has been defined as human conflict expressed in action. Stage movement lies at the heart of dramatic action. Through stage composition, the director can create meaningful pictures; with movement, the director is able to bring those pictures to life.

Definition of Movement

Movement may be defined as *the process of shifting a character or characters through space on a stage,* as differentiated from stage business, the complex of smaller movements that do not carry the character through space. For example, the cross a character takes to a table to get a cigarette is *movement*. The process of picking up the cigarette and lighting it is *business*. This differentiation is worthwhile because the director usually creates and rehearses movement and business at different stages in the production process. Stage business is discussed in detail in the next chapter.

THE PRINCIPLES OF MOVEMENT

Movement is one of the most powerful means at the director's disposal for projecting the playwright's meaning to an audience. In any final accounting, this projection of meaning, be it intellectual or emotional, is the sole purpose of movement.

In each dramatic situation the director selects movement that will best express the motivational forces operating in the situation. By way of illustration, an argument between John and Mary:

> JOHN: Mary, I can't stand any more of this. I will not tolerate it another minute. (*John exits.*)

This little scene so obviously calls for movement that there appears to be no problem. Actually there are many. Why does John move? Where does he move? How fast should John move? How do John's characteristics affect the movement? What quality should the movement have? The answers to these and other similar questions are found by searching for the motivation in the scene.

There is still another battery of questions to be answered before the director can complete the little scene above. How will John turn away to the door? Should John go upstage or downstage of Mary? Should John cross to the door before the line, during the line, or after the line? These questions raise the technical considerations of movement. If movement is to express the meaning of a scene, it must both reflect the motivation in the situation and fit the technical requirements of the theatre.

There are six easily observed reasons for moving. These kinds of movement are all based in the motivational pattern of the play. Without motivation no movement can be meaningful, regardless of how perfect it may be technically.

Movement Must Have Purpose

Since humans are naturally lazy, they never move without having a reason for doing so. In life we interpret man's reason for moving the moment he begins to move. The reason may be the result of internal motivation, such as the restless activity of the prospective father pacing in the hospital corridor; or the movement may result from some outside or external motivation, as going to the door because one is asked to do so. Therefore, purpose is the first test of all movement in life or on the stage. Purposeless movement on the stage confuses and distracts. The spectator is disturbed because he can't assign a reason to the movement, or the reason is at odds with the nature of the situation. Action does speak louder than words.

Movement Catches Attention

The psychologists have proved that the human being attends to that which moves in preference to that which is static. For example, in the grade school Christmas tableau, we watch the young angel who loses her balance, momentarily, even though she is not the most important character in the scene. We watch her because she is the only moving object in an otherwise static picture. We are immediately attracted to any movement. On the stage where emphasis is tremendously important, movement is a powerful device for attracting and controlling attention. Through movement the auditor is told where to look.

Note how this factor relates to the preceding discussion of purpose in movement. Purposive movement will direct our attention where it belongs. Non-purposive movement will lead our eyes astray.

Movement Should Tell a Story

Anyone who has seen a silent moving picture will readily agree that effective movement has storytelling value. Charlie Chaplin needed no words to carry the viewer through the entire plot of a play. Movement has such obvious story value that nothing more need be said.

Movement Should Convey Emotion

Most activity has an emotional quality. As critics in life, we are experts in assessing the connotative values of movement. We judge the way a man enters a room. We can determine whether he is angry, depressed, excited, or pleased. Many of our cues come from the movement.

Movement Should Delineate Character

A man's character is expressed in the way he moves. The play, *Detective Story*, concerns the comings and goings in a precinct police station during a single evening. Many of the characters have few or no lines, yet we can determine what kind of individuals they are from their movement.

Movement Should Explain Character Relationships

In static compositions, we ascertain the relationships among the characters by noting the bodily tensions present. Movement is a more effective way of determining these relationships because it is the picture of the resolution of the physical tensions into overt activity. For example, in Noel Coward's *Private Lives,* the love and hate that Amanda and Elyot alternately express for each other is constantly reflected in their movement. One moment their movement is gentle, easy, flowing; the next, it is sharp, violent.

SHOULD THERE BE MOVEMENT?

Every beginning director and many experienced directors are perplexed by the question, "When should a character move?" Many directors slavishly follow the movements suggested in the script by the author or the printed instructions found in the publisher's acting edition. Either of these courses is to be deplored. Many times these instructions are a poor record of the movement in a poor production. More important, these printed movements fit a particular production, with a specific set, with a particular group of actors, with a particular furniture arrangement, with one director's interpretation of the play, and, in the professional theatre, with a star or stars who were handled in a particular way because of their professional prominence. Your production should be individual. It should be directed to fit your interpretation, your actors, your set, your furniture arrangement. Your production should be an imaginative creation, not a labored carbon copy.

So again we ask the question, "When should a character move?" The answer to the question must depend upon each director's interpretation of the motivational forces in the scene. Stated differently, movement is determined by the impulse or energy in the line or situation. The director must decide whether action will help project the meaning of the line or situation. Movement is always the resolution of tension. What tensions are present in the line? Does the line imply aggression, submission, withdrawal, or no emotion? Is the line the result of pleasant or unpleasant tensions? Is the line forceful enough to demand action? Can action increase the emotional force of the line? These are some of the questions the director must ask before deciding to move a character.

For example, in Ibsen's *Hedda Gabler,* Hedda finds herself the slave of Brack and rebels.

HEDDA: No, I cannot endure the thought of that! Never!

Should Hedda move? The answer is, probably, yes. An impulse to move is contained in the line. The line is forceful, aggressive, dynamic, the result of unpleasant tensions. Movement will help to show how the desperate struggle within Hedda has been resolved by aggressive decision.

After the director has decided that there should be movement, there are other problems. Where, when, in what manner should the character move? How can the movement be made to convey to the audience the exact meaning the director intends?

The answers to these questions lie in a knowledge of the characteristics of movement. Movement on the stage has the same characteristics that it does in everyday life. These characteristics convey both denotative and connotative meanings. Careful analysis of the characteristics of movement will help the director select movement that best projects the playwright's story to the audience.

THE CHARACTERISTICS OF MOVEMENT

All movements have five specific characteristics: (1) direction, (2) strength, (3) speed, (4) duration, and (5) timing. In determining the meaning of the movement, the audience judges each of the specific meanings of these qualities. On the stage, these qualities are applied much as they are in life, with the exception that theatrical limitations create certain artificial aspects. The motivational and technical characteristics of movement are considered in the following sections.

Direction of Movement

Direction in movement is always related to a character or object. Thus, direction may be defined as the approach to or withdrawal from a point of interest. In a purely technical sense, movement has direction relative to the parts of a stage, such as moving left or right, upstage or downstage. This meaning of direction is used by the director in moving his characters. However, it is the approach or withdrawal that signifies to the audience the motivational forces operating in the situation.

Almost all movement in life is forward movement. We seldom back up unless to avoid being struck or to retreat from some distasteful object. In life, we almost never side-step. Watch a milling group at a party. Side-stepping is avoided even in the unconscious adjustment of position within a group. Unconsciously, the audience is aware of these life patterns, and any stage interpretation that runs counter to them is immediately recognized as false. Actors who are unfamiliar with the principle of forward movement will consistently side-step or back into their stage positions. This must be corrected.

Since the direction of movement is related to a particular character or object, the spectator can assess the meaning of the direc-

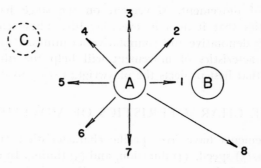

FIG. 17. DIRECTIONS OF MOVEMENT WITH RESPECT TO ANOTHER CHARACTER OR OBJECT

tion. Actually, the actor can move in only four directions in relationship to a point of interest: toward, away from, across and away from, or neutral movement neither toward or away. These possibilities are illustrated in Figure 17.

If we analyze these different directions as problems in approaching and withdrawing, we find that numbers 1 and 2 are approaching movements, 3 and 7 are essentially neutral movements; 4, 5, and 6 are withdrawing movements, and 8 involves passing the other character, then withdrawing. These directions represent the sum total of the possibilities.

At first glance, the addition of another character may seem to complicate the pattern. In reality, it doesn't, for we have defined direction as moving in relationship to a specific character or object. If character A in Figure 17 is moving in relationship to C rather than B, then the possibilities of direction are related to C. For example, if A and B have been talking, and C enters and says, "Hello," A may move toward C in response, saying, "Well, it's good to see you." Note the statement "move toward C." C becomes the point of interest, and the movement is related to him. B is no longer important.

Each of the eight directions illustrated in the drawing has meaning for the audience. The approaching movements show a positive relationship. This relationship may either be pleasant or unpleasant, but it is positive. For example, the following extremes: (1) "I think you're wonderful" (positive and pleasant) or (2) "I'll rip you to pieces" (positive and aggressive). In a like manner, movements of withdrawal suggest negative relationships. "I won't do it." "Why, that's ridiculous." Both are examples of lines usually calling for withdrawal movement. These negative lines may, of course. be interpreted positively and aggressively depending upon the context of the script. The movement changes direction to denote the attitude expressed.

Thus far we have considered movement as it is related to approach and withdrawal in life. Let us now examine the effect which the stage has on direction in movement. Since the audience is sitting on the one open side of the stage, the possible directions of movement are decreased.

In the chapter on composition it was stated that an open body position is emphatic because the audience can see the actor's face. This principle holds when a character moves. The audience must still see as much of the actor as possible. On this basis, directions 3 and 4 are usually avoided in stage movement when the moving character is dominant. It is a simple matter of seeing. Each of these movements calls for the actor to turn his back to the audience.

Direction 2 creates a special problem. It is basically a weak movement, having a closed body position; but because of the actor's strong body position at the end of the movement—it is probably the most used movement in the theatre. The technical details of this movement will be discussed later.

Direction 8 is frequently used to indicate negative relationships, for it has two technical advantages. It is easily seen, and it reverses the positions of the characters on the stage.

Frequently negative movement and positive movement may coincide. The little scene at the opening of the chapter illustrates this. John exited in rage. Whether the movement is a sharp withdrawal from Mary or a positive movement toward the door is unimportant; both are logical.

Strength of Movement

Just as any movement has direction. it also has strength. Strength of movement may be defined as the force or energy of the action. Physical tensions provide the cues by which the audience can determine the amount and kind of emotion present in a situation. (See Chapter 10.) Since movement is the resolution of tensions, the amount of energy in the movement will denote the amount of emotional tension present.

The strength of a movement may range from strong to weak. Strong movements are sharp and forceful. They result from strong emotion. In opposition, weak movements lack tension and denote an absence of emotion.

Some directors feel that strength or intensity in movement is, in part, related to the stage area in which the movement takes place. From the standpoint of emphasis, this is probably true. If there are two movements of similar energy, that action which occurs in a strong area or moves from a weak area to a stronger one will appear to the audience to have greater intensity than the action occurring in a weak area or progressing from a strong to a weaker area.

Strength in movement is, for the most part, a motivational concept. There are no technical restrictions imposed by the stage. The director must learn to sense the relationship of emotion in dialogue to strength in movement.

Speed of Movement

Another characteristic of movement is speed. The quickness of an actor's movement aids the audience in judging his character and the situation. In general, fast movement is more exhilarating for the spectator than slow movement. A feeling of excitement or vitality may be generated with quickly paced movement; or a feeling of solemnity or even tragedy may be associated with slow movement.

The principles governing speed in movement are similar to those affecting tempo or speed in other aspects of production. A detailed discussion of the use of time is found in Chapter 11.

Duration of Movement

Duration in movement may be defined as the *length of the movement in time and in space*. In most cases, the duration of movement has less connotative value than the characteristics previously discussed.

From a technical point of view, the duration of movement is closely related to length of the line. In an earlier section, it was stated that the spoken line catches and holds attention. Movement will also capture attention. It is important, therefore, that the length of the movement and the length of the line coincide unless special emphasis is to fall on one or the other.

Long movements are hard to sustain. The audience quickly judges the meaning of the movement. If the movement takes too long, interest wanes. For this reason, most stage movements are short. On the other hand, length of movement does have some emotional value. If all movements are short and staccato, a feeling of crisp, sharp tension may develop. Long, graceful crosses give a feeling of ease and harmony, though speed is probably a more important factor than duration.

The length of the movement is also controlled by the distance between players or between a character and an object. Remembering that humans are prone to conserve effort, the player should take the shortest distance to the point of interest. Any lengthy detour will be hard to sustain. It will also be difficult for the audience to determine the direction and the motivation.

If it is impossible for the length of the line and the length of the movement to be identical, the actor should arrive at his destination prior to the end of the line. A short line accompanied by a long movement will usually appear false, for the meaning in the line generally determines the movement.

Timing of Movement

In the preceding section, we have discussed one type of timing wherein the movement coincides with the line. Two other time relationships may be used. The movement may precede the line, or the movement may begin after the line has been concluded. In each of these cases special emphasis will result.

The rule may be stated as follows: *If the movement precedes the line, the line will be emphasized. If the line precedes the movement, the movement will be emphasized.*

Examine the possibilities in the following scene.

> *Ralph is standing by the fireplace right. Ellen enters center. They speak for a moment. Ralph crosses to Ellen. They embrace.*
>
> RALPH: Hello. Thanks for coming.

There is only one line, but there are at least three possibilities for movement.

(1) Ralph says, "Hello," then crosses to Ellen on the speech, "Thank you for coming," and they embrace. This procedure does not place particular emphasis on any part of the situation.

(2) Ralph says, "Hello," then crosses to Ellen. After he reaches Ellen he says, "Thank you for coming," and they embrace. This procedure emphasizes the line.

(3) Ralph says, "Hello. Thank you for coming," then crosses to Ellen, and they embrace. The third movement sharply emphasizes Ralph's movement and the embrace.

Timing lines and movement can be used to point up or emphasize any aspect of a situation.

Amount of Movement

Most of the preceding characteristics of movement have been discussed as they pertain to the connotative meaning of a single movement. The number of movements in any single time sequence will also have an emotional meaning for the audience.

One of the first questions asked by the beginning director is, "How much movement should I use?" Unfortunately, there is no standard answer to this question unless it be, "As much movement as the material requires." This answer is not very helpful.

The amount of movement depends in part upon the kind of play and the way it is produced. Some plays are strengthened by great numbers of movements; others lose their meaning if too much movement is introduced.

In general, large numbers of movements create a feeling of vibrant energy, breathless hurry, even excitement and violence. Little or no movement may, depending upon the context of the play, suggest static dullness, quiet languor, solemn depression, or at the other extreme, an emotional tension so great that all activity is suspended.

Most beginning directors have too little movement rather than too much. Since movement is somewhat difficult to handle, the beginner is satisfied to get his characters comfortably seated on the stage, so that they may chat. The result is a static picture which does not hold the interest of the audience. Remembering the power of movement to catch and hold attention, to tell a story and convey emotion, the director might do well to err, if err he must, on the side of too much, rather than too little, movement.

SUMMARY OF THE GENERAL PRINCIPLES
OF STAGE MOVEMENT

The following summary of the basic principles of stage movement may be used as a check list for the director as he plots the movement of a play.

Movement holds attention. In any static picture a moving object will catch attention. Thus, movement becomes an active force in directing a play. Through movement, the director is able to direct and control attention.

No movement without a purpose. Since movement holds attention, any purposeless movement will confuse the audience. Every movement must be logically motivated.

Move the character on his own lines. Speech holds attention. Movement holds attention. Therefore, a combination of speech and movement will strengthen the focal point. Any split between speech and movement will result in a division of attention.

Move one character at a time. Since movement holds attention, any confusion in movement will distract. If the director wishes to focus the attention of the audience through movement, he should move only one character at a time. Certain technical exceptions to this principle will be discussed later.

Move the shortest distance to a destination. Avoid detours. People do not make detours in life. Detours confuse the audience because changes in direction indicate changes in motivation. Gracefully curved movement may be employed.

Use a single movement for a single motivation. Direction, strength, speed of movement may not change without a change in the motivation. The audience attaches meaning to movement. Any change in the characteristics of the movement without a change in the motivation will appear false.

Stage movement is forward movement. Whether the movement is toward, away from, or past and away from the point of interest, movement should be forward. This is a part of the normal life pattern. Any deviation from this pattern except in special cases will appear false.

Select the direction, strength, speed, duration, and timing in movement for the best interpretation of the line. Each of the characteristics of movement has a meaning for the audience. Balance the selection so that the best possible interpretation is given to the line.

SPECIFIC TECHNIQUES IN STAGE MOVEMENT

The following sections are devoted to the theatrical techniques of movement. These techniques seem artificial when judged in terms of what people do in life. Because of the peculiar requirements of the stage, however, they appear completely real when handled effectively.

Taking, Giving, and Stealing Stage

In the chapter on composition, a method was suggested for establishing the dominance of one character over another character by a modification of body position. It was observed that profiles are harsh and that the older fashion of characters partly facing the audience, rather than one another, appears unreal. This problem was solved by placing the dominant character slightly upstage of the non-emphatic character.

A very logical question may occur to the director. How does the dominant character get upstage? This process of going upstage is called *taking stage* and is illustrated in A, Figure 18.

A. Taking

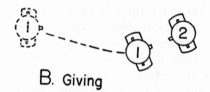

B. Giving

FIG. 18. TAKING AND GIVING STAGE

At first glance, the process seems to be merely one of Character 1 walking upstage and turning to face 2. This is not quite the case. Note the slight curve in the line of 1's movement. This curve allows 1 to go upstage of 2 or to take stage without side-stepping or turning into place. In taking stage, the audience, with its largely two-dimensional view of the stage, cannot see that 1 is gradually working his way upstage during the cross.

To *give stage* is the reverse of *taking stage*. It means *to give up the dominance of a superior body position by moving slightly downstage so that the opposing character will be left in a dominant body position.* In B, Figure 18, Character 1 may give stage to 2 by moving downstage of 2 while he is speaking and then turning to 2 at the end of the speech. When 1 faces 2, he will have partially closed his body position.

Another theatrical term closely related to the above is *stealing stage.* When an actor steals stage, he makes himself dominant at a time when the script does not call for his being dominant. To take stage at the wrong time is to steal stage. There are any number of ways of stealing stage. The actor may move about or fidgit, he may make noise, he may open his body position, he may make use of any devise to attract attention.

Most non-professional actors steal stage without being aware that they are doing so. They inadvertently change body position, move randomly, or through carelessness in crossing find themselves in the upstage position. This problem should be explained carefully by the director.

Crossing Another Character

The term "cross" has two meanings in theatrical parlance. A cross is any movement on a stage; for example, Robert crosses down left. A second definition concerns the passing of another character. *To cross another character means to pass the other character:* Robert crosses Jane to the table. The principles discussed in this section refer to the second definition of the cross.

The principle of crossing may be stated as follows: *When crossing another character on stage, the moving or crossing character should pass in front of the stationary character unless the stationary character is seated.* Passing in front of or behind a seated or prone character is not technically considered a cross.

The reason for crossing in front is easily discernible. The moving or crossing character is dominant. If he passes behind a non-moving character he will be lost from sight. During the period that he is behind the non-moving character, the audience cannot see or hear him well. More important, by passing behind, the moving character leads the eye of the spectator to the non-moving character, and the spectator's eye tends to remain with the stationary character.

In exceptional cases, the back cross, passing behind another, is used to provide variety. In this situation several other factors must be changed. They will be discussed later.

But the director may say, "Many times the moving actor has to detour if he is to pass in front, and detours should be avoided." The answer to this problem lies in the preparation for the movement. In the preceding movement or composition, the actor who is to cross should be placed so that he need not detour in order to cross in front.

Dressing or Balancing the Stage

Compositions are set up so that the stage is in balance. Any movement to the left or right will shift the masses in the composition and destroy the balance. The *dress* or *balance* may be defined as *a compensatory movement made by a player who has been crossed, used to re-establish stage balance.*

In dressing the stage, the actor who has been crossed moves a short distance in an opposite direction. The dress must begin at the exact moment that the non-moving actor is covered or hidden from the audience by the moving or crossing character. The elements of the dress or balance may be seen in Figure 19.

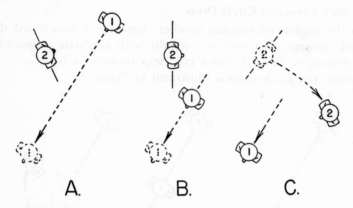

Fig. 19. The Dress. (A) At Beginning of Cross. (B) At the Moment of Covering. (C) The Dress

The spectators do not perceive a well-executed dress because their eyes are following the dominant moving and speaking character. Even if the audience's attention is distracted momentarily by the dressing movement, no harm is done because the movement of the dress has excellent motivation. The actor who has been crossed will naturally turn and move down stage slightly, so that he can better see and hear the dominant actor.

The dress can serve several purposes in addition to balancing the composition. It helps keep the action near the center of the stage, since the characters are moving in opposite directions. It helps to separate the actors. The clumping or bunching of actors is one of the major difficulties of the beginning director. And it helps maintain a logical upstage-downstage relationship. The cross-ing actor usually moves downstage as he crosses. The dressing actor also moves downstage, thereby maintaining a balance in depth. If the cross is from downstage to upstage, the dress usually is merely a turn.

Particular emphasis must be placed on the time of initiating the dress. If the dress begins too soon, that is, before the dressing actor is covered by the crossing actor, the movement of the dress will catch the eye of the audience and confusion in attention will result. If the dress begins too late, it will appear as a regular stage movement, and there will be confusion in attention.

The Back Cross and Circle Dress

In the section on crossing another character, it was stated that a back cross may be used occasionally with adequate preparation and execution. A circle dress can help to make a back cross acceptable. The circle dress is illustrated in Figure 20.

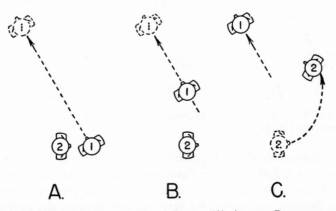

FIG. 20. THE BACK CROSS AND CIRCLE DRESS. (A) AT THE BEGINNING OF THE CROSS. (B) AT THE MOMENT OF COVERING. (C) THE CIRCLE DRESS

The principle of the circle dress is similar to that of the regular dress with the exception that the attention of the audience changes from Character 1 to Character 2 and back to 1. The technical process is as follows: The dominant Character 1 begins the back cross and disappears behind 2. At the exact moment he is covered, 2 dresses in a circle carrying the eye of the spectator with him.

Character 2 then stops in a partially closed body position, throwing attention by visual focus on dominant Character 1, who concludes the cross.

The back cross is used to provide variety in crosses and is par ticularly useful in moving characters upstage. Note that in making the circle, 2 has also moved farther upstage. Since the back cross with a circle dress is a somewhat complicated maneuver, it should not be overused, for it may stand out as a technique.

The motivation is perfectly logical. It is natural for 2 to follow 1 in his movement, for he is interested in what 1 is saying.

Turning on Stage

Turn means the same in the theatre as it does in everyday life. It is the process of changing or reversing the body position. Since it is part of the process of moving the actor through space, it is included in the discussion of movement. Most turns are used to initiate movement. As such, they are usually taken by the speaking character and will catch attention. Turns made during a dress are not seen by the audience, so the following principles governing turns do not apply to them.

Two principles may act as guides for making turns: (1) The actor should take the *open* turn, and (2) the actor should take the *shortest* turn. At first glance these principles may seem in conflict. The open turn is not always the shortest turn. This apparent conflict can be eliminated by correct preparation before turning.

The *open turn* is defined as *a turn made toward the audience.* The reasons for advocating the open turn lie in the advantage of body position and audibility. The speaking character is usually the turning character. If the turn is made toward the audience, the speaker's voice will be projected into the audience. If the closed turn is used, the actor's voice will be lost upstage. Following the same line of argument, the open turn provides an open or dominant body position.

The *shortest turn is that turn which requires a minimum of turning.* Since turning is always related to some point of interest, the short turn is a turn of less than 180 degrees. The selection of the short turn is based upon the logic of normal movement. The short turn requires little energy and is the quickest way of turning. Thus, it is the normal way of turning.

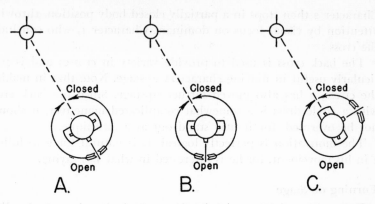

Analysis of the drawings in Figure 21 will show how preparation for the turn can make the open turn the shortest turn. The body position of the actor prior to turning is the key in preparation. The body position must be related to the point of interest and to the audience. Move the point of interest in Figure 21; the problem remains the same. The body position must always be opened sufficiently to make the turning arc less than 180 degrees. In A, the open and closed turns are equally easy, as the actor has turned his back squarely to the point of interest. By shifting his body position, as in B, the open turn is the easiest turn. In C, the body position of the actor makes the closed turn the shortest turn. If a choice *must* be made between the open and short turn, the short turn should be chosen. Any turn of more than 180 degrees will appear false.

The reader may have gotten the impression from the preceding discussion that the closed turn is taboo. The closed turn can be used to give variety to the movement pattern, but it should be used sparingly, since it deprives the audience of maximum visibility and audibility.

Entering and Exiting

The comings and goings of characters create special problems for the director. The entrances and exits of the set are usually placed at some distance from the centers of action. This means

that the entering character must move a considerable distance before he is able to join the players in the principle acting areas.
This problem is further complicated in that the entering actor is
usually the dominant character in the scene.

Intelligent playwrighting helps to solve the problem. The first
speech of the entering character is long enough to carry the actor
to his destination. Another type of entrance is based on a short
entrance line. The character appears in the doorway and speaks.
Lines or reactions from the actors on stage shift the attention of
the audience to the new character. Then he moves into the centers
of action on his second speech. Since the entering character usually
dominates the action, doorways must be placed so that all of the
audience can observe an entrance.

The problem of exiting is similar to that of entering. As in the
entrance, the exiting character is usually dominant. The distance
from the center of action to the door must be covered by dialogue.
The playwright usually provides an exit line composed of two
parts: a cover line which is long enough to carry the actor to the
door and an exit tag or punch line which covers the actual exit.
On the cover line, the actor goes to the door and opens it. Then
the actor gives the exit tag and leaves the set immediately. Extensive rehearsal is necessary to time exits effectively. The actor
must disappear from sight at the conclusion of the exit tag. If
the attention of the spectator is supposed to revert immediately to
the actors remaining on the stage, any pause between the tag and
the actual exit becomes a meaningless gap in the play.

The principle of the simple exit is illustrated in Helmer's lines
from *A Doll's House.*

> HELMER: ... Now you go and play through the Tarantella and prac-
> tice with your tambourine.
> *(He goes to the door and opens it on the following cover line.)*
> I shall go into the inner office and shut the door, and I shall hear
> nothing; you can make as much noise as you please.
> *(He turns back at the door for the exit tag.)*
> When Rank comes, tell him where he shall find me.
> *(He exits, closing the door.)*

Another common type of exit involves a line spoken by another
character between the cover line and the exit tag. This is illustrated

by Paula Tanqueray's exit at the end of the second act in *The Second Mrs. Tanqueray.*

> AUBREY: And could you, after all, go back to associates of that order? It's not possible!
> PAULA: What, not after the refining influence of these intensely respectable surroundings? We'll see!
> *(Goes quickly to the door.)*
> AUBREY: Paula!
> *(Paula turns back in the doorway for the exit tag.)*
> PAULA: We'll see!
> *(Paula exits.)*

Note how the exit in this scene would be weakened if the author had not provided the interchange which permitted the exit tag. In each of the preceding scenes, the actor turns back to deliver the exit tag after reaching the door. This movement preceding the line emphasizes the line.

Sometimes it is desirable to emphasize the process of exiting. In these cases, the exit tag is read while the character is still a considerable distance from the door, since movement following a line emphasizes the movement. This principle is used in the following lines from Odet's *Golden Boy.*

> MR. BONAPARTE: . . . Now I see what you are . . . I give-a you every word to fight . . . I sorry for you.
> *(He stands in silence, the roar of the crowd is heard.)*
> TOKIO: I'll have to ask you to leave, Mr. Bonaparte.
> MR. BONAPARTE: *(holding back his tears)* Joe . . . I hope-a you win every fight.
> *(He slowly exits. As he opens and closes the door the roar of the crowd swells up for an instant.)*

Entrances and exits involving more than one character are more difficult. Most of these exits are handled in one of two ways. Either the characters enter or exit together, moving so that they are seen as a single unit, or the movements are staggered so that one character moves to the door, the second character moves up on the next line, and they exit together.

Entrances and exits are keystones of the play. They frequently open and close motivational units. They add life and variety to the play. They point up emotion and resolve conflict. As such, they are usually high spots of action and must be directed with care.

Simultaneous Movement

Most of the preceding discussion has been based upon the principle of moving only one character at a time. Obviously, there must be exceptions to this principle. The playwright may insist that more than one character move simultaneously. Several people may rush to greet a newcomer. Two people may enter or exit together. Everyone may go to the window to see some startling event take place.

When we watch two people move across the room at a party, we are not concerned with balance because they are not appearing within a frame. Transplant that same movement to the stage, and the picture will seem to tip in the direction of the movement. When a single character moves, we are often able to maintain stage balance by compensating with a *dress*. This is seldom possible with simultaneous movement.

A second problem of simultaneous movement arises when two characters who are some distance apart move across the stage at the same speed and in the same direction. The effect is excessively regular. The players look like soldiers on parade.

For the above reasons, it may be stated that two characters should never be moved simultaneously in the same direction, at the same speed, if the illusion of reality is to be preserved.

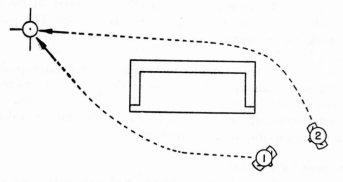

FIG. 22. SIMULTANEOUS MOVEMENT

If two characters must be moved in the same direction, they may be handled in one of three ways. First, the two characters may be moved as a single unit; that is, arm in arm or partially covering one another, so that the audience gets the impression of a single person moving. Second, they may be moved at different speeds. For example, one character starts for the window, the second character waits for a moment and then, moving more quickly, catches up. The third method is to have the two characters follow two different courses to the point of interest. This is illustrated in Figure 22.

In the illustration, the two characters do not at any time move in the same direction. During the time that Character 1 is moving parallel to the footlights, 2 is moving upstage. When 1 turns upstage, 2 moves parallel to the footlights. This procedure is the most satisfactory of the three possibilities because it does not throw the stage sharply out of balance. Movements toward and away from the footlights do not affect stage balance. In Figure 22, only one movement is affecting the balance of the stage at any one time.

Simultaneous group movements are affected by the same principles. The powerful surge of a crowd in a single direction will throw the stage out of balance. To compensate for this, some sharp movements in opposition to the general direction should be included. These atypical movements will soften the connotative value of the surge and help to keep the stage in balance. Such movements are called *counter movements*. (Also, see below.)

Parallel movement. Occasionally for comic effect, two characters are moved in the same direction, at the same speed, at the same time. This movement is called *parallel movement*. The comedy rises from the incongruity of excessive regularity and the radical changes in balance.

Counter movement. Counter movement is the exact opposite of parallel movement. It is the process of moving two characters in opposite directions, at the same speed, at the same time. As in parallel movement, the effect will be comic. The humor is derived from the artificiality of the movement.

Movement for Position

Movements for position are highly arbitrary movements which the director introduces to improve compositions, prepare for entrances, exits, or turns, prevent covering, or increase the use of the stage. From the director's standpoint, they are highly technical movements. These movements are somewhat difficult to execute, in that there must be a dual motivation. The director moves the character for a technical reason, but the audience must be able to find a logical reason behind the movement.

Routine Movement

Routine movement is an exception to the rule that all movement will catch and hold attention. On the stage as in the drawing room, a servant may go about his business without attracting constant attention. This is possible because his movements are routine. The audience expects and accepts them without any particular curiosity.

The audience's attention is directed to the entering servant, just as it will be to any entering character. The audience perceives that it is a servant. If the servant continues into the center of action to deliver a note, for example, he becomes a dominant character. If he follows a pattern of routine activity and does not become involved in the focal point of the scene, the audience's attention shifts back to the focal point.

Even with routine movement, there is, without question, a conflict in attention values between the speech of the dominant character and the movement of the servant. In order to create as little distraction as possible, the director should keep the servant out of the dominant areas and have him close his body position while picking up glasses, emptying ash trays, or going about his duties. The rules for turning and crossing should be ignored since these principles are aimed at making the character dominant.

SUMMARY OF THE TECHNICAL PRINCIPLES OF STAGE MOVEMENT

The following summary of the technical principles, coupled with the summary of general principles on pages 129, 130, should provide a basis from which the director may devise an attractive and logical movement pattern for any play.

The dominant character should take stage if he is to be dominant at the end of his movement. If the moving character gives up dominance at the end of the movement, he should give stage and finish the movement downstage with a slightly closed body position.

The moving character should cross in front so that he may be seen and heard at all times during the movement.

The character who is crossed should dress in the opposite direction so that the stage will be held in balance. The dress must begin at the exact moment of covering.

The turning character should take the open turn and the shortest turn so that he can be seen and heard. Preparation of body position made prior to turning will make the open turn the shortest turn.

The entering character should move well onto the stage so that he may be seen.

The exiting character should disappear from sight after the exit tag, so that the action of the play will not be stopped. Exceptions to this principle occur when the process of exiting is to be emphasized.

Simultaneous movement of two or more characters should not be in the same or opposite directions, at the same speed, except for comic effect. The excessive regularity of the movement and sharp changes in balance will make it appear unreal.

The principles of movement laid down in this chapter should be used with discretion. They are by no means the be-all and end-all of good stage action. They have been set up as guide posts. The imaginative and experienced director will quickly find ways to break the rules with perfectly satisfactory results. The beginner would do well to adhere to the rules with some care, for they represent the experiences of hundreds of directors over many years.

Above all, the director must not become so engrossed in technique that he loses sight of meaning. When a character enters a room, the first and foremost requirement is that the movement be that of a real person entering a real room for a real reason. The director must take the place of the spectator. He must learn to sense the truth in movement, for one false movement can so confuse the audience that it spoils an entire scene.

The imaginative and artistic director can create varied, colorful, exciting action patterns which will give vitality to the meanings of the play. In any play the director has literally hundreds of opportunities to select, develop, and intensify movements that will dynamically project the appropriate meaning. The skillful director makes his choices wisely.

9

Stage Business

STAGE BUSINESS fills out the production. It completes the visual picture. It adds the nuance, the light, the shadow, to the dramatic action. For example, the manner in which a mother clutches her child can tell us more about the mother and the child than a dozen speeches.

Many discussions of stage business are found in books on acting. Doubtless it was included because the writer felt that business and pantomime are the province of the actor—as indeed they are. But business is also one of the finer aspects of direction, for the director must sift and select, intensify and expand, limit and crystallize the pantomime of the actor so that every action is filled with meaning and emotion.

Definition and Purpose of Stage Business

Stage business may be defined as all visual activity not involving movement from one place to another. Composition deals with the grouping of characters on stage; movement concerns shifting characters from one place to another; stage business, as suggested above, involves activity that helps to complete the expression of the idea without words. In some texts, it is called *pantomime.* Actually, *pantomime* is a somewhat broader term which encompasses all expressive action and often includes movement as well as business.

The purposes of business are identical with those of composition and movement. It is used to aid in the expression of the motivational pattern. It has storytelling implications. It is employed to intensify emotion. It is one of the best means of delineating character. It may be used for comic effect, and, finally, it is frequently used for purely technical reasons. These purposes define the different types of business of which the director must be aware. The specific meaning of each is discussed below.

TYPES OF STAGE BUSINESS

One of the problems in any classification is the overlapping between and among various divisions. Many bits of business are representative of more than one type. The purpose of the list is not to provoke arguments about classification but to point out the principle jobs stage business can perform.

Storytelling Business

Storytelling business, sometimes called *integral business,* is usually provided by the playwright, for it is essential to the advancement of the plot or conflict of the play. Puck must cast his spell in *Midsummer Night's Dream* if the play is to proceed. Aubrey in *The Second Mrs. Tanqueray* must read the letter to project the crisis. The stabbing of Caesar is basic to the conflict in *Julius Caesar.*

Integral business is usually the easiest to conceive and perform, for the playwright has provided the motivation and made a place in the script for the action.

Character Business

All well-written characters fit within the background of experience of the audience. There must be some link of understanding that makes the character comprehensible. Sometimes the character evokes sympathy, sometimes antagonism; but the character must be recognizable and conceivable. The characteristics differentiating one character from another usually involve business. The selection of business to elucidate the character may be trite and hackneyed, or it may be fresh and exciting, an artistic elaboration which increases the meaning and power of the role. Often by providing specific activity, the playwright helps to delineate the character, but usually the careful addition of business to fill out the character is the responsibility of the actor and the director. Examples of specific activity are Lady Macbeth's concern for her hands, the consumptive cough of Trock in *Winterset,* Algernon's appetite for cucumber sandwiches in *The Importance of Being Earnest,* Uncle Willie's propensity for pinching in *The Philadelphia Story.* Additions to the galaxy of character business developed by the actor and the director will be seen in every superior portrayal of character. Depending upon the imagination of the actor and the director, business may be limited to the broad overused stereotypes— lollypop sucking to indicate youth, or a wobbly cane and a bent back for age, or it may be a subtle elaboration of character.

Business for Emphasis

A third type of business is created for emphasis. It may be used to emphasize conflict as in O'Neill's *Anna Christie,* when Anna slaps Matt. The use of the hat box in *Night Must Fall* creates suspense. The fearful handling of the paw in *The Monkey's Paw* intensifies the mood of the scene. Or it may be used to emphasize the incongruity in comic scenes, as the eating of the Indian nuts in *Once In A Lifetime.* A complete discussion of comedy styles and techniques will be found in Chapter 25. The impact of any line, object, association, or situation may be increased by the addition of stage business with visual appeal for the audience.

Arbitrary Business

Much of the business in a play does not specifically advance the story, make character more clear, or emphasize any specific aspect of the play. It is business used as a filler. It is added to round out the normal activities of the characters, to fill up gaps in the action, to provide characters with something to do. The tea party scenes, the eating and drinking scenes, the flower arranging sequences, the numberless cigarettes which are lit and extinguished after a few puffs are examples of this kind of activity. Although the handling of each of these activities is important to character portrayal, the business is not placed in the play primarily for this purpose.

Arbitrary business is almost completely the job of the director. The playwright may provide the situation and a few covering lines, but the rest is up to the director and the actors. In many ways this is the most difficult type of business to perform. It must not get in the way of the idea, yet it is extremely important to the feeling of completeness and reality. The director must be sensitive to the amount of arbitrary business to be employed. Too little may make some scenes seem stiff and uneasy; too much can clutter the scene with distracting activity.

Technical Business

This final type of business should always pass under the guise of one of the other kinds. The audience must never see the technical reason. But many times business is added to accomplish a purely technical purpose. For example, one character may become engrossed in fitting a paper into his briefcase, so that another character in the scene will have time to leave. One character may warm his hands at the fire, so that others can say something that he is not supposed to hear.

Time and time again the director will insert business so that the compositions or the movement pattern can be rearranged. The development of technical business is totally within the province of the director.

CREATING AND PROJECTING STAGE BUSINESS

Most stage business does not just happen. It is carefully created to project a distinct meaning to the audience. The steps to be considered in either creating or evaluating a piece of stage business can be set forth in detail.

Motivation

The basic rule for all visual activity—that there can be no movement without a purpose—applies with equal force to stage business. All activity that catches the eye of the audience has meaning. Any cue that reaches the audience must further the idea or emotion being expressed. The actor who does not know how to smoke a cigarette will use many false, random, and non-purposeful movements in trying to imitate the process. The audience will note the lack of reason in the activity and be distressed by it. Opening a letter, sipping a drink, closing a door, embracing a friend will appear false, unless the reason for the total action and each of its segments is made perfectly clear and logical to the audience. For example, a stage kiss may appear false, even though there is every reason for the characters to embrace. The actors may fail because they are embarrassed by the business and do not make the physical proximity of the embrace seem logical. The director is the only person who is in position prior to performance to see that every detail of stage business stems from the external and internal motivational pattern.

Selection

Stage business must be selected with care. Not only must it be conceivable to the audience, but also it must make some concrete contribution to the production. An imaginative actor can think of literally hundreds of things which his character might do, ranging from picking lint off his coat to manicuring his finger nails. All logical or motivated stage business is not necessarily good stage business. Good stage business presupposes an addition to the production as a whole.

Since stage business usually involves activity, it will catch attention. The director must select items of business that add to, rather than detract from, the focal point of the action. To pluck lint from a coat sleeve may be a fine way of describing a particular character; however, if such an action detracts from the meaning that is being projected at a particular moment, it is poor stage business.

Definition

Meaningful stage business is distinct and definite. For example, there are probably a dozen ways of answering a telephone. One of the brightest spots in *The Voice of the Turtle* is the telephone sequence in which the young soldier calls the girls in his little black book. Much of the humor in the scene is derived from the way the telephoning is handled. The telephone becomes more than a mechanical device for covering space in a hurry. The longing, the consternation, the irritation, the excitement, all are communicated by the way the telephone is used. The telephone is caressed; it is cajoled; it is beaten. Every action has a precise meaning. The action is definite.

Any piece of business, from writing a letter to shouldering a gun, must have a precise denotative and connotative meaning. Clear-cut activity without random or wasted motion will make stage business meaningful.

Intensification

After selecting and defining, the director must intensify the business. The visual activity must be projected to the audience. There are several ways of intensifying business. The actual size of the activity may be expanded. For example, a telegram may be opened with small, quiet movements, or it may be opened with large, broad movements. The size of the movement will be determined, in part, by the circumstances surrounding the opening of the telegram and, in part, by the distance the business must travel. A movement visible from the front of the house may be no movement at all in the back of the house. All business must be gross enough to be seen.

Another method of intensifying the business is to increase the vigor of the action. A gesture may be pallid and indefinite or enthusiastic and strong. Of course, the strength of the action must reflect the motivation. At the same time, business indicating weakness or indecision must be projected with vigor.

A third way of intensifying stage business is through focus. If the movement must be small, the meaning of the movement may be greatly emphasized by focusing the audience's attention on the action. For example, suppose that the unauthorized opening of a letter is important to the conflict in a play. The business may be intensified by picking up the letter, looking at it for a moment, setting it down again, glancing about the room, picking it up again, studying it, listening for the sound of an intruder, and finally opening the letter with infinite care. The curiosity of the audience has been aroused; the suspense of waiting to have the letter opened has increased the letter's importance; every eye is focused on the action.

The director's problem in some cases is to soften business rather than to intensify it. Sequences involving brutality such as stabbing, strangling, or shooting are so powerful emotionally that they may cause the audience to lose its detachment. This kind of action may be softened by reversing any of the above-mentioned procedures. The action may be covered, moved to a weak area of the stage, slowed in tempo, reduced in strength, or confused by momentarily distracting the attention of the audience.

Timing

Timing, though really a method of intensifying stage business, is so important that it warrants separate mention. The meaning of time as it applies to lines and action is discussed in detail in the chapters on movement, comedy, and tempo. The same principles apply to stage business.

The pause focuses attention. Just as movement may coincide, precede, or follow a line, so may business. Normally business coincides with the line it illustrates. Such a relationship establishes a balance in emphasis. If the business follows the line, the business will be stressed. The same relationship holds for the key point in the business. For example, if the actor focuses the audience's attention on a knife and allows a pause to develop before handling it, the importance of the knife will be emphasized. Or in reverse, if the actor grasps the knife immediately, the possible use to which the knife may be put will be emphasized by a pause following the action.

Visibility

The most obvious requirement of good business is that it be seen. Strangely enough, many directors spend time developing complicated bits of business which cannot possibly be seen by the audience. The first essential of visibility is an open body position. The actor must never stand between the business and the audience.

There is, as a matter of fact, a difference between a piece of business being visible and its being seen. It may be within view of the audience and still not be perceived. All essential business must be brought to the attention of the audience. Many plays call for the audience to see a particular piece of business which is not at the focal point of the action. For example, in the classic melodrama, *Dracula,* the legend that vampires cannot see their own images is used by the doctor who wishes to prove, by holding a mirror before his face, that Count Dracula is a vampire. The audience's attention is focused on a drawing room conversation with the Count. How can the spectator be made aware of the business with the mirror when his attention is on the conversation? In one production, the mirror was withdrawn from the doctor's pocket, so that it was deliberately flashed in the eyes of the audience. Immediately, attention shifted to the mirror. The business with the mirror became the focal point.

Balance

In some productions, the director introduces so much business that its rightful position as a complement to the rest of the action is destroyed. In other productions, one imaginative actor fills his role with business, but the portrayals of other less ingenious actors are barren. The director is responsible for maintaining a balance. Business may have to be cut out of some scenes and amplified in others. The basis for decision must lie in the specific contribution that each action makes to the play as a whole.

TECHNICAL PROBLEMS IN HANDLING BUSINESS

Action on a stage gives the appearance of reality when it is handled with technical perfection. Some of the specific techniques, often largely unreal, which give the illusion of naturalness are discussed below.

Gesturing

The gesture implies the movement of a part of the body. In one sense, all business not involving the handling of an object is gesturing. For that matter, one can gesture with an object. Gesture includes movement of the torso, shoulders, and face as well as movement of the arms and hands. The principles of motivation hold for the gesture. The gesture should be definite, vigorous, and relaxed. The principles of timing for stress also govern gestures. The gesture normally coincides with the line. Placed before the line, it emphasizes what is said. The mistimed gesture, a gesture placed after the line, appears strange and is deliberately used for comic effect.

Ideally all actors should be ambidextrous. Gestures of the arm and hand, particularly those at face level, should be performed with the upstage arm. The reason for this simple rule is obvious. Since most gestures accompany speech, the audience should see the player's face while he is speaking. A gesture with the downstage hand covers the actor's face and often tends to close his body position. It is the director's job to fit the gesture to the words and the scene.

Rising and Sitting

Modern acting dictates that the motivation arising from the situation and the personal attributes of the character govern the process of sitting. An uneducated boor will not sit down in the same manner as will the dilettante lord of the manor. The child of ten will not get out of a chair in the same way as will a man of fifty. Appropriateness to the situation and the character is the key.

In addition, the process of rising or sitting must not call attention to itself unless there is a special reason for its doing so. Ease in rising is important. The picture of the actor fighting his way out of a deep chair can be effective comedy, but it adds little to the serious play. The rules of timing for emphasis also apply to rising and sitting. The director will usually have to teach the unexperienced actor how to sit and rise.

Opening and Closing Doors

The business of opening and closing a door on stage requires distinct technical finesse. The action must appear completely natural. Doors which are hung so that the door panel swings up and offstage are the easiest to manipulate.

The actor should reach the door prior to the tag on the exit line. Standing so that he faces the audience, he should place his nearest hand on the doorknob. On the exit tag he opens the door and walks through it in one movement. After the actor is out of sight the door may be closed in any appropriate manner.

Entering the stage through a door involves a somewhat different procedure. The player standing offstage grasps the doorknob with his upstage hand. This causes him to step back slightly to avoid the door as it opens. As he walks through the door, he must let go of the door, allowing it to swing free. When he reaches the threshold, he should take an open turn back to the door, catch the knob with his upstage hand and pull it shut.

Awkward entrances and exits draw attention to themselves. The business of opening and closing a door must be accomplished with complete ease. Any struggle with a door emphasizes the process of handling it rather than the dramatic action. The director must plan rehearsal time to teach this piece of stage business.

Lighting Cigarettes

Cigarettes can be the bane of the director's existence. Actors like them, if they are smokers, for it gives them something to do. Quite apart from lighters that won't work and matches that won't light, cigarettes can cause trouble. The lighting of a cigarette must be timed within the action of the play. The play can never stop for the business.

The director should find a place in the script where all of the necessary action can be handled during lines spoken by a character who is not smoking. There is more to lighting a cigarette than striking a match and applying it to the cigarette. The cigarette must be removed from the package or case. The matches must be opened and a match torn out ready to strike. Then there must be time during a single speech for the cigarette to be placed in the mouth, the match struck, and the flame applied. The cigarette should be lit in the same sequence, at the same spot in the play, at every rehearsal and every performance.

Many experienced directors may smile at the naïveté of the preceding remark, but if one had a dollar for every time a cigarette has interrupted a stage scene, he would be a wealthy man.

Eating and Drinking

The problems of stage eating and drinking are similar to those of lighting a cigarette. The process of eating must not interrupt the action of the play. Small bites of very soft foods, eaten when others have the lines, will usually suffice. Careful rehearsal of eating and drinking scenes will ensure smooth play. Prop crews don't like to supply food until the last minute. This is unfortunate, for food should be introduced fairly early in the rehearsal period. No matter how much practice an actor has had in pantomiming eating, when he actually takes a bite, chews, and swallows, his timing will be off. Society dictates and audiences agree that persons with mouths full of food may be seen but never heard.

Embraces and Kisses

The kind of embrace or kiss is determined by the motivation in the situation and the individual traits of the characters. Many years ago, the motion pictures instituted a stylized embrace which had little to do with reality. After the days of the great screen lovers, the kiss which was extreme in form lived on in the theatre as comedy business. It looked ridiculous because it did not honestly reflect the emotion.

The embrace or kiss is always a touchy business because audiences embarrass easily. An embarrassed spectator either writhes in his seat or laughs to release his nervous tension. If the auditor laughs, he has withdrawn from the scene. He is no longer able to empathize with the characters. The aesthetic distance has been broken. It means that he is no longer viewing characters from a play, but rather is watching actors, perhaps some he knows personally, indulge in intimate conduct in public. The problem is further complicated in that not all of the members of the audience will react in the same way. Some persons, by virtue of their backgrounds or mores, embarrass very easily, others less so. The director, unfortunately, must have his actors execute an embrace or kiss in such a way that it will not embarrass the most sensitive spectator. If a single shy or nervous playgoer giggles, the response of the rest of the audience changes immediately. Their attention is drawn to the embarrassed member. Empathy collapses.

For the beginning director who has had little experience with audiences and therefore is unable to judge the potentials of response with any degree of accuracy, the following suggestions may be helpful. Direct embraces with utter simplicity. The depth of the character's emotion does not have to be portrayed by a scale of violence in the business. A simple and intense scene, in which the actors merely hold hands and look at each other with honest adoration, can be more powerful dramatically than the most passionate kiss. If the director needs a more arbitrary set of standards, experience would dictate that the most intense embrace should never be held more than three seconds, preferably a little less. If the script demands a greater length of time, change the position; that is, break the embrace quickly and come together again. The break will relieve the tension and allow it to be built again.

During the embrace, have the actors stand close together with the dominant character placed slightly upstage of the less important character. Be certain that the embrace does not give the impression that the characters are bending over to reach each other. Have the actors stand so that they can embrace in a completely upright position. Discourage the tendency for the man to bend the woman backward. Above all, make sure that the actors stand still. In an embrace, weaving resembles struggling. If the players can be placed in some position other than profile without destroying the balance of dominance between the characters, the embrace will look more graceful and easy.

The position for a kiss is similar to that for the embrace. Place the characters so that they stand in a position natural to dancing. Have the man stand slightly downstage of the girl. During the kiss the man's head will be turned slightly away from the audience. If this procedure is carried a bit farther, the kiss will be masked entirely by the man's head. This is called a *closed kiss,* because the head positions are such that the audience cannot see the kiss. Most theatrical kisses are closed kisses. The same principle may be used for the kiss when the characters are seated. If the man leans downstage and across the girl, the kiss will be covered. Incidentally, the director should not assume that the closed kiss will be less powerful in its meaning, for the audience will imaginatively complete the picture.

Struggling and Fighting

Since most dramatic action is based in conflict, the dramatic struggle frequently manifests itself in hand-to-hand combat. The basic problem is to determine how a fight can give the impression of reality without damage to properties and persons. On the one hand, an obviously faked fight calls attention to the pretense, and on the other, a violent fight may well break the illusion for the spectator who becomes concerned about the physical welfare of the actors.

One characteristic of the real fight, overlooked by many directors, is its sporadic nature. Fighting is not a continuous procedure. A sharp melee is followed by several moments of inactivity in which the fighters reorganize the attack.

A second factor for the director to consider is the type of fighting. Since wrestling has much grosser physical activity than boxing, wrestling, with a few carefully masked blows, will create a more violent impression than boxing. An additional advantage of wrestling is that the players are able to thrash and roll without actually hurting each other.

The important thing to remember about striking a blow is to mask the impact. If the audience cannot see the blow land, it may be thrown with great force and the spectator will imagine the impact. This is much more satisfactory than allowing the audience to see a feeble blow which is parried.

The struggle between a culprit and his captors is hard to direct so that it appears real. Many directors allow the victim to thrash about continuously, assuming that this will create an illusion of reality. The sustained thrashing merely weakens the action and confuses the focal point. Important lines may be lost. The struggle will appear much more real if the victim makes occasional violent attempts to free himself. The director may rehearse this type of activity so that the lines are read during the quiet moments and are climaxed by bursts of violent activity.

Stabbing and Shooting

The motion picture director has made an art of scenes of stabbing, flogging, and the like. Direct personal violence is censored from motion pictures. As a result, the director relies upon the imaginations of his audiences. Shadows, sounds, blows which were started and never finished, expressions of terror on the face of those about to be hit, or stabbed, or kicked, or trampled create via the spectator's imagination a far greater violence than could conceivably be perpetrated before the eyes of the audience.

The same principles must be used on the stage, though for different reasons. On the stage, the possibilities of representing violence are greatly reduced because the audience can clearly see the mechanics of the action. Sequences involving stabbing are more effective when the actual impact of the blow is hidden from the audience. The raised dagger, stopped just before it reaches its mark, appears ridiculous. If the characters are arranged so that the spectator sees the dagger start and then loses sight of it when it hits with tremendous force, the effect will be powerful.

The rules governing the business of shooting on stage are similar to those covering other types of struggle. However, the action can be more open, for if the gun is actually fired, no one can trace the course of a bullet. If the gun is to be fired offstage, and this is by far the wisest course of action, the prop gun held by the killer must be masked at the instant of firing. This can easily be done by distracting the attention of the audience at the critical moment. For example, the victim may scream a fraction of a second before the shot, thereby shifting the audience's attention from the gun.

All of the rules for handling firearms must be obeyed, whether the stage gun is loaded or not. The director must make absolutely certain that no gun is ever pointed toward the audience. The spectator who sits looking up the barrel of a rifle carelessly slung over an actor's arm is bound to wish he could move.

Stage Falls

The stage business of falling is complicated by the necessity for making the fall appear real and yet graceful enough so that the audience does not question that it was intentional. The example in Chapter 4 of an actual tumble down a flight of steps illustrates how a poor fall may destroy the illusion. If the fall is too brutal, the audience will worry about the actor rather than the character in the play.

At the opposite extreme is the fainting maiden or dying man whose fall doesn't have the semblance of reality. If the spectator sees the fainting actor reach out to break his fall, it will be impossible to maintain the illusion. Obviously, the ideal fall will lie between the extremes.

The mechanics of falling are relatively simple. The execution takes a great deal of practice. As the player topples over, the shock of the drop must be absorbed in several places. The usual sequence involves turning slightly and allowing the knee, hip, shoulder, and hand to hit the floor in succession. A good stage fall can be very abrupt with no material damage to the actor.

Death Scenes

Playwrights often put some of their best lines into the mouths of characters who are dying. These scenes are extremely hard for the director to handle because the playwright asks the character to follow a very illogical course to his doom. The characters must die a little, speak a little, die a little, speak a little, sometimes ad infinitum. For example, the death scene in *Cyrano de Bergerac* is so protracted that most directors have given up any attempt to make it seem real.

The director must follow the dictates of the playwright as gracefully as possible. Actually, the dying and speaking can be alternated. Place the actors in a comfortable and yet conceivable position. Let the dying character experience some pain which will notify the audience that he is dying. Then let the character have a reprieve from his pain and talk. Continue to alternate the process. Be certain that the pattern or sequence is not observable to the audience or the scene will seem ridiculous.

Two other aspects of dying must be handled with discretion. It takes time to die, even to die quickly. Audiences frequently laugh at the final scenes of some of Shakespeare's tragedies because the deaths come so quickly, both in the sense of quick succession and quick submission. The audience should not be blamed for laughing; it is the director's fault for allowing the audience to objectify the scene. The final scene of *Hamlet* will test the ingenuity of any director, for it has four deaths in less than a minute.

A final suggestion. Dead bodies should be removed as soon as possible. The audience knows that the player isn't dead. As such, the spectator becomes more and more conscious of the actor lying on the stage. This objectivity cannot in any way strengthen the production.

With the chapter on stage business, we complete the discussion of the visual principles of play direction. Well thought out, imaginatively conceived, perfectly executed business can give a production roundness and depth unobtainable in any other way. Poor stage business can deprive a production of the nuance of meaning and emotion it deserves. Good stage business is a sign of the master craftsman and the creative artist.

IO

Emotion and Key

HUMAN CONFLICT is the foundation upon which this book is built. Conflict causes an upset in the equilibrium of the individual or, in the case of the play, an upset in the balance of motivational forces. The result of the impaired balance is a disorganization in the responses that may be called emotion. By following this simple chain of reasoning, we may conclude that the projection of emotion becomes one of the major concerns of the director.

Emotion in drama may be approached in still a different way. The director wishes the spectator to suspend his critical, rational judgment and respond subjectively. The desired audience response is emotional rather than rational. Laughter, tears, and thrills are expressions of emotion. Thus, the second task of the director is to stir an emotional response in the spectator. How may this be done? By expressing the emotion in terms which the audience can understand and recognize. To accomplish these ends the director must understand what emotion is, how it may be projected, and the factors limiting spectator response.

A Definition of Emotion

The psychologist defines emotion as a pattern of disorganization. It has been observed that when a person is faced with a conflict situation, muscular tension tends to increase. If the individual is able to solve the problem at hand, the tensions decrease or dissipate. If, on the other hand, the individual is unable to regain an adjustment to his environment, the tensions increase. During emotion, many of the bodily changes which take place are under the control of the autonomic nervous system. These changes are similar to changes which occur as a result of extreme muscular exertion, except that the amount of energy released is much greater than that needed for the solution of the problem. Part of this increased tension is the result of excessive endocrine activity which causes an almost immediate increase in muscular tension, blood pressure, respiratory and pulse rate.

The physiological changes in emotion seem to be similar, if not identical, regardless of the emotion experienced. The basic emotional reactions appear to be an awareness of pleasantness or unpleasantness. Most psychologists agree that three basic emotions can be differentiated. These are: anger, fear, and love. Both so-called pleasant emotions such as love and anger (we enjoy the outburst) and unpleasant emotions such as fear and anger (we hate our opponent) have identical physiological bases. Both are patterns of disorganization. Even extremely pleasurable emotions indicate a pattern of disorganization. For example, "I'm so happy I don't know what to do!" Or the person who cries both when he is happy and when he is sad.

Let us recapitulate. Emotion is the result of a pattern of disorganization depending upon personal involvement which excites the autonomic nervous system and the endocrine glands, with a resulting physiological response that may be interpreted as pleasant or unpleasant.

Of what possible value can such a definition be to a play director? It should serve to point out a major problem. All emotion considered physiologically is essentially the same. If this be true, how can delicate differentiations in emotion be projected to an audience?

Recognition of Emotion

Let us take another step in the examination of emotion and determine the spectator's ability to recognize differences. Several studies have shown that spectators are unable to recognize with any reasonable accuracy different emotional states. Since the physiological changes in respiration, pulse rate, blood pressure, etc., are the same whether one has been kissed, frightened, or insulted, some other basis for recognition must be found.

Now suppose a new clue to the emotion is added. The situation which provoked the emotion is explained. With this information, the ability to judge the emotional response is greatly improved. This increase in the accuracy of judging emotion is not based upon the differences in the visible emotional pattern, but rather upon the judgment of the situation provoking the emotion.

Dockeray and Lane sum up the bases upon which emotions are named and classified in terms of the following factors: [1]

1. We must have some information concerning the nature of the visceral elements of the response. This aids us in determining the character of our own emotional behavior.
2. We must be able to see a considerable sequence of the behavior of the person experiencing the emotion.
3. We must have some knowledge of the stimulating situation.
4. We must have been through a similar experience ourselves in order to be able to ascribe correctly our own responses to those we observe.

In the theatre, most of the factors suggested above are provided. A differentiation in actual emotion can be perceived. However, several other studies have indicated that simulated emotion is more readily perceived than actual emotion. This leads to a discussion of conventionalized emotional expression or the emotional stereotype.

The Emotional Stereotype

Stereotypes may be simply defined as the "pictures we carry in our heads" to simplify, clarify, and complete our fragmentary information. They are little kernels of information which may be fallacious but are nonetheless the basis of our judgments of situations in which we have had little actual experience.

Just as there are stereotypes of ideas, classes of things, and situations with which we have had little experience, so there are stereotyped ideas concerning emotion. The point is that although little or no actual difference exists among various emotions, the spectator has a mental image of what each emotion "should look like." These stereotypes are meaningful in projecting stage emotion because they are conventionalized expressions of emotion.

Several studies have shown that the ability to identify emotion

[1] Floyd C. Dockeray and G. Gorham Lane, *Psychology* (2nd ed.; New York: Prentice-Hall, Inc., 1951), p. 354.

accurately is much greater when actors simulate the various emotions than when real emotional states are judged. Why? Because
the actor creates an emotional stereotype when he simulates emotion. He employs a conventionalized pattern of expression. By
using bodily tension, postural attitude, facial expression, and hand
gesture, the actor's portrayal, more closely approximates the stereotyped picture of the emotion which the spectator uses as the basis
for his judgment, than actual emotion does. It should be noted
that some rather uniform mistakes occur even with conventionalized expression. For instance, the portrayal of excited expectancy
is confused with fear; reverence is confused with love. The reason
for this confusion is readily discernible. The conventionalized
expression of each of these pairs of emotions is extremely similar.
In each case, the muscular tensions resulting in posture, facial
expression, and gesture follow the same general pattern.

Summary of Emotion

The success of a theatrical performance depends in a large
measure upon the ability to differentiate, project, and communicate
subtle differences in emotion. Little or no physiological differences
are observable; therefore, communication depends primarily upon
two factors. First, the spectator must be acutely aware of the
motivational forces that provoke the emotion. Second, the actor
must portray emotion in a conventionalized or stereotyped manner
to coincide with the spectator's concept of how the emotion should
appear.

Note that the first of these requirements fits exactly into the requirements of play production as outlined thus far in this text.
Repeatedly, the need for explicitly projecting the reason or cause
for each action, the motivational pattern, has been emphasized. Let
us assume, therefore, that this requirement needs no further discussion.

The second requirement, that the expression of the emotion
coincide with the audience stereotype of the emotion, warrants
further consideration. The succeeding sections of the discussion
are devoted to a re-definition of emotion, the principles of creating
and projecting emotion, and the technical relationship of emotional expression to the dramatic production as a whole.

DEFINITION OF CONVENTIONALIZED
EMOTION

The argument concerning the amount of emotional involvement the actor should experience has long since waned. Most of our leading actors observe that they do experience physiological excitement during the playing of a role. But at the same time, they maintain a rational perspective toward the role. Whether the actor actually experiences fear during the portrayal of the emotion fear is, as we have seen, of little consequence, for all emotions are basically alike. Any emotional arousal may serve as a base from which the actor can more forcibly assume the conventionalized attitudes of the stereotype, but probably it will do little more than that. In fact, some psychologists maintain that emotional arousal experienced by actors on stage is the result of the excitement of the performance and has little to do with the stage emotion the actor is supposed to be experiencing. If this be true, how can the actor communicate the qualities of a specific emotion to the audience?

The spectator has only two bases for evaluating emotion: (1) that which he can see, and (2) that which he can hear. The bases for projecting emotion, therefore, will depend upon visible and audible symbols. The studies in which actors simulated emotion show that language symbols, while helpful in differentiating subtle variations, are not necessary. For instance, the audience is not dependent upon the actor's saying, "I hate you" in order to identify hatred. In fact, the line, "I hate you," may serve to confuse the audience if the visual attitudes symbolizing hate are missing.

The conventional cues to the recognition of emotion all stem from a single base, muscular tension. The muscular tension or tonicity of the actor is reflected in the contraction or relaxation of the body, including the vocal mechanism. Even the emotional relationship between characters is identified in the muscular tensions of the individual characters.

Visual Projection of Emotion

The visual cues by which the spectator identifies emotion are related to the amount of contraction, relaxation, or extension in the musculature. Specifically, the spectator can see the muscle tension found in the posture, the facial expression, and the hand movements. This accounts for the importance of visibility in establishing a focal point in composition, movement, and business.

Two extremes of muscular tonicity are possible. The *contracted* or tensed state, usually associated with unpleasant emotions such as fear and anger. And, in opposition, the *expanded* state, associated with pleasant emotions such as joy and love. An additional comment is necessary to explain the term, *expanded*. Actually, it is a misnomer, as muscles cannot be expanded. A better term might be *extended*, as the extensor, rather than the contractor muscles, are in play.

Portrayal of anger. What are the visual symbols expressing anger? Contraction is the key. It may be seen in a general tension of the bodily musculature. The posture is usually tense and contracted. The facial muscles are distorted in tension. The hands and fingers are contracted and tense. Gesture is energetic, sharp and quick, all results of tension. Movement is aggressive and dynamic, also the result of extensive tension.

Anger is one of the basic emotions which can be identified with reasonable accuracy in its natural state. How can the actor communicate irritation or rage, variations upon the same base? The only procedure available to the actor is a change in the tension pattern. Irritation and rage are essentially degrees of involvement in the anger pattern. They will be portrayed by variations in the tension pattern.

Portrayal of joy. Just as anger results in a conventional expression of contraction, joy may be portrayed by relaxation or extension of the musculature. The feeling of well-being or expansiveness is communicated through a different set of tension characteristics. The posture shows either relaxation or extension. Facial expression, gesture, and movement are relaxed or animated in the sense of freedom and openness. Again, variations in the basic tension pattern will communicate subtle differences in the basic emotion: love, happiness, even ecstasy.

Note that the descriptions of emotion are essentially conventions or stereotypes. The spectator has learned to anticipate such expression. These muscle states are not necessarily representative of the differences in emotion. Actual anger may be expressed with no visible tension whatsoever. The angry person may respond to the stimulus with complete immobility. Likewise, the person who is happy may, in life, give no external evidence of the emotion.

Vocal Projection of Emotion

A second clue to the recognition of emotion arises from the changes in the vocal characteristics. The vocal changes, like the visual changes, are the result of differing muscular tensions accompanied by changes in respiration.

The violent changes in the respiratory pattern resulting from intense emotion affect the voice. Any intense emotion tends to leave the subject breathless. Again, the change in respiration is not a good key to identification of the emotion. We may be breathless from joyous excitement, breathless from inarticulate rage, or breathless in romantic expectancy. A knowledge of the situation is imperative to the recognition of the emotion.

The same is true of catches, breaks, or a complete breakdown in the voice. Our voices may break because of rage, grief, joy, or love. Carried to the extreme, it is difficult, if not impossible, to differentiate the vocal characteristics of any extreme emotion. Extreme joy may result in tears. Extreme grief may turn tears to laughter. We may cry in insensate rage. The vocal pattern of hysteria is similar, regardless of the kind of hysteria.

Short of the extremes, conventions in vocal expression can be found. Pitch, force, rate, and quality, the four variables of voice, reflect the muscular tensions in emotion.

The pitch of the voice tends to rise as a result of tension. Thus, in unpleasant emotional states with considerable tension, a raised pitch results. In situations involving pleasant emotional states, the vocal mechanism is relaxed with a corresponding tendency toward a lower pitch. Scenes of anger and fear are frequently characterized by high pitch. The emotions of love and simple grief, since they lack tension, are played in low pitches.

Rate, a second vocal variable, also responds to tension. Tension implies excitement, which usually results in an increase in the rate of speaking. In reverse, relaxation is related to slower pacing. For example, love scenes are seldom hurried.

Force also reflects muscular tension. Increases in tension call forth increases in force. Decreases in tension result in decreases in force.

The quality, timbre, or resonance characteristics of voice are also useful in portraying emotion. Assuming that the actor can speak with a full, resonant normal quality, changes in quality will suggest changes in emotional tension.

Just as in the case of the visible cue to emotion, the suggested vocal characteristics are essentially conventions. Under the duress of actual emotion, no two people, probably, will respond in the same way. Certainly not all angry people speak with high pitch, fast rate, great force, and a harsh quality. Indeed, it would be a shame to interpret all stage characters in this way. On the other hand, these vocal characteristics do appear in varying degrees frequently enough so that a general convention or stereotype has developed. The imaginative actor and director will embroider the stereotype while retaining the basic characteristics accepted and expected by the spectator.

Emotional Key Defined

Since muscle tension is the basis for the spectator's recognition of emotion, it should be apparent that every scene, indeed every line in a play, will evidence some degree of emotional tension. A measure of the amount and kind of tension is useful to the director who is as much concerned with the ebb and flow of emotion throughout the play as he is with the individual emotional tensions of the actors.

Emotional key, the amount and kind of tension shown by an actor or revealed by a scene, is such a concept. The term, *key*, is taken from popular parlance. It is common to refer to a person as being "keyed up," showing emotional excitement of one kind or another. The relationship between individuals may show the same characteristics. Thus, we may say that a scene is played in a high key or a low key, denoting the amount of emotional tension in the scene.

SOURCES OF EMOTIONAL KEY

The emotional key of either a scene or a character is found by analyzing the underlying emotional pattern. Since emotion has been defined as a pattern of disorganization with accompanying changes in muscular tension, the cause of the disequilibrium in a character or characters is traceable to its natural basis, the motivation.

Individual Emotional Key

The basic drives determine the amount and kind of tension affecting a character. The term, *drive,* implies a dynamic force urging the individual to action. Whenever the individual is frustrated in his attempt to satisfy the drive, emotional tension increases. By evaluating the strength and force of the drive, the director can ascertain the amount and kind of emotional tension.

In a similar way, the physical, social, and psychological situations create tension. At any point in the play, a set of circumstances is in force. These circumstances influence the behavior of the characters. As a result, tensions are revealed. For example, the socially inferior person experiences emotional complications when in elite society.

Perhaps the most important source of emotional tension in the play results from the interaction between the characters. Interaction was defined as a serial response in which each of the responses of the reacting individuals acts as a stimulus to further action. Even a simple exchange of the social amenities will reveal a tension relationship between the characters. In more extreme situations, and these are the situations of which a play is composed, the interaction of human personalities and drives creates sharp changes in the keys of the characters.

Finally, the amount and kind of emotional tension aroused in a character is the result of the individual character complex. Typical responses of characters with different individual traits are considered in Chapter 2.

The Key of a Scene

A combining of the keys of the various characters will, in a large measure, determine the emotional tension or key of a scene. Few scenes are played in a single key. The playwright provides changes in the unfolding of the motivational pattern. On the other hand, if you examine any play as a whole, you will find that different scenes or motivational units have different keys. These basic changes in key are essential to exciting drama. Chapter 4 discussed the importance of recognizing changes in the meaning and purpose of adjacent motivational units. Change in key from scene to scene is another of the playwright's ways of keeping an ever-changing stimulus before the spectator. No play can be produced in a single key, no matter how intense the key might be. The resultant monotony would be undesirable.

Frequently, an analysis of the key relationships between scenes will influence the interpretation of the individual scene. The director who understands the need for variety will avoid similarities in interpreting the emotional tension in adjacent units insofar as the motivational pattern permits.

An example may indicate how the relationship between scenes can influence the director in his interpretation of key in one particular scene. Let us suppose that the tension characteristics of three units in sequence are as follows: unit one, violent conflict causing a high key; unit two, social conversation, low key; unit three, romance in a low key. If the director follows the pattern suggested above, the unit involving the social conversation will be emphasized because of the contrast to the preceding scene. But perhaps the director wishes to emphasize the love scene. This may be done, assuming the motivational pattern permits, by raising the excitement and tension of the second unit of social conversation. In the new interpretation, the conversation will receive less emphasis because the drop in key from the conflict unit is slighter, and the romantic unit will be emphasized because of the definite change in key following the conversation.

The Motivational Unit and Key

The motivational unit provides the starting point in the evaluation of key, just as it serves that purpose in directing composition, movement, and business. The procedural principles are also similar. First, the director should determine the characteristic key for the unit. This must be done with particular concern for the relationship of the unit to surrounding units and to the play as a whole. Second, the director should evaluate the motivational forces causing tension at the initial moment of the unit. From that point forward, the key will be controlled by the interaction of the characters in the scene.

THE CHARACTERISTICS OF EMOTIONAL
TENSION

Emotions may be hard to identify, but they do have certain rather specific characteristics that are useful to the director in composing the emotional picture.

Emotional tension usually expresses itself in action of one kind or another. The body is stirred up and the musculature is tensed; whether it be contracted or extended, physical activity will result. This quality may be projected in the visual pattern of the play.

Emotions are pleasant or unpleasant. As a result they tend to give rise to either favorable positive, or unfavorable negative responses. This aspect also can readily be interpreted through movement and business.

Frequently, emotional tension is dissipated upon surrounding objects or persons who have had no part in stirring up the emotion. For example, a happy man is generous to everyone in sight. In anger, his tension may resolve itself into an action such as kicking the furniture or striking a youngster.

Finally, one of the most important characteristics of emotion is its manner of coming and going. Emotional tension may arise very suddenly or quite slowly. Since it is the result of glandular activity, small amounts of the stimulant may be gradually infused into the system, or a large quantity may be released with a sudden upsurge in tension. Probably more important to the director is the fact that emotional tension always dies away slowly. It takes time for the effect of the stimulant to wear off. This characteristic determines many of the time relationships in changing key.

PRINCIPLES FOR CONTROLLING KEY

At first glance one might assume that the determination of key and the process of handling key are dictated solely by the motivational pattern. It must be remembered that there are numerous ways of interpreting any single set of motivational factors. These differences are coupled with the need for selection, arrangement, and intensification of the emotional responses into a compelling dramatic pattern. The result is a group of principles that give the illusion of reality but are in some ways highly artificial.

Key Within the Single Speech

The procedure for establishing the key of a single speech is to determine the motivation at the beginning of the line. This indicates the amount and kind of tension. Next, determine the key at the end of the line and notice whether the key changes within the line. Then observe any possibilities for changing the key within the line. In most short speeches, the key remains unchanged through the line, except, perhaps, for the stress given emphatic meanings.

The long speech always demands key change within the speech. An angry tirade, eight to ten printed lines in length, must not be read in a constant key, for the monotony of the tension would impair the power of the speech. A speech of this length should not be read with a constantly increasing tension (this is the way most inexperienced and almost all unimaginative actors will read it), for the expression of increasing anger seldom follows a constantly increasing pattern. And, finally, the actor cannot begin on a high key and move to a higher one, because there are limits to the amount of vocal and visual tension that can be expressed.

The solution to the reading lies in finding in the speech spots at which the key may be raised and lowered. No matter how the speech is written, such moments can be found. If the actor begins in a high key, he must find a place to decrease it, so that he may build again to an even higher key. The contrast and variety put into the reading of the speech will greatly enhance its power. The key can be changed by varying the rate, force, and pitch patterns, by the use of pause, by modifications in quality, by changing the posture, movement, and gesture patterns. The next time you see a motion picture or a play, analyze the use of key in some of the longer speeches. As a director, you should be able to sense the changes which make the speech eloquent.

Key Relationships Between Characters

In Chapter 2 the importance of *interaction* was emphasized. Examine this word carefully: *inter*—between, *action*—response. By definition, it is the *response between* characters, the affect of one character upon another.

Interaction is the foundation of the concept expressed in every acting text: *an actor must be a good listener*. Only by listening acutely to the key in which a line is read can the actor respond in a fashion that will indicate his *reaction* to the line.

If characters are interacting, each is responding to the emotional tension of the other. Note this relationship of emotional key in life. In every instance, some logical relationship is present. Listen to two persons in angry conflict. They usually respond to one another in similar keys. Listen to two lovers. If they are responding to each other, their keys will be related. Listen to an irate mother berating her sullen child. The high key of the mother and the low key of the child express the relationship. This interaction is of primary significance on the stage. The relationship between the emotional keys of interacting characters is perhaps the best clue the audience has to the characters' relationship.

Suppose we examine this relationship in a negative sense for a moment. Think of the times during tryouts when one actor correctly portrays the emotional key of the character he is reading, while another actor participating in the reading goes his own way with no response whatsoever to the first actor. The meaning of the emotional relationship between the characters is lost. Indeed, the superior actor soon finds it impossible to read the lines well because he receives no stimulation upon which to build his responses.

The most significant points of contact between the speeches of two interacting characters are found at the cue and at the attack. A cue is the signal to respond, usually the last few words of a speech. (Chapter 11 contains a detailed discussion of cues.) The attack is the immediate response, which comes on the first few words of a speech. Thus, the cue and the attack represent the points of juncture between speeches. Any speech ends at the cue with a characteristic key. The responding character attacks his speech in a related key. Three of the four possible key relationships between speeches are shown in Figure 23.

Topping. Illustrated in A, topping is the process of interacting so that the emotional key is raised a step with each new response. Topping is employed to indicate a sharply increasing tension between the characters. Typical dialogue might read as follows:

CHARACTER a: Put the letter down.
CHARACTER b: I'll do nothing of the kind.

CHARACTER a: I insist that you put the letter down at once!
CHARACTER b: I won't!

Comparison of the dialogue with *A* in Figure 23 shows the relationship. The key is raised between the cue and the attack.

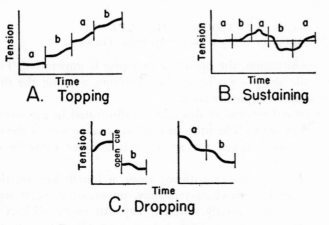

FIG. 23. INTERACTION IN EMOTIONAL KEY

Sustaining. The key relationship between characters is sustained if the cue and the attack are in an identical emotional key. This relationship is shown in *B* of Figure 23. Note that the key may change sharply within the speeches, but that it is identical at the cue point. Almost all dialogue is handled in this manner. The actor who listens to the tension in the cue responds in his attack by using the same amount of tension. Sustained key gives the extremely necessary impression of a flow in the dialogue. The tempo factors discussed in Chapter 11 further accentuate the flow between speeches.

Dropping. A decrease in tension between characters is called *dropping.* Dropping is seldom, if ever, merely the reverse of topping. Tension does not dissipate itself in this regular fashion. In the drawing *C,* two methods of decreasing the tension in a scene are indicated. The first method involves a sharp change in tension with an opened cue. The time lapse between the highly keyed cue and the low key attack is tremendously important. In an earlier section it was stated that emotional tension takes time to dissipate.

Let us suppose that the dialogue shown for topping is continued. The speech of character *a* in illustration C is raised in tension and attached to the end of the topping sequence, drawing A. The continued dialogue with a sudden drop in tension might appear as follows: (Read dialogue on preceding pages and add the following.)

CHARACTER a: PUT DOWN THE LETTER!!
CHARACTER b: (*After a pause*) All right. I'm sorry.

In this situation, the open cue or pause is imperative. Time indicates the sharp drop in tension. Without a pause the dialogue would sound completely false.

The second method of dropping is illustrated in the second section of drawing C. The drop in tension is taken within the speech. The juncture between the speeches is another example of sustaining the key.

Opposite keys. In exceptional cases, a fourth key relationship may be found. Two characters may, on occasion, react together, each displaying a totally different key. An angry military officer might dress down a completely submissive soldier. The officer's key would be high; the soldier's key would be low. This key relationship will be credible only when the context of the script clearly indicates such a relationship.

I wish that there were some way of driving home the importance of exact key relationships as one of the guiding principles of play production. An appallingly large number of productions are ruined because the director has not taught his actors to listen and respond to the emotional tensions of other actors. The correct use of key will not save a poor production, but it can cover up a great many other faults.

Emotion is, in many ways, intangible, yet it must be expressed with clarity and force on the stage. Knowledge of the conventional means of expressing emotion will help; the emotional arousal of the actor will help; but above all, a carefully conceived, well-controlled flow of emotional key is necessary to an integrated powerful production.

II

Tempo

CONSIDERABLE CONFUSION exists concerning the meaning and use of tempo in dramatic production. Some of the leading authors of works on play production disregard the concept entirely. Unfortunately, this may lead some directors to think of tempo as a perfectly natural and simple use of time. In many ways, the timing of a play does reflect the natural timing relationships found in the life situation. In other ways, it is a highly artificial concept resulting from the peculiarities of the drama and the stage.

Stop for a moment and listen to the time factors found in an ordinary drawing room conversation. Notice that the real tempos of life are singularly undramatic. In average conversation, people take time to think. The time relationships between bits of conversation are erratic and without purpose. Without any apparent reason, pauses develop in the conversation. Frequently, several people speak simultaneously, completely obscuring the meaning. Even in an argument, which should have dramatic elements, the time sequence often has a sporadic quality that does not clearly indicate the course of the conflict.

In contrast, listen to the tempo pattern of a play. It sounds logical enough, but upon closer examination the artificial qualities can be observed. The playwright has eliminated the random and purposeless aspects of the usual conversation. He has telescoped his events into a clear-cut pattern. As a result, the time relationships have been altered. In the play, the characters know when to speak. They do not fumble for words, interrupt and excuse themselves, allow meaningless gaps to occur between speeches. The playwright writes in tempo and rhythm patterns which are pleasing to the ear and dramatically effective. Every interruption in the flow of the dialogue has a purpose and meaning which can be interpreted by the spectator. If characters in the play do interrupt each other or fumble for words, there is a specific dramatic reason for it. Stage characters are highly articulate; they seldom have the universal human problem of struggling with the composition of a sentence. Tempo on the stage serves a very specific series of dramatic purposes.

THE STAGE USE OF TEMPO

It has been said that a "good" use of tempo can cover a multitude of sins in a play. Or, in reverse, a play that lacks effective timing will appear ragged and unfinished. These statements are largely true. The effective dramatic use of time can direct attention, lessen fatigue, provide excitement, help convey emotion, intensify conflict, aid in changing mood, point up lines and situations, and provide variety in the dramatic production.

Tempo Should Direct Attention

In reality, this heading should be reversed. One might better say that a lack of control of tempo may misdirect attention and create a corresponding fatigue. In the play there is a continual, though varied, flow of dialogue among the characters. This flow is particularly important at the juncture between speeches. The spectator usually directs his attention to the speaking character. Therefore, at the end of a speech the attention of the spectator must be shifted to some new point of interest, usually the speech of another character. At the juncture of the two speeches, the time factor is of extreme importance. If the new speech is not begun immediately, the spectator is confused. For that moment when the gap occurs, the playgoer does not know where to look. He will undoubtedly be completely unconscious of this momentary confusion, but it will take energy for him to redirect his attention. As these little frustrations mount into the hundreds, excessive fatigue sets in, and enjoyment of the play is reduced.

Time may be used to direct attention in a positive sense also.

One of the best methods of pointing up lines, situations, objects, and relationships is through the manipulation of the timing pattern.

Tempo Should Convey Emotion

Time has a connotative value. Note the implied meaning in the adjectives *quick, brisk, clipped, nimble, fleet,* as compared with the adjectives *slow, sluggish, dull,* and *lazy. Speed* has emotional meaning. In discussing movement, it was noted that a quick movement held for the spectator a meaning different from that of a slow movement. In a similar way, the speed of a line or scene can provide the audience with clues to its emotional meaning. For example, in scenes of arousal and activity, the tempo will quicken. Anger and violence are usually accompanied by an increased tempo in activity and speech. At the other extreme, scenes of tenderness and pathos are usually characterized by a retarded sense of speed. In a happier vein, the spirit of gaiety and frivolity will be reflected in a quickening beat. In drama, as in life, the use of time reflects the basic tenor of the emotional key. (See Chapter 10.) Time is, in part, determined by the motivational pattern of the scene.

Tempo Should Intensify Conflict

Since time has an emotional connotation, it is logical to assume that it may be used as a factor contributing to changes in emotional meaning. As the emotional key changes, the tempo will change. Time, speed, pace are an integral part of every activity. Thus, changes in tempo are important to the projection of a change or intensification of emotion. In fact, if time is misused, the impact of an emotional key or a change in keys may be impaired or destroyed.

Tempo Should Provide Variety

Throughout the discussion of the bases of dramatic production, the need to vary the stimulus from the stage was emphasized. Changes in tempo can help the director to provide a changing stimulus. Changes in speed within lines, between lines, between motivational units, between characters, all contribute to a varied effect. Through variety, the interest of the audience can be maintained.

Definition of Tempo

Tempo may be defined as an *impression of speed*. Strange as it may seem, fast tempo and high speed are not synonymous terms. This apparently paradoxical phenomenon is based on the fact that the impression of speed depends largely upon the feeling of excitement which emanates from the stage. To illustrate: A director may be accused by the spectator of having produced a "slow" show. Frequently the so-called "slow" performance is one in which the elapsed time has been extremely short. The critic is confusing the terms "slow" and "dull." The speed actually may have been terrific, but the spectator felt that it was slow because the scene did not hold his attention.

In a general sense, scenes which have large portions of dramatic interest or excitement may be paced slowly, for the tension will sustain the scene. In reverse, scenes with little interest value should *appear* to move quickly or give the *impression* of high speed.

Note that both fast tempo and slow tempo are deliberately controlled impressions of speed. These terms may be contrasted with the terms poor tempo or no tempo, which imply that the control of time in the play does not have a dramatic purpose. The spectator who observed that the show was "slow" in the sense of being "dull" was in actuality referring to a lack of meaningful tempo or to a badly selected tempo.

CHARACTERISTICS OF GOOD AND FAST TEMPO

Tempo can be any speed ranging from very fast to very slow. The characteristics distinguishing good tempo from poor tempo can be analyzed. In most dramatic situations, good tempo will also be fast tempo.

Speed

In defining tempo, it was emphasized that a high speed does not guarantee a fast tempo. A machine gun delivery of lines is usually an indication of poor acting. The meaning and emotion of the lines are lost in the speed. Moreover, the audience does not have an opportunity to respond to the line. And, most important, a continuous speed in line delivery eliminates the nuances of feeling and becomes monotonous by virtue of its constancy. Therefore, speed is one of the least effective methods of establishing fast tempo. At the same time, it is obvious that a line briskly paced gives more of an impression of quick tempo than a line read in a generally retarded fashion.

Cue-pickup

One of the most significant elements in creating an impression of a fast tempo is cue-pickup. *A cue is defined as the signal given by word or action for the beginning of a new set of lines or actions.* Cues may be of any nature. There are sound cues, light cues, curtain cues. In each case, the cue is the signal to introduce the sound effect, change the lights, or pull the curtain. The most common cue is the line cue. This is a signal for the actor to begin speaking. Usually the cue or signal is the last few words of the preceding line.

Cue-pickup may be defined as the speed with which the response comes to the signal. In the case of the line cue, the pickup refers to the time lapse between the cue and the actor's attack on the speech. Accordingly, a slow cue-pickup implies a large time lapse, and a fast cue-pickup suggests no time between the signal and the response.

Good tempo, whether it be fast or slow, is dependent upon high speed cue-pickup. As suggested earlier in the discussion, gaps between the cue and the attack create confusion and fatigue in the audience and destroy the flow of the dialogue. Slow cue-pickup results in the ragged impression characteristic of poor tempo.

When the director says, "Pick up the tempo!" he usually means, "Pick up the cues!" Unfortunately, the beginning actor usually reacts to such a request by increasing the speed with which he reads his speech rather than by closing the gap between the speeches.

The procedure for picking up a cue instantaneously is purely mechanical. Most actors sense the cue coming, hear the cue, breathe, and then deliver the line. Ideally, the actor should do his breathing on the cue, not after it. With a little practice, this procedure becomes automatic. The resultant change in the tempo will be surprising.

The stalled cue. If the tempo is to be slow, the stalled cue is

frequently used. *The stalled cue may be defined as a pause introduced immediately after the pickup of the cue.* Let us suppose that
a character must think before speaking. If the director allows the
gap to open up between the cue and the attack, the audience may
be confused. The character should pickup the cue by word or action immediately, so that the audience will know where to look.
After picking up the cue, the actor may pause as long as is desirable.
The attention of the audience will remain focused upon him. For
example:

> CHARACTER a: I don't understand how you can believe that.
> CHARACTER b: Well ... I can't explain the reason; I just do.

In this situation, the second speaker picks up the cue immediately.
The stall comes after the cue. The audience will not be aware that
its attention has been redirected; therefore, despite the extended
pause, no confusion will result. The tempo is slowed down, but
the continuity of the scene is maintained.

*The open cue. An open cue, somewhat different from a stalled
cue, is a deliberate pause between the cue and the attack.* It is
used in exceptional cases in which the spectator's attention has
already been directed to the responding actor. If the attention has
not been transferred, an open cue will appear as a meaningless
gap between lines. In Chapter 10, an open cue is indicated in
the dialogue about the letter.

> CHARACTER a: PUT DOWN THE LETTER!!
> CHARACTER b: (*After a pause*) All right. I'm sorry.

In this case, there can be no question as to the focal point of the
scene. Every spectator will watch Character B to see if he will lay
down the letter.

Projection

Another factor which aids the impression of brisk pacing is
projection. *Projection* means, literally, *to throw out.* In stage
terminology, projection implies the creation of a visual and auditory stimulus of sufficient energy to be seen and heard without
strain by the audience. This may be accomplished by pure loud-
ness or any other combination of factors which will give a forceful
impression. (See Chapter 18.) Just as in the case of slow cue-pickup,

a lack of projection requires an excessive expenditure of energy on the part of the audience. The result of weak projection is the impression of slowness or dullness.

Again it should be noted that tempo is related to excitement. Underprojection appears to decrease the excitement. For this reason, scenes with a low emotional key need greater projection than scenes of great emotional upheaval. With an increase in the projection, the impression of speed is increased, and scenes which might otherwise seem static come to life.

Emotional Key

Apropos of the preceding discussion of the characteristics of tempo, the emotional key of the scene not only establishes the tempo requirements, but also can create an impression of tempo by itself. Scenes with great tension will appear to move quickly for the audience because they are exciting. The director may deliberately slow the pace, since the tension of the scene will sustain the interest of the audience. In reverse, it may be necessary in some low-keyed static scenes, to raise the speed, tighten the cue-pickup, and increase the vitality of the projection.

Visual Characteristics

The preceding remarks all concern the auditory aspects of tempo. Good tempo is just as much a matter of pantomime as it is of speech. Everything that has been said about speed, cue-pickup, projection, and key applies with equal force to the visual aspects of the production. To summarize briefly, the actual speed of the movement and business will affect the impression of pace. Variety in the speed of the action will be more significant than sustained speed. Cues may be picked up by movement as well as by speech. Since cue-pickup concerns the redirection of audience attention, it follows that a movement or gesture which will catch the spectator's eye can be used to pick up a cue. Frequently, simultaneous speech and action are used to forcibly redirect attention.

Projection of visual activity, explained in Chapters 8 and 9, can convey an impression of vitality which will, in turn, enhance the pace. In a similar way, emotional key, shown through physical tension and activity, can create excitement in the audience and, as a result, increase the impression of speed in the scene.

Dramatic Pause

Good tempo makes full use of dramatic pause. Pause is the best method of providing variations in tempo. Most inexperienced actors and many directors are afraid to make a maximum use of pause; yet pause is a more powerful means of emphasizing and creating change than are variations in the force or speed with which the dialogue is read.

Dramatic pause creates suspense. For example, what happens when a line is forgotten? The audience, possibly restless prior to the pause, quickly quiets down. With anticipation, the tension grows. Apparently the audience stops breathing, for the air becomes electrified, and the silence is complete. A well-planned dramatic pause will cause exactly the same response.

Note that the pause must be dramatic; that is, it must have some reason and purpose. If the pause is not motivated, it becomes a gap. Slow cue-pickups are meaningless little gaps. Pause that breaks the illusion is a gap. Any time lapse to which the audience cannot assign a dramatic meaning is a gap. There should be no gaps in the dramatic production.

GENERAL CONSIDERATIONS IN DETERMINING TEMPO

Offering specific suggestions for the determination of tempos in a play is a virtually impossible task. The selection of the right speed for a scene depends upon the special characteristics of the scene, the relationship of the scene to the preceding and subsequent scenes, the tempo characteristics of the characters in the scene, and many other variables. Nonetheless, a few general observations can be made, to give the director some clues to the possible use of tempo.

The Motivational Pattern

The tempo of any scene is decided largely by the motivational forces. It was stated earlier that speed has an emotional meaning; therefore, the tempo of any scene must conform to the total impression which the scene is to produce.

Technical Considerations

Unfortunately, knowledge of the motivational pattern is not sufficient to determine all of the tempo changes in the production. The director frequently uses changes in the tempo pattern, which are alien to the motivational pattern, to create specific impressions.

If the director follows the motivational pattern entirely, the tempo will normally be slowest in those scenes with the least excitement. For example, in a static intellectual scene in which the characters talk without deep emotional involvement, the tension or key is low. Based upon the motivational pattern, a corresponding slowness of tempo would seem to be indicated. The result of this combination would be undramatic. In such a scene the director often must introduce some factor to increase the dramatic effect. One procedure at his disposal is to increase the tempo. A faster tempo will hasten the undramatic scene and, at the same time, give it a brilliance which would otherwise be lacking.

Highly dramatic scenes of great tension call for a quickening of the pace, yet frequently these scenes are dramatic enough without the added impetus of a fast tempo. In such cases, the speed of playing may be retarded. It cannot, of course, ever be slowed down to a point at which it no longer reflects the motivational pattern, for the scene then would lose its meaning. Slowing the dramatic scene may, in certain situations, actually increase the excitement.

If the director wishes a rule-of-thumb for pacing a play, it might read as follows: Use a fast tempo as the base. Vary the pace whenever the motivational pattern or heightened emotional tension permit. This principle is meaningless unless the director can apply it with imagination and sensitivity. On the other hand, many, many plays are ruined for the audience because they seem to lag. Fast tempo with variety will eliminate this impression of dullness.

Variety in Tempo

Speed is relative. It can be recognized only when it is compared with slowness, and vice versa. The director must be fully aware of this concept if the tempos he sets for the play are to have meaning for the audience.

Any sensory impression loses its force when it is continued over a period of time. At the start of a trip, sixty miles per hour may seem dangerously fast. After driving for a time, the same sixty miles an hour will seem slow. When you slow down to a crawl while going through a town, a glance at the speedometer may show that you are still going at a forty mile an hour clip.

So it is with the play. Even the fastest tempo, held constant, soon loses its impression of speed and appears to drag. The director must provide changes in the pace. He must constantly search for opportunities to retard the tempo, so that when he increases it again the exhilaration of the speed can be felt and enjoyed by the audience. Time and again, one sees productions in which the director has used every means at his disposal for increasing the pace; every means, that is, except variety, the most important device of all. The individual tempo factors were all handled well; the running time was short; the cue-pickup was superior; the projection was vital; but the production still seemed dull and lagging. Changes in pace would have made the production sparkle. Some of the procedures for assuring variety in tempo are discussed below.

TECHNIQUES FOR GAINING VARIETY

The director must be aware of the places in the script where he may find justification for changes in tempo. Credible reasons for changes in pace can be found in literally dozens of places from the single line to the motivational unit.

Variations Between Motivational Units

Most motivational units have specific tempo characteristics. Since the motivational pattern is modified with each new unit, the tempo may also change. For example, a unit with violent conflict as its basic emotion will probably be interpreted with a moderate to fast tempo because of the high key of the scene. If the next unit is one of reconciliation, the change in mood can be shown by a change in tempo. By tracing the sequence of motivational units, the director can determine in advance the general possibilities for variety in pace throughout the play. This over-all application of the major tempo changes, if handled effectively, will give the show as a whole a sense of pace, which the audience will never recognize but will enjoy.

Variations Between Characters

A second likely place for tempo variation is found in the individual differences of the characters. The individual character complex fixes an underlying tempo pattern for each of the characters. Some of the characters in the play are steady, deliberate, contained people; others are excitable, distraught, and nervous. These differences are present in a good play because the playwright is aware of the need for variety.

As these different characters interact, variations in tempo can be an important way of differentiating them. At this point a word of warning should be inserted concerning the tempo responses of the inexperienced actor. Many actors tend to respond to the tempo of the individuals who surround them. To the extent that this tendency to copy the tempo characteristics of others is a reflection of the emotional key of the scene, it is proper. However, the actor must avoid changing his tempo to the extent that he impairs the tempo pattern of his character. Frequently, an over-all impression of monotony arises because the tempos of all the characters are the same. The director can provide variety in the pacing of the play if he can maintain tempo differences among the characters.

Variations Between the Lines

Some of the tempo differences between lines result from the different time patterns of the characters. Apart from these differences, the director will find that the playwright often includes tempo sequences. These sequences are small rhythmic or speed units that fit together. Normally, they are emotional key units as well as tempo units. A good example of such a unit is found in the second act of Noel Coward's *Private Lives*. Amanda and Elyot are arguing about nothing in particular in the privacy of Amanda's apartment.

ELYOT: It's a pity you didn't have any more brandy; it might have made you a little less disagreeable.
AMANDA: It doesn't seem to have worked such wonders with you.
ELYOT: Snap, snap, snap; like a little adder.
AMANDA: Adders don't snap, they sting.
ELYOT: Nonsense, they have a little bag of venom behind their fangs and they snap.
AMANDA: They sting.

ELYOT: They snap.
AMANDA: I don't care, do you understand? I don't care. I don't mind
            if they bark, and roll about like hoops.

Note the feeling of tempo as the lines fit together. They go chit—
chat—chit—chat—chit chat. Then there is a shift in tempo as the
subject changes. The gradually increased tempo at the cue points
builds the little unit to its logical conclusion. Units of this type
are found in most plays, though the device is more obviously used
in comedies. The time relationship between the lines, more than
the speed of the lines, gives these units their enjoyable quality.
Assuming a logical motivational base, the director can vary the
pace of the play by changing the tempo characteristics between the
lines. If fast cue-pickup is considered the norm, any device which
retards or increases the speed will provide variety. In an earlier
section, stalled and open cues were discussed. Both of these devices
may be used to slow down the tempo.

Telescoping cues. The director can increase the impression of
speed beyond that of the fast cue by telescoping the cues. *Telescoping a cue may be defined as an overlapping of the cue and the
attack or beginning of the following speech.* The following line is
started before the preceding line has been completed. Telescoped
cues create an impression of excited interruption.

Simultaneous speech. A final procedure for gaining variety in
tempo between speeches is simultaneous speech. Simultaneous
speech occurs when two or more people talk at once. The meaning
of the lines is usually lost, but at times the director is more concerned with creating an impression of chaotic excitement than with
precise meaning. With simultaneous speech the emotional and
tempo qualities of the scene supplant the meaning of the lines.
For example, in a party scene the director may be more interested
in giving the impression of gaiety and enthusiasm than in communicating the particular ideas expressed. Or in a scene of violent
struggle, the impression of vicious action may be all that is important.

In summary, the director may establish any pace he desires by
controlling the time lapse between lines. Diversified cue-pickup
provides variety.

Variation Within the Line

The final and most powerful tempo variations are derived from changes of pace within the line. Actors caught up in the tempo of the scene frequently read lines, particularly long speeches, at a constant tempo. It may be said with finality that any speech several sentences long will have changes in the emotional meaning. These changes must be interpreted by tempo variation as well as by changes in emotional key. Monotony in the tempo characteristics of the play, more frequently than not, is the result of poor timing within the individual speeches. The director must explore every speech for possibilities of breaking up the timing pattern.

Just as variety can be obtained between speeches by the use of pause and telescoping, so variety may be developed within the speeches by the same devices. After the actor has picked up the cue, he may deliver the speech in any manner that gives impact to the thoughts and emotions contained in the lines. Many actors are afraid to slow down or to use pause within a speech. They feel that any letdown in the delivery may reduce the dramatic value. The exact opposite is true. Variety in the pacing of the speech will increase the meaning and the emotion.

Now that there are so many recordings of great plays interpreted by famous actors, the value of variety within speeches can be brought home to most actors. Select an excerpt recorded by a superior professional actor. Have the student actor read the same selection. Record it if possible. Time the length of the speech as it is read by the student. Then compare the student's time with that of the experienced actor. If they are recorded, run the two simultaneously. Hundreds of trials have shown that the inexperienced actor takes considerably less time to read the speech than does the professional. The conclusion: Constant speed within the lines is more of a deficit than an asset.

The conclusions to be drawn from this chapter should be obvious. First, time has meaning in the theatre. Its use must reflect the motivational patterns if credibility is to be maintained. At the same time, it is a technical device for facilitating dramatic effect. Second, speed by itself is of little value in creating the impression of vibrance necessary to a successful dramatic production. And finally, variety is the key to good tempo.

If the director realizes that time must be integrated with sound and sight to make a meaningful whole, many more plays will stimulate numberless audiences to greater imaginative enjoyment.

Part Three

The Procedures of Play Direction

12

Play Selection

MANY THEATRICAL PRODUCTIONS fail because they are unable to rise above a poor script. True, some productions have succeeded because magnificent acting or extravagant technical effects have compensated for weak playwriting. But all things considered, it is difficult to create a production that is better than the material of which it is made.

Many directors have a ready answer for this problem. They say, "Select a good play!" This is easier said than done. What makes a good play? Analysis of the critical comment indicates that even the theatrical critics are often unable to agree upon the ingredients of a good play.

Does the fact that a play is superior literature make it a good play? Not necessarily, for many literary masterpieces written in dramatic form make very poor plays when they reach the stage. If a play pleases the audience, is it good drama? Not necessarily. Often it may be extremely poor drama. Cheap, sensational claptrap frequently appeals strongly to the crowd. Does a successful Broadway production guarantee superior drama? Not necessarily. Broadway producers are more noted for their interest in box office receipts than for their support of good drama. Does the fact that it is a new play by an unknown author make it a good play? Some directors seem to think so. However, there are far more poor original plays than good ones. If the play appeals to the director, is it a good play? Not necessarily. Directors are human. They have prejudices, biases, special interests. Many directors who produce only those things which appeal to them, regardless of the require-

ments of the production situation, do their theatres a real disservice.

This series of questions could be greatly expanded without finding the key to the good play, though each of the questions does
provide a clue to the selection of a superior play.

A further difficulty greatly complicates the problem of play
selection. A play may stand all of the tests of good drama but still
be a poor choice for a particular producing group. A fine choice
for a college may be a poor choice for a high school. A play ideally
suited to one community theatre may not serve the needs of another community theatre. The specific local conditions have a
tremendous bearing upon the determination of the "good" play.

We have defined the "good" play in two different ways: as a
superior theatrical fare, a play which has theatrical worth, and in
terms of the practical strengths and weaknesses of the particular
theatre in which it is to be produced. The following list of questions may be helpful as guideposts in determining the good play as
drama and the good play for a specific production.

DETERMINING THEATRICAL WORTH

Will the Play Be Dramatic?

Most experts agree that a script becomes a play only after it has
been brought to life by production. Many scripts read well but
play badly. Reference to Part I of this text will refresh the reader
on the bases of drama. To be dramatic, the script must deal with
human problems and conflict. It must present the action in the
form of conflict which can be seen and heard by the audience. It
is not enough that conflict be talked about by the characters; it
must be acted out before the spectators. Some great pieces of
dramatic literature have little dramatic value. Literary merit is not
to be disdained, but literary artistry is only one of the elements
that go into the making of a great play. If a choice must be made
between fine literature and compelling dramatic action, the latter
is of greater importance. The ideal play will, of course, contain a
full measure of each.

Does the Script Have Individuality?

Someone once proved that there are fewer than twenty plots
about which all of the dramas of the world have been written.

Thus, the possibilities of conflict are limited. The characters may change. The situations may change. The basic mood may change. But the story and the conflict remain much the same.

The prospective director must choose a script that has individuality. This bit of advice should not be construed as an appeal to select something different simply because it is different. Rather, it is an appeal to select a script with some distinguishing and distinguished characteristics.

The non-professional play director can select his scripts from hundreds of distinguished dramas. He can select plays that have stood the test of time. He can choose plays that have received critical acclaim. He can choose plays introducing new and experimental procedures. There is no reason for him to consider the cheap and tawdry substitutes which flood the dramatic market.

Does the Script Have Universality?

Great plays, which have stood the test of time, have broad general appeal. Molière's comedies are as humorous today as the day they were written. Why? Because they have universality. In Chapter 4, the audience was examined in some detail and found to attend the theatre for rather specific reasons. Every play should be considered in terms of the spectators who are there because they wish to participate.

Many productions misfire because the director or the committee choosing the play has failed to consider the play's appeal to the audience. This does not mean that every play must please every member in the audience. That is impossible. It means rather that the play must have dramatic worth and meaning for the major proportion of the attending group. Most great drama can be produced for any audience because of its universal appeal.

A word of warning. Don't trust the audience's own choice of plays too implicitly. A rash of audience polls in the college theatres has unearthed some interesting facts. Audiences only vote for the plays they have heard about or know. A poll at the University of Wisconsin placed Lillian Hellman's *The Children's Hour* at the top of the list. When the play was produced, a storm of protest arose from the very individuals who had voted for it on the poll. Analysis of the reasons for the play's high rating on the poll indicated that many people selected the play with no idea whatsoever of its subject matter, a theme of children's gossip about homosexual activities. They remembered Longfellow's little poem which begins:

> Between the dark and the daylight,
> When the night is beginning to lower,
> Comes a pause in the day's occupations,
> That is known as the Children's Hour.

They thought that it must be a pleasant little comedy about children.

Does the Play Challenge the Audience?

The good play should do more than please the audience. It should also challenge the audience. The theatre can be more than a palace of laughter and tears. The terms *entertainment* and *enjoyment* can have a broader meaning. The high school, college, and community theatres have a responsibility that goes beyond pure entertainment. A play should contribute to the growth of the spectator. This does not mean that it must be a lesson in sociology, or history, or politics, but the impact upon the audience should have some lasting value. Perhaps the play has a thesis which can be discussed afterwards. Perhaps it will leave the audience with a better understanding of human kind. Perhaps it will merely convey a mood or feeling which is meaningful to the spectator. Perhaps it will purge the trials of the day through laughter or tears. Whatever the purpose may be, good drama should add meaning to the life of the spectator.

Do not misunderstand. The preceding statements are not a plea for the production of arty or obscure drama. They are, rather, a plea for plays with powerful dramatic impact, drama serious enough to strike with force and honesty, comedy bubbling with laughter at the foibles of mankind.

Does the Play Challenge the Actor?

The non-commercial theatre has a responsibility to the participants which is seldom considered in the commercial theatre. The actors participate in dramatic activity for reasons other than a weekly paycheck. For some, participation means a study of drama; for others it implies an interest in better self-expression. Whatever the reason the actor needs a play in which the characters are written honestly and well. The actor should find a challenge in the creation of the role. Well-written roles are easier to portray than inadequately sketched or poorly motivated characters. The well-developed character, comic or tragic, stimulates the actor's imagination and encourages his best efforts. It will intrigue the actor and serve as a constant stimulus throughout the rehearsal period. Poorly written plays seldom hold the interest of the actor or provide an opportunity for study and growth. Poorly written characters can be difficult to portray because there is no clear-cut personality for the actor to grasp.

Does the Play Challenge the Director?

Just as the play should challenge the actor, so it should call forth the best efforts of the director. Superior directors will not be creatively stimulated by the silly claptrap which parades across the play production scene. Plays which have depth and subtlety are exciting to produce. The director must be careful, however, to avoid rating his own interests and desires too high on the scale. If his interests are allowed to control the play selection of a given theatre, the one-sided result will lessen the value of the entire play production program.

In summary, we may say that the "good" play is based on the best in dramatic values. It has a broad appeal for the audience yet maintains individual characteristics which differentiate it from the run-of-the-mill product. It can provide a breadth of experience and growth for the audience, the actor, and the director.

PRACTICAL PROBLEMS IN PLAY SELECTION

The play of great dramatic worth may be a poor selection for a particular theatre. Each play must be tailored to the needs, facilities and abilities of the producing group. Each of the following questions should be answered in the affirmative if the play is to succeed in the local playhouse.

Can the Play Be Cast?

Limitations in acting personnel cast a shadow over the production of many plays in the school and community theatre. Play selection must be determined in part by the availability of talent. *Cyrano de Bergerac* is a good play in the dramatic sense, but it is a miserable choice for the dramatic group without a Cyrano. The problems of casting are discussed in considerable detail in Chapter 15. After studying the principles of casting, the director should be able to compare the character requirements of any play with the talent potential available in his group and reach a decision as to whether the play can be produced successfully.

Can the Play Be Staged?

The ability to stage the play must be considered when selecting any play. If the equipment and technical facilities of the theatre are modest, the basic technical requirements of the play should be studied carefully. Note that the basic technical requirements of the play may be very different from the technical requirements listed in the author's description or shown in the pictures of the Broadway production. Many plays gain from simplicity in staging. Drapery settings with simple properties may highlight the playwright's message. Shows written for two or three sets frequently may be played in a single setting.

The problem of staging is essentially one of establishing the necessary illusion. Imaginative direction can do much to create the desired feeling. Visualize the play on the available stage. The possibility of production is not always limited by the number of spotlights or flats available.

Can Production Costs Be Met?

Almost every theatre must make its own way financially; therefore, it behooves the director to examine the cost of the production. A play of great dramatic worth is a poor choice if it plunges the theatre into debt to the extent that other plays cannot be produced. Assuming that equipment and facilities are adequate and no new capital expense will be incurred, royalties, costumes, and settings will be the major items that make one play more expensive than another.

Royalty. Royalties vary with the prestige of the author and the popularity of the play. The royalties on contemporary successes run from $35 to $50 for the first performance with discounts of from $10 to $15 for succeeding performances. Many publishers will adjust royalty rates in accordance with the size of the theatre and the potentials of income. In fact, one publisher charges royalties on the basis of a percentage of the theatre's income. This procedure offers a distinct advantage to small theatres.

Copyrights usually expire in 56 years. For this reason, much of the finest world drama can be produced without charge. In addition, several manuscript services release new plays for a nominal fee, to cover mimeographing and mailing. A list of these services is included in the bibliography.

Costumes. Costumes are expensive to rent or to make. For this reason, a careful cost analysis should be made when a costume show is considered for production. The rental prices of costumes are constantly changing. However, a safe estimate would include a budget of from $7 to $20 per costume for a week's rental, depending upon the elaborateness of the costume and the price scale of the costume house.

Settings. Scenery and properties are economical or costly, depending upon the size of the carry-over from previous productions and the possibility of using the pieces in future productions. If theatres produce several plays a year, they can re-use the same basic scene pieces in several shows, thereby prorating the cost.

Does the Play Encourage Maximum Participation?

The small cast, one-set show may be economical to produce, but it may not contribute greatly to the internal success of the producing organization. Since actors and crew members are participating in dramatic activity to learn, work, and play, it is essential to choose a play which provides a maximum opportunity for every kind of creative endeavor. The large cast play provides experience for more actors. The play with elaborate scenery, music, or dancing offers opportunities for the expression of every kind of talent.

In summary, the practical problems of play selection represent a series of tests that any play must pass, regardless of its artistic merit, if it is to be a superior choice for a particular theatre. Thus far, we have considered the selection of a single play. The difficulties are magnified when a season of plays is selected.

CHOOSING A SEASON OF PLAYS

If the theatre offers a season of plays, it is in a stronger position than if it sells plays individually. With a season bill, the director is able to sell his patron a package containing a wide variety of goods. If the patron is displeased with one item, he may look forward to others more appealing to his individual taste. On a season bill, the theatre can include plays that represent a strong diet for the average patron, as well as plays that will please almost everyone. The selection of a season of plays is complicated by the need for variety and balance.

Variety in Selecting the Season

When one considers the manifold possibilities for variety within a season of plays, it is hard to understand why some theatres limit their fare to a single type of play. Some community theatres do nothing but contemporary comedies. Some college groups produce only the experimental and academic. Presumably, unless the circumstances are strange indeed, any audience can profit from a profile or cross-section of all that is good in drama. Different kinds of variety are suggested below. The following list does not claim to be exhaustive, for the number of categories depends upon the method of classification.

Kind of drama. Farce, tragedy, romantic comedy, satire, fantasy, social drama, drawing room comedy, melodrama—all have a place in the season of plays. A variety of types gives the season patron a broad experience in the forms of drama. This kind of variety is important for still another reason. Many patrons prefer a particular type. Everyone can be pleased if different kinds of drama are offered throughout the season.

At the same time, a balance must be maintained within the season. It is unwise, for example, to put all of the serious plays at the beginning of the season and conclude with all the comedies. In a season of six plays, one might begin in the fall with a play that is light and entertaining, follow it with a serious drama, lighten the program with a meaty comedy as the third play, insert a new or experimental play next, follow this with another serious play, and wind up the season in the spring with another light and charming piece.

Style of production. A season replete with realistic or naturalistic styles can be varied by including fantasy or even more abstract forms. Style in setting can be varied also. Box settings, drape settings, cutaway settings, non-realistic settings should be included in the season, so that the patron always adds to his experience as he enters the theatre.

Plays from different periods. Great drama is found in almost every period in the history of the theatre. Consistent dependence upon one period in drama, whether it be contemporary or classic, seriously hampers the audience's enjoyment and education.

Plays from different areas. Recent studies, which are mentioned later in this chapter, suggest that vast areas of world drama have been largely untouched by the high school, college, and community theatre. America and Great Britain have not produced all of the worthy playwrights. Programs should draw upon the talents of the world to broaden the spectator's view of the drama.

Balance in Selecting the Season

For practical as well as aesthetic reasons there should be a balance among the various plays on any theatre season. In the interests of economy, costs can be balanced over a season of plays. Costume shows, multiple set shows, high royalty shows push costs upward. Throughout a season of plays, economical shows can be alternated with expensive shows. Also, a show which is very expensive in one item, such as costumes, can be economical in another, such as royalties. Any number of combinations can be used to control costs over a period of time.

Balance in the size of casts is another important consideration. In presenting a season of plays, most theatres have the problem of overlapping rehearsal periods. If two large cast plays are placed next to each other, each play may suffer because of lack of talent.

For technical reasons, some balance should be maintained between shows with elaborate settings and property plots and shows with simple technical effects. Most scene shops have a maximum capacity which dare not be overreached.

SOURCES OF PLAYS

The greatest obstacle to superior play selection is a weak background in dramatic literature. It is impossible to select good plays if your knowledge of drama consists of the two or three plays you have seen and the ten or twelve which were read in a sophomore English literature course. There is no substitute for reading.

Surveys of high school, college, and community theatre play selection clearly indicate that most directors begin and end their play selection chores by thumbing through the catalogues of the play publishers. There is no doubt that the play catalogue is a worthwhile source of dramatic material, but total dependence upon any single source can lead to a badly balanced program.[1]

The best starting point (though it will require some time and effort) is the comprehensive dramatic history. In these volumes, plays are considered on their merits by scholars of dramatic literature. Critical comments are especially meaningful to the director who has a limited background in drama.

Another source of good drama is the anthology. Plays are selected for publication in an anthology only after careful evaluation by a scholar. They are included because they have specific values to recommend them. In addition, anthologies encourage systematic play reading.

A fourth fund of knowledge is the dramatic bibliography. Contemporary bibliographies rapidly become dated, but the annotated digests can be helpful in suggesting directions for play study.

A final and relatively new source of dramatic material is the manuscript play service. These services are dedicated to introducing new plays which have merit. The offering of the manuscript services should be studied with care.

A list of major sources of plays is included in the bibliography. The listing is by no means all-inclusive. It is presented with the hope that it will encourage the director with a limited background to explore the field of drama more thoroughly in his search for his next play.

As we said at the outset, the selection of a good play is difficult and the responsibilities of the director are great. To qualify for the task, the director should develop a broad background by ex-

[1] For a thorough analysis of the play selection practices of the college, high school, and community theatres in America, examine the articles suggested below.

John E. Dietrich, "Survey of Dramatic Activity in American Colleges: 1946-47," QJS, XXXIV (1948), 183-190.

Ronald C. Gee and John E. Dietrich, "A Survey of Dramatic Activity in Wisconsin High Schools: 1947-48," QJS, XXXVI (1950), 65-70.

John E. Dietrich and William Work, "Dramatic Activity in American Community Theatres: 1949-50," QJS, XXXVII (1951), 185-190.

tensive reading. He should be able to evaluate critically the dramatic worth of the play. He should understand his audience, his actors, and himself. And above all, he must assess the limitations of his own theatre correctly. A well-chosen play is the first major step in successful play production.

13

Interpreting the Script

THE DIRECTOR has selected the play. We may assume that the play has dramatic value and can be produced with the available talent and production facilities. The first step in the process of creating a dramatic production is to analyze and interpret the script.

Throughout our discussion we have emphasized that play production is a creative and interpretative process. Numerous interpretative decisions must be made at the outset. The purpose of the play, the author's intent, the emotional and intellectual meanings, the kind of production, the method of staging must be considered in detail. In addition, the director must make a number of practical decisions. He must adapt the script, plot the production, and make the prompt book. The following discussion deals with the interpretative and practical decisions which face the director.

THE PURPOSE OF THE PLAY

We have observed that the primary task of the director is to interpret the meaning and intent of the playwright for the audience. The first step, therefore, in the analysis of the script is to determine the playwright's purpose.

The over-all purpose should be easy to ascertain. First, is the play a comedy or a serious drama? Does the playwright merely wish to evoke laughter or tears? Or is the intent more specific, such as the presentation of a social message or the evaluation of an important character? Obviously, the playwright may wish to communicate many things, but usually he has some reasonably specific purpose for writing the play.

The purpose of some plays is obvious after the most cursory analysis; others have more obscure specific meanings. The playwright's intentions in many of the greatest plays have been the subject of critical controversy for decades or even centuries. In determining how the play should be interpreted the director may be aided by the background of the play and the play itself.

The Background of the Play

To many of his plays, George Bernard Shaw added prefaces which are as long as or longer than the plays themselves. Their inclusion suggests that Shaw felt a need to suggest to the reader and the producer a point of view or, indeed in some cases, a manner of interpretation. If other dramatists had been as thoughtful or as specific, problems of interpretation would be minimized.

The professional has a great advantage over the non-professional in this matter of background. Most contemporary producers have the playwright at hand during the production of the play to aid in the interpreting process (though some complain that frequently the author is more of a hindrance than a help).

The non-professional director has at least three sources of background material: the history of the play, the background of the author, and the critical comment.

The history of the play. If the play has a history, it may be of great help in determining the interpretation. Plays are written to be produced in a contemporary environment. They reflect the manners, customs, ideas, and mores of their time. The historical play can best be understood in terms of the social and cultural events of the time. Even contemporary plays reflect the culture in which they are written. Plays of the 1930's give indications of the social, economic, and philosophical environments of that decade. Today, we say that these plays are dated. Ideas, traditions, customs, even languages have changed to such a degree that the play has a "foreign" flavor, proving that the play reflects its place in history. A study of the social, cultural, and historical backgrounds of the play will help in its interpretation.

The background of the author. A second source of material which may influence the interpretation of the play is knowledge of the author. Just as the social milieu in which the play is written influences its meaning, so does the kind of man who wrote it. The meanings and purposes of Ibsen's plays are more clearly revealed if one has a clear-cut knowledge of Ibsen's social and cultural attitudes. Even the analysis of a modern play can be strengthened by a knowledge of the author's background.

If the director will take the time to learn and understand what provoked a man to write a particular play, many confusions in meaning can be eliminated.

The critical comment. Most worthwhile plays have been carefully analyzed by the scholars of the time. A collection of the critical comment can provide the director with an objective evaluation of the play's purpose and meaning, its strengths and weaknesses. Where the critics cannot agree, the director must select the particular meanings he believes to be significant. It is certainly wiser for the director to consider the points of view of the scholars than to depend solely upon his own intuitive judgment.

The Study of the Play Itself

Many of the clues necessary to a considered interpretation of the play can be found in the play itself. The well-written play should powerfully express much of its meaning by itself. The poorly written or obscure play will probably only confuse the audience, regardless of the interpretation, and should not be produced at all.

Directors employ different procedures in studying scripts. One procedure which may be useful, particularly to the director who lacks experience, is suggested below. It is a procedure which gradually gets "inside the skin" of the play.

THE FIVE READINGS

Each of the first five readings has a different purpose. These initial readings are of tremendous importance, because the director quickly loses perspective on the play as a whole when he becomes involved in the specifics of production. The first impressions are important guideposts that will be helpful throughout the production process.

The First Reading: General Impression and Audience Response

The first reading should be a quick run-through of the play. If at all possible, the play should be read at a single sitting. It should give the director the general feeling of mood, meaning, and audience response. In a sense, this reading is comparable to the experience the audience will undergo. In most cases, the spectator sees the play only once and has to form all of his impressions from this single experience. If the first reading does not stir the director's imagination, he should be wary of producing it.

The Second Reading: Story and Theme and Situation

In reading the play a second time, the director can be somewhat more analytical. At this point, his study of the script really begins. The second reading, which traces the story line, the development of the theme, subject, or proposition, and the growth and use of situation, should be much slower and more careful than the first.

In many plays, both story and situation may encompass materials beyond the director's immediate knowledge. Additional research is needed. If the play is laid in a historical period, the director should study the manners, customs, traditions and attitudes of the time. If the play concerns a jury trial, the director should understand the basic elements of courtroom procedure. If the play uses psychiatric principles, the director should know something about psychiatry. In other words, the director must be competent to deal with the story and situation at hand.

The Third Reading: Conflict and Crises

Since drama is the story of human conflict, careful analysis of the development of the conflict is in order. It was emphasized earlier that no play is written with a single crescendo of conflict to a climax. The playwright develops several lines of action at the same time.

During the third reading, the director should trace the structure of the play. A knowledge and understanding of the major sections, the exposition, the inciting moment, the climax, the resolution, and the conclusion are helpful in creating a production which has an over-all increase in tension.

During this reading the director should also isolate the motiva-

tional units. A study of the motivational forces in the play will
elucidate many of the important elements that should be projected
to the audience. The director should record his analysis of the
motivational units as he studies the play. The principles and procedures for this analysis are discussed in Chapter 6. The entire
pattern of the play can be revealed by a careful motivational
analysis.

The Fourth Reading: Characterization

The reading specifically for characterization has been postponed
until now because the bases of character lie in the story and situation and the conflict and crises. During this reading, the director
can trace the development of the important characters, noting the
forces which motivate them and the clues to their individual character complexes. The bases for defining character were discussed
in Chapter 2. At this point the director is responsible for interpreting the characters in accordance with the playwright's wishes.

The director can find many clues to the character complex in
the script. The first, simplest, and frequently least satisfactory
source of information is the playwright's description of the character. Inexperienced actors are prone to lean heavily upon the
playwright's two or three line description of the character. Actually far more valuable clues to the individual character complexes
can be found in the script. What do other characters say about
the character? We often judge people in life on the basis of what
others say about them. The playwright recognizes this fact and
often paints a clear-cut character by this means. How do other
characters respond to the character? Actions speak louder than
words. The way other characters respond to a particular character
is often more important in developing a character profile than
what they say about him.

A fourth clue to characterization lies in the character's attitudes
and actions toward others. The spectator judges the character
largely in terms of what he says and does. Therefore, the words
and actions of the character serve as a prime source of information
about him.

Finally, the individual character complex may be analyzed in
terms of the character's reason for being. Since a play is a carefully
formed work of art, each character will serve a specific purpose in

he development of the story and conflict. Good plays do not have dangling characters. Careful analysis of the relationship of the character to the play will explain many of the elements in the individual character complex.

The Fifth Reading: Problems of Production

By the time the director has read the play four times, he should be ready to deal with the complexities of the actual production. He should now plan the production in terms of style, manner of staging, adaptation of the script, blocking the action, and details of technical production. Since these are major steps in interpreting the play, they will be discussed separately.

PLANNING THE PRODUCTION

The director should be thoroughly acquainted with every aspect of the playscript before he attempts to plan the production. As he reads and rereads the play, his imagination should be deeply stirred. Dozens of ideas of how the play might best be produced should have occurred to him. Now that he is fully acquainted with the story and situations, the conflict and structure, and the characterizations, the creative process of turning the script into a play begins.

The Style of Production

The style of production must be settled early in the producing process, as it will influence most later decisions. The majority of plays demand realistic illusion, yet a great many variations are possible within the framework of realism. (See Chapter 23.) The fact that the original production was produced in a particular manner need not govern all succeeding productions. Decisions concerning production style are controlled by the purpose of the playwright. If the director feels that he can better project the author's ideas with a new production style, let him try it.

The Manner of Staging

The manner of staging is determined by the style of production. The director, with the aid of the designer if one is available, should lay out floor plans and settings that effectively project the mood and meaning of the play. In Chapter 19 the basic requirements of a superior floor plan and setting are considered.

Adapting the Script

The professional director, as mentioned previously, has the advantage of having the playwright available to correct inadequacies in the script. The non-professional director usually works without access to the playwright. His problems are usually complicated by inadequacies in acting, and limitations in staging facilities, plus a strict moral code imposed by his audiences. As a result, most plays require some adaptation before they can be produced in the non-professional theatre.

The problem of adaptation is essentially one of how much. Where is the point in adapting the script past which the director dare not go? When should the director choose another play rather than try to adapt the one in hand? The answers to these questions depend so much upon the specific play and the particular situation, that only the most general observations are possible.

Most provincial audiences object to drinking, profanity, and references to sex. If such are the attitudes, offending lines should be cut or the play discarded. Some directors rationalize offensive behavior by saying "that's the way these people talk and act; it gives the play a flavor of reality." If this is truly the case, if the play depends upon these elements, then discard the play. Nothing is gained by shocking the audience. So-called shocking activity draws such attention to itself that the true message of the play may be lost. By cutting the objectionable material, the director insures concentration on the play as a whole.

Several other reasons exist for cutting a play. Occasionally an actor cannot read a line intelligently as it is written. It is better to cut or change the line than to attract attention to the poor reading.

Some plays are too long, have too many settings, or have archaic word play or humor. If the meaning of the play is not impaired, cutting may actually strengthen the production.

Blocking the Action

Considerable difference of opinion exists on the question of blocking the action of the play prior to the rehearsals. Some directors believe that blocking should develop spontaneously from the creative efforts of the director and the cast. They feel that time spent in blocking on paper is time wasted. For the experienced director who has a complete and facile control of the techniques of composition, movement, and business, there may be no need to block during the interpretative process. For the inexperienced director, blocking action on paper in advance of rehearsal is imperative.

The advantages of at least roughly blocking the play in advance are manifold. Blocking out the action on paper encourages the director to visualize the production. Visualization, the process of picturing the two dimensions of the printed page in the three-dimensional form of the stage, is one of the most difficult processes for the beginning director. The hours spent in blocking the action in the quiet of the director's study can increase his ability to think in three dimensions. A second advantage of blocking in advance is the saving in rehearsal time. Tangles in the blocking are bound to occur when the director is moving actors under the pressure of a rehearsal, but many may be eliminated if the director knows what he plans to do in advance. And a third advantage lies in allowing the director to experiment with innumerable combinations in his search for the best arrangement. Such experimentation is more difficult during the rehearsals.

Procedure in blocking the action. When the director has completed his analysis and interpretation of the play he is ready to block the action and record it in the prompt book. His tools should be: a scale floor plan showing exact furniture arrangement (see Chapter 19), a set of three-dimensional figures in approximately the same scale as the floor plan, and the playscript.

The matter of scale in the floor plan and figures is of considerable importance if the director is to visualize compositions correctly. The larger the scale, the clearer will be the picture of the compositions. For example, one may use a scale of one-half inch equals one foot. Assuming a playing opening of thirty feet, this scale is large enough to be clear and yet small enough to be practical. If the proscenium opening is much larger or smaller, a different scale will be more satisfactory.

The figures to be moved about the floor plan may be chessmen, tin soldiers, or any other three-dimensional figure. As mentioned above, the scale of the figures is important. If the figures are either too large or too small for the floor plan, effective visualization is impaired.

Starting with the first motivational unit (see Chapter 6), the director should determine the meaning and emotion (see Chapter 10) which are to be projected. Then he should arrange the first composition (see Chapter 7) by placing the figures in positions that project the motivation and can be seen. When he is satisfied with the composition, he should record it in the prompt book, which is discussed in detail in a later section.

When plotting the movement, the director must be careful to consider the length and the timing of the movement in relation to the scale of the drawing. Until the director becomes accustomed to the scale, he might "feel out" some of the movements by actually pacing them off in the room. If the scale of the movement is not reasonably accurate, confusion will occur in the rehearsal room when the director attempts to move his actors.

After the movement has been completed, a new composition will be formed. Both the movement and the second composition should be recorded in the prompt book.

Since the compositions and movements in the unit are dependent upon the meaning and emotion of the scene, the director will have to make rough decisions concerning the emotional key and tempo of each unit. (See Chapters 10 and 11.) The changes in key and tempo should be noted in the prompt book at the same time compositions and movement are recorded. After the first motivational unit has been set, the director may block out the next and continue throughout the play.

Technical Production

The final step in planning the production is to work out the technical aspects of production. In large theatres, this may be the job of the technical director; but even in this situation, the ultimate responsibility lies with the general director.

The technical plot of a production involves laying out, in addition to the floor plans and settings, the costume, property, light, and effects plots.

The costume plot is the responsibility of the director. The color, style, and texture of the costumes will affect the playing of the show and reflect the quality and mood of the characters.

The property plot must be an integral part of the direction. The director must specifically lay out the requirements. Since movement and composition depend upon pieces of furniture of particular size, shape, and style, the stage properties must be selected with great care. The same is true of the hand properties. The stage business depends upon the properties involved.

The light plot includes all light cues and details of the effect desired. It may, but need not, show the actual instrumentation. Remember that the intensity, placement, and color of light will have a distinct effect upon the mood and tone of the play. It is therefore incumbent upon the director to provide the technical crews with the information necessary to setting the lights.

The special effects plot, like the light plot, must show the cues and the effects desired. Good effects can improve a show; poor effects can ruin it.

THE PROMPT BOOK

The prompt book is a record of the production from the selection of the play through the final performance. After the final performance, it is the only existing record of the production, other than the program and possibly some photographs. If the great producers and directors had taken the time to record their productions, the study of dramatic history would have been greatly enhanced.

Apart from recording a particular production, the prompt book can serve many purposes. It provides the director with a record of his pre-production efforts which may act as a source book for the production. The drawing together of all of the research on the play into a single book may help the director formulate his ideas before casting, and a record of the steps taken in the director's interpretation of the play and blocking of the action saves rehearsal time. A detailed prompt book supplies the technical crews with all the data they need to work the production. And finally, the prompt book may be used as the name implies, to prompt.

During the rehearsals many changes will be made in the preproduction decisions. A rehearsal assistant should record these changes in the prompt book. A complete prompt book facilitates

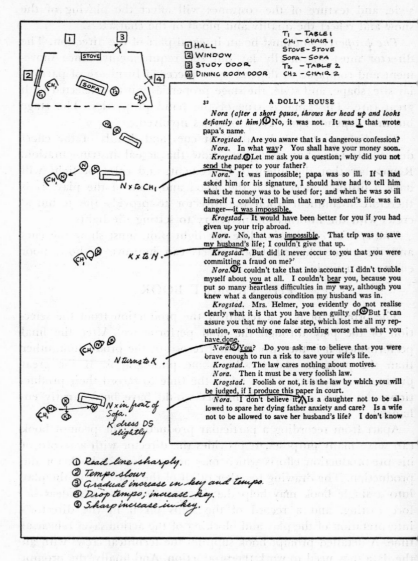

3²   A DOLL'S HOUSE

*Nora (after a short pause, throws her head up and looks defiantly at him)*❶No, it was not. It was **I** that wrote papa's name.

Krogstad. Are you aware that is a dangerous confession?

Nora. In what <u>way</u>? You shall have your money soon.

*Krogstad.*❷Let me ask you a question; why did you not send the paper to your father?

Nora. It was impossible; papa was so ill. If I had asked him for his signature, I should have had to tell him what the money was to be used for; and when he was so ill himself I couldn't tell him that my husband's life was in danger—<u>it was impossible.</u>

Krogstad. It would have been better for you if you had given up your trip abroad.

Nora. No, that was <u>impossible</u>. That trip was to save <u>my husband's life</u>; I couldn't give that up.

Krogstad. But did it never occur to you that you were committing a fraud on me?'

*Nora.*❸I couldn't take that into account; I didn't trouble myself about <u>you</u> at all. I couldn't <u>bear</u> you, because you put so many heartless difficulties in my way, although you knew what a dangerous condition my husband was in.

Krogstad. Mrs. Helmer, you evidently do <u>not</u> realise clearly what it is that you have been guilty of.❹But I can assure you that my one false step, which lost me all my reputation, was nothing more or nothing worse than what you have done.

*Nora.*❺You? Do you ask me to believe that you were brave enough to run a risk to save your wife's life?

Krogstad. The law cares nothing about motives.

Nora. Then it must be a very foolish law.

Krogstad. Foolish or not, it is the law by which you will be judged, if I produce this paper in court.

Nora. I don't believe it.⋀Is a daughter not to be allowed to spare her dying father anxiety and care? Is a wife not to be allowed to save her husband's life? I don't know

Marginal notes (left margin):

N x to CH₁

K x to N.

N turns to K.

N x in front of Sofa. K dress DS slightly

❶ *Read line sharply.*
❷ *Tempo slows.*
❸ *Gradual increase in key and tempo.*
❹ *Drop tempo; increase key.*
❺ *Sharp increase in key.*

FIG. 24. SAMPLE PAGE FROM PROMPT SCRIPT

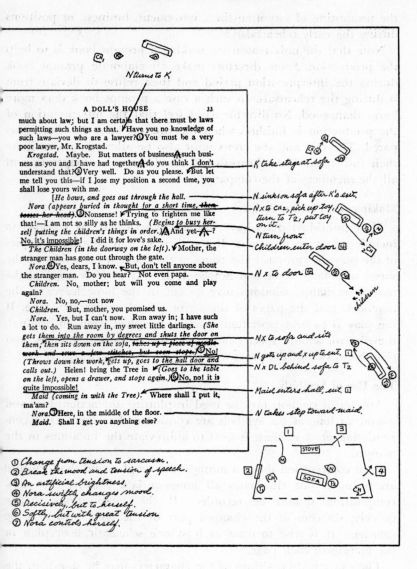

N turns to K

A DOLL'S HOUSE 33

much about law; but I am certain that there must be laws permitting such things as that. ✓Have you no knowledge of such laws—you who are a lawyer?⓵You must be a very poor lawyer, Mr. Krogstad.

Krogstad. Maybe. But matters of business⌐such business as you and I have had together⌐do you think I don't understand that?⓶Very well. Do as you please. ✓But let me tell you this—if I lose my position a second time, you shall lose yours with me.

[He bows, and goes out through the hall.] ——— *K take stage at sofa*

*Nora (appears buried in thought for a short time, ~~then tosses her head~~).⓷*Nonsense! ✓Trying to frighten me like that!—I am not so silly as he thinks. *(Begins to busy herself putting the children's things in order.)*⌐And yet—⌐? No, it's impossible! I did it for love's sake.

The Children (in the doorway on the left). ✓Mother, the stranger man has gone out through the gate.

*Nora.*⓸Yes, dears, I know. ▸But, don't tell anyone about the stranger man. Do you hear? Not even papa.

Children. No, mother; but will you come and play again?

Nora. No, no,—not now

Children. But, mother, you promised us.

Nora. Yes, but I can't now. Run away in; I have such a lot to do. Run away in, my sweet little darlings. *(She gets them into the room by degrees and shuts the door on them; then sits down on the sofa, ~~takes up a piece of needle work and sews a few stitches, but soon stops.~~)*No! *(Throws down the work, gets up, goes to the hall door and calls out.)* Helen! bring the Tree in ✓*(Goes to the table on the left, opens a drawer, and stops again.)*⓹No, no! it is quite impossible!

Maid (coming in with the Tree). ✓Where shall I put it, ma'am?

*Nora.*⓻Here, in the middle of the floor. ———

Maid. Shall I get you anything else?

N sinks on sofa after K's exit.
N x to CH2, pick up toy, turn to T2, put toy on it.
N turn front
Children enter door ⬜
N x to door ⬜
children
N x to sofa and sits
N gets up and x up to ent. ⬜
N x DL behind sofa to T2
Maid enters hall, ent. ⬜
N takes step toward maid.

⓵ Change from tension to sarcasm.
⓶ Break the mood and tension of speech.
⓷ An artificial brightness.
⓸ Nora swiftly changes mood.
⓹ Decisively, but to herself
⓺ Softly, but with great tension
⓻ Nora controls herself.

the prompting of forgotten lines, movement, business, or positions during the early rehearsals.

Note that the only reason for making a prompt book is to help the production. Some directors make an elaborate prompt book during the interpretation period and then refuse to deviate from it during the rehearsals. In such a case a prompt book does more harm than good. No director dares feel that the interpretation of the production is finished when the prompt book has been prepared. The cast and the crews must also be allowed to contribute their full share. The rehearsals call for the creative cooperation of all the members of the company.

Making the Prompt Script

Most published plays have insufficient space in the margins to include adequate notations. If the director can afford two copies of the play, he can paste the pages of the play on both sides of the sheets of a large loose leaf notebook. If only a single copy of the play is available, windows may be cut in the loose leaves of the notebook and the pages of the script affixed with scotch tape. If the play is to be typewritten or mimeographed from an original, the director should specify large margins at the top, bottom, and right-hand side of the pages.

The Use of Symbols

Any set of symbols may be used in plotting the action, key, and tempo, as long as the symbols are consistent. In Figure 24, a conventional set of symbols is used to abbreviate the notations in the margins.

Each composition shows a miniature floor plan and the furniture arrangement but eliminates all nonessentials. Ideally, each new composition should be recorded. If the compositions change quickly, sketches of the changed part of the floor plan may be sufficient. It is wise to draw at least one schematic floor plan in the margin of each page.

The exact body positions of the characters may be shown in the compositions by using the symbol which has been employed throughout this book; for example, Figure 11. The "nose" on the symbol shows the direction the character is facing. If the character is seated, the symbol will be placed over the piece of furniture involved. If the character is prone, a small *p* may be placed beside the symbol. The initial of the character's name placed in the center of the symbol will identify the character.

Movement may be symbolized by dotted lines showing movement to be taken or by solid lines indicating a completed movement. Before the actors have completed the movement, it should be sketched on the floor plan. If this is done, the director, when blocking actors during rehearsals, is aware in advance of the next movement. The conventional symbols for the cross (X), entrance (En), and exit (Ex) are used. The direction of the movement can be symbolized by the usual stage directions such as "cross down left" (XDL). The final position after the movement may be designated by either the symbol for the appropriate area or by the player's relationship to a particular piece of furniture. For example, "Mary crosses down left of davenport" may read (*Ma XDL of Dav*). Even greater abbreviation may be used if the entrances are numbered and the major pieces of furniture are lettered.

Changes in key may be shown by underlining the stressed or emphatic elements. Degrees of emphasis may be symbolized by increasing the number of lines in the underlining.

Tempo and tempo changes can be indicated by marginal notation. Dramatic pauses may be shown by the caret ($\bigwedge_2$). The number placed under the caret indicates the approximate length of the pause.

Any other notes which the director feels are necessary may be cued to the script by placing a number at the point in the script with which the comment deals and numbering the comment in the margin.

By interpreting the play, the director has obtained a tremendous head start. He should now be ready to tryout and cast his show. Later, during the rehearsals, he will be prepared to fulfill his responsibility to the cast as an expert and guide. Though the hours spent in interpretation may be long and the research exhausting, the time and energy are well spent. The director is prepared to produce the play.

14
Tryouts

TRYOUTS ARE ONE of the most important and least pleasant aspects of the play production process. Innumerable systems are in use, but each system is essentially a variation of the same basic process: judging actors after hearing them read. The principal variations are discussed later in the chapter.

Frequently more important than the specific procedure are the criteria which every tryout must satisfy if it is to be considered a success.

CRITERIA OF THE TRYOUT

Each of the criteria for tryouts considers one phase of the basic human relations problems of the tryout. The tryout is probably the most touchy moment of the entire play production process. It is the first meeting of the director and his would-be players. The ultimate success of the entire theatre program depends upon this meeting being a pleasant one.

The Tryout Procedure Should Be Efficient

Tryouts are, at best, a tedious procedure. Frequently in the larger theatres, the aspirants will number in the hundreds for a single play. This means that no matter how the tryout is conducted, it is exceedingly time consuming for both the director and the players. A satisfactory tryout system reduces the expenditure of time to a minimum. More important, the actor must be made to *feel* that a minimum of his time is being wasted. All too often potentially good actors are discouraged because of the laborious tryout process. The director may say, "If the actor isn't interested enough to wait his turn, then *I* don't want him." This may be true. But as a one-time actor, I can assure the director that endless hours of sitting while the tryout meanders aimlessly, with little or no sense of direction, do little credit to the theatrical organization represented.

The Tryout Procedure Should Be Clearly Explained

The actor, particularly the newcomer, has a great many questions when he appears at tryouts. He wants to know the specific steps in the procedure to be followed. He wants to know exactly what is expected of him. He wants to know something of the director's interpretation of the play and particularly his interpretation of the individual characters. And finally, the actor wants to know how the director expects him to portray the role.

Each director conducts his tryouts somewhat differently. For example, some directors want the actor to portray the character with both visual and vocal completeness. Others are annoyed when the actor moves about the stage. These directors want the actor to stand quietly and read as though at a radio audition. Some directors are very particular about attire; others do not care. Some directors require full stage projection; others are satisfied with a quiet reading. Some directors want the actor to choose the roles for which he wishes to read; others resent any such boldness on the part of the actor. Therefore, it is essential that the actor be told explicitly all of the rules of the game.

The Tryout Should Provide Maximum Opportunity

Many directors are loath to spend time with players who have little ability or do not fit the play being cast. As a result, some of the more promising aspirants read again and again and the less promising actors are not given an adequate opportunity to show their talents, however meager they may be. A superior tryout system must include a time allowance that permits every actor to read as much as he desires. Moreover, the actor should be encouraged to read for any role he may choose. Most actors do not take unfair advantage of this consideration on the director's part.

The Tryout Should Be Completely Fair

Each actor must leave the tryout feeling that he has been treated fairly. The actor is a human being, usually a rather sensitive person, who is eager for a part in the play and is often frightened by the tryout procedure. This combination of attitudes means that he is vulnerable to real or imagined hurt.

The director must be extremely careful to treat every aspirant with the same friendliness and courtesy. It is often easy for the director to be congenial to those actors with whom he has worked previously. This attitude makes the new actor feel uneasy. The director must conscientiously treat every actor in the same way, for new actors, the life blood of any theatre, must be made to feel that they are a necessary and important part of the play production process.

The Tryout Should Encourage Each Actor to Try Again

No play will have roles for all available acting talent. Rejection creates a problem. Humans do not like to risk repetitions of failure; therefore, the director must continually encourage actors to try again. One of the most helpful procedures in this respect is to explain carefully at the outset that good people will be rejected, that rejection does not represent a judgment against an actor's ability.

It may seem that human relations in tryouts has been overstressed. It cannot be overemphasized. The tryout procedure is a strain for everyone involved and must be handled with great finesse.

PRE-TRYOUT ORGANIZATION

Many tryouts fail because they are improperly organized. Careful organization can mean as much to the success of the tryout as the choice of procedure.

Scripts and Cuttings

Scripts of the play should be made available prior to the tryout period. Most actors who are sincere in their interest wish to read the play before they try out. The director who does not make the play available often loses actors who might have been stimulated to try out by reading the play.

Short sections, typed from the play, are more useful for the readings than the playscript itself. The typed cuttings can be of uniform length for each reading, and they can be typed without the complicated stage directions which clutter most acting editions. Most actors have sufficient difficulty reading at sight, without complicating the process. For the same reason, the cuttings should be limited to dialogue with two characters. Scenes of five and six characters can seldom be read well at sight.

The tryout cuttings should be selected with care. The selections should cover key dramatic moments, reflecting the general tone of the play and showing the characters in typical situations. The number of selections should be large enough to include all principal characters in the play.

Tryout Forms

A carefully prepared tryout form saves hours of needless confusion after the readings. The form must carry the data necessary to the identification of the actor and the recording of the reading. A 4" x 6" or even a 6" x 8" card is not too large for the necessary information.

The name, address, and telephone number are obvious necessities. Age, height, weight, color of hair will aid identification of the actor. A record of the actor's experience is sometimes helpful in comparing your judgment with that of previous directors. (See tryout blank, Figure 25, p. 218.)

One of the most important sections on the tryout blank is the schedule of commitments. Actors may have jobs, out-of-town trips, responsibilities in other productions, and the like, which may conflict and seriously hamper the rehearsals of the play. Experience also reveals that some actors are prone to "discover" commitments after they have been cast. The initial enthusiasm slackens once the grueling work of rehearsal begins. By requiring the actor to state all obligations in advance, a great deal of unnecessary dissatisfaction can be avoided.

A special section for recording eligibility is necessary on the college form, and knowledge of special talents such as the ability to sing, dance, or play a musical instrument is often useful.

Some theatres attach an identification picture to the blank. In major universities, a musical comedy may draw as many as three hundred aspirants. No director can successfully identify that many

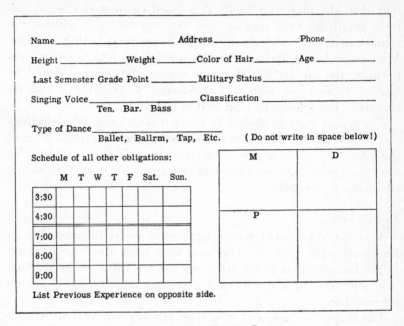

FIG. 25. SAMPLE TRYOUT BLANK

actors. In such a situation, a picture is a necessity. The picture may be taken immediately before or after each reading. A 35 mm. contact print costs little if taken by a local camera enthusiast. Finally, space must be left on the blank to record the results of the reading.

Recording Results of the Reading

The director keeps the characters of the play in mind as he watches the tryout. He tries to fit each actor who reads into one or more of the roles. Ultimate casting depends upon differentiations among actors, which the director cannot make during the initial tryouts without a great waste of time; therefore, it is essential that he record upon the tryout blank only information that will help him decide whether he wishes to call the actor back to the final readings.

At least five basic characteristics of the reading should be recorded: (1) reading ability, (2) physical and vocal control, (3) personal tonality, (4) ability to project, and (5) the general physical and vocal character type. Each of these characteristics is discussed at length in Chapter 15. They are considered here only to indicate the need for a satisfactory system of recording the characteristics necessary to successful evaluation of the actor.

Four criteria should be satisfied by an adequate recording system: (1) The system should be sufficiently exact to give the director a clear picture of the actor. (2) There should be a range in classification sufficient to differentiate the actors. (3) The system should have a high degree of reliability, so that the indicated differences among actors are meaningful. (4) The system should be in some kind of private code.

The director must be extremely careful to avoid letting his own mood or attitude on a particular evening affect his grading. The actors' readings on the last night of tryouts must be judged on the same scale as those of the first evening.

Always record at the time of the reading whether or not the actor is to be called back to the final tryouts. This clearly indicates the director's attitude at the time of the reading. An outsized final tryout list may be reduced after the readings have been completed.

The Production Assistant

A responsible student production assistant can be invaluable in the handling of the tryouts. He or she can take over the mechanics of the tryouts, pass out cards, arrange chairs, and be generally useful. He can also handle many of the human relations problems of the tryouts. As official greeter, he can make newcomers feel at ease by seating them and explaining the procedures. As doorman, he can deal with latecomers who would either interrupt the tryout or perhaps be too shy to enter.

TRYOUT PROCEDURES

The great majority of theatres follow essentially the same pattern in handling tryouts. A general elimination is conducted to cut the total number of aspirants down to a workable size. A smaller group is called back to a final tryout from which the show is cast.

The following sections consider the principal tryout procedures, including some of the more useful innovations and variations.

General Open Tryouts

An open tryout is so named because any interested person may come, and the readings constitute an open competition with all aspirants present. The basic procedure is as follows. The group is convened and fills out tryout forms. The director discusses the play in some detail. He tells the basic plot, discusses the qualities of the characters, and explains the style of the production. The actors read, singly or in pairs, excerpts from the script.

The great majority of theatre groups use the open tryout system because it has certain very definite advantages. The competition is completely free and open. Each actor can assess what every other actor does. The psychological pressure is identical. Each actor reads in exactly the same situation. And good actors stimulate less experienced actors to give better readings, an advantage with disadvantageous ramifications to be discussed later. Succeeding actors may improve their readings by assimilating some of the aspects of the excellent reading.

The open tryout also has some very distinct disadvantages, the greatest being the slowness of the procedure. With large groups, the time consumed is disheartening. There is also the handicap of having actors read with little or no previous preparation. The effectiveness of the reading is decreased and it is difficult for the director to determine the real potential of the actor.

Another disadvantage in the open tryout system is the tendency to copy or imitate superior readings. Since almost any actor recognizes good reading, a candidate who is unsure of himself often makes the mistake of trying to copy another's style, usually to his own disadvantage. Thus, a good reading early in the tryout may stimulate a series of poor imitations which last throughout the entire reading period.

The Screening Tryout

The screening tryout, a variation of the open tryout, is fast and efficient. Description of this procedure is included to help directors who feel that their tryout procedures lack efficient organization. It is important to note that the screening tryout succeeds or fails depending upon the acceptance of one assumption, namely, that the director can evaluate the vocal control, physical flexibility, and general personal tonality, regardless of the role being read. For example, it is assumed that the director can recognize a character man even though he is reading the lines of a leading man.

In this system, the selections from the play should be chosen with an eye to the possibilities for flexibility in interpretation. The actors are paired at random. One pair is asked to read. At the same time, the next pair is told to stand by. After the first pair has finished, those who were standing by step to the platform, and still another pair is asked to stand ready to go. Thus, a continuous stream of readings is assured.

If the play cuttings are about one and one-half minutes long, and thirty seconds is allowed between couples, approximately sixty actors an hour can be read.

An essential addition to this procedure is the provision that after all the new aspirants have been heard, any actor may read again for any role he chooses. The process of recording the data and determining the recall is identical to other tryout procedures. Screening has the advantages of speed and fairness, for every person is offered the same opportunity. Since it is a high speed process, however, the director, in recalling actors to final tryouts, should be more generous than is necessary with a system which reads the actor for a longer time.

The Closed or Personal Interview Tryout

The closed tryout system may be used for either seasonal casting or the casting of a single play. The fundamental difference between the closed and open systems is that the tryout interviews or readings are held in private. In addition, the method of handling tryout materials is also somewhat different. In the closed system the tryout selections are usually made available beforehand. If the tryout is to determine a season casting list, stock cuttings are provided. Stock cuttings are scenes selected from well-known plays in which each scene includes characters of specific types. The actor is allowed to select the characters he wishes to portray.

A schedule of ten- to fifteen-minute interviews is set up, and the actor is allowed to choose a convenient tryout time. The actor appears for the tryout, fills out a tryout blank, and is interviewed by the director. The director tells the candidate a little about the tryout system and the play to be cast and asks the actor to read. Most directors who employ this method have an experienced actor present to read with the person trying out for the play.

The interview tryout system has some distinct advantages. In the first place, the director can establish a greater rapport with the actor. Since the interview is private, the director has a chance to observe the actor's responses during the interview as well as during the reading. This increase in personal contact may facilitate judgment of the actor's temperament and ability.

Another advantage of the closed system is its convenience for the actor. The actor spends ten to fifteen minutes, at his own convenience, rather than hours at the open tryout's scheduled time.

Each candidate is assured a competent partner at the interview. In the open system with its random pairings, superior actors are often severely hampered by having to read with very poor actors. In the closed system, a good actor is present to help the newcomer do his best.

Obviously, the personal interview tryout encourages previous preparation. Only the most conceited and brash actor will waste the director's time with an unprepared reading. As a matter of fact, experience shows that many actors not only prepare but memorize the material.

The final advantage of the closed system lies in the reduction of competitive pressure. The reader does not have the problem of reading before his competitors. The director may put the reader at ease and make him feel at home. It must be admitted that this last advantage may turn out to be a disadvantage. Some actors who have never been through the interview tryout become so frightened before they ever enter the tryout room that no amount of consideration on the part of the director can put them at ease. There is something comforting about hearing others read, knowing that you will be treated just as they were treated, and feeling that you can do a better job than some who have preceded you. The closed system offers no such reassurance.

Apart from the matter of fear, the closed system has three other disadvantages. The greatest criticism of the method lies in the fact that the tryout is *closed*. We may fear and dislike what we cannot see and judge for ourselves. An analogy may be drawn with the closed trial or private police procedure. Americans traditionally dislike secrecy. Actors want to judge for themselves the equality of opportunity and treatment and the degree of proficiency of the readings. Some of the most unpleasant criticisms of the theatre I have encountered have arisen from the closed tryout system.

Another real disadvantage of the interview system is the expenditure of the director's time. Obviously this system takes a great deal more of the director's time than the open tryout method. In open tryouts the director can probably hear from twenty to thirty pairs of readers per hour, forty to sixty individual actors. In the interview system this number is decreased to five or six. If the tryout group is large, the closed system is not very feasible.

Because the director cannot describe the play and the characters days or weeks before the tryouts, the actor may be at a disadvantage. In the interview procedure some actors spend a great deal of time and energy developing a character which is completely false in interpretation. If the actor has prepared the material with great care, the mistakes have probably been deeply ingrained. In the open system, the actor may gain in interpretation by listening to others.

A final disadvantage of the interview method is that the actor usually has only one opportunity to read. In a well-conducted open tryout, the actor may read as many times as he wishes.

Final Tryouts

Each of the preceding methods leads to a final tryout period, during and after which the play is cast. The closed system may also be used to develop a seasonal casting list, to be discussed in a later section. Generally, if the seasonal casting or talent list is used, a final tryout period for each specific play will still be necessary to effective casting.

All of the actors who are even remotely possible for a part in the play are called back to final tryouts. The final tryout should be by invitation only. As a rule of thumb, we may say that the larger the tryout the larger the final call back. A large group does not necessarily assure a larger percentage of superior actors, but as the number of candidates increases the director's ability to differentiate between actors decreases. A final call sufficient in number to equal two or three actors per role is common. The opportunity to read at final tryouts usually stimulates participation in future tryouts, so it is better to call too many than too few.

At the final tryouts, actors are asked to read in all possible combinations, for the director is now trying to cast the play. He should feel free to read the more promising actors as frequently as he desires. New cuttings must be chosen for these readings. The selections read at the general tryouts will now be stale and tiresome.

At the beginning of the final tryout period, it is wise to have each actor record on his tryout blank his willingness to play a small role or walk-on in the play. Some actors wish to try for a lead or nothing. This is certainly the actor's right. Considerable embarrassment can be avoided for all concerned if the actor's wishes are known in advance.

SPECIAL TRYOUT TECHNIQUES

Pantomimes

One of the weaknesses of any reading tryout is the director's inability to judge adequately the physical control and flexibility of the actor. Actors who try to move about in response to the motivation in the lines are seldom successful. For this reason, directors request actors to assume the stance, posture, and basic tensions of the character without any elaborate pantomime.

A simple pantomime assigned at the end of the final tryout period provides a sound basis for judging the physical abilities of the actors. Ideally, the pantomimes should be built upon characters, plot, and situations selected from the play. Through pantomime the director can assess the coordination and, indeed, the imagination of the actor with a minimum of wasted time. The pantomime quickly reveals basic faults in timing and physical control, which otherwise might remain hidden.

Improvisations

The brief selections used for the readings often give the actor insufficient opportunity to indicate his imaginative grasp of the situation. Improvisations based upon the play and its characters give the actor a chance to use his imagination. Assign actors to small groups, give them a situation, characters, and the major conflict in the scene. Then allow the actors to improvise the dialogue, the specific elements of character, the movement. This method quickly sifts the talented, imaginative, and dynamic from those who lack inventive ability. Remember that the ability to improvise improves with experience, however, and the work of actors who are accustomed to the procedure must be judged accordingly.

SEASONAL AUDITIONS VERSUS INDIVIDUAL PLAY TRYOUTS

Some schools have a single general tryout or audition period at the beginning of the year. At the end of this tryout period a casting list is posted, from which the casts of all of the season's plays are selected. In some cases the casting list is used as the basis for calling actors to final tryouts for specific plays; in others, the plays are arbitrarily cast by the director from the casting list. The materials used in seasonal auditions are either stock characters or cuttings selected from the plays to be presented during the year.

In certain highly specialized situations the casting list may be satisfactory. For example, it is used with success by many radio stations that have a great many plays to cast and cannot afford the time to hold new tryouts for each production.

The disadvantages heavily outweigh the advantages for most theatres. The seasonal audition allows the actor only one chance to read each year. There are many obvious reasons why an actor may read more effectively one time than he will another. Multiplying the chances to read gives both the actor and the director a better casting opportunity. With the seasonal audition, a select talent group is set apart at the beginning of the year. This is psychologically bad for the person who is on the talent list and the one who is not included. An even greater disadvantage of the casting list is the tendency to form a cliquish stock company. The same people are cast again and again. A proficient group may be developed, but certainly the educational need to give broad opportunity for participation suffers.

Tryouts are probably the least pleasant part of the entire play production process. Every director approaches them with some foreboding. Although actors look forward to playing in a show, they anticipate the tiresome and frightening process of trying out with something less than enthusiasm.

Remember that the superior tryout does more than enable the director to pick a fine cast. It provides an equality of opportunity and encouragement for each actor, be he a potential star or the most fumbling spear-bearer.

15

Casting

CASTING THE PLAY is said to be fifty per cent of the directing. This may be an exorbitant claim, but there is little doubt that superior casting is necessary to first rate production. With a good cast, the director can show his capabilities as an artist. With a poor cast, the director's job may well be insurmountable.

Casting may be defined as *fitting the actor to the role*. A perfect match between the requirements of the role and the capabilities of the actor is ideal casting. The director's task is three-fold. He must study each role in the play and assess its requirements; he must judge the abilities of the actor during the tryouts; and he must match the actor to the role.

THE RANGE OF THE ROLE

Range is a measure of variability. This concept may be applied with meaning to both the acting role and the actor. Range of the role is the variability or spread in the possibilities of playing the role. Range of the actor is the variability or flexibility of the actor.

The first step in the casting process is to determine the range of the role. This is accomplished by carefully analyzing each role in the play.

Analysis of the Role

The requirements of any role will be based upon three factors: (1) the demands of the script, (2) the requirements of the audience, and (3) the interpretation of the director.

The clues to characterization which are to be found in the script were analyzed in the discussion of interpreting the script. (See Chapter 13.) They are to be found by evaluating the motivational forces, analyzing the physical and social situation, and studying the individual character complex.

The requirements of the audience are those qualities which the audience must find in the portrayal if the character is to be conceivable. These also are found in the script. They are the amount of sympathy which the character should elicit and the amount of stereotyping necessary to make the character credible.

The interpretation of the director also affects the range of the role. After the studies of the script and the audience are completed, the director still has considerable leeway in deciding the specific characteristics of the role. It is improbable that two directors would draw an identical picture of a given character even though their methods of research and sources of information about the roles were identical.

The Profile of the Role

Analysis of the role will suggest a rather clearly defined picture or profile of the character. It is important to realize that these qualities are not necessarily a set of absolutes. For each of the qualities there is a range or spread in the possibilities of portrayal. The profile of the character usually consists of the physical, vocal, emotional, tonal, and interpretative characteristics of the role.

The physical characteristics. The physical requirements may be very exact and precise, or they may be so general that they provide a generous range for casting. Well-known historical characters have an extremely limited physical range. For example, the physical portrait of Abraham Lincoln is so firmly fixed in every American's eye that an actor playing the part of Lincoln must conform almost exactly to a specific physical pattern. It is mandatory that the actor portraying the role be tall and lean, have a face that can be made up to look like Lincoln, etc.

In contrast, the characters of many plays are not defined with physical exactness. Old Chris in O'Neill's *Anna Christie* must show age but may have almost any other physical qualifications. He may be heavy, thin, tall, short, grey, or bald; it makes little difference.

The character of Cyrano de Bergerac is well known to every theatre lover. He is a romantic swashbuckler. Except that he must be virile, physically mature and must be made up with a large nose, the physical playing range is large. Walter Hampden and José Ferrer created two of the most famous portrayals of this character. Physically, these two men are of radically different types; yet each was able to project the character to the audience.

The director must determine the physical characteristics demanded by the role. Perhaps more important in the case of the non-professional director who doesn't always have unlimited selection in actors, the director must determine the range in which the role can be played physically.

The vocal characteristics. The vocal range of most roles is broader than the physical range. But in some cases—characters who have dialects or speech defects—the range may be extremely limited. Old Chris Christopherson, mentioned above, is identified more because of his vocal than his physical characteristics. The actor playing Chris must be able to reproduce a Scandinavian dialect. Such a limitation sharply decreases the vocal range. Actors who cannot handle the dialect cannot be considered for the role.

Voice is important in defining a character. The quality of the voice is one of the prime means by which an audience judges character. Light, thin voices connote a lack of vitality and brute strength. Coarse, rough vocal qualities are frequently associated with uncouth or violent characters. The analysis of the role determines the range of possible voices which could portray the role believably.

The emotional characteristics. Some roles run the gamut of emotion during the course of the play; others are shallow emotionally and require very little flexibility on the part of the actor. Many parlor or domestic comedies need little emotional depth. Most serious dramas or tragedies require a vast range. After analyzing the role and finding the emotional extremes present, the director must be certain that the actor can portray all of the emotional phases of the character. Again the range of the role should be determined.

The tonal characteristics. Tonality may be defined as the quality, feeling-tone, or timbre of the character. It is the over-all feeling projected by the character. In essence, the tonality includes the easily judged aspects of personality displayed by the character. We say of one character the moment we see him, "There is a hateful person." If we are asked to explain why, we may supply a number of reasons to justify our decision, but the reasons come after the decision has been made. The truth of the matter is we "just don't like him."

The tonality of a character is more than merely a set of positive or negative reactions to that particular person. It is the aura which the person projects. Frequently we describe people in terms of their tonality. He is a dynamic person, or a pallid person, or a coarse person. She is a brittle person, or a languid person, or an unctuous person. In actuality we are judging the physical and vocal characteristics, but for some reason the whole often is greater than the sum of its parts.

The tonal characteristics of the role should be carefully defined by the director. Some roles are simple and clear-cut in the feeling tone they give off. Some roles are deep, complex, and confusing. Some roles have a very limited range in the tonal values. Some roles are so general and apparently nondescript that the particular feeling tone which they project is not important; however, one of the keynotes of drama is the fact that every character must project some distinct tonal value.

The profile of the role is a summation of the physical, vocal, emotional, and tonal values of the character. The director may develop a profile of each role to be cast by analyzing the characteristics and the range. His next task is to judge the actors at tryouts.

JUDGING THE ACTOR

Psychological studies show that actors, even at the non-professional level, are somewhat atypical individuals. These differences in personality apparently are related to the bases of acting. Before judging the actor, the director should read Chapter 18 for its discussion of many problems of the actor.

During the final tryouts the director should consider each of the seven qualities discussed below. They reveal the potentialities of the actor and determine his range.

Dramatic Personality

A dramatic personality, sometimes called a sense of theatre, is basic to successful acting. This quantity may be defined as the individual dynamics, energy or vitality radiated by the actor. It is evidenced in the sensitivity and imagination with which the actor approaches the reading of the role. Some actors give the immediate impression of being phlegmatic, stolid, unimaginative people. This impression can be misleading, but it is frequently corroborated on watching and listening to the actor read. The actor who has a dramatic personality unconsciously makes himself felt even before he reads. A sense of the theatrical is hard to define but easy to recognize.

Projection

Directly related to the dramatic personality is the ability to project, the process of throwing out or casting forth. Theatrical projection involves the ability to get impressions across to the audience. During the tryouts the director should place himself as far from the actors as possible and ask: What does the actor project as he reads the role? Does the vocal impression of the character come across clearly and forcefully? Are the visual aspects of character presented with clarity and vigor? What tonal feeling, if any, does the director perceive? Is the vitality of the actor immediately apparent? Even the pallid and colorless character must be projected with vigor.

The significance of projection should not be underestimated. With the exception of the intimate central stage, the motion picture, and television, with their mechanical devices to help intensify the portrayal, projection is the key to the transfer of ideas and emotion from the actor to the audience. No matter how beautifully an actor may read, no matter how sensitive the interpretation, without the ability to project the beauty and sensitivity to the audience, the actor is lost.

Acting Experience

Previous experience is a difficult commodity to judge. Previous experience can be harmful or helpful. The value of previous experience depends upon where, when, in what, and with whom.

Breaking bad habits acquired in actors' previous contacts with the theatre often consumes as much time as is spent teaching beginners the rudiments of acting.

Good previous experience is helpful. Most actors who have played several roles have acquired some technique, some poise, some maturity in things theatrical. If the actor has learned his elementary lessons well under a competent director, past experience in the theatre makes for better acting.

Experience seems to be a highly rated factor in getting a role in many theatres, both professional and amateur. Most directors are unwilling to take a chance on the rank beginner. The director fears that the actor may crack under the strain of the first role. He may feel that the necessary elementary training will take more time than is available. In professional radio, actors and announcers are advised to get experience in some small station before trying the networks. In the commercial theatre, experience is rated almost as high as a recommendation from some leading theatrical personality (which, of course, is usually a guarantee of experience).

Every director wishes that he might see the actor upon the stage before he casts him in a major role. It may be advisable, unless the inexperienced actor appears to be outstanding, to break him in with a small role. Once the director sees the actor on the stage even as a member of a crowd, he can judge his potentialities with greater certainty.

Cooperative Attitude

Dramatic production is a cooperative group endeavor. Unless the actors and the crews work with the director for the good of the production, unity of production cannot be obtained. A cooperative attitude on the part of each actor is a necessity.

One procedure for determining the cooperativeness of the actor is, as was suggested in the material on tryouts, to find out whether he is willing to play a small part in the play. There is the old saying that there are no small parts in the theatre, only small actors. If an actor is interested in playing only a leading role, the director may well question whether he has the interest of the group at heart. The highly egocentric actor is frequently a noncooperative actor. One dissident voice can destroy the unity of the entire production.

DETERMINING THE ACTOR'S RANGE

The qualifications of dramatic personality, projection, and co-operative attitude are basic ingredients of acting, necessary to the playing of any role. In addition, we have seen that previous experience may be helpful. The actor's range depends upon a group of more specific individual qualities: physical appearance and control, vocal flexibility and control, emotional depth and flexibility, and tonal projection. The director should make some provision for recording these qualities when he listens to the actor at both the initial and final tryouts.

Physical Appearance and Control

The general physical appearance of the actor will determine to a considerable degree his qualifications for certain roles. Physical appearance can be camouflaged to some degree, but the basic physical characteristics of height, weight, and age do tend to limit the actor's range.

Often more important than general physical appearance is physical control. Physical poise and ease are essential to acting. The energy which the actor commands should be observed during the tryouts. The flexibility with which the actor can command and control his walk, carriage, stance, and gesture helps define his range. His sense of timing in his physical activity also should influence casting.

The director can learn a great deal about the actor's coordination by watching his activities in the tryout room before and after his reading. The flexibility and control of his physical activity may be easily determined by assigning simple pantomimes and improvisations. The actor who can project the impression of youth and age, of grace and fluidity of movement as well as solid, heavy, plodding activity, can control his body. Control and flexibility define the breadth of the physical range.

Vocal Control and Flexibility

The actor's vocal range can be determined in the same manner as the physical range. The range is based upon the native characteristics of voice and the actor's technical facility in handling his voice. The flexible actor should be master of the vocal variables of pitch, force, and rate. He should be able to produce different vocal qualities instantly.

One other vocal characteristic to watch for during tryouts is the tendency toward vocal patterns. If the director notes such a pattern, he should point it out to the actor immediately and encourage him to break it. If the actor is unable to break the pattern, the director should be careful about casting him in a major role in which the repetition of the pattern may become monotonous and distracting to the audience.

Finally, the director must judge the actor's sense of timing. Many actors apparently read intelligently but have little awareness of the importance of time. The use of dramatic pause, the handling of stress and inflection, the ability to express the impact of emotion in the speech, the ability to deliver the comic line, all help the director to evaluate the actor's sense of time and, in turn, his vocal range.

Emotional Depth and Flexibility

Since drama depends upon emotional expression, the actor's facility in portraying depth of emotion helps determine his playing range. A story is told about one of America's leading actresses who often graciously auditioned actors. At each audition she made one request. She asked each actor to make her laugh and cry with but a single minute allowed to accomplish each. Obviously, any actor would need great emotional facility and control to succeed in this situation.

The director should be aware, however, that emotional facility is not always a clue to good acting. Some actors need time to work themselves into the mood before they can express emotion well. Unfortunately, the tryout system tends to militate against these actors, another reason why the director can judge the actor more accurately if he has had a chance to see his work. Lack of emotional facility is frequently the reason for misjudging the actor.

Many actors are limited in their emotional range because they are unable to express emotional depth. Their attempt to express powerful emotion is superficial. Since emotional depth is important in many roles, the director must test for this quality during the readings.

A final emotional quality is flexibility. There are a great number of ways of expressing the same emotion. Many actors drop into a physical and vocal pattern which reveals a complete stereotype of the emotion. Any tendency to patternize emotion severely limits an actor's emotional range.

Tonality

Inflexible personal tonality, usually a reflection of the actor's own personality, frequently limits the actor's range. The motion picture actor or personality is selected because of the particular feeling-tone he happens to communicate. For example, the Hollywood leading lady may change the costume she is wearing or perhaps even the dialect she speaks, but seldom does she change any aspect of her own personality. After all, the movie-going public pays to see *her,* not a character in a play. Happily, more and more examples can be cited to show exceptions to this rule. Would that it might be broken for good.

Flexibility in the actor's range is largely dependent upon his ability to change his tonality. Tonality is in reality the sum total of the physical, vocal, and emotional characteristics. To the extent that the actor is limited in any of these qualities, so will he be limited in the type or quality of character he can play. The great actor is the one who is able to assume new characteristics and provide a tonality different from his own.

CASTING THE INDIVIDUAL ACTOR

Assuming that the director has carefully developed a profile of the role, noting its physical, vocal, emotional, and tonal range, casting the role is the simple process of matching to the profile of the role an actor who has a sufficient physical, vocal, emotional, and tonal range.

Type Casting

A perfect matching of the actor and the role is called type casting. With certain distinct exceptions, all good casting is type casting. Every director who has the good of the production in mind aims to cast the roles as perfectly as possible.

In the non-professional theatre, however, some exceptions to pure type casting exist. In addition to a top-notch production, the director in the non-professional theatre is interested in providing the actor with educational and individual personality values. He never sacrifices the individual to the play. In other words, the director should never cast an actor in a role if he believes that playing the role will be detrimental to the actor's own well-being. For example, the male actor who has distinctly effeminate characteristics will certainly gain nothing by playing an effeminate character. In fact, playing such a role may further crystallize the deficiency. Similarly, the educational director should never capitalize on a physical deformity or a speech defect.

Educational Casting

Educational casting, sometimes called anti-type casting, is practiced by some directors. It may be defined as casting the actor in roles at the extreme limits of his range. Some directors even encourage actors to play roles completely outside their ranges.

The advantage of educational casting, according to its proponents, is the opportunity given the actor to increase his flexibility by working outside his present range. An extreme example would be casting an effeminate youngster in the part of an aged ruffian. It is assumed that the actor may be able to adjust his personal problems by acting out the qualities that would be desirable in his own personality. In theory and in classroom practice, this procedure may be valuable if applied carefully. For example, leading mental institutions have found that role-playing is helpful in treating certain psychoses.

If, on the other hand, anti-type casting is conducted in productions meant for public performance, another psychological factor must be considered, and it may more than negate the benefits of educational casting. That factor is *success*. More often than not, the actor who is cast at the fringe of, or completely outside, his range fails to create a meaningful character. He knows he has failed, the rest of the cast is impatient with the failure, and most important, the audience and the critics recognize and condemn the failure. I would contend that a youngster who fails in the eyes of his friends and the public will lose infinitely more, psychologically, than he can possibly gain, physically or vocally. Many actors are sensitive and insecure. They enter the theatre because they believe it will give them a chance to express themselves successfully. If the experiment fails, the resultant increase in insecurity may be disastrous.

In summary, educational casting is an excellent idea if it is confined to the classroom or the acting laboratory. Conducted in public performance, it may not only spoil the show but also injure the actor.

CASTING THE ENSEMBLE

In discussing the casting of the individual actor, we have not mentioned the relationship of the individual to the cast as a whole. This relationship frequently affects the individual casting.

Unity in the Cast

The production cannot have unity unless the cast fits together. Time and again, the director has an actor whose range fits the profile of a role, but who cannot be cast because he is out of key with the other actors. The members of the cast must appear to belong together visually. A tall leading woman playing opposite a short leading man will appear ridiculous despite the fact that both actors may play their roles capably. The cast members must be able to play together vocally. Wide disparities in vocal mannerisms or range can be detrimental to the total effect of the play. Similarly, the emotional and tonal ranges of the actors must create an impression of unity.

Variety in the Ensemble

Without destroying the impression of unity, there must also be variety in the ensemble. A community theatre production had three young women who looked and sounded so much alike that the audience found it virtually impossible to differentiate them. Even the variety written into the role by the playwright was insufficient to make them distinct entities. Physical, vocal, emotional, and tonal variety is essential to a vivid production.

Perhaps an example can clarify the apparent paradox of unity and variety in a cast. Let us suppose we are to cast a family. The casting will have unity if the audience can believe that the actors belong to the same family. They may have similarities in action, in speech, in social background, and attitude because they represent a group that belongs together. Within the framework of this unified family there must be physical, vocal, emotional, and tonal variety, for contrast is basic to clear-cut and dramatic characters. In other words, the similarities and the differences are essential to the production.

The Tentative Cast

At the conclusion of the tryouts and casting, the director posts his cast list. It is imperative that this list be labelled *tentative*. No director can be certain of his choices until he has heard the cast read the play together several times. When the director cannot choose between two actors during the tryouts, it is probably advisable to ask them both to the first few rehearsals with the understanding that one of them will be dropped.

Actors are prone to be proprietary about roles. When an actor reads his name on the cast list, he frequently feels that he has "got" the role. It belongs to him. The director should make it perfectly clear at the final tryouts that every member of the tentative cast is on probation and may be dropped or switched to a different role if necessary. Actually, the responsible director will seldom change the members of his cast. Tentative casting allows any necessary changes to be made with a minimum of hard feelings between the actor and the director.

If the director feels that he needs a precedent for the tentative cast procedure, he may explain the option principle employed in the professional theatre. The professional producer and director have a five-day option period during which the cast is completely tentative. At any time during the five days the director may drop an actor without having incurred any obligation. Or the actor may withdraw from the cast during the same period with no penalty. Beginning with the sixth day, the producer is obligated to the actor, and vice versa. The producer must pay the actor two weeks' rehearsal salary if he drops him from the cast. If the actor withdraws from the cast, he must pay the same amount to the producer.

SPECIAL CASTING PROBLEMS

In addition to the casting procedures already discussed, two other casting methods are employed. These are double casting and pre-casting.

Double Casting

Many high school directors double cast their productions. Few college and community theatres follow the practice except in casting the leading singing roles in musical productions. Double casting may be defined as employing two casts for a single play or casting two characters in a single role.

The advantage of double casting lies in the increased opportunity for participation. Many high schools produce only one or at most two plays a year. The director double casts so that a maximum number of students have the opportunity to play in a production. The proponents of double casting maintain that several other advantages result from the system. First, it saves the director's time. He is able to increase participation without having to go through all the steps necessary to the production of an additional play. Second, it is cheaper. Most high school productions have monetary gain as a primary motive. One show is obviously cheaper to produce than two. Third, two actors in the same role can help each other in developing the role. Fourth, the problem of understudies is solved. If illness or accident claims a member of the cast, the other actor can play all of the performances.

Directors who are opposed to double casting answer these arguments in somewhat the following manner. It might be noted that many of the directors who oppose double casting are persons trained in dramatics rather than harassed mathematics teachers who have been assigned dramatic duties. The opposition claims that first, the additional participation provided by double casting is not adequate. Neither cast gets a good opportunity to go through the production process, since one of the two casts is always sitting by watching the work of the other. Second, two plays are always better than one. Third, while some time is saved, the quality of the director's work is bound to suffer when there are two casts. Moreover, the help that a director is able to give the individual actor, which is one of the primary benefits to be derived from dramatic participation, is cut in half, or more by double casting. Fourth, since two plays can be produced before two audiences, they can make twice as much money. Fifth, the two actors cast in the same role are seldom cooperatively competitive. Jealousy, envy, bickering over who is going to play which night make the idea of the double cast unsound. Sixth, if one actress proves to be much better than her counterpart, the poorer actress may be judged a failure.

The decision to double cast will, of course, depend upon the individual situation. A review of the arguments may help the director make a considered decision when the question arises.

Precasting

Most professional plays are precast, that is, cast in advance of tryouts. For that matter, they seldom have an open tryout in the sense that it has been discussed here. Readings are usually held by invitation, for the play is selected with certain actors in mind.

Almost the exact reverse is true in the educational and community theatre. The play is selected without any clear idea of who will try out. Tryouts are opened to everyone who is eligible under the rules of the organization, and the cast is selected from those who try out.

The non-professional director who precasts is almost certain to incur trouble. Word travels down the dramatic grapevine almost with the speed of light. "Jones is going to play the lead." The immediate reaction is, "Why bother to tryout? No one else has a chance." Once a director gets a reputation for precasting, he begins to lose valuable talent because actors feel they don't have a chance. Furthermore, select groupings and cliques develop. Those who are cast form a tight little nucleus and further exclude outsiders. Such a situation is antithetic to every aim of the educational or community theatre.

On the other hand, every director occasionally must at least tentatively precast certain parts in his own mind. If he does not permit himself to do so, there will be many plays which he dare not attempt. No director, unless he knows that he has unlimited talent at his disposal, will dare do *Hamlet, Macbeth, Peer Gynt, Cyrano de Bergerac, Medea, Antigone, Hedda Gabler,* or any other play which depends almost completely upon the magnificent portrayal of a single character, without having some idea of who may be possible for the leading role.

Even the most tentative precasting should be the exception rather than the rule. It is easy to get into the habit of mentally casting a show from the known, available talent, but this is a dangerous procedure if there is any possibility that the director may close his

mind to the efforts of the newcomers at tryouts. Finally, the director
will have to take his chances that the person he has in mind plans
to come to tryouts. Special invitations to the tryout are as dangerous as precasting itself.

Having selected the play, analyzed the script, conducted the tryouts, and cast the show, the director is ready to enter the exciting
process of building the production. The rehearsals will test the director's imagination and his knowledge of theatrical technique.

16

Rehearsal

IN THE REHEARSAL room, the script is turned into a play. The director and his actors assemble with a single purpose: to breathe life into the cold type of the printed page. The director brings his knowledge of every aspect of play production. The actors bring their creative abilities and disciplined techniques. Together they create the cooperative team so necessary to successful play production.

During the rehearsal period, most of the bases, principles, and problems of play direction are called into play. Although this chapter is primarily concerned with the mechanics of planning and conducting rehearsals, frequent references are made to other sections of the book. These references should make clear the manner in which the bases, principles, and problems are related to the rehearsal plan.

PLANNING REHEARSALS

The final performance of a play reflects the efficiency of the rehearsals. Poor rehearsal procedures may seriously impair what otherwise might have been a superior production. Before rehearsing a play, every director should consider the problems of planning, scheduling, and conducting rehearsals.

The Number of Rehearsals

It is difficult to be specific about the number of rehearsals because of the number of variables operating in the production of a play. In general, it may be said that a one-act play will require from 15 to 25 rehearsals, while a three-act play of average difficulty will need from 30 to 45 rehearsals. Approached from a different point of view, it may be said that after each section of the play is rehearsed 30 to 35 times, it should be ready for performance.

The actual number of rehearsals which are desirable for a specific play depends upon the complexity of the play, the style of the production, the size of the cast, the length of the play, the experience and ability of the actors, the experience of the director, and the continued growth in the production.

Some plays are very complex; others are relatively simple to produce. A classic poetic drama needs a good deal more rehearsal than a contemporary drawing room comedy. In the former, the tasks of understanding the drama and learning to read the poetry take extra time. A difference is found, also, in the rehearsal necessary for stylized production as opposed to realistic production. The rehearsal time should be increased whenever elements which are alien to the normal backgrounds of the cast are introduced.

Obviously, the size of the cast, the number of scenes, and the over-all length of the play should be taken into consideration. An elaborate play such as Marc Connelly's *Green Pastures* may require almost half again as much rehearsal as Patrick Hamilton's *Angel Street* with a very small cast, a single setting, and virtually continuous action.

One of the most important variables affecting the amount of rehearsal is the experience of the actors. Some advanced summer stock companies do a good job of simple plays with one to two weeks of rehearsal. One of the factors operating in such situations, to be sure, is the number and length of the rehearsals; yet the speed with which their productions are assembled can be maintained only because every actor has experience and ability. Play production in this situation is not really a learning process. At the opposite extreme is the high school production with brief afternoon rehearsals three or four days a week. These young actors may have to be taught how to read, to speak, to move, to stand, indeed to fulfill each step of the production process. Such a production may take most of a sixteen-week semester for rehearsal.

The experience of the director should also be taken into consideration. A director with twenty or thirty full-length plays behind him probably has little difficulty in blocking out the action of a play. With average actors it can be done in a week of one rehearsal per day or less. The beginning director who does not have the technical facility may find that blocking is a long and complicated process.

A final test for determining the number of rehearsals needed will be meaningful to the director only after he has produced several plays. It is growth of the production. A play should be rehearsed only as long as it continues to grow. At the final dress rehearsal, many directors wail, "Oh! If I had just one week more!" More often than not, this merely signifies that the director has misused his rehearsal time, but in some cases it results from the sincere belief that the play is still developing. The director is saying that the actors and he are adding new strengths and values at each additional rehearsal. Not every play will continue to grow, regardless of the length of the rehearsal period. Depending on the director and the actors, a play may stop growing, may jell or crystallize, at any time after the lines and movement are learned. Rehearsing a play that has ceased to grow is useless. The rehearsals become mere repetitions. The actors become restless. The play might just as well be performed. Additional rehearsals will merely reduce the spontaneity of the production.

Why does a play cease to grow? Probably because the director and the actors have insufficient imagination to go any further. I have watched rehearsals of plays which had stopped growing despite the fact that the play was not ready for performance. The director, evidently, was unable to see the inadequacies in the production. The actors were unable to add any further meaning to their characters. Even though the production was destined to failure, the director was content to sit back and "let 'er run." Such a situation obviously implies gross inefficiency on the part of the director, for he must be the stimulus to growth in the production.

The Length of Rehearsals

The feasible length for a rehearsal is pretty well agreed upon by experienced directors. Rehearsals should run from a minimum of one and one-half to two hours to a maximum of two and one-half to three hours. It will not be possible for all groups to fit their rehearsals within these time limits, but there are good reasons for suggesting the limits.

The rehearsal which is less than two hours is too short to accomplish a maximum of work. Some time will be lost at the beginning of the rehearsal period, regardless of how strict the director is about starting rehearsals on time. Even if the rehearsal room is arranged and the people begin on the minute, it often takes thirty minutes or so to get into the feeling of the play. Most actors come to rehearsals from classes or jobs. It takes time to shake off the effects of these responsibilities and begin to concentrate upon the creative aspects of a play.

Fatigue is the enemy of accomplishment in the rehearsal which runs over three hours. The concentration necessary to create, digest, and commit to memory the emotional and technical elements of a play is tiring. No matter how much the actor may wish to continue to produce at full capacity, fatigue produces diminishing returns at the long rehearsal.

Another important reason for limiting the length of the rehearsals is the criticism often leveled against the dramatic group by parent and school officials. Frequent short rehearsals provoke little comment. One long rehearsal running far into the night will arouse a storm of protest. Careful planning of the rehearsal schedule will obviate the necessity for the long and fruitless attempt to make up time.

The Conduct of Rehearsals

The professional rehearsal has a single purpose. It aims to produce a superior play at a minimum cost to the producer. Every moment of the expensive rehearsal time is devoted to improving the production.

The non-professional rehearsal has the same primary aim as its professional counterpart. At the same time, several subordinate purposes must be kept in mind. Rehearsals in the high school and college should serve as training periods. Training in cooperation and teamwork, training in individual adjustment, training in effective use of time, training in organization, all are as much a part of the non-professional rehearsal as training in dramatic production. Although the preparation of the play is the focal point from which all of these other experiences arise, they affect the conduct of rehearsals.

The director must take the time to answer questions of all kinds.

He must work to help the individual actor adjust to the group. He must help the player bring to the fore the best that is in him.

Is the rehearsal a work period or a play period? Is it a time for a coffee *klatsch* or concentration upon the job at hand? Most directors agree that the rehearsal should be a period of concentration on the job at hand. The businessman who tries out for a play does so with the thought that the process of putting on a play will be fun. He derives his pleasure from working hard in the play. Usually he is annoyed by a desultory rehearsal at which little or nothing is accomplished. Directors who have been afraid to get down to business should take solace in this fact. Certainly producing a play should be a social experience, but the recreation and fun arises from producing the play. The same principle holds for the high school and college rehearsals. Rehearsals are fun because everyone in the group is working hard at something that each enjoys. The director who conducts his rehearsals in the spirit of "hard play" will please all but the shiftless few who do not belong in the theatre.

The Time and Place for Rehearsals

Selection of a rehearsal room depends largely upon the facilities available to the group. Some groups rehearse on the stage where the play is to be performed. This has some advantages but is not necessary. Other groups rehearse in classrooms, in private homes, in church basements. The location of the early rehearsals does not matter if it meets the three simple requirements of size, solitude, and atmosphere.

The rehearsal room should approximate the size of the stage upon which the play is to be performed. Much of the rehearsal time is spent in working out the compositions and movement of the play. Both composition and movement depend upon space relationships. There is little sense in trying to block the action to one scale, knowing that every move will have to be doubled in size when the cast gets on the stage. Length, speed, and duration of movement all have specific connotative meanings for the audience. If the movement pattern has to be changed when the play reaches the stage, the emotional connotations of the movement will also change. Select a room of the right size.

The second requirement of the usable rehearsal room is solitude.

Rehearsals require intense concentration; thus, they cannot be carried on effectively in a room that is a center of distracting activity.

Atmosphere is important. If the rehearsal room reflects the atmosphere of the play, direction will be easier. A neutral room is the most that many groups can hope for. A large, quiet, reasonably secluded room with tonal characteristics similar to those in the play is the ideal.

Rehearsal Units

Should the play be rehearsed in sequence? Should all actors attend every rehearsal? Should crowd scenes be rehearsed separately? These and many comparable questions can be answered only by studying the structure of the play to be produced. A play like Irwin Shaw's episodic *Bury the Dead* has very little overlapping of the acting personnel and can best be rehearsed in small segments without regard to sequence. On the other hand, if the play depends on group action, it probably should be rehearsed in sequence.

The problem of dividing a play into practical rehearsal units is a matter of finding a functional unit of suitable length. In some plays, scenes involving two or three leading characters are units which stand by themselves. In others the characters come and go with such rapidity that it is impossible to work any small group of characters without affecting the others. Frequently the best division can be found in a study of the motivational units.

The director should strive to make the best possible use of the actor's time. In the non-professional theatre, acting is an avocation rather than a vocation. Actors have other things to do. To require that one actor sit hour after hour, while small bits of business are worked out for other characters, is a needless waste.

If a principle is needed, it might be stated as follows. Require every actor to attend the early rehearsals so that he may gain a perspective on the place of his character in relation to the whole play. During the more technical blocking and polishing rehearsals, request an actor's presence only when he is needed. All actors should attend the final mounting rehearsals. After the first rehearsal or so dismiss members of crowd scenes until such time as their scenes are to be rehearsed. In planning the schedule of rehearsal, do not underestimate the time necessary to direct the crowd scenes (see Chapter 20).

The Rehearsal Schedule

Every director introduces variations into the rehearsal plan, yet all rehearsal plans follow the same general pattern. Usually, it includes four types of rehearsals: (1) the reading or interpretation rehearsals, (2) the blocking rehearsals, (3) the polishing rehearsals, and (4) the mounting rehearsals. Each of these types of rehearsal is discussed in detail in later sections.

The wise director lays out his rehearsal schedule before the rehearsals begin. A carefully organized schedule helps the actor budget his time and insures an adequate distribution of rehearsal time for each section of the play. Without the pressure of a rehearsal schedule, it is easy to become so involved in rehearsing some particularly complicated scenes that time slips away and other scenes get little or no attention. Even with a rehearsal schedule, this may happen; therefore, some open periods for making up lost time should be included in the schedule. Too many rather than too few rehearsals should be planned. It is much easier to cut rehearsals than add them.

The sample schedule reproduced below might be used for the production of a contemporary prose play of average length and difficulty with average college actors and a moderately experienced director. The schedule probably won't fit any specific production, but it may serve as a rough pattern for working out a schedule that can be tailored to the requirements of an actual production.

REHEARSAL SCHEDULE

READING REHEARSALS

First Week

1. Read entire play. Discuss meanings and problems of production.
2. Read Act I twice. Study interpretation and characterization.
3. Read Act II twice. Study interpretation and characterization.
4. Read Act III twice. Study interpretation and characterization.
5. Read entire play. Run play for total interpretation.

BLOCKING REHEARSALS

Second Week

6. Block first half Act I, set action, review blocking.
7. Block second half Act I, set action, review first half Act I.
8. Block first half Act II, set action, review second half Act I.
9. Block second half Act II, set action, review first half Act II.
10. Run Acts I and II, review all blocking.
11. Block first half Act III, set action and review blocking.
12. Block second half Act III, set action, review Act III.

Third Week

13. Run Acts I, II, and III, review all blocking.
14. Open Period.

POLISHING REHEARSALS

15. Polish first half Act I by motivational units, lines learned, review.
16. Polish second half Act I by units, lines learned, review Act I.
17. Run Acts II and III.
18. Polish first half Act II by units, lines learned, review.
19. Polish second half Act II by units, lines learned, review Act II.

Fourth Week

20. Run Acts I and II, review all polishing.
21. Polish first half Act III by units, lines learned, review.
22. Polish second half Act III by units, lines learned, review Act III.
23. Run entire play, review all polishing.
24. Open period, polish weak spots Acts I and II.
25. Run Acts II and III.
26. Open period, polish weak spots Act III.

Fifth Week

27. Run entire play.

MOUNTING REHEARSALS

28. Technical Rehearsal, add lights, costumes, props, etc.
29. Technical Rehearsal, continuity for technical effects.
30. Technical Rehearsal, continuity.
31. Dress Rehearsal.
32. Dress Rehearsal.
33. Dress Rehearsal.

PERFORMANCES

The sample rehearsal schedule breaks each of the acts into two working units. This is an arbitrary procedure. The working divisions in a real rehearsal schedule will be based upon functional units or scenes in the play. The number of rehearsals per week obviously depends upon the time available to the actors and director. A schedule as heavy as seven rehearsals per week presupposes several rehearsals during each week-end.

The amount of time and stress placed upon each of the four divisions differs considerably with different directors. Some directors dispense with the reading rehearsals entirely, believing that interpretation of the play should grow gradually throughout the entire production period. These directors plunge immediately into the blocking rehearsals. Others believe that reading and interpretation must precede blocking and polishing. They spend a considerable period reading and discussing before they try to block the action. No one plan is the answer to all problems. The individual director must experiment and find out which plan works best for him.

A REHEARSAL PLAN

The following portions of this chapter are used to lay out a sample rehearsal plan. The purposes and procedures for handling each of the four different types of rehearsals are discussed in detail. The beginning director may find the plan a basis for action. The advanced director may find that the plan crystallizes his own procedure and offers some challenging suggestions with which he may agree or disagree. It should be clearly understood that this sample plan does not pretend to be the only or even the best method for rehearsing a play. It is presented because it is a procedure that has stood the tests of time and practice.

Preliminary Preparation

We may assume that the director enters the rehearsal arena completely prepared. Not only is he imbued with an enthusiasm for producing the play, but also he has taken the time to analyze the play and prepare a prompt book. (See Chapter 13.) He has sketched the basic compositions and the gross movement pattern into the prompt book (Chapters 7 and 8). He has decided upon the style of the production (Chapter 23). He has made general decisions concerning interpretation and characterization (Chapters 6 and 10). He may have worked out the basic elements of business and tempo (Chapters 9 and 11).

None of his ideas are so firmly set that they cannot be altered by the stimulation and imaginative interplay between himself and the actors during the production period. His plans are all tentative. They are subject to modification, even complete change, depending upon the ideas arising during rehearsals. But he must have plans. Even the most experienced and inspired directors owe it to their actors to come prepared.

THE INTERPRETATION REHEARSALS

The first reading rehearsals should introduce the actors to one another as individuals and as characters in the play. Play production is teamwork. The early rehearsals build the team. The interpretation of each character in the play affects the interpretation of every other character. Early decisions on basic interpretation provide a basis for creating the balance and unity necessary to successful production.

During the first reading rehearsals the director should analyze and interpret the play with and for the actors. Since play production is a creative process, the basic decisions must be reached by collective thinking, with the director as the leader and the final authority but never the absolute autocrat.

The first rehearsals should be used to explain the style of the production, to analyze the structure of the play, to determine the meanings of the play, to trace the development of the conflict, to examine the interrelationships of the characters, to define in considerable detail each of the characters, to study the motivational units. If these problems are solved in the first two or three rehearsals, later readings of the play can be devoted to the more technical considerations of interpreting lines and roughing in emotional key and tempo.

The advantage of the reading rehearsal for the actor is obvious. He has an opportunity to orient himself to the production. He can ask questions, clear up any confusions concerning the play and his character, and discover new meanings that will facilitate his creative contributions to the production. Without this knowledge, the actor may become a mere automaton responding to the commands of the director.

The number of reading rehearsals depends solely upon the amount of time necessary to make the decisions and solve the problems of the production. A simple and transparent play such as *Dear Ruth* may require only two or three reading rehearsals to decide upon and set the basic interpretation. A complicated play like *Hamlet* may have many undefined problems of meaning and interpretation after eight or ten reading rehearsals. The number must be determined by the time needed for this first phase of growth. If the job of interpretation has been accomplished and the cast is champing to go ahead, further reading may harm the production more than help it.

Procedure

A specific procedure for conducting interpretation rehearsals might include the following steps. At the first meeting the director introduces the members of the cast, distributes the rehearsal schedule and finds out if any unforeseen conflicts have arisen. He may then profitably spend some time explaining his directing procedures: what he expects of the actors; what the actors may expect of him. After these preliminary comments, he should talk about the play in detail in order to stimulate thought in and discussion by his actors. In other words, he must make the actors realize from the beginning their importance as agents in the production.

The next step is to read the play. The first reading may be without interrupting comment from the director. Such a reading serves two purposes: it gives the director an opportunity to assess the levels of acting ability, and it permits the actor to sense the continuity of the production. After the reading, the director and the actors should discuss the play together. At this point, major questions of meaning and interpretation can be resolved. The director may feel that he wants to make specific comments concerning the interpretations of character. Such comments are best saved for the next rehearsal. After the first rehearsal, the director may ask each actor to read the play by himself prior to the next meeting and bring with him any specific questions relating to his character and the play.

The second reading rehearsal may include another reading of

the entire play. At this rehearsal the director and the actors should feel free to stop the reading at any time to consider problems of meaning, conflict, or character. During this reading the director can outline the structure of the play, pointing out the playwright's techniques of development.

Assuming a complicated play, the next three or four rehearsals may be devoted to the concentrated study and vocal interpretation of smaller units. The motivational units should be studied in detail. If the play is rehearsed by acts, one act per night will probably be sufficient. Each act may be read more than once. The director should never become so involved in the minutiae of interpretation that the actor loses sight of the whole. For instance, if an act is read by fits and starts with numerous interruptions, it should be read as a whole at the end of the evening. This procedure re-establishes the feeling of unity and permits a review of the decisions made in interpretation.

The final reading rehearsal should be a run-through of the play. By this time the basic interpretation of the play should be set. The actors as well as the director should have solved all of the fundamental problems of author's intent, mood and meaning, plot, conflict and character interrelationships. Even a rough development of individual vocal interpretation, of key and tempo levels, and changes should be apparent. In many ways the final reading rehearsal should approximate an unpolished radio show. As a matter of fact, the procedures for the reading rehearsals are very similar to those used in radio production. In both kinds of rehearsals the whole play must receive greater stress than the parts.

In summary, the reading rehearsals are exploratory in nature. Their primary purpose is to acquaint the actor thoroughly with every aspect of interpretation. At the end of these rehearsals the actor should be as well acquainted as the director with the play as a whole and his responsibilities in the play. With this knowledge he is able to enter the period of blocking and polishing as a creative force.

The director, in turn, should be thoroughly acquainted with the potentials of his cast. Except for the visual aspects, he should be able to see the strengths and weaknesses in the production. With this knowledge, he can do a more effective job of creating a balanced and unified production during the succeeding rehearsals.

THE BLOCKING REHEARSALS

Blocking constitutes the most difficult period for most inexperienced directors because composition and movement require technical facility as well as imagination. Every beginning director should anticipate confusion in building compositions, dissolving them with movement, and re-forming new compositions. Care and time are needed to make the visual picture appear perfectly natural.

Since blocking is a highly technical process, every director is advised to conserve rehearsal time by rough-blocking compositions and movement into a prompt book (Chapter 13). In most cases, compositions and movement designed at home without the pressure of waiting actors are superior to those originating in rehearsals. In opposition, it should be stated that an overconcern for the exact plottings of the prompt book may also impair the vibrancy and spontaneity of the production. A balance should be maintained. The director should feel free to add new ideas that occur to him as a result of seeing the actors perform the sections of the play. No director can afford to freeze the play within the confines of the covers of a prompt book. It has been emphasized that the actor as well as the director is a creating agent. The actor should have many worthwhile ideas about when and how he should move. These feelings about movement stem from his knowledge of the play and his interpretation of the role. Quite often they are better motivated than the movements set up by the director prior to the rehearsals. Also, many times an actor cannot perform the movement suggested by the director, even though the movement itself is a good one. There is an old saying in the theatre, "A good actor can make a poor movement look natural; a poor actor can make a good movement look artificial." Movements the actor creates will usually appear well motivated.

Many directors are distressed when they see the interpretation set at the reading rehearsals break down during the blocking rehearsals, but this is to be expected. No actor can concentrate on both interpretation and movement at the same time. The breakdown, however, is temporary. The carefully created interpretation constantly acts as a firm basis for making decisions in the compositional and movement pattern. Above all, the director should resist the temptation to return to a study of the interpretation at this point. He must stick to the job of blocking.

A final suggestion before turning to the procedure in blocking. A balance should be maintained between the extremes of under-rehearsed blocking and over-rehearsed blocking. Some directors block out the play with such speed that the actors cannot be expected to remember much of what has been done. Others become so interested in particular bits of action that they stop and fill in the details or polish it immediately. Neither course is to be recommended. The blocking period should be used to rough in the visual pattern of the show. At the same time, the director and the actors should be reasonably satisfied with the rough pattern when it is set. If large sections of the action are changed again and again during the rehearsal period, the movement pattern will always be in a state of flux. The actors will be unable to remember which of the many experimental patterns is the right one. As a result, the movement pattern will not jell. Once the movement pattern is fixed in the actor's mind, it is wise to avoid major changes. A neural trace has been established; the movement is automatic. The actor has difficulty in making changes after blocking has crystallized, for he must consciously break the old habit pattern before he can build a new one.

As in the case of the interpretation rehearsals, each director has his own special procedure for handling blocking. The following procedure is general in nature and admits the possibility of change.

Procedure

The number of rehearsals necessary for blocking will depend upon all of the basic factors set forth at the beginning of the chapter. Before the blocking rehearsals are started, the actors must be thoroughly acquainted with the floor plan. Since it acts as a source of motivation, the floor plan should, if possible, be laid out in full scale on the floor of the rehearsal room. (See Chapter 19.) At this stage of the rehearsals, most groups will not be able to obtain the furniture to be used in the production, but it is not really necessary. Substitute furniture, however, should approximate the size and shape of the actual furniture. The movement pattern cannot be worked out satisfactorily if the distances on the stage are not reasonably exact.

At what point in the play should the blocking begin? Most beginners would do well to block the play in sequence. The gains in continuity will probably offset any advantages derived from other procedures. The possibility of over-rehearsal of the first act can be avoided by a carefully organized rehearsal schedule.

The most satisfactory blocking unit is the motivational unit. It is a logical division of workable size. The procedure for blocking in rehearsal is identical to that used in paper blocking (Chapter 13). Arrange the opening composition in the unit; move the characters as the motivation dictates to form another composition. Repeat the procedure until the unit ends with the introduction of new characters or a change in situation or theme.

The actors should write every movement into their scripts even though they may know the lines. The production assistant records the action in the prompt book. After the unit has been completed, the actors should run through it. Correct any flaws in the general blocking and run it still another time. Then the director can turn to the next unit, and the procedure is repeated.

Always leave time at the end of the rehearsal to review all of the blocked units. The actor's concentration during blocking is usually focused on small bits of action, a single movement at a time, when to sit, what body position to hold. Actors and even the director quickly lose touch with the whole. A review helps reestablish the continuity of the scene.

Every repetition of the blocking while it is fresh in the actor's mind plants it more firmly. However, the director should never make the mistake of assuming that once a piece of blocking has been set and reviewed, the actor will remember it from that time forward. The motor pattern has to be repeated at frequent intervals over a considerable period of time before it becomes habit.

At the end of the blocking period, the play should be ready for polishing. The interpretation must be set, the visual and vocal expression of the interpretation should be roughed in, and all lines must be learned. If any of these elements lags behind at the beginning of the polishing period, polishing will be impossible until it catches up.

Some directors unnecessarily demand hand properties at the beginning of the blocking period. If the actor is still carrying a book, he will waste time trying to manipulate a coat or a teacup simultaneously. Small props may be added during the later blocking rehearsals when the actor is reasonably free of the book. Any property essential to the movement or the timing of a scene should be added prior to the polishing rehearsals. At this stage, substitute properties—a block of wood for a cup or a pencil for a dagger—are perfectly satisfactory. The only reason for properties during the blocking rehearsals is to help the actor create a rough visual approximation of the scene.

THE POLISHING REHEARSALS

Many plays are produced at the end of the blocking rehearsals. At this point, gross characterization, rough visual and vocal interpretation, and memorized lines do give the play a crude form. Many of the high speed, sloppily produced summer stock plays never get beyond the blocking stage. Some high school, community theatre, and even college directors honestly feel that when the compositions and movement are set and the lines learned, the play is ready to go. This attitude accounts for much of the miserable drama produced in the non-commercial theatre.

The conscientious director realizes that the polishing rehearsals represent the artistic starting point in the direction of a play. It is comparable to that point in painting at which the sketch has been roughed in with color; to that point in instrumental work at which the musician has learned to finger the notes of the tune in the correct tempo; to that point in dressmaking at which the seamstress has basted the materials together. Most of what is art rather than craft lies ahead. From this point forward, imagination and sensitivity on the part of the actors and the director are at a premium.

The purpose of the polishing rehearsals is to develop a finished artistic product. Each composition should be checked and re-checked to determine whether the focal point is clear, whether it tells the story, reflects the emotional content, helps to delineate each character, shows the exact interrelationships of the characters, and is pictorially attractive. Every movement should be polished until its force, speed, direction, duration, and timing connotes the exact meaning and emotion called for by the playwright. Stage business should be selected, enriched, elaborated, intensified, and timed until it carries the precise tone and value necessary to the scene. The rise and fall of emotional key, the numerous variations in tempo, the force and balance of visual and vocal projection should be perfected to give the nuances of mood and expression. Each character should be judged as an entity and in relation to every other character. The vitality and spontaneity of the characters should be adjusted and fitted together. Every sound and move should be tuned to indicate the motivation or reason for the conflict, the crises, the climaxes.

The number of polishing rehearsals depends upon the potentials of growth within the group producing the play. In the professional theatre, the process of polishing may be an unending one. When Alfred Lunt and Lynn Fontanne opened S. N. Behrman's *I Know My Love* at the Wisconsin Union Theatre, it was one play. After almost a year on the road the play opened in New York. By this time it was a different play. An entire year had been used to polish it to perfection. This example is in some ways an exception, but the principle is clear: the length of time for polishing depends upon the possibilities of growth within the group producing the play.

Obviously the non-professional cannot take a year to polish a play. Indeed, after ten to fifteen rehearsals the capacity for creation is exhausted in many groups. In addition, the pressure of time and other responsibilities permits only a limited polishing period. Regardless of the time devoted, the polishing rehearsals can make or break the play. At the same time, it should be noted that a piece of lead can be polished forever without outstanding results. The result of the polishing process will depend upon the material in hand and the foundation of interpretation and blocking which has been laid.

Procedure

The mechanical procedure of the polishing rehearsal is comparable to that of the blocking rehearsal. Divide the play into motivational units. Study and work over each unit in detail. At the end of the evening, review everything which has been worked.

Just as in the blocking rehearsals, the director should budget his time so that no single section of the play is more polished than any other. The director may protect himself against the possibility of unevenness by polishing the most important parts of the play first.

During the polishing period, a seeming paradox exists. Polishing is concerned with detail. At the same time, continuity increases in importance as the play approaches the mounting rehearsals and performances. A careful balance between the two must be maintained. For every period in which the director takes the play apart, he must provide a comparable period for reviewing the material. During the run-throughs, good, bad, or indifferent, the director should never interrupt. The actor must develop a sure feel for the development of the play as a whole. The director can take notes and make his suggestions at the end of the review.

In the later polishing rehearsals, use all properties and costumes that directly affect the action. For example, in a period play it is advisable for the women to practice standing, sitting, and moving in the skirts of the period. If the costumes are not completed, find and use some comparable substitute. The substitute hand properties employed during the blocking rehearsals should be replaced with the real articles during the polishing rehearsals. If sound cues affect the timing of the play, these effects should, if possible, be introduced during the polishing period. The finish of the production improves with the addition of every technical device that affects the action.

At the end of the polishing rehearsals the show should crystallize. This may seem an ambiguous term to the student who has never produced a play. Crystallization occurs often at a single rehearsal, when the play suddenly becomes set, in much the same way that concrete does. Before this, the play has been fluid; now it becomes rigid. When the play jells, real growth stops and repetition begins. If, for some reason, the play drops into a rigid pattern too soon, the play might as well be performed—unless the vocal and visual patterns can be jarred loose. The rigidity can be broken up by taking the play apart again and making major changes, but such a breakdown is usually inadvisable at this stage because there is not enough time to rebuild the play.

One way to stimulate growth is to objectify the play for the actors. Sometime during the latter portion of the polishing period, tape, wire, or disc record the play. The results can be helpful and may be startling. The mechanics of recording the play are discussed in Chapter 17. A recording provides an auditory picture of the production. The actor who hears himself becomes more aware of his relationship to the other characters. Frequently, points that have never been clear in the discussions between the actor and the director will suddenly make sense. Some directors use recording equipment throughout the rehearsal period. This procedure has advantages and disadvantages. Both relate to the matter of objectivity. The actor who listens to himself can make corrections on the basis of an objective analysis of what he hears; but through parts of the rehearsal period, the director wants a subjective, emotionalized response from the actor, rather than objectivity. Most actors cannot balance the two types of response.

At the end of the polishing period, the play should be ready for production as a vocal and visual unit. No further major changes should be made. We may assume that the play has crystallized and has had sufficient repetition in its final form to be ready for the stage. Interpretation, blocking, and polishing are complete; the production is ready for mounting.

THE MOUNTING REHEARSALS

Few non-professional drama groups have a stage of their own to use for all of the rehearsals. During the reading, blocking, and polishing rehearsals, this lack of stage facilities is not as important as many directors believe. If the director can get his actors on stage occasionally during the early rehearsals to check sight lines and projection levels, he should be satisfied. For most of the rehearsals the director benefits from the intimacy of a room of stage size.

At the beginning of the mounting rehearsals the play must be moved to the stage. Those drama groups allowed on stage for only the final dress rehearsal operate under a severe handicap. Stage time serves many purposes. It allows the actor to become acclimated to the feel of a stage and auditorium. The technical crews need time to learn to work the curtain cues, light cues, and sound cues and to set, strike, and shift the settings. The director needs time to fit the production to the stage and gain the perspective only distance can provide.

The specific number of mounting rehearsals depends largely upon the technical complexity of the production. A play with four or five settings and thirty to fifty light cues requires numerous mounting rehearsals. A total of from four to eight mounting rehearsals is sufficient for the average play. This number provides a minimum of two technical rehearsals and two dress rehearsals. A more satisfactory number for the average play is five technical and three dress rehearsals.

Technical Rehearsals

The technical rehearsals, as the title implies, deal with the technical and mechanical problems encountered in adapting the play to the stage. The director who has been pleased with the final polishing rehearsals will be discouraged after the first technical rehearsal. The play will come apart at the seams, no matter how well it has been rehearsed. This is perfectly logical. The actor is upset by the scenery, the lights, the properties, the doors that must be opened and closed, the furniture that is lower or higher than usual, the sounds of bells, clocks, and crowds, and above all, by the feeling of the great void that is the auditorium. The director should not worry about the collapse of his play. It will come back together again quickly, providing it has been thoroughly rehearsed and has crystallized.

The first technical rehearsal should be devoted to adjusting the cast to the stage and settings. Everything the actor must handle, sit on, move, or touch should be in place. Furniture, hand props, rugs, steps, doors, windows, and levels or platforms are essential. Without them the play cannot be mounted.

The procedure at the first stage rehearsal is to work slowly through the play without regard for complete interpretation or characterization, allowing the actor to feel his way. Business dealings with the setting, such as opening and closing doors, has to be timed. Compositions with poor sight lines have to be modified. Some entrances and exits may have to be reworked. If the distances on the stage are different from those in the rehearsal room, considerable time will be needed to readjust the movement pattern. At this rehearsal the curtain, light, and sound cues may be run, merely to acquaint the respective crews with the play.

The second technical rehearsal should include a costume parade. Every character in the play should have his costume checked for any necessary refitting. The parade should precede the rehearsal, so that any incomplete or offending costumes can be returned to the costume crew immediately. The rehearsal itself should be devoted almost exclusively to the technical crews. Some directors wisely jump from one sound or light cue to the next without going through all of the intervening dialogue. Each technical cue should be rehearsed until it is perfectly timed and executed. A complex show may require more than one evening for this technical work.

The third technical rehearsal should be a run-through which gives the cast and the technical crews an opportunity to work together as a team. The director should avoid interrupting any run-through. The actors and the crews need the experience of continuity. The timing of costume changes, for example, is based upon the running time of the scene. After the run-through, the bad spots can be reworked until they are perfect.

Dress Rehearsals

The final mounting rehearsals are dress rehearsals. Make-up and costume as well as all technical effects should be complete for the dress rehearsals. Ideally, they are performances in every sense of the word. The production should begin on time. It should run without interruption through each act. Intermissions should be observed to the minute. The director should be in the front of the house, leaving the stage manager in charge of the show. The director should take notes during the performance and make his comments either at the end of each act or at the end of the evening.

Some directors like to invite a test audience to the final dress rehearsal. There are several distinct advantages and one or two problems in this procedure. The greatest advantage of the test audience is the stimulation it gives the cast. A group of no more than twenty or thirty people in the house changes the entire mood of the cast.

The test audience is particularly helpful in comedy. The actors can tell by the response where some of the large laughs in the show will come. In addition, the actor is able to establish a rapport with the audience. The test audience is less important in the production of serious plays because the serious play involves less overt interplay between the actor and the audience.

The greatest disadvantage of the invited audience is that it may not represent a typical cross-section of the regular audience. If this is true, the audience reactions can mislead the cast and the director. Two specific illustrations may clarify this problem. Some years ago, a major university presented the classic melodrama, *Dracula*. Some three hundred high school students were invited to the final dress rehearsal. The youngsters had a marvelous time. They shrieked, chattered, and giggled. They hissed the villain and cheered the hero. The director was surprised at the response but, because of his inexperience, assumed that it was typical. He changed the projection levels of the acting. The next night, when the drama opened before an audience composed of townspeople and college students, not a sound could be heard in the auditorium. This audience responded with tense and rapt attention. The projection levels had to be changed back again.

At another university, a production of John Van Druten's drawing room comedy, *There's Always Juliet*, was tested before a group of building maintenance men and their friends. The delightful subtleties of the play were missed completely. The only laughter of the evening was provoked by several *double-entendre* remarks. The cast was dejected. The next night, before the regular audience, the play was a success. The purpose of these illustrations is not to discourage the use of the invited audience, but rather to encourage careful selection of the audience. Atypical audience reactions must be discounted accordingly.

With the final dress rehearsal, the director's *work* is done. The die has been cast. No amount of worrying can change the end result. The director's *responsibilities*, however, continue into the performance period.

17

Performance

THE PERIOD BETWEEN the final rehearsal and the first performance
is a trying one for the director and the cast. Assuming that the play
has been rehearsed on schedule, there is no further work to be
done. It is a period of suspense and mounting excitement. No
matter how much experience a director or the actors may have had,
the tension preceding the first performance becomes severe. Several
thousand man-hours of conscientious work, hundreds of imaginative ideas, and endless striving for a cohesive production await
testing. Since play production is a creative process, no director,
actor or technician can really be certain that success lies ahead.
The highly suggestible, often volatile, sometimes kind and occasionally cruel audience will soon cast its ballot. The critics with
the power of the printed page behind them will soon make their
decision. No wonder professionals and non-professionals alike await
an opening night with bated breaths.

THE RESPONSIBILITIES OF THE DIRECTOR

The director's work is done. He can no longer tamper with the
production. Any last minute changes cannot be crystallized through
repetition. New instructions would be forgotten in the excitement
of the first performance. The responsibilities of the director lie in
the realm of psychology. He must control the affects of the tension
upon his actors and crews and judge the affect of the production
upon the audience. Before the performance he belongs backstage,
where he can act as a steadying influence. During the performance,

the director's place is in the auditorium, where he can watch the reactions of the audience.

Controlling Excitement

Some excitement prior to the opening of the play is important. Controlled tension adds to rather than detracts from the performance. After all, this excitement, sometimes called stage fright, is nature's way of preparing for a new situation. The excitement of an opening night usually results in a more dynamic portrayal of the characters. The emotional level of the show is intensified. In popular parlance, a "spark" is added. In some cases a play which has never jelled suddenly drops into a precise form as a result of the stimulation from the audience. Other productions which have lost some of their spontaneity in the final rehearsals suddenly come to life again.

At the opposite extreme, excessive excitement can wreak havoc with the inexperienced cast or the under-rehearsed play. The play has been rehearsed four to eight weeks to establish patterns so ingrained through repetition that no amount of pressure or excitement can dislodge them. There is the possibility with an inexperienced cast, however, that a mild sort of panic may cause some actors to change their characters. As a result, the unity and balance of the production are destroyed. If the play has been under-rehearsed and few patterns have been clearly and firmly set, chaos can result. Usually, however, the director will be pleased by the unifying effect of performance excitement.

A note of warning should be included. Even the best rehearsed show may not receive the audience response expected by the director and cast. Let us suppose that the play is a comedy. The first comic situation or line in the script, which the actors have always thought very funny, gets little or no response from the audience. This may upset the cast. The next gag line or humorous situation passes without getting the anticipated response. After this has happened several times, some inexperienced groups may panic and try harder and harder to be funny. Of course, the humor is destroyed. The harder the actors try to be funny, the less funny they are.

Occasionally, the response may be greater than expected, with just as deadly results. The inexperienced actor who gets bigger

laughs than he expected often forgets the careful balances established during the rehearsals and sets out to be even funnier.
He can spoil both his own character and the play. Still another
problem arises from the fact that some inexperienced actors respond more violently to the excitement than others. These deviations can also throw the play out of balance. The director cannot
eliminate either the excitement or its effects, but he must maintain
control over the actions resulting from the excitement. How may
this be done?

The director must appear calm and collected, regardless of his
own feelings. The excited, often frightened, members of the cast
and crews are quick to sense anxiety on the part of the director.
The resultant rise in general tension in the group is undesirable.

The director should avoid the pep talk. Many a football game
has been fumbled away by players who were trying too hard. The
same is true of the play. Sufficient excitement is already present; a
pep talk does nothing more than increase the tension. In place of
an emotional peroration, the director should talk quietly with his
cast and crews and explain dispassionately the problems of dealing
with an audience.

The director should insist that the actors play the show as it was
rehearsed. Inspiration, in the form of new patterns of visual or vocal
activity, has no place in the first performance. The play was rehearsed with great care. The form of the final production is not
happenstance. The projection levels, emotional key, compositions,
movement, and business represent the group's judgment of how
the meaning and the emotion of the play may best be projected to
the audience. This judgment may be faulty, but any changes should
be left until later performances. The actors and crews should be
encouraged to approach the performance in a workmanlike manner.
Precision rather than inspiration is the goal.

The Director's Place

No director can successfully evaluate a performance from backstage. He must be in a place where he can gain the same perspective
on the production that the audience does. The director belongs
in the auditorium. As a matter of fact, the director who scurries
about pushing actors on stage at the right moment, prompting
lapses in memory, signalling sound and light cues, or acting as a

costume mistress, can easily harm the performance. The actors and
crews will be tremendously conscious of the director's activity and
may center their attention on the director rather than the job at
hand. The backstage area during a production should be a place
of quiet concentration. The director's presence usually upsets this
balance.

Some high school directors say that they have to be backstage to
run the show. My personal feeling is that these directors underestimate the initiative and resourcefulness of the high school
student. They are unwilling to accept the fact that anyone other
than themselves is competent to run a performance. However, if
some adult must be present, it should be some person other than
the director.

The Responsibilities of the Stage Manager

Ideally, full backstage responsibility including complete authority over the cast should be delegated to the stage manager at
the dress rehearsals. The stage manager in both the professional
and non-professional theatre is tactical head of the production. He
checks the readiness of properties, costumes, lights, and other equipment with the appropriate crew heads. He is responsible for calling
actors to their positions. He signals the house when the production
is ready to begin. He either runs or assumes the responsibility for
running every backstage aspect of the production. By this delegation of authority the director is free to assume his duty of evaluating
the effectiveness of the production.

EVALUATING THE PERFORMANCE

Prior to the performance, the director can only guess what effect
the production will have on the audience. Throughout the rehearsals, the director has tried to see the play through the eyes of
a spectator. He dares not judge the production from his own expert point of view, for the audience is not composed of experts.
Obviously, there can be no substitute for experience and a knowledge of audience psychology. Even with considerable experience,
the director is at a disadvantage because he often loses perspective
upon the production as an entity. During rehearsals the director
becomes so engrossed in the techniques of production that he is

unable to evalute the spontaneity and freshness of the production.

Hard as it may be to accept, the director must view his work with a calculating objectivity when it is performed before an audience. The director who is willing and able to set aside his own feelings can learn much about his work by watching the reactions of his audience. Unfortunately, many directors subjectively watch a performance. When the audience responds negatively they are upset and unable to analyze objectively the reasons for the failure. When the audience responds enthusiastically they are so pleased that they don't use the fleeting moment of the response to evaluate the basis for the reaction.

Evaluation of the production can be of two types. One, the evaluation of the meaning and emotion projected and, two, the analysis of the audience response to the play. Actually these are two different ways of approaching the same problem. The director has evaluated his play throughout the rehearsal period. During performance the director can sense the audience's responses. Since he is in the house with the audience, the director can feel the changes in tension run through the audience. If the director can place himself in a position where he can observe the faces of a segment of the audience, he can read the reactions of the crowd even though the spectators never laugh, weep, or shriek.

Does the Play Hold Attention

The first requisite of the performance is that it hold attention. The director has tried to set up a precise focal point for every moment of the play. He knows where the attention of the audience should be placed at all times. He has used composition, movement, business, speech, light, color, and other devices to highlight and intensify the focal point. Sometimes the focal point isn't where the director believes he has placed it. Distracting elements, overlooked by the director, may steal the audience's attention. Observe the audience during the performance. Confusions in the focal point are readable in audience responses.

The silent audience. An attentive audience is a silent audience. In moments of high tension the audience may be so quiet that it is difficult to believe that the spectators are breathing. Such silence is a real tribute to the effectiveness of a scene. However, since attention with its resultant tension is an energy expending process, the audience cannot be silent at all times. The spectator must be given an opportunity to release his tension occasionally. During the periods of release the director can hear a slight rustling sound, yet there is no apparent change in the audience's attitude. This rustling is quite different from restlessness, which we will discuss in a moment. If the rustling occurs during dramatic moments in the performance, something is wrong. For some reason, either the actor or the script is not holding the audience. Remember: the performer must control the response of the spectator. The experienced actor can react to the responses of the audience and control them. The inexperienced cast, playing the show as it was rehearsed, is dependent upon the magic of the director who has anticipated the response of the audience at every moment of the play.

The restless audience. If, for some reason, the audience is not reacting well to the stimulus from the stage, the director should be able to sense it immediately. The rustling sound grows in intensity until it becomes overt restlessness: the spectator shifts in his seat. Some shifting is, of course, inevitable, as it helps relieve the stiffness from sitting in one position. If large groups of people begin to shift at approximately the same time, the director should immediately examine the stimulus from the stage and ascertain what is wrong.

The facilitation that helps to maintain attention can work in reverse. If the people sitting next to you in the theatre are restless and shifting, it will tend to facilitate you to writhe and shift. Restlessness can be contagious. Therefore, the director makes an immediate note of uniformity in the non-attentive responses and changes the stimulus in later performances.

Coughing. Another sign of the uneasy audience is coughing. Some coughs or sneezes are involuntary, but most of them result from paying prolonged attention to a scratchy throat or a tickle in the nose. If the spectator is distracted by a tickle, it means that the stimulus of the tickle has become greater than the stimulus from the stage. Thus, a cough is frequently a sign of inattention. The isolated cough means little; but in a restless audience, one cough facilitates others. There is a spread effect. A cough sounds like a pistol shot to the sensitive director. If it is followed immediately by other coughs, the director should determine what is wrong on stage.

Can the Audience See and Hear

Frequently, inattention results from the spectator's inability to see or hear. Attention breaks down because both listening and watching take energy. If the auditor has to strain to catch the lines of the actors, he will soon tire and ultimately give up listening. The inability to hear may also act as a distraction. The spectator becomes conscious of the fact that he can't hear. Frequently, he turns to his neighbor and asks that a line be repeated. Obviously, no spectator in this predicament can be expected to participate in the production.

The inability to see adequately causes reactions similar to those mentioned above. If the compositional focal point is not opened so that every member of the audience has a clear view of it, or if the lighting is reduced to a point wherein the spectator cannot see the actors clearly, restlessness will result.

A strange relationship exists between seeing and hearing. If the spectator cannot see, he finds himself unable to hear, even though the amount of sound projected is perfectly adequate for reception. An illustration may make this point more clear. The mood for a mystery show was established by raising the curtain on a dimly lit stage. The audience evidenced considerable inattention, maintaining that they could not hear. At the next performance the sound levels were raised. Still the spectators couldn't hear. Few objected to the inability to see; hearing was the problem. In later performances, the lights were increased at the opening; and after the audience had a chance to see everything clearly, they were dimmed to exactly the same level used at the first performance. No one complained about not being able to hear. In other words, a psychological deafness was operating in the first case. The spectators had literally decided that they couldn't hear. Once the spectators convinced themselves that they could hear, the problem no longer existed.

Hearing is a very real problem in handling comedy. Many times laughs are lost or are small rather than large for the simple reason that the audience doesn't hear the funny line. The student is referred to the chapter on comedy for a detailed discussion of the characteristics of laughter and the laugh response. The director can easily tell when the audience is unable to hear the comic line by noting the fullness of the reaction. If only one segment of the audience laughs, it means that others in the audience didn't hear the line. Usually this is a result of faulty timing. The pause before the gag line helps insure hearing. The punch of the line should be gauged so that every member of the audience hears the line. The director should assess the timing and projection of each comic line and situation during the performance. Those missed should be studied in detail and corrected before the next performance. The number and size of laughs can sometimes be doubled.

In the serious play, problems in hearing may manifest themselves in restlessness in the sections of the audience unable to hear. If the director watches the audience, he can see the line of demarcation between those who can hear and those who can't. The major aspects of this problem should, of course, be solved during the rehearsal period.

Note that the director should never depend upon his own ability to hear as a criterion of whether the audience can hear. The director is a poor judge because he is acquainted with the lines and is able to fill in any indistinct segment from his own memory. The same is, in part, true of seeing. He sees what he expects to see rather than what is actually happening. He knows what the actors are doing and, therefore, is able to see satisfactorily even when the lighting is inadequate. The director should ask someone who has never seen the play before to sit in on one of the final rehearsals and test the levels of sound and visibility, to compensate for his inability to judge.

In establishing projection levels, one more factor should be considered. The auditorium acoustics change when it is filled by an audience. The clothing of the spectators absorbs sound. This damping effect cuts down the carrying power of the actor's voice. Usually, vocal projection must be raised to compensate for the presence of an audience. This factor alone may account for the inability to hear during performances although the projection was adequate at the final rehearsal in an empty auditorium.

More non-professional productions fail because they cannot be heard than from any other cause. When the playgoer pays to enter the theatre, the least the director can do is to make certain that he is able to see and hear everything that might contribute to his enjoyment.

Is the Audience Participating in the Performance

In Chapter 4 the ideal balance between identification and detachment was discussed. The director should be able to sense whether the spectators are responding *to* and *with* the characters. Over-identification makes itself apparent by overt sounds and actions on the part of the spectators. Shrieks and screams are usually undesirable unless the play is a melodrama designed to elicit responses of this sort. In other types of plays, over-participation causes a breakdown of the artistic detachment. It is evidenced by embarrassed laughter at places in the performance where it is undesirable or by excessive unrest which develops during tense scenes.

The breakdown of the participatory response may also arise because certain scenes lack credibility. If, for example, a messenger hurries in with a letter for the king, and the audience breaks into laughter, the participatory response has been broken. The audience has withdrawn from the play for some reason. The director must analyze the reason for the negative response. Frequently, the director can recognize immediately the incongruity causing the laughter. Time and again the director will note obvious discrepancies that went unnoticed during the rehearsals but upset the audience.

The director should be particularly careful to determine whether spectacular scenic effects are serving their purpose. The fact that the audience "ooohs" and "aaahs" may please the technical director, but usually it means that the effect is calling attention to itself. If this is true, the effect should be reduced in its intensity, for it is impairing the total audience response to the play.

Does the Play Have Unity and Balance

Every play must have a unity of purpose. All of the parts must contribute to the whole. In addition, all of the parts must be in balance. No single aspect of the production may overshadow any other aspect. These elements should have been considered throughout the rehearsal period; yet, when the play is actually performed the director gains a new perspective by observing the response of the audience. Elements which seemed perfectly unified during rehearsal often seem to be out of balance in the performance.

One of the most frequent faults is a difference in the acting styles. Part of this difference may be the result of varying reactions to the excitement of the performance. The actor who is carried away by his own success may destroy the unity of the production. Sometimes this problem may be solved immediately. The director can go backstage and pull the actor into line. If this is not possible, a balance may be regained in the next performance by discussing the discrepancies after the initial showing.

A spectacular scenic effect may also destroy the unity of the production. In a production of *The Petrified Forest*, the gasoline pump, visible through the restaurant doorway, was rigged up so that it would buzz, whirr, and pump gas like a real one. The audience was so attracted to this bit of naturalism that other aspects of the scene were forgotten. To this day, some of the spectators remember that production of the play more for the pump than for the ideas of the author. The director can easily overlook this type of disparity during rehearsals. He should be able to catch them during the first performance.

Another destroyer of unity, about which the director can probably do little while the play is in performance, is overuse or overemphasis of certain elements of production. For example, some directors stress the visual and overlook the auditory; others do the reverse. In some cases, a particular pet movement or bit of business is used again and again until it calls attention to itself. I don't know why such things, overlooked throughout rehearsals, suddenly become apparent during performance, but it frequently happens. Perhaps the director is able to see more clearly with the new perspective provided by the audience.

Does the Play Have Variety and Spontaneity

There is a definite tendency for inexperienced casts, mesmerized by the excitement of the performance, to take the variety out of a production. The director has labored throughout the rehearsal period to develop a shifting stimulus capable of holding the attention of the audience. He has used contrasts in key and tempo to create hills and valleys of excitement which alternately generate excitement and provide release for the audience. Unfortunately, casts under the stress of the performance frequently allow both the key and the tempo to run wild. The result is a plateau of speed and tension that tires the audience. The pre-performance emphasis upon playing the show as it was rehearsed can often stifle any such eventuality. If this does not suffice, the problem must be dealt with after the performance, during the discussion of the show.

The one quality in which the amateur production can always surpass the professional one is spontaneity. The verve and vitality of youth cannot be matched by the weary professional. Often the inexperienced actor does not make use of this advantage. Some actors respond to the tension of performance by fading out vocally and visually. The director must try to free the frightened actor. The vivid spontaneous impression of the first time depends upon vitality. The well-directed play is spontaneous and vital.

MAKING CHANGES IN SUCCEEDING PERFORMANCES

It has been stated several times in the preceding sections that the director usually cannot make any really effective changes during the performance. At best, he can make the actors aware of certain very general problems, such as under- or over-projection, excessive speed, or monotonous pacing. Even these general faults should be considered only in so far as they deviate from the way the play was rehearsed.

Specific or detailed corrections cannot be made until after the performance. The actor has too much to think about to heed advice given to him between entrances or between acts. Most actors under pressure have sufficient difficulty remembering the rehearsed pattern. To introduce new types of activity is foolhardy. Two factors are responsible for the inability to change immediately or to remember mistakes after the performance. First, the actor is unable to objectify his acting. He is a part of the whole and cannot stand apart and observe himself in the play. Second, most actors are so excited about what comes next that they cannot remember what was done in earlier scenes.

This problem is particularly complex in that the non-professional must make his corrections immediately or not at all, since most amateur productions run only two to four performances. The professional has the advantage of time. He can experiment with a production over dozens of performances. Any method that can objectify the play for the actor will help condense the correction period.

Recording the Performance

The simplest and most inexpensive permanent record of the strengths and weaknesses of the performance is a tape or disc recording of the play. A microphone placed in the footlights or suspended behind the act curtain can pick up both the dialogue of the play and the reactions of the audience. Since the microphone is a considerable distance from the actors, the quality of the recording will be inferior, but this in no way hinders the analysis of the performance.

Some directors call the cast immediately after the performance while the experience is fresh in their minds. Others feel that the actors are too tired to make good use of the recording after the performance and prefer to save the critical session for the next day. The cast's reaction to the recording is frequently one of amazement. For the first time, the actor is able to step aside and view his work as the painter, sculptor, and composer does. He may hear not only every inflection, pause, and change of pace in his reading of the lines, but more important, he can hear the audience's response. An entirely new, thoroughly objective point of view is possible.

A recording of the performance facilitates corrections. If the actor has inflected a line badly, the line can be played again and again until the mistake is recognized and the correction made. If unwanted laughter has occurred, analysis of the recording usually indicates the exact cause for the response.

The director who has also been excited by the performance will find that a recording gives him further opportunity to evaluate the effect of the performance. He need no longer perceive, digest, and analyze the play's actions in the fleeting moments of their occurrence.

The Succeeding Performances

If the attitude of the director and the cast is a wholesome one, concerned with improving the production each time it is played, the succeeding performances should, in a large measure, take care of themselves. However, the acute director is prepared to handle the differences in audiences, the possibility of a second night letdown, and the problems of closing the show.

Audience differences. Although audience differences are often overrated, the beginning actor may not realize that there is any difference whatsoever between one audience and the next. The homogeneity of each new audience in the high school, college, or community theatre may be reasonably constant, yet responses from one performance to the next may vary considerably. These changes in response are largely the result of changes in the production.

To be specific, the fact that an actor received a laugh of a particular intensity, duration, and pattern does not in any way guarantee that the laugh will have identical characteristics at a second performance. Many beginning actors anticipate the audience response to a comic situation by throwing the line, then stopping to wait for the audience. Unless the laugh has been proved by a number of performances, the actor may be caught off balance when the line does not provoke any laugh at all. Each new audience must be dealt with on its own merits.

The second night letdown. The opening performance is usually characterized by terrific tension. After the first audience has been met and conquered, most actors experience a severe letdown. This is a perfectly natural reaction. Excessive expenditure of bodily energy is followed by a release of tension when the cause for the excitement has abated. Many productions experience a general letdown during the second performance. The actors feel tired and sluggish; they find it difficult to regain the tension necessary to an effective performance. The director may compensate for this condition by focusing the actor's attention on improvements needed in the second portrayal of the role. In accordance with good psychological practice, the director should not mention the possibility of a letdown. He may plant the idea in the minds of the actors.

The closing performance. Ideally, to experience any material growth, a play should be performed more than three times. The first performance is usually an overly tense opening, the second performance is a letdown, and the third performance, if it is the final one, is a gala closing. The performances between the letdown and the closing are often the best from the director's as well as the spectator's point of view. The closing performance provides a new series of problems for the director. The excitement of producing the play and meeting the challenge of the audience has almost completely vanished. The actors are concluding many weeks of hard work. They are searching for some new and exciting way to finish the run of the show. Frequently, amateurs (in the worst sense of the term) feel that they must resort to clever horse-play. The results can be ruinous. The cast and crews have a wonderful time playing jokes upon one another, and the spectator wonders why he wasted his money.

The director can take several courses of action. Certainly, he should never discuss the possibilities of trouble until rumors of it arise. If and when the director hears of the ingenious pranks under consideration, he should bring the situation to the attention of everyone. Usually an appeal to the mature judgment of the group is sufficient. If not, he should point out that the theatre is a business, not a game; that an audience has paid admission to see a show, and they deserve to see the best that the group can offer; that only the rankest amateur would consider ruining the play. If the actors still act up during the performance, the director should go backstage immediately and deal harshly with the problem.

Would that there were no reason for the preceding paragraphs. The good of the play comes first to any sincere actor or crewman. Unfortunately, there are occasionally those who are not sincere. They must be handled severely.

SPECIAL PERFORMANCE PROBLEMS

The Prompter

A controversy has long raged as to the advisability of using a prompter during the performances. Depending upon the background of the director, the answer may be a dogmatic "yes" or a didactic "no." Each director must make the decision for himself, but the arguments pro and con may make the decision easier.

Those who believe that the prompter is a necessity argue that the prompter gives the actor support both moral and literal. This is probably true. Most inexperienced actors and many very experienced ones worry about memorization. The presence of the prompter acts as a moral support for the actor. Those who argue against the use of the prompter emphasize that moral support is unnecessary. The actor should learn to stand on his own feet. He should concentrate on the interplay between the characters rather than on his own lines. These directors maintain that some actors (and I am sure that this is true) forget lines because the prompter is there to save the day.

Those who believe in the prompter feel that he insures against the possibility of the play coming to a complete and dreadful halt. Those who are against maintain that every time a prompt is given, the play does come to a complete and dreadful stop, for the prompter is always heard by the audience; the actor in his excitement is unable to hear the prompt; he is worried about hearing an offstage voice rather than reacting to the onstage scene, and his attention is directed away from the play. Without a prompter at the moment of a lapse in memory, the actors direct their attention to getting the play back on the track. Every actor pitches in to help the stranded actor. Those who stand against using a prompter maintain that the ad-libbing used to bridge the gap in the production, however weak it may be, is superior to the complete stop that comes while waiting for the prompt.

In the opinion of the author, the choice depends upon the experience of the group. At the high school level, where experience is minimal, a prompter may serve the very useful purpose of providing moral and literal support. At the college and community theatre levels, the more mature and experienced casts should stand on their own feet without a prompter. Once a theatre group has become accustomed to doing without a prompter, the results are eminently satisfactory.

There is, of course, a final possibility. One college director told me that he had solved the problem. He always used a prompter who had the strict order, "Don't prompt!"

Reviews of the Play

Some high schools and most colleges and little theatres have their plays reviewed by the local press. Frequently, the reviews are merely feature articles about the play and the actors. They tell the story of the play, the cast, and the director. They are innocuous and are good publicity. In large cities and notably in the colleges, the newspaper assigns a reviewer to criticize the production. Unfortunately, many of these self-styled critics have practically no background in drama or production. In addition, many of them feel highly important in their positions as guardians of the community's culture. Since they have the very real power of the printed word at their command, they often constitute a problem for the director.

The theatre asks but two things of the critic: a considerable knowledge of things theatrical, and a completely objective honesty. If both of these requirements are fulfilled, the director should be happy to have his play stand the test of a review. If the play is bad, the reviewer is expected to say so in simple, honest terms.

Unfortunately, many of the local critics try to emulate Alexander Woollcott and George Jean Nathan. Their acid remarks personalize what should be a clean-cut, objective evaluation. They hurt the actors, the director, the theatre, and, in the long run, themselves. The director who realizes that his play must face this kind of reviewing should explain the possibilities to his cast *before* the review comes out. In this way he can improve the objectivity of the actor's attitude toward the review. This advice applies to the lavish review as well as to the unkind review. The director should explain the nature of reviewing to every cast, whether the reviewer is known to be fair or unfair.

The Understudy

The understudy is an important and necessary part of professional theatre organization. When a play runs fifty to a hundred or more performances, it is to be expected that certain members of the cast will be unable to appear at one time or another.

The advisability of the understudy in the non-professional theatre is not as clear. In the professional theatre, a person may be paid a good salary for doing nothing or playing a very minor role. In the non-professional theatre, where a chance to participate is the prime reward, it is hard to ask a youngster to spend long hours learning a role with only a small probability of being allowed to play it. The non-professional director is faced with a dilemma. If he uses understudies, he probably cannot give them a chance to play. If he doesn't have understudies and one of his cast members is unable to appear at the last moment, he has a major problem. Some directors solve the understudy problem by double casting. The strengths and weaknesses of this procedure are discussed in Chapter 15. The director who does not use a double cast must answer several questions. Can someone in the cast do the understudying? Is he eager to do it? If the talent is available within the cast and actors with small parts are willing to assume the responsibility of understudying with full knowledge of the limited potential, understudies for major roles may work out. On the other hand, if the possible understudy is an actor not already cast in the play, it would seem inadvisable to use one. The extra person will never really feel that he is a part of the group.

What can the director do in case of illness or accident if no understudy is available? This problem, which will confront most non-professional directors at some time during their careers, deserves individual consideration.

Illness and Accident

There was a delightful motion picture about theatrical business, some years ago, in which an aging trouper asked the question, "Why must the show go on?" He asked people connected with every branch of theatrical activity and did not receive a sensible answer from any of them. Tradition is probably the only reason that "the show must go on." Every other type of spectator event is cancelled if something goes wrong. The actor and the mailman are about the only ones who always carry on. If a boxer is ill, the match is cancelled. If it rains, the baseball game is called off. If the speaker is indisposed, the meeting is postponed. But "the show must go on."

The only real reasons for this persistence that the writer can think of are related to the intricacies of the box office. Since the number of seats in a theatre is limited, a rain check serves no purpose. Road companies can't stop, for they have new commitments ahead. If the need to postpone the production arises just prior to the opening of the show or even earlier, it is virtually impossible to reach the members of the audience. Therefore, it was probably a producer, worried about his purse, who started the rumor that the show must go on. At any rate, the director is stuck with this glorious tradition, and the show, for better or for worse, does go on. There are, of course, in the history of the theatre many cases of cancelled performances (which are not discussed above a whisper), but usually some type of substitution is made.

Assuming that there are no understudies, what shall the director do when the leading actor breaks his leg three hours before the curtain rises? First, the performance can be cancelled. Second, the audience may be given a choice of having their money returned or having someone, perhaps even the director, read the part, script in hand. Given such a choice, the audience usually enters into the spirit of the occasion and enjoys the play with the substitute performer.

If the director has 24 hours in which to prepare a substitute, he may recast the part. The thought of having an actor do in one day what it has taken the rest of the cast four to six weeks to accomplish may seem absurd. Try it. You will be amazed at the speed with which a single actor can be absorbed into the production. If the new actor can memorize quickly, interpretation, movement, and business can be learned in a hurry because every other member of the cast knows exactly what the missing character does at every instant. The new actor is moving through a pattern in which every element is set. The regular cast members can straighten out any deviations from the prescribed pattern.

Twice in fifteen years, the writer has had to substitute new actors in major roles with less than twelve hours in which to do it. In each case the audience was completely unaware of the substitution.

Curtain Calls

The curtain call is a theatrical tradition which many non-professional theatres have eliminated. A good case can be built for either retaining or rejecting the call. The directors who insist upon the curtain call assert that it should be included because it is a part of theatrical tradition, audiences expect it, and actors want it. Another and perhaps better reason for the curtain call is that it gives the audience a chance to express its appreciation.

The directors who have eliminated the call can also argue well. They maintain that the curtain call breaks the mood and feeling of the play; it destroys the illusion the production has created; and the audience suddenly forgets the play and directs its attention upon the actors. A second objection is that the curtain call tends to stress the actors over the other members of the play production group. In the non-professional theatre the technical crews are as much a creative part of the production as the actors. The directors who take this position rightly suggest that the crews should appear for a curtain call also. A third objection to the curtain call is that it stresses one of the least desirable aspects of the professional theatre—the star system. Most non-professional directors have trouble enough making bit actors and extras feel a part of the production without the additional problem of "star" emphasis resulting from the curtain call.

The decision to have or to eliminate the curtain call should depend upon the circumstances at hand. If the curtain call is to be used, several suggestions for making it meaningful follow. First of all, be certain that the curtain call is blocked and rehearsed as carefully as the other visual elements of the production. A shabby, restless, meaningless line of uneasy actors is never a satisfactory way to conclude a production. One good way to take a company call is to arrange a single composition with the actors remaining in character and maintaining the same relationships to other characters that they had in the play. This procedure was used with great success in the professional production of *Life with Father*. Instead of a company call, small tableaux were posed as nineteenth century daguerreotypes. The non-professional production should be limited to a single *company* call. It is always wiser to leave the audience unsated than to force polite applause. If curtain calls are eliminated, a note in the program to that effect helps avoid confusion in the audience.

Flowers

Flowers across the footlights. Never! This tradition of the professional theatre has no place in the high school, college, or community production. Flowers emphasize the persons receiving them. The actress in the non-professional production does not receive flowers because of her recognized superiority as an actress but rather because she has affluent friends. Flowers across the footlights not only break the continuity of the production but are hard on cast morale. Not everyone receives flowers. The young lady who does not get them cannot help but feel either envy or hurt. If flowers do appear (and they will), have them sent to the dressing rooms, preferably after the performance.

In the preceding five chapters, the director has been led through the maze of procedure surrounding the production of a play from the selection of the script to the final curtain. Not every directing experience will be a success, but every directing experience should be a lesson which can help assure greater success on the next venture. When the final curtain falls and the current production is a matter of record, the director should eagerly await his next opportunity to apply his new knowledge.

Part Four

Problems in Play Direction

18

Handling the Actor

THIS CHAPTER does not propose to develop a small text in acting. It is, rather, a study of the specific techniques with which the director must be conversant if he is to help the actor give the best possible dramatic portrayal. The relationship of the director and the actor, the approaches to acting, the common faults in acting with methods for correcting them, all are subjects the director must understand and cope with if he is to fulfill his responsibilities as a director.

THE RELATIONSHIP OF THE DIRECTOR AND THE ACTOR

In Chapter 5 it was emphasized that the actor is the greatest creative force in the drama. The director's job is to stimulate the spark of creation and to mold the dynamic results into a single entity called the production. To do this, the director must be teacher and friend, motivator and critic.

Actors Are Human

Why do highly sensitive, imaginative young people try out for a play in the first place? It is because they feel, consciously or unconsciously, that being in a play can contribute something to them as human beings. Some appear, of course, who have false or misdirected values. They believe that the theatre is a place to show off or gain prestige. Some are led to the theatre by false notions of glamour stimulated by movie magazines and rotogravure sections.

But most actors timorously enter the arena because they believe that the theatre can help them solve their own problems, aid them in expressing themselves, provide a new and deeper experience. These are the director's charges. Experimental studies show that actors are more sensitive, less well-balanced emotionally, more creative, less well-adjusted than their non-theatrical brothers.

Many directors feel their only job is to produce a play. The play is important, to be sure. But more important, at least in the non-commercial theatre, is the help and guidance which the director can give the actor while they cooperate in producing a play. Do not misunderstand. This is not a plea to turn the theatre into a psychological laboratory, but rather it is a plea for the director to recognize that the actor is more than a puppet. He is a human being, worthy of note, worthy of consideration, worthy of the best that the director can give.

Actors Differ

Some directors make the mistake of handling all actors in the same way. If actors were blocks of wood to be fitted into a puzzle, this sameness of approach would be logical. But actors are human and thus different from one another. No two humans have the same background, the same reaction patterns, the same complement of habits, the same sensitivity, the same ability to respond; therefore, the first responsibility of the director is to get to know his actors. This factor is emphasized as one of the bases of casting. (Chapter 15.) This is particularly true in the case of the new actor. The director's job is to motivate a series of highly dynamic vocal and physical responses from his actors. This cannot be wisely and successfully done until the director knows something about the personality with which he works. Complete cooperation depends upon establishing a rapport between the actors and the director. Each must understand the other. Each must respect the other. The director and the actor have come together to accomplish the same end—the production of a play.

Actors Have Ideas

If the actor is worthy of the title, he will have ideas to contribute to the production. The director must make full use of the actor's talent. He should encourage the actor to experiment. Since most actors are eager to learn about dramatics as well as act in a play, the director should try to explain the "why" as well as the "what" of his directions. Only with a director who encourages questions, discussion, and initiative can the full possibilities of the play be realized.

Actors Have Strengths and Weaknesses

Players are chosen because they potentially fit within the range of the role. In the high school, college, or community theatre, however, the director seldom finds an actor completely trained, fully experienced, and greatly endowed. If such an actor were available, the commercial theatre would soon deprive the director of his talents. The student actor is almost always limited. He may have a magnificent imagination but a poorly coordinated body. He may have great vocal flexibility but lack sensitivity.

The director must find the strengths and weaknesses of the actor quickly. He must capitalize on the strengths and either eliminate or hide the weaknesses. This need accounts in part for the tendency of the director to cast actors whom he has seen act. Even if the actor has had no opportunity to show his wares on the stage, the director tends to choose the actor whom he knows. Not because he likes the actor, but rather because he has determined from the contacts of everyday life some of the actor's strengths and weaknesses.

The director will find that there is no substitute for a close knowledge of the actor. Only by knowing the actor can the director determine his individual needs and goals and make the necessary adjustment to his divergent individual characteristics. Only by knowing the actor can the director help him help the production.

KINDS OF ACTORS

There are many different theories of acting, each having its individual variations, but, essentially, there are two methods by which an actor may approach the creation of a character. He may tackle it from the outside or from the inside. The ideal end result is the same. One procedure works for some actors; the second is the solution for others. Unfortunately, each of the seers of the various schools of acting has preached his method as the only satisfactory one. As a result, actors tend to be apostles for one or the other approach to acting.

The director should ascertain the method the actor uses, for the problems of direction depend in part on the procedure the actor follows. Perhaps the best way of illustrating the difference between the methods and the concurrent problems is to cite the extremes.

The Technical Actor

The technical actor develops his character from the outside. He creates his character by mechanically assuming a particular stance, walk, style of speech, and other mannerisms until he has filled in each detail of the character. He portrays emotion by external signs. In playing rage, he tenses his muscles, contracts his body, tightens his throat, changes his vocal quality. Since the audience can react only to what it can see and hear, the portrayal will be as perfect as the technique of which it is built.

This technical procedure is based upon the famous James-Lange theory of emotion. Expressing the theory in simple terms, we do not run from a bear because we are afraid, but, rather, we are afraid because we run. In other words, emotion is merely the conscious awareness of the physical activities involved in response to a stimulus. Carried to its logical conclusion, we may anticipate that by assuming the physical characteristics of hate, emotional arousal will follow. The pretense results in actuality.

Think of the times within your own experience that you have pretended to be angry or sad. You have gone through all the motions of anger or grief. Frequently this pretense, which started as a game, results in actual rage or despondency. The technical actor follows this procedure exactly. By assuming the outward characteristics of the character or the emotion, he generates the inward feeling. Once the feeling has been aroused, the process is reversed. The feeling helps determine the outward appearance. Note from the discussion of the characteristics of emotion in Chapter 10 that emotion is merely physiological arousal. Since all emotions are similar if not identical in origin, the problem is to bring about the physiological changes basic to all emotion. *Inner feeling* explains the state exactly.

The failure of this procedure lies in the fact that many times the inner feeling does not follow the outward manifestation. This is particularly true of the inhibited or unimaginative actor. When no inward feeling arises to support the external technique, the audience senses the lack of completeness in the portrayal. Shortcomings in the technique can be observed. In addition, the character has a cold quality; it lacks the so-called inner spark which gives life and vibrancy to the portrayal.

Directing the Technical Actor

Many actors are technical in their approach because they are afraid of appearing foolish; they are unwilling to make a display of their carefully repressed emotions in public. These actors can be helped. Any procedure which can break down this inhibitory barrier will provide a new dimension to their acting.

Establishing the correct attitude toward the rehearsal procedure is the first step in freeing the inhibited actor. Professorial formality or stiffness has no place in the rehearsal room. Rapport with the actor can be created only if the actor is made to feel completely at ease. The director who acts as a general commanding his troops can never make his actors feel free to express themselves fully. The attitude of everyone toward rehearsals should be one of warmth and kindness, enthusiasm and understanding. Every actor should be made to feel that he has complete freedom to try out every new idea. Above all, he must feel that the director and the other actors are eager to work with him. The ideal cast is a cooperating group. The actor who feels that everyone is experimenting together toward a common goal will lose his inhibitions. The actor who senses that others are standing apart watching, criticizing, even laughing at him will seldom do his best.

Assuming a warmth and freedom in the attitude of everyone at the rehearsal, the director may proceed to stir the inner feelings of the mechanical actor. This may be done by bringing powerful suggestion to bear, by inducing emotion with emotion by direct stimulation, by using the stimulation from the feeling of other actors, and, finally, as a last resort, by creating a model for the actor to follow.

Every reasonably mature person has experienced, either actually or vicariously, the emotions necessary to the creation of any character in almost any situation. A lack of awareness, sensitivity and concentration, or deep subjective involvement at the time of the impact may have deprived the emotion of specific meaning to the individual, but the background of experience is there. The director must establish the connection between the experience and the portrayal. The connection can be made by employing the methods of the emotional approach to acting. Assuming that the actor intellectually understands the character and the motivation or reason for the feeling, the director can stimulate the actor's emotional memory by painting vivid, moving, colorful pictures of the character and the situation. Imaginatively the actor should be able to transport himself from the rehearsal room to the place, time, and feeling of the event. The sensitive actor can be stirred and can with careful concentration transfer his feeling to the role.

Let us suppose that the script calls for the actor to portray a grief-stricken parent. The director can help him recall and intensify for him the actor's own moods and feelings of grief, or the director may describe a scene involving the emotion so vividly that the actor is caught in the spirit of the scene. In either case, the actor draws upon his own past experiences.

A second method of creating feeling in the actor is inducing emotion with emotion. The director involves himself and, in turn, the actor in the desired emotional state. If, for example, the scene requires that the actor project the feeling of nervous excitement, the director, by expressing nervous excitement, can catch the actor up in the swirl of the emotion, with the result that the actor begins to respond in the same manner. This procedure is usually coupled with the preceding one.

A third method is to stimulate the actor directly until he experiences the desired emotion. As an educational practice it is not recommended, but it does get results. In *The Silver Cord* by Sidney Howard, the emotionally unstable youngster, Hester, has hysterics after her engagement has been broken. Let us assume that the actress playing the role has never been hysterical, has not even witnessed hysterics. Endless rehearsal may produce the same hollow imitation. By direct stimulation, the actress may be prodded into hysterics. Once she has experienced the emotional outburst, she can simulate it at will.

Fourthly, the stimulation of feeling in an actor can frequently result from intense feeling on the part of other actors. The principle of transferring emotion is operating, but in this case the other actors rather than the director act as the stimulus.

Finally, and as a last resort, the director may literally provide a model for the actor. The great disadvantage of this procedure is that it stifles inner feeling. The actor concentrates on matching the external qualities of the model. It is difficult, if not impossible, to study the externals of walk, stance, vocal quality, etc. and, at the same time, arouse inner feeling. The directors (and there are some) who feel that this is the best method say that after the actor has learned to mimic the externals, the emotional inner tensions will arise. Perhaps. However, one always suspects that the director who plays every part for his actors is in reality only indulging his own frustrated desire to act.

This discussion of creating emotion raises the age old question in the minds of many directors: how much emotion? Ideally, the actor should "feel" during the portrayal, but the physiological arousal should not be so deep that he loses conscious control. Complete indulgence in emotion belongs in the rehearsal room rather than on the stage. The profound emotional experience should be the basis upon which a character is created. On stage, feeling should be used to fuse the techniques into a whole.

Having aroused the actor, the director should re-direct the actor's attention to the external vocal and visual techniques which project the character to the audience. Assuming that the director is a good critic of what will create the illusion of reality for the spectator, the course of action should be clear. He can evaluate the vocal and visual cues upon which the audience must depend. He can help the actor select, order, and intensify the externals.

The Emotional Actor

The emotional actor develops his character from the inside. He thinks the thoughts and searches for the inner truth of the character. He stimulates himself imaginatively by putting himself in the character's place. He looks for the fundamental motivation. Usually by purely mental rather than physical stimulation, he arouses an inner feeling. This method of creating a role is just as logical as the approach through the externals. Successful application does, however, require a particular type of person.

The truly emotional actor is usually one who has a very low

threshold of emotional excitability. He is extremely sensitive. Frequently, though not always, he is a person who lives predominantly in an emotional rather than a rational world. By most conventional standards the truly emotional actor will be considered unstable, as indeed he probably is. The greatest strength of the emotional actor lies in his ability to feel deeply with minimal stimulation. The greatest weakness of most inexperienced emotional actors lies in their sincere belief that deep feeling is all that counts in acting. They scoff at technique.

Let us take the analogy of the violinist. Suppose the beginning violinist has the spirit, the sensitivity, the depth of feeling, the emotional fire, the imagination that differentiates the great artist from the run-of-the-mill musician. Is this artistic stature enough? It is not. Until the player has perfected all of the techniques of fingering and bowing his instrument, he will be unable to produce more than squeaks and squawks from a violin, no matter how deep his feeling may be. So it is with the actor. Depth and fire are important; but unless he has a superbly trained and controlled voice and body, his technical instrument, he will not be able to project his feeling to the audience.

Any director knows that the flow of real tears down the cheeks of an actress in no way guarantees a similar flow of tears from the eyes of the spectator. As a matter of fact, the presence of tears can destroy the illusion, for the spectator may turn to his neighbor and say, "Look at that—real tears!"

Another weakness of the completely emotional actor is a lack of control, which may destroy the balance of emotional keys in the production. It is said that Elinora Duse at times became so deeply stirred emotionally that she fainted on stage and had to be hauled from the footlights for fear that her hair might catch fire in the open flame lamps used at the time. I cannot help but feel that such an emotional display, although it might be exciting to watch, contributed little to the production as a whole.

A third weakness of the highly emotional actor is his inconsistency. The director can never be sure of what to expect from the emotional actor. At one performance he may be inspired; the next, he may be unable to transcend his own mood. The resulting unevenness of performance works a very real hardship on the other actors of the cast who are striving to keep the play in balance.

The emotional actor usually rebutts the preceding remarks by claiming that complete submersion in the character results in the true vocal and visual manifestations of character. Occasionally this may be valid, but more frequently it is erroneous. Complete indulgence in emotion usually results in the vocal and visual patterns of the player rather than the character.

Directing the Emotional Actor

The task of directing the emotional actor is not so much one of curbing his emotion as of perfecting his technique. As the actor becomes more aware of the meaning and affective value of the external character that the audience can see and hear, his attention is divided between emotion and technique. Since the technique must be rationally controlled, the depth of the emotional involvement decreases. Once the actor accepts the worth of selection and intensification of technical elements, he usually begins to experiment with new and different technical devices for projecting his emotion to the audience.

The Balanced Actor

The balanced actor is usually the ideal actor. He stands at the midpoint between the extremes of technique and emotion. He feels deeply but has complete rational control. He has a sure knowledge of the technical elements necessary to effective expression. The particular approach to acting which he chooses makes little difference. He may attack the character externally, with deep inner feeling as the result, or he may begin with sensitive emotional responses that are implemented technically to project a precise effect.

Most of the great players of the contemporary theatre are balanced actors. Morton Eustis, in his little book, *Players at Work,* reports the methods of Alfred Lunt, Lynn Fontanne, Burgess Meredith, Helen Hayes, and several others. No two methods are alike, but a mixture of feeling and technique is present in each.

Directing the Balanced Actor

Since the balanced actor combines technical facility with emotional depth, he is the easiest actor to direct. The balanced actor can give the director a deep emotional base upon which the ex-

ternals of character can be built, or he can absorb the technical
aspects during the early blocking rehearsals and later infuse the
character with emotion.

The desired procedure is determined by the method of direction. The director who is first and foremost concerned with the
total interpretation of the play may encourage the actor to indulge
himself emotionally early in the rehearsal period. The director who
begins with the mechanics of composition and movement may
prefer the addition of feeling later in the production. It should be
noted that few actors can do both at once. If the actor is learning
the movement pattern, he cannot concentrate on arousing feeling,
and vice versa.

COMMON FAULTS IN ACTING

Most faults in acting arise from either the inability of the actor
to express the emotion of the character in a way that projects
the motivational pattern to the audience or a lack of the technical
control necessary to make the character sound and appear real.
These two basic sources of difficulty are too general to be of much
use to the director. Many directors sense that something is wrong
in the actor's portrayal but are unable to define the specific difficulty. The following sections provide a helpful checklist of common faults in acting. Each of the faults can destroy the illusion
of the character for the audience. Since the audience is able to
perceive only the visible and audible, the faults are classified in
terms of their visual and vocal characteristics, regardless of whether
the cause of the difficulty stems from emotional or technical
inadequacy.

Visual Activity Lacks Motivation

The most common fault in acting arises from a breakdown in
the chain from cause to effect or from motivation to expression.
Frequently, the movements or business of an actor may seem logical enough in a general way, but they do not ring true; they don't
really reflect the motivational pattern. For example, if the situation calls for the character to shake hands, the problem lies in the
way the character shakes hands. Because of the motivation in
the situation and the individual characteristics of the character,

the hand shake must have a certain vitality, quality, and duration if it is to seem real. Furthermore, the activity must fit within the spectator's preconceived notion of how the character would shake hands.

Meaningless or random activity also breaks down the motivational pattern. Many actors, particularly beginners, carry personal mannerisms into the playing of a role. The audience sees this activity and is unable to find a reason for it. Frequently, the movement is nothing more than the actor's attempt to release the tension caused by the excitement of being on a stage in front of people. Directing the actor's energies into useful channels will correct the difficulty.

A third difficulty results from a lack of visual activity. The audience derives its impression in part from what it sees. The static actor connotes nothing. The audience is frustrated by an inability to assess the qualities of the character. The director must stimulate the actor to meaningful activity.

Dropping Out of Character

Character must be sustained throughout the performance. The character is sustained by maintaining the physical tensions, regardless of whether or not the character has lines. Many players express emotional tension while they have lines and visibly relax when others are speaking. This behavior gives the character an intermittent realness which is not conceivable. If a man is engaged in an argument, his annoyance does not cease when he stops speaking. It is present until some new motivational factor either increases or decreases it.

One of the best ways to eliminate dropping out of character is to teach the actor to listen. Listening is a normal response when others speak. If the actor can learn actually to hear what the other characters are saying rather than merely waiting for his own cue, a sustained character can be realized.

Visual Overacting

Overacting may be defined as the expending of a greater amount of energy than is logical within the motivational framework of the situation. The audience is quick to perceive this excess. Overacting is associated more often with the listening character than with the speaking character. Listening requires a continuity of tension but not necessarily an abundance of activity. The player who continuously nods in acquiescence—fidgets in irritation, smiles, and shrugs—draws attention to himself through such excessive activity. Such actors must be toned down until their activity is commensurate with their character's requirements in the scene.

Visual Underacting

Underacting implies a lack of visual projection. The character is static and meaningless. The director is referred to Chapter 9, "Stage Business," in which the bases of visual projection are discussed in detail.

Patterned Visual Activity

In the normal activity of everyday life, most people reveal physical idiosyncrasies. They continuously repeat little actions. Some of these mannerisms attract attention. One woman twists a handkerchief, another fingers her throat, a third unconsciously fusses with her hair, a fourth flutters her hands. Even in life, these repetitive visual activities are annoying. On the stage, such mannerisms become much more emphatic and, accordingly, more irritating.

Mannerisms are basic to character portrayal; but if they are repeated to the extent that they call attention to themselves, they subtract rather than add to the characterization. On stage, where every action is highlighted, variety must be emphasized.

Quite apart from the little specialized mannerisms is the general physical pattern or way in which we handle our bodies. Frequently, the character and the actor have different patterns of activity. If the actor is unable to break up his own individual pattern, the character may seem confused and out of focus.

Lines Lack Motivation

The common vocal faults are really counterparts of the problems encountered in visual activity. Lines may lose their meaning because of poorly placed stress or emphasis which indicates that the actor does not understand the line. This difficulty can usually be cleared up by discussing the meaning of the line. Occasionally, an actor reads a line with a false inflection and is unable to change it, despite repeated readings by himself and the director. It is wiser to skip over such a line for the time being rather than to create a block which can never be repaired.

Frequently, lines sound false because the actor reads them exactly as they are written in the script. Most playwrights use a formal written style. They do not indicate all of the desirable contractions and gradations of stress. For example, the following line may be read in several different ways. Each of the readings gives a completely different impression; yet the line is usually written as it appears in the first sample.

1. "I do not want to see them."
2. "I don't wantta see th'm."
3. "I don' wanna see 'em."

Occasionally, the precise and equal stress shown in the first sample may be desirable. In most instances, however, the second sample, which more closely approximates everyday speech, should be chosen. In the third example, still a different impression of character is created by using a greater condensation and disregard for diction. If the line has a false quality, the director should make certain that the reading reflects the character and situation rather than the formal written style.

A lack of vocal tension is a third reason for lines not giving the effect indicated by the motivation. Emotion is expressed in part by physical tension. Tension cannot affect one part of the body and not another. If the members of the audience can see tension, they must also be able to hear it. The spectator cannot help but be confused when the actor's body projects one set of meanings and his voice projects a completely different set. The voice and body must always represent a single unit of expression if the emotion portrayed is to appear real.

Lack of Vocal Projection

Many actors share the misconception that the projection of sound depends solely upon volume. Volume is only one of the means of projecting. Vowel sustention, rate, articulation, and quality also determine how far the voice will carry.

Since most theatres have doubtful acoustics, the sustained vowel is an important means for increasing projection. Careful enunciation and sustention of the vowels allow the slight echo present in most theatres to dissipate itself upon the vowel rather than upon the following consonant.

Similarly, the rate of speaking affects audibility. Slow speech is more distinct than fast speech. As the speed increases, the overlapping of the sound and the echo becomes greater, with a resultant decrease in distinctness.

Clear articulation of the consonant sound also aids projection. If the actor drops either the initial or the final consonant sound, the ability to recognize words is sharply decreased.

The director must check the projection levels and correct any inaudibilities by explaining which aspects of projection are causing the trouble.

Lack of Vocal Variety

Two types of vocal variety should be considered in evaluating the actor's work. The first involves variety in rate, force, pitch, and quality. Vocal monotony kills expression in the role. These variables of voice must change as the coloration of the material changes.

A vocal pattern is far more noticeable to an audience than a monotony of rate, force, or pitch. Just as many of us have physical mannerisms, we also have vocal mannerisms. This habitual pattern can be observed whenever any single aspect of speech is overused. For example, some speakers finish every sentence with a downward inflection; some break up each line or phrase in a repetitive pattern; some attack or release each line the same way. These habits can make the difference between the presentation of a believable character and one which is not conceivable.

The director can expect difficulty in handling problems in monotony because most actors merely transpose their own speech characteristics onto the stage. In order to change the pattern, the actor must be aware of the monotony, break up the pattern, and practice the new variations until they become an unconscious part of his being.

Problems in Ensemble Playing

One of the most common faults in ensemble playing is a lack of interaction among characters. Expressed differently, the actors are not responding one to the other. This is particularly true of beginners. The novice actor is so concerned with the process of creating a role that his concentration is directed inward toward his own character rather than outward toward the other characters. He is so concerned with the way he appears and sounds that he is unable to stimulate and respond to the other characters. Ideally, the concern with self belongs in the early part of the rehearsal period. As the play grows, each character must begin to act and react with others. Until this is done the play can never have unity.

A second problem in ensemble playing is balance among characters. If the technical actor and the emotional actor have not balanced their playing, they will not fit when they appear together on the stage. The audience will be jarred by the differences in acting.

There must also be a balance in styles of play. If one character is fully developed visually and vocally and the next is not, the difference between the two is readily noticeable. There must be a balance in projection. If one character roars and another character whispers, the auditor cannot adjust to the difference. There must be balance in emotional key. Chapter 10 is devoted to explaining the causal factor in a play, how one character affects another character who, in turn, stimulates the first character. If the two players are not playing at the same emotional level the result is meaningless.

The actor cannot tell when he is in balance with the other characters. That is the director's job. He is completely responsible for the balance and unity of the ensemble.

Stereotyped Acting

In discussing emotion, the stereotype was defined as images that are carried in our minds. The need for playing within the emotional stereotypes was explained in Chapter 10. Although the stereotype is necessary to acting, it may also serve as a stumbling block.

One of the most common faults in acting is excessive dependence upon the stereotyped image. The characters in most American radio programs typify this error. They are stock types. For example, gangsters all sound alike because of the stereotype built up around them. Few of us know any gangsters; therefore, we create a stock image of how a gangster should look and sound.

The poorest acting is usually a cheap imitation of the stock stereotype. Frequently, the director can improve the playing of the role if he can teach the actor to elaborate imaginatively upon the stereotype.

Another fault in acting is found at the opposite extreme. In trying to avoid the stock character an actor may play the role completely outside the stereotype. To illustrate, the character labelled "a princess" by the playwright creates an image in the minds of the audience. To be sure there are many kinds of princesses, some saucy, some weary, some bright, some stupid. But all of them have certain basic characteristics which the spectator recognizes as "princess." If the actor creates a character which doesn't in any way fit within the stereotype, the audience is disappointed and refuses to participate in the play with the character. The spectator will say, "That's no princess; she doesn't act, look, or sound like a princess."

The actor must be directed to play between the extremes. His characterization must be conceivable to the audience; it must fit the audience's image of what the character is. At the same time, the actor must always search for new ways of elaborating his characterization so that it doesn't fall into the category of the stock type.

CRITICIZING THE ACTOR

The term *criticism* is misleading. In popular parlance, it has developed a negative connotation. To criticize means to disapprove. Actually, criticism is the process of rendering a judgment according to certain standards. The judgment may be either favorable or unfavorable. Approval is criticism just as much as disapproval. The term, *criticism,* throughout this discussion is used in its broader sense.

Criticism of the actor presents a difficult problem in obtaining objectivity. In almost every other type of artistic endeavor the artist can stand apart from his work and examine it objectively. When the painter has finished a canvas, he is able to step back and look at it. He may not be able to disassociate his own feelings from the work, but at least a critic can point to specific strengths and weaknesses in the work. The true artist should be able to establish an objective attitude toward his work. Acting cannot be separated from the actor. Since the actor is subjectively involved in the process, it is impossible for him to stand aside at the time of creation and evaluate his art. Nor can he stand back from it later, for the art is fleeting and disappears the moment the process of acting ceases.

Since the actor is unable to disassociate himself from his work, another factor frequently confuses the process of criticizing acting. His art is so personal that he is prone to construe criticism of his acting as a criticism of himself. It is said that some actors take criticism very well; others, badly. The source of the difficulty when the actor is balky about the evaluation of his work is almost always found in the actor's inability to separate himself from his work. When the character he is creating is judged, he feels that he, as a person, is being judged. If the judgment is unfavorable, he is hurt personally. If we add to this difficulty the tremendous sensitivity and emotional excitability of most actors, it is not surprising that the criticism of acting is a difficult job.

Procedure in Criticism

All criticism should be in terms of the play rather than the actor. Assuming the common goal of a fine production, each action of the actor must be judged in accordance with its contribution to the whole. The director should always maintain a completely objective and impersonal attitude himself. If the director treats one actor with a consideration not shown the next, the actors soon lose faith in his fairness. Since any artist tends to fall in love with his own work, the actor who senses partiality will erect a barrier between himself and the director.

Be liberal with praise, but be careful to praise the acting, not the actor. Be certain that objective reasons are given for the favorable criticism. Many directors neglect the positive aspects of criticism. It is as important for the actor to know what he is doing well as it is for him to know what he is doing badly. If they can see and understand the reasons for their improvement, most actors, being human, will work harder than if they are notified only of their failures. Positive criticism of one piece of work may also stand as a goal for other actors to achieve. As a matter of fact, this is one of the best ways to establish an objective attitude. Any actor can be painfully objective about another actor's work. If the strength of one actor is set as a model for other actors to work toward, a clear objective goal can be set before them.

Never make purely negative criticisms. They serve no purpose other than to demoralize the actor. Minimize the failure and emphasize the solution to the problem. A good rule of thumb for directors and also a good rule for everyday living: Never make a negative criticism until you can couple it with a positive or constructive suggestion.

The thesis of the preceding discussion should be apparent. The actor is not a machine, a puppet; he is a sensitive, imaginative, creative being. Treated well, stimulated to creative heights, taught to express his emotional depth with technical sureness, the actor makes the show.

19

Floor Plans and Settings

EVERY DIRECTOR should be vitally interested in the settings for his production, regardless of whether or not he is responsible for designing and building them. Assuming the cooperation of a technical director who is responsible for the specific design and construction of the sets, the play director must be able to evaluate the artistry and practicability of a particular design. In addition, he should take an active part in the creation of the floor plan.

Remember that a good setting can do much to help the play. A poor one can create insurmountable obstacles to direction. This discussion does not aim to provide the answers to scenic design or construction. The director who has complete responsibility for the settings should turn to one of the many books in the bibliography covering this subject.

THE STAGE

The modern stage is the result of the increasing need for illusion and the complication of technical devices. As the stage machinery increased, the acting areas were gradually withdrawn behind the proscenium arch. The modern stage is a "picture frame" stage because the spectator views the scene through a picture frame made by the proscenium arch. The modern stage is sometimes called a "peep hole" stage because the spectator is set apart from the stage and looks through the peep hole of the proscenium into the lighted box of the stage area beyond.

A revolution against the picture frame stage is in progress in

many quarters. This "new" staging, now called *central staging,
staging-in-the-round, arena style, ring staging,* etc., is a reversion to
the earliest stage arrangement in which the playing area is placed
in the center of the audience. Since central staging has many things
to recommend it and is coming into ever increasing vogue, a
separate chapter is devoted to a discussion of this style (see Chapter 22).

Despite the trend toward the central stage, most modern plays
are written for and produced on the picture frame stage. Therefore, this standard staging procedure merits first consideration.

The Physical Stage

A floor plan view of the picture frame stage and auditorium is
shown in Figure 26. The stage is delimited at the front by the
footlights and an apron, the last vestige of the earlier forestage.
On either side, the proscenium arch rises as a vast picture frame
enclosing the opening. Directly behind the proscenium opening is
the front or act curtain which may be raised and lowered much
like a guillotine, from which it takes its name, or may be opened
laterally, in which case it is called a *traveller.* Behind the front
curtain are the devices for adjusting the size of the playing opening to fit the playing requirements of a particular setting. These
are: the teaser, an overhead drapery obstructing the audience's
view of the rigging and top of the stage house; the tormentors,
which are standing pieces that slide on or off the stage to cut
down the width of the proscenium opening; and the returns, masking pieces attached to the front edge of the setting and run offstage
behind the tormentors. In many modern productions the lateral
masking is accomplished by attaching the tormentor to the downstage edge of the setting, thereby eliminating the return. It should
also be noted that in many small theatres the traveller hangs
behind a grand drapery or permanent teaser. Back of the masking
pieces is the setting, which encloses the playing area. The setting
may take many forms; it may be a bare stage enclosed by draperies;
it may be a wing and drop setting (see Chapter 21); or it may be
a "box" setting composed of the three walls of a room with a
ceiling.

Numerous variations are possible in the structure of the stage,
in the arrangement of the masking pieces and the type of setting,

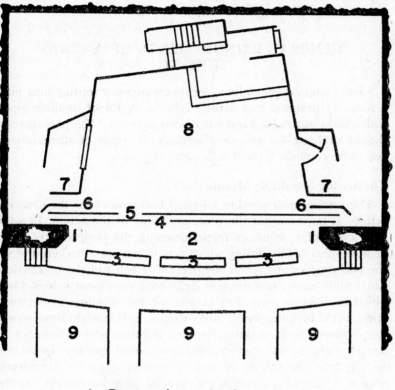

1. Proscenium Arch
2. Apron
3. Foots
4. Teaser
5. Curtain Line
6. Tormentors
7. Returns
8. Box Setting
9. Seats

FIG. 26. FLOOR PLAN OF STAGE AND AUDITORIUM

but the conventional arrangement seen in Figure 26 is typical of most modern picture frame stages.

GENERAL REQUIREMENTS OF A GOOD SETTING

Scene designers generally agree that a superior setting must meet a series of practical and artistic criteria. A list of qualities upon which most authorities agree is discussed below. The play director should evaluate his proposed settings in terms of these criteria before he commits himself to a particular plan.

The Setting Should Be Meaningful

The setting must provide a logical background for the dramatic action. It must suggest the place and time of the action. In addition, every play, comic or tragic, demands the projection of mood or atmosphere. The setting which acts in part as a background for the performers must reflect the prevailing spirit of the production. Line, mass, color, texture, and light have emotional values. Combined in different ways, they project specific meanings to the audience. In the broadest terms, bulky masses, bold straight lines, strong deep colors, harsh textures, somber lighting project a heavy or serious tone. In varying combinations, more specific moods may be created. The feeling of power, majesty, austerity, decadence, even a feeling of bitterness and squalor may be created. At the opposite extreme, delicate use of mass, fragile curved lines, light vibrant colors, smooth textures, and vivid lighting project a feeling of gaiety and vivacity, of brightness and life. The implication should be obvious. The setting can aid the production by complementing the mood of the play, or it can seriously hinder projection of the proper mood. The director must be certain that his settings denote the proper meanings.

The Setting Should Be Attractive

In design and execution the background which appears as the curtain rises should be pleasing to the eye. Either improper design or poor taste can invalidate the worth of a setting. Regardless of the style in which the setting is created, nothing in the setting should distract from the central theme or idea of the production.

Some settings are so ornate, grandiose, or beautiful that they attract attention and even acclaim. The setting should act as an integral part of the production, not compete with the production. Beauty without meaning is to be decried. Competition between the director and the scene designer can destroy the unity of a production.

The Setting Should Be Practical

Several times in the preceding discussion the setting has been referred to as a background. It should be more than that. It must facilitate the action. The director should be vitally interested in the practical aspects of the setting.

The setting must have a workable floor plan. Despite beauty and expressiveness, it may still be a poor setting if the arrangement does not permit adequate movement, meaningful entrances and exits, and satisfactory playing areas. The superior setting actually motivates the action. Let us assume that the place of the dramatic action is a drawing room and the characters are a family. This stage family must do more than parade before the background of a room. They live in the room during the action of the play. The performers should be able to use the room as easily, comfortably, and efficiently as any similar group does in everyday life; yet the three-sided room of the stage setting is actually very unlike life. Because of the peculiarities of the stage, the arrangement of doors, windows, a fireplace and a staircase can aid in creating the illusion of natural, comfortable living, or it can destroy it.

Just as the arrangement of the setting affects the performance, so does the placement of the furniture. People tend to cluster on, near, or about furniture. If a feeling of naturalness is to be created, the stage people must appear to follow the same patterns of living that actual people do. The single open wall of the stage creates difficulties. Furniture should be placed so that it creates a feeling of reality and, at the same time, meets the needs of the stage action.

PLANNING THE SETTING

The director is interested in the beauty and meaning of the stage setting, but its practicality or usefulness may spell the difference between success and failure of the production. Every director, therefore, should be conversant with the steps in planning the setting.

Most of the discussion in this section concerns the box setting, for a major proportion of the plays produced call for box settings or simple variations of this form.

The Form of the Setting

The form of the setting, whether it be a wood and canvas box setting, a drapery setting, a formalized platform or a bare stage, must be determined by the need for expression, the demands of beauty, and the requirements of practicality found in the play. Many directors are distressed by the sameness of form in settings and search frantically for scenic novelties. Scenic novelties, if they do not serve a real, expressive purpose, are meaningless and disruptive, however attractive they may be.

The Shape of the Setting

Most settings are rectangular for the simple reason that more serviceable acting space is provided by the rectangle than by any other shape. Manifold variations of the rectangle are possible for variety, but the basic form is usually maintained.

One other shape deserves consideration—the triangle. The playing space of the triangle is comparatively limited, for the downstage points of the triangle are not serviceable playing areas. This limitation in space makes the triangular setting ideal for small, intimate scenes involving two or three people.

The Size of the Setting

The ideal basis for determining the size of a setting is the impression that the setting must give and the number of people it must accommodate. For example, if the scene is the cramped tenement basement home of the Esdras family in Maxwell Anderson's *Winterset*, the opening will be restricted. It may be narrow and shallow with a low ceiling. Cluttered with heating pipes and crowded by the seven people who congregate during the scene, the desired tight, confused, stifled impression will be created. The exterior setting from the same play, a street scene laid under the Brooklyn Bridge, ideally needs vast width, depth, and height. The contrast between the cramped tenement and the freedom of the outside is basic to the meaning of the play. If only a small stage is available, the director will have to compromise or occasionally avoid plays that make immoderate demands on the stage. In most cases, imaginative ingenuity can make up for a lack of equipment.

Numerous Settings

Any play with several settings should be studied to find out whether some of the settings can be eliminated. Many shows written for Broadway production before the inflation concurrent with World War II called for more numerous and more lavish settings than were necessary to the successful production of the show. Elimination of settings reduces the visual variety, but it may make possible the production of plays that were previously discarded for economic reasons.

If the play to be produced has several sets, however, the director's prime concern is the speed with which they can be shifted. Any change of setting, if it stops the action of the play within an act or lengthens the intermission between acts, handicaps the projection of the play's moods and message. In Chapter 22, several methods for handling multiple settings in the musical show are analyzed. The shifting principles are similar in the regular production.

Change in the style of the setting can make multiple settings more economical and easier to handle. The unit setting provides economy and speed. Large prop pieces set in front of a cyclorama setting suggesting locale and mood are also economical and easy to shift. Exploration of different scenic styles may facilitate the production of the multiple set play.

The Sight Lines of the Setting

A sight line may be defined as the line of vision from any seat in the house to the stage. The poorest sight lines are those from seats at the extreme sides or at the top of the balcony. Except for scenes with high staircases or platforms that cannot be seen from the top of the balcony, the director is most concerned with lateral sight lines, those drawn from the worst seats on the sides. Actually, the usable portion of the stage is determined by the sight lines. In Figure 27 the limitations imposed by poor sight lines are indicated. The shaded areas in the figure cannot be used for any important action because they cannot be seen. Note that if the opening of the setting in Figure 27 is made narrower, the sight lines grow steadily worse. Since sight lines determine the playing

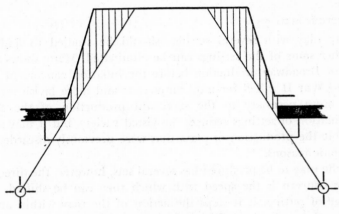

FIG. 27. LATERAL SIGHT LINES

areas, they also affect the placement of furniture, doors, windows, in fact any part of the stage to be used. Every director must check the sight lines of his theatre before planning the settings for the play.

Architectural Logic in the Setting

Any stage room must be planned with at least a semblance of architectural logic. An interior door cannot be in the same wall as an exterior window unless some suggestion is given that the house has a wing. The hallway to the kitchen cannot logically also be the hallway to the front of the house without explanation. In planning a setting, visualize the architecture of the whole and be certain that the segment represented on the stage is reasonable.

PLANNING THE PARTS OF THE SETTING

After the form, shape, size, and number of settings have been planned with consideration given to the sight lines and architectural logic, the parts of the setting must be selected and arranged.

This selection and arrangement can materially affect the direction of the play.

Placement of Entrances

Entrances serve an important function in the play. The entering or exiting character is usually a dominant character; therefore, principal doorways and arches should be placed to give maximum dramatic value to the entering character. Usually, the principal doorway is placed in the back wall. This permits the entering character to be seen by the entire audience as soon as he comes onto the stage. An upstage center doorway is called a *center door-fancy*. Its presence strengthens the upstage center playing areas by framing characters who stand in front of it.

Additional doorways should be placed with architectural logic in the side walls to provide variety in the movement pattern of the entrances and exits. The director should avoid having all of the entrances on one side of the stage. Such an arrangement creates an almost insurmountable problem in movement. The rest of the setting becomes a cul-de-sac from which it is virtually impossible to extricate characters.

Unless there is a specific reason to the contrary, doors should be hinged on the upstage edge, so that they swing up and off stage. This placement of the door panel serves two purposes. It is self-masking, the opening of the door masking the area upstage of it, and the exiting character may stand in an open body position with his hand on the door knob. When the door is opened the actor can leave the stage immediately. If a door is hung so that it opens into the stage area, the actor has to step back as he opens the door, walk around it, and reach in to close the door behind him.

Doorways should be labelled for the audience by the action of the play. The kitchen area of the house can be defined by the coming and going of servants. A study doorway may be labelled by reference to it in the dialogue. Stairs to the second floor may be toward the front or the rear of the house, provided they are carefully defined. Consistent use of the doorway for the purpose indicated is essential. The audience will accept any reasonable designation for a doorway until a character appears through a door when it is not logical for him to do so. Then the door acts as a distraction.

Finally, it is essential that doorways be used. The audience is curious about a doorway that is not labelled or used. It acts as a constant distraction. In a recent production, it took over two hours for the audience to discover that a rather prominent down-stage doorway was an additional bedroom. Fertile imaginations had by that time created all kinds of mysteries concealed by the unopened door. Needless to say, the auditors' attention was not on the play.

The principles that have been discussed are illustrated in the conventional drawing room shown in Figure 28. Analyze the principles and practice laying out different combinations of entrances, maintaining architectural logic, dramatic emphasis, good visibility, variety, and proper hinging. Study the play at hand and label the doors, noting their consistency of use. Remember, too few entrances rather than too many!

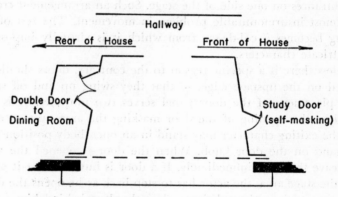

FIG. 28. CONVENTIONAL ENTRANCES

Placement of Windows

The arrangement of windows is determined by the desirability of having the audience look through them. If a window is placed in an upstage position, especially if it is on the back wall, the problem of masking or providing a view through the window is much greater than that for a window in a side wall downstage. Despite the difficulty, it may be desirable to create a picture window. An upstage window may enhance entrances, for the entering character can be seen by the audience before he comes through the doorway. The need for such a window is exceptional rather than usual. One further difficulty is created by the picture window. A character who looks through it will unavoidably have his back at least partially turned to the audience (see Figure 29, Character 1). Also, the audience will be able to see everything that the character sees unless he places the offstage events well to one side of the window.

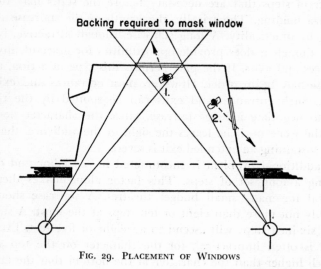

FIG. 29. PLACEMENT OF WINDOWS

Usually the disadvantages of the upstage window decisively outweigh the advantages. For this reason, most windows are set in the side walls, where the audience is unable to see much through them (see Figure 29, Character 2). Such placement allows a character in the play to describe outside events that would be impossible to stage. An additional advantage of the downstage window is the position of the character who is looking out the window. If he stands at the upstage edge of the window his body position is partially open and his face may be clearly seen by the audience. One disadvantage of the window in the side wall is the poor sight line. The farther upstage the window is placed, the poorer the sight line will be. The advantages and disadvantages are illustrated in Figure 29.

Placement of the Staircase

Staircases add dramatic motivation to a setting by allowing the director to arrange compositions with differences in level. This adds variety to the playing and provides opportunities for establishing compositional dominance by placing one character higher than another.

The length of the staircase is determined architecturally by the number of steps that are necessary before the stairs may turn or end in a landing. Theatrically, the length of the staircase is controlled by practicality. A long staircase, though attractive, is hard to use, though it does provide opportunities for graceful, involved entrances and exits. If the play permits this type of action, a long staircase may be in order. However, most entrances and exits are abrupt. Such entrances and exits can be spoiled by the time it takes to negotiate a long staircase. Since the character does not leave the scene until he leaves the sight of the audience, the problem of sustaining an extended exit is severe.

An additional problem is encountered in the labor and cost of building a long set of steps. This factor alone makes them impractical for many small budget theatres. A staircase should be probably not more than eight or ten steps at the most. A staircase of ten six-inch steps will ascend to a height of five feet. Even this height is often impractical, for the character on the top step is so much higher than the character at the bottom that the arrangement appears awkward. For compositional purposes, a landing raised 18 to 24 inches is sufficient to establish a pleasant difference in height. Short staircases that stop at a low landing and then turn out of sight are ideal for playing purposes.

Frequently staircases are placed in the hallway back of a center arch. They serve little or no purpose in the playing but do give the impression of an upstairs area. Usually no more than three or four steps are necessary to give the impression. If a staircase is to be used in the action, it should be placed either on the back wall or on an upstage section of the side wall of the set. A notable exception was the staircase in the original setting for *The Innocents*, which ran the entire length of one side wall and projected well onto the stage. In this instance, the setting was built around the staircase. Generally, the staircase is merely a part of the setting.

Several practical and impractical staircase arrangements are pictured in Figure 30.

The most frequently used staircase arrangement is shown in A. A deep hall with the projection of one end of a staircase suggests an upstairs area. As mentioned before, it is too far upstage to materially affect the action. The staircase in B stops on a landing

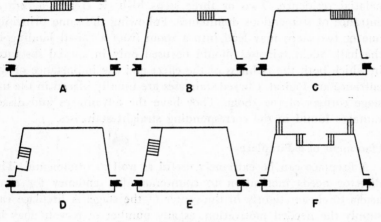

FIG. 30. STAIRCASE PLACEMENT

in sight of the audience. The landing can be eliminated by building a wall which begins at the top of the steps. This has a playing advantage over the staircase shown in C, for the staircase has been brought onstage far enough so that all of the audience can see it. In C, the staircase is lost in the upstage left corner of the setting. It is in a weak area with poor sight lines. On the other hand, the staircase in C does not take up as much stage space as the one in B. Stairs are bulky pieces. The tread, the part of the stair on which you step, is usually one foot deep. The amount of lost playing space can be readily calculated. The stair arrangement in drawing D should usually be avoided. Note that the rising framework of the staircase tends to cover the person who is climbing. This negates the purpose of the staircase. In exceptional instances, in which an extremely dominant downstage area is needed, the staircase shown in D may be used if it is no more than three or four steps high. The staircase shown in E is practical because it uses a minimum of playing space. Note, however, that any side staircase is superior for entrances but inferior for exits. The entering character is in full view of the audience. The exiting character will have his back turned to the audience. Thus most exits up a side staircase are handled by having the character run up a few steps and then turn back to speak.

The double staircase in F is a novelty which might fit into a palatial residence. Two or three steps high, it creates a central entrance of tremendous dominance. Following the same principle, one or two steps may lead into a room from a raised landing in the hall. Such staircases should be used only in special instances in which both the richness of the effect and the importance of the entrance are logical. Curved staircases are usually placed in the upstage corners of the room. They have the advantages and disadvantages found in the corresponding straight staircases.

Placement of a Fireplace

A fireplace can be extremely useful as well as ornamental. The director needs motivation to counteract the tendency for characters to cluster tightly in the center of the stage. A fireplace can supply the needed motivation, as any number of reasons may be devised for a character's movement to the fireplace or the mantel. In addition, it has a logical attraction for the character who is supposed to reflect while others carry on the action.

The usefulness of a fireplace depends largely on its placement. A fireplace located well downstage on a side wall is close enough to the centers of action so that characters may frequently turn to it. In addition, the character can easily stand at the fireplace so that his face can be seen.

The ornamental fireplace is better placed in the center of the back wall. In this position it dominates the entire setting and creates a delightful impression. The upstage position, however, decreases its usefulness. Since most action is played in the downstage areas, a character has to turn his back to walk to the fireplace. In addition, the natural positions for standing at the fireplace will force him into closed body positions. The choice of the two locations depends upon whether the fireplace is more important as a motivating force or as a set decoration.

The fireplace, like the staircase, is a great consumer of space.

Every director should consider carefully whether the size of the stage area can accommodate a six to eight-foot fireplace.

Balance in the Setting

The principles for balancing the setting are identical to those employed in balancing the composition (see Chapter 7 for a detailed discussion of balance). The setting must be in balance within the proscenium frame. An unbalanced setting acts as a constant distraction to the audience. Doorways, windows, staircases, fireplaces, and bulky props such as pianos are heavy masses that must be equally distributed in the setting if balance is to be maintained. Always examine the distribution of mass while the setting is in the paper and pencil stage. Care at this point will save money and grief later on.

PLANNING THE FURNITURE ARRANGEMENT

Furniture is functional in life and on the stage. The primary function in each case is to provide a logical place for people to gather and converse. Since the purpose is apparently similar in life and on the stage, one might logically assume that the arrangement should be similar. Nothing is farther from the truth. Normally, furniture is arranged to conform to the contours of the room. On the stage some pieces are placed primarily to create an illusion of reality, but the key pieces are placed with regard to their motivational possibilities and their relationships to the acting areas, the traffic lanes, the conversational groupings, the entrances and exits.

Conventional Arrangement

In Figure 31 a conventional theatrical furniture arrangement is shown. Variations are possible, but they must satisfy the criteria of acceptable furniture arrangement. Some directors may be annoyed by the conventional arrangement of furniture in the theatre, but there are some very good reasons for it. In the first place, the stage must be kept in balance. Second, the actors who use the furniture must be seen; therefore the furniture should be set so that it partly faces the audience. Third, furniture is used as the center of much of the stage action; therefore, it must be placed at the centers of action and within the sight lines of the house. A fourth reason for traditional placement is to provide more than one reasonably intimate conversational grouping. Fifth, the furniture must leave effective traffic lanes to and from the entrances and the centers of action. And finally, furniture is set downstage so that audibility can be kept at a maximum.

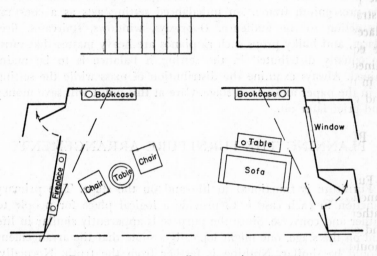

FIG. 31. CONVENTIONAL FURNITURE ARRANGEMENT

Examine the arrangement in Figure 31 in terms of these criteria. Hypothetical sight lines are shown by dotted lines. The conventional arrangement centers the furniture well within the audience's view and within the principal playing space. This arrangement provides two distinct conversational groupings. People may either cluster about the davenport or about the chairs and table. Note also that the chairs and table are placed close enough to the fireplace to make it a part of the conversational grouping. The three entrances are uncluttered by furniture. Just as in any house, there is room for a free flow of traffic. And finally, the furniture is placed somewhat downstage so that conversations can be easily heard. These are the reasons for a conventional arrangement. Let us examine the strengths and weaknesses of some of the possible variations.

Variations in Arrangement

The most popular variation is to place the davenport center with chairs flanking it on either side. This arrangement is satisfactory, but it increases the dominance of the davenport and makes it the only real conversational unit. Note in Figure 32, A, how the furniture acts as a fence separating the downstage and upstage areas. If the davenport is set center, the upstage center entrance is wasted. It loses its emphatic value because anyone entering through the doorway is cut off at the waist by the davenport and runs into the furniture fence as he comes downstage. The entrance should be changed if such a furniture arrangement is desired. The preceding discussion is not meant to discourage use of the centrally

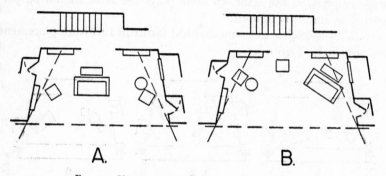

A.   B.

Fig. 32. Variations in Furniture Arrangement

placed davenport, but rather to encourage study of the play to see if it is helped or hindered by such an arrangement. An intimate play involving three or four characters may gain by having one extremely dominant piece of furniture. Another arrangement is suggested in Figure 32, B. Apply the criteria suggested above, and the faults of this furniture plot quickly manifest themselves.

Common Faults in Furniture Arrangement

There are at least eight common errors in furniture arrangement. Each of these faults causes pictorial or motivational problems.

Too much furniture. The director, eager to provide lots of opportunity for creating new business, may clutter his stage with furniture. Pictorially, the stage picture is spoiled because the simplicity and grace is gone. In addition, the actor feels cramped by the furniture; movement patterns become illogical; entrances and traffic lanes are blocked. Some pieces of furniture are covered by other pieces. The players seem to wend their ways through a maze. Even in arranging a fussy Victorian room, elaborate styling is more important in creating the desired impression than the number of pieces.

Too little furniture. In most cases a lack of furniture gives a barren quality and creates a psychological hazard for the actor. Most inexperienced actors feel lost on an open stage. They are unable to sustain emotion without things to do and places to go. Furniture helps them feel at home. On the other hand, extreme simplicity—indeed, bareness—may at times be desirable. The bare stage emphasizes the actor. In some plays the actor should be permitted to stand by himself.

Some of the other more mechanical faults in furniture placement are shown in Figure 33.

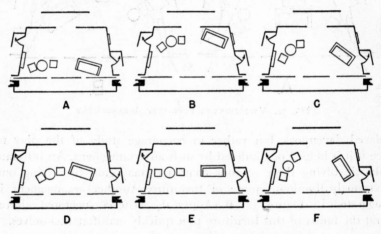

FIG. 33. COMMON ERRORS IN FURNITURE ARRANGEMENT

Furniture crowded downstage. In Figure 33, A, the furniture forms a wall between the actors and the audience. The strong downstage acting areas are eliminated. Frequently directors place the furniture on the playing line for maximum vocal projection. Any gain in audibility is far outweighed by the losses in illusion and practicality. The furniture appears to fall out of the picture frame. It is hard to get to and to play on. Finally, such an arrangement discourages a logical pattern of movement.

Furniture crowded upstage. In B, the furniture is arranged so that a void is created in front of it. This open area is difficult to use as the characters tend to gravitate toward the furniture. In addition, actors who are placed on or near the furniture appear to be withdrawn from the audience.

Furniture crowded to the sides. In C, the scene is split down the middle. It is difficult to motivate action in the bare area, center stage. The conversational groupings are separated by an unbridgeable chasm.

Furniture crowded to the center. In D, the central placement limits the effective use of the strongest acting area on the stage and emphasizes the side areas. Pictorially, an impression of an island of furniture in a sea of space is created. In addition, the traffic lanes are pushed to the sides, and a fence is established.

Furniture set in a line. The line of furniture in E limits the action. Compositions will have little depth. The players logically drawn to the furniture will work into a line conforming with that of the furniture. Finally, such an arrangement is dull and uninteresting.

Furniture set at sharp angles. In F, the angle or rake of the furniture hinders successful playing. If two characters are placed on the davenport, the downstage character will cover the upstage character, no matter how deep the former sits or how shallow the upstage character sits. In addition, the downstage character must talk upstage when addressing his friend, thus sacrificing both visibility and audibility. In fact, the sharp angle at which the furniture is placed makes it difficult to see or hear either character clearly.

Problem Pieces of Furniture

Certain pieces of furniture are pictorially attractive but functionally impractical. The chair with a low seat may be comfortable, but it is impractical on the stage if a good deal of sitting and rising is necessary. The same is true of the lounge chair or davenport with a very deep seat. The actor disappears from sight as he sinks back into it and appears even more foolish when he struggles to extricate himself. Have the property crew check the sitting qualities as well as the style and appearance of each piece of furniture.

The coffee table is an attractive addition but often turns out to be a bugaboo in direction. The davenport must be placed farther upstage to make room for it. An aisle large enough for easy passage must be left both above and below it. Finally, it hampers a quick, forceful rise and cross from the davenport because the actor must detour around the table. If tea scenes are mandatory in the play, a butler's tray can be brought on and later removed.

Lamps are needed to give the impression of a light source in evening scenes. They are also attractive ornaments on the setting, but they may make composition difficult. Floor lamps should not be set in their normal positions behind chairs. If they are so placed no one can stand back of the chair without being covered by the lamp. The same principle holds for tall table lamps. Light source can be adequately indicated by a chandelier or wall brackets. Torchiers standing against the upstage walls or very low table lamps which do not obstruct the action are two other possibilities.

THE FLOOR OR GROUND PLAN

Almost every drawing in this book is an example of a floor or ground plan. The floor plan may be defined as the view of the stage one would have if he were suspended directly above it. In the floor plan, walls appear as lines; furniture has only its top side showing.

The floor plan has many uses. It is fundamental to designing the setting and arranging the furniture. It may be used to determine sight lines. Prior to rehearsal, the director may use a floor plan in plotting the action. It should be laid out in actual size on the floor of the rehearsal room to aid in blocking the movement. The director should always approve the floor plan of the setting before construction begins.

The Use of Scale

Any ground plan must be drawn to scale to be meaningful. Many students shy away from the use of scale as though it implied some magic formula. Actually, drawing to scale is very simple. The actual size of objects can be reduced to smaller proportions by substituting a fraction of the full size throughout the measurements. Suppose that we are interested in plotting the proscenium opening of a stage thirty feet wide. A line showing the actual size of the opening would be thirty feet long. This line may be reduced to any desired scale. Suppose the scale is one inch equals one foot ($1'' = 1'$). The line showing the proscenium opening will be thirty inches in length. Every measurement on the setting will be correspondingly reduced. A practical scale which fits a large piece of paper is one-half inch equals one foot ($\frac{1}{2}'' = 1'$). Using the scale, the line representing the thirty foot proscenium will be fifteen inches long.

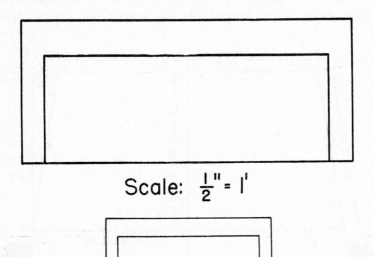

Scale: $\frac{1}{2}'' = 1'$

Scale: $\frac{1}{4}'' = 1'$

FIG. 34. A DAVENPORT IN TWO SCALES

In Figure 34, the floor plan view of a davenport is shown in two scales. Use a ruler and check the measurements. The davenport is seven feet long and three feet wide; the arms are six inches wide and the back is nine inches thick.

Many beginning directors have considerable difficulty in laying out a setting because they have no accurate idea of the size of various parts of a room and pieces of furniture. Measure several fireplaces, staircases, doorways, chairs, tables, even people. The ability to visualize should begin to develop.

Laying Out a Floor Plan

One method for making a floor plan is discussed below. Follow each of the steps in order (see Figure 35).

1. Draw a floor plan view of the proscenium opening to some practical scale.
2. Find the center of the proscenium opening. Decide upon the desirable opening for the setting. In Figure 35, the opening of the setting is the same size as the proscenium opening. Move

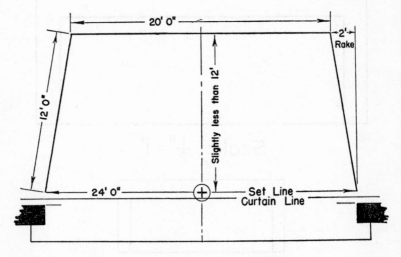

FIG. 35. FLOOR PLAN OF A SIMPLE BOX SETTING

sufficiently upstage so that there is room for the curtain. Then draw in the set line.

3. Determine the length of the side walls and the amount of rake desirable. *Rake* is the angle at which a piece of furniture or scenery is placed in relationship to the footlights. Most side walls are raked slightly to help accommodate the sight lines. Lay out the side walls.

4. Connect the side walls with a line which forms the back wall. The length of the back wall depends upon the amount of rake in the side walls. Usually the rake is determined in a ratio of one foot of rake for each four to six feet of wall. Note that the depth of the setting is slightly less than the length of the side wall. This is caused by the rake. The length of the side walls rather than the exact depth of the setting should be laid out first so that no odd-sized flats are needed.

5. Masking pieces may be added to the downstage edges of the side walls. These tormentors or returns carry the setting off behind the proscenium arch. At this point you will have a perfectly plain three-walled setting. Any number of variations in shape may be drawn following the same basic procedure. For example, the setting in Figure 26 has radically different dimensions.

6. Lay out entrances, windows, staircase, fireplace, and other features. Examine other drawings in this chapter for the method of symbolizing these pieces. The beginner can save time and erasures by laying out to scale on a separate sheet of paper the doors, windows, etc., which are called for in the play. These pieces may be cut out and moved about on the floor plan until a pleasant arrangement is obtained.

7. Arrange the furniture. Again, the director can save time if he will draw the different pieces of furniture to scale on a piece of light cardboard. They may be cut out and juggled on the floor plan until an ideal arrangement is reached. Draw in the furniture arrangement, and the plan is complete.

The Scale Model

Many directors cannot visualize the actual setting from a floor plan. A three-dimensional model can clear up this difficulty. The walls for the model may be cut from a stiff paper and fitted over the floor plan. The entrances and windows can be cut out of the paper. Furniture may even be constructed to scale with a little imagination.

There is no doubt that a complete model of the setting is helpful. On the other hand, model making is a time consuming process. With a little practice, anyone can lay out a useful floor plan in a minimum of time.

The character does not play in front of the scenery; he is surrounded by the scenery. The scene establishes his environment. If this stage environment is not conducive to the kind of living demanded by the script, the character is lost. The director must make certain that the scenery actively promotes a better production.

20

Crowd and Group Scenes

MANY DIRECTORS avoid plays with crowd scenes as they would avoid the plague. If the crowd cannot be eliminated from the script the play is discarded. Why? Probably because the director has been distressed at one time or another by his inability to make a stage crowd seem real. His extras stood about the stage like wooden puppets, looking uneasy and uncomfortable. They cheered on cue with doubtful enthusiasm. They fidgeted and fussed between outbursts. They stumbled over each other on entering and exiting. They blocked the audience's view of the principals. The crowd subtracted from, rather than added to, the play.

Most of the difficulty in staging crowd scenes stems from a lack of knowledge of crowd activity in life. Before the director can create a good stage crowd, he must understand the reason for the crowd's gathering, the make-up of the crowd, the bases for activity in the crowd, the psychological principles underlying all crowd reaction.

Why Crowds Gather

The hour is midnight. The city is asleep. At a quiet intersection the screech of brakes, the shriek of torn and twisted metal, a human scream—silence. The crowd gathers. By ones and twos—some silent, some garrulous, some eager, some furtive—they come. In a few minutes a hundred people may surround the wreckage. After the ambulance and the police have performed their duties, the crowd dissolves. By ones and twos—some silent, some garrulous, some eager, some furtive—they go. Why did they come? They responded to a stimulus. They felt a need, an urge, a desire to come.

Each man had his own reason. Some were merely curious. Some thought they might help. For some there was a morbid fascination in disaster. For others it was a chance to see real drama in action. They came for the same reasons that people go to the theatre, in response to their individual needs. Each crowd member's actions while at the scene were based upon his reason for coming, his individual characteristics, his background of experience.

In *Winterset*, Lucia, a good-hearted Italian, hauls his street piano back to its shed under the Brooklyn Bridge. He has been evicted from the street. Before putting the piano away, he decides to play one more tune. Out of the silence of the night a crowd gathers: an applewoman, two urchins, a sailor and his girl, a hobo, a radical, two other girls, two pedestrians, the two young lovers Mio and Miriamne, and a policeman. Why has this crowd gathered? Because they felt a desire to come. Each was attracted by the stimulus of the music. Some came to dance, some to watch, some to laugh and deride, and one came to perform his duty. As in the previous scene each member's actions are governed by his reason for coming, his individual characteristics, and his background.

So it is with every crowd. Whether people gather to see a hanging or to drink and dance in a Viennese garden, they come because they, as individuals, are responding to a stimulus. They may even be brought against their wills, as a group of prisoners dragged before the court. But still they are present for a reason. Each individual responds and reacts to the situation in terms of his own reason for being a member of the crowd.

THE MAKE-UP OF THE CROWD

Too often a director thinks of a crowd as a mass. As a result, his direction is limited to instructions to the group. This procedure overlooks the make-up of the crowd. The crowd does not react as an entity except in a time of great excitement. The crowd's reactions to a single stimulus are as varied as the components of which the crowd is made.

Individual Motivation

Every crowd is composed of individuals. Each individual, as we have seen, has his own reason for being a member of the crowd.

In a like manner, each individual differs from every other member of the crowd in his reaction to the stimulus. One of the differences between the two crowds that have been described is that Anderson has given identities to the members of his crowd. Each of these labels depicts an individual who may respond differently from others to the same stimulus. When the policeman tries to silence Lucia's music, the applewoman defends Lucia's right to earn a living; the sailor jeers at the cop; the radical makes a speech on capitalistic oppression; one girl retreats fearfully into the background; another pleads for music to dance; the urchins run; Mio vents his hate for policemen. Each person responds within the framework of his own individual motivational pattern. In this instance, the playwright has provided the director with all the individual characteristics. The clarity of this motivation makes the crowd in *Winterset* one of the best in all drama.

Most playwrights are not so considerate. They treat the crowd as an indistinguishable mass. It then becomes the responsibility of the director to provide the labels and the motivation for each of the individuals in the crowd. To tell a member of the crowd that he is a villager is not enough. He must be given a specific role to play. The more varied the people who gather in the crowd, the more variety and excitement the reactions of the crowd can convey.

The Integral Unit

In one sense, a crowd is composed of individuals; in another sense, it is not composed of individuals at all. This may seem to present a paradox, but it is true. The integral unit in the crowd is not the individual but the small cluster of two or three people. In the crowd at the accident, most of the people came in small groups; some family units, a husband and wife, a parent and child, a brother and sister; some social units, a fellow and his girl, two couples who left a game of cards. In the scene from *Winterset,* note the groupings: a couple of girls, a couple of pedestrians, two or three youngsters, a pair of lovers, the pianoman, and the applewoman.

In each case, the members of the small clusters or integral units are bound together by some common tie. The presence of this tie affects the way each responds to the principal stimulus. The crowd members respond as individuals, and they also respond within their own small groups, for motivational forces are present within this unit.

The director must determine the integral units within his crowd. When this is done he has established two levels of reaction: the individual response to the major stimulus and the response within the unit.

Still a third level of response is found in the crowd, the response between integral units. Many of the clusters will not extend their responses beyond their own units. Other clusters, however, depending upon the power of the stimulus, may react with other groups. This interaction between integral units breaks down the units and causes a new type of response. In the case of the young man and his girl at the accident, *at the individual level of response* the man is curious, the girl is frightened; *at the unit level of response,* the young man, being interested in the girl, comforts her in her fear; *at the third level of response,* the young couple approaches another couple, and they talk together about the accident. The motivation has changed again. The integral unit has dissolved into a larger group. The young couple will conduct themselves differently with these strangers than they would if they were alone. If the strangers withdraw, the unit re-forms.

Mass Reactions

It was stated at the outset that in exceptional instances the crowd may respond as a mass. In almost every case, even the mass reaction is modified by the unit response. Although there is some uniformity in the response of the integral units to the primary stimulus, the responses within and among units may vary. The clusters in a crowd watching a street fight may, in general, sympathize with and respond to one of the fighters, yet many of the individuals continue to respond as members of their respective integral units. This situation exists in most stage crowds. Considerable uniformity of response results, but there is still sufficient variety within the unit responses to create the diversity of reaction that lends credibility to the crowd.

One final level of crowd response is the total mass reaction. To get a mass reaction, a crowd must be psychologically blended into a single entity. In a lynch mob, for example, the integral units break down. The stimulus of the leader or the situation is so great that each person in the crowd ceases to react as an individual or as a member of an integral unit and becomes a member of the largest possible unit, the mob.

The preceding discussion of crowd characteristics and the levels of response through which the crowd may progress is basic to the directing of any stage crowd. Only after absorbing and understanding these factors can the director efficiently proceed to the consideration of the general and technical problems of staging a crowd scene.

GENERAL PROBLEMS IN CROWD SCENES

The playwright's suggestions for handling the crowd are often vague and confusing. Sometimes the advice consists of such meaningless phrases as "The crowd enters" or "A street scene with normal activity" or "The passersby stop to listen." The playwright has not gone to the trouble of actually visualizing the kind, size, and specific characteristics of the crowd. He has added a crowd to "build the scene up a little." This weakness in the writing forces the director to make all of the decisions concerning the crowd.

When to Use a Crowd

The first question that should enter the director's mind is, "Should there be a crowd?" If the crowd suggested by the playwright does not contribute to the dramatic action, it may be wise to eliminate it. In other situations, the director may want to add a crowd in spots where the playwright has merely suggested that a few pedestrians pass by or has made no suggestion at all. Most playwrights write for the commercial theatre where cost is a paramount consideration. They do not include crowd action, though it may be highly desirable, for fear that the script may be rejected by a producer as too expensive to produce.

In the non-commercial theatre, participation may be a more important factor than cost. Since one of the purposes of the high school, college, and community theatres is to give everyone as great an opportunity as possible, the director may, with perfect justification, create crowd scenes where they did not before exist. Obviously, such a decision must be based upon the dramatic value of a crowd as well as the opportunities for acting that it provides.

The Size of the Crowd

A second basic consideration is the size of the crowd. Cost and participation figure in this decision along with several other factors. The dramatic impression which a crowd projects is, in part, a result of size. In a street scene, for example, hordes of people will give an impression different from that of a scattered few. The director, therefore, must consider size in terms of its dramatic value.

The size of the stage is another factor to be considered. Crowd scenes are usually of short duration. If the setting is enlarged to accommodate the crowd, much of the rest of the play may seem dwarfed by the huge setting. The size of the setting should be determined by the play, and the size of the crowd worked out accordingly.

Another consideration in determining the size of the crowd is the amount of time available for rehearsal. Crowds are complicated to direct. The greater the size, the greater the number of problems. With no levity intended, one may say that the difficulties in handling a crowd increase in a geometric rather than an arithmetic progression.

A final consideration in resolving the size of the crowd is the levels of response through which the crowd must pass. Mass or mob reaction, as opposed to integral unit reactions, depend in part on size. It is almost impossible to create a feeling of mob hysteria with a crowd of four or five people, for the audience perceives a small group as individuals. Individuals seldom react as a mob.

Writing in Crowd Scenes

The crowd scene in *Winterset* is a classic example of superior crowd writing. Anderson has provided every step in the development of a crowd with fidelity to the facts of crowd behavior. Most playwrights cannot claim a superior knowledge of crowd activity. They simply write dialogue between the leading character and the crowd. This usually appears in the form of a speech from the lead and an ad lib from the crowd. Note that this procedure assumes that the crowd is an entity, which we have positively shown it is not. This failure is, however, not always the result of a lack of knowledge on the playwright's part. The difficulty may arise from certain problems inherent in writing a scene involving a stage crowd.

In each of the two illustrations at the beginning of this chapter, a good deal of time was spent assembling the crowd, developing the crowd reactions, and finally dissolving the crowd. The running time for the crowd scene in *Winterset* is something over eight minutes from start to finish, much longer than most crowd scenes. Many plays do not justify this extended development of the crowd action. Thus the playwright telescopes the scene, compresses it. As a result, the scene is difficult to motivate. Insufficient time is allowed to overcome the inertia present in any large gathering. Another reason for hurrying the scene is that a gradual increase in crowd reaction is not particularly dramatic. However, the spectator will sense that the scene is unreal if insufficient time is allowed for development. Some playwrights solve the problem of time in an even more unsatisfactory way. Instead of telescoping the development, they omit it altogether. In either case, the director must compensate for the weakness in the writing by including all of the elements which are part of a crowd's make-up and response.

Insufficient or stereotyped dialogue is another deficiency found in the writing of crowd scenes. Many playwrights are apparently unwilling to take the time necessary to write forceful dialogue for the members of a crowd. They merely suggest cheers or boos. The director can effectively overcome this barrier to reality by requiring that each actor supply specific dialogue motivated by the individual characteristics of his role. A crowd in which each member speaks the lines that would be natural to him will sound much more real than if the cast mutters, "Rhubarb, rhubarb, rhubarb."

Acting in Crowd Scenes

Effective acting in an ensemble scene often requires more talent and experience than playing in a scene with two or three characters. The reasons are obvious. The crowd actor usually writes his own dialogue. He must react through long stage waits between lines, one of the theatre's most difficult arts. Because of the numbers, he must often be his own director. And he must maintain a balance in his acting so that he will be noticed for neither his overacting nor his underacting. A good crowd demands poise, maturity, and imagination in the actors. Far too frequently the least experienced make up the cast for the crowd, another reason for so many poor crowd scenes. The director who can convince the members of the ensemble of the necessity for hard work and imagination will have taken a major step in making his crowd scenes successful.

Directing the Individual Crowd Member

The steps in directing the individual actor in the crowd scene may be detailed as follows. First, acquaint the actor with the purpose of the crowd. Explain what the crowd as a whole must contribute. Assign a specific role to each crowd member. The role must be detailed. It is not sufficient to say, "You are townspeople." For example, tell the actor that he is the town blacksmith, age 55, uneducated, surly and taciturn by nature, disliked by others in the community. Provide the actor with a profile of the role which will stimulate him to develop a complete character. Assign the actor to an integral unit. The blacksmith may have come with his wife and daughter or with two drunken friends. Establish a dominant character within the unit. In any cluster of people who have a common bond, one person is usually the leader or key member in the group. This procedure adds meaning and purpose to each of the clusters in the crowd. Encourage the actors in the unit to improvise a complete motivational pattern or reason for the group's existing and reacting together from the beginning of the scene to the end.

The actor who has been told in detail the who, what, and why of his character will be prepared to take direction relating to composition, movement, business, emotional key, and tempo.

TECHNICAL PROBLEMS IN STAGING THE CROWD

Crowd direction is complicated because the normal technical problems in using a stage are amplified as the number of persons on stage at one time is increased. By precise application of certain crowd direction techniques, the audience can follow the essential action in the crowd scene as easily as in a scene with two or three characters. Without precise directing, the result can be chaotic.

Establishing the Focal Point

Crowd scenes without a specific focal point are rare. Occasionally the director may want to establish a feeling of confusion, of people laughing, of bustle in a street, in which the audience is not supposed to find any particular point of interest. An example of this is the opening of the carnival scene in Molnar's *Liliom*. As the curtain rises the audience is struck by the general gaiety and confusion of a carnival. After this mood has been established, the director emphasizes certain aspects of the scene and, finally, sharply focuses the attention of the audience on one character. The duration of a scene without a focal point must be short. The audience has been trained to find a point of interest. The spectator is confused if none exists.

The focal point in the crowd scene as in any scene is established by the use of speech, movement, light, vitality, or any of the compositional factors; however, the presence of ten to twenty animate crowd actors makes focalization more difficult. The factors giving emphasis must be more forceful here than in the small group scene.

Level and space are the compositional devices most frequently used to define the focal point in crowd scenes. For example, the dominant character may be placed on a level that raises him above the heads of the crowd; or the crowd may be tightly packed in one group and the leading character set apart. The emphatic character may also be given broad, full movements in contrast to the crowd's small movements. And, of course, the dominant character can be emphasized by the visual focus of the crowd.

Changing the Focal Point

In changing the focal point from one part of the stage to another, the eye of the spectator must be forcibly led from one point to the other. The carnival scene in *Liliom* may have several carnival acts which take place in front of booths. By using space, level, speech, and action, the attention of the spectator may be transfixed on one booth. A change in the focal point to another booth can be accomplished by a simple procedure. The new focal point must suddenly be made more emphatic than the preceding one. A sudden burst of sound, vigorous activity, the calling of the barker will shift attention. The activity at the first booth must be closed out, the sound diminished, the emphasis of level, space, and body position eliminated. The surge of the crowd toward the second booth will carry the attention of the audience to the new focal point. Most of the spectators will cast a glance back to the first booth to see what is happening. If the attention factors have been eliminated, they will immediately return to the dominance of the second booth.

A more subtle method of shifting the focal point makes use of the movement of a single character who leads the spectator's eye to the new point of interest. Suppose that in a party scene there are several conversational clusters alternating in dominance. The dominant cluster should be opened so that the audience can see and hear the players. The vocal projection level is raised; the vigor of the activity is greater in this group. To shift the focal point, one actor moves from the dominant group to the other group, speaking as he moves. This actor holds the audience's attention because of the movement and speech. As the actor approaches the new group, the players' body positions are opened to receive the new actor; the animation of the new group is increased; a new focal point has been established. The formerly dominant group decreases its activity and closes itself out of the action. Obviously, the techniques mentioned here are merely illustrative. Dozens of others are possible, but in each the principle is the same. The success of the procedure depends upon the finesse with which the focal point is changed.

Sight Lines in Crowd Scenes

No member of the crowd should ever obscure the sight lines to the focal point. In crowd scenes, the problem of clearing sight lines is complicated by the large number of actors. The three or four people involved in a small group composition can be arranged so that an open side is toward the audience. The composition seems real. When a large group is involved, an open pocket on one side of the composition strains the credibility. In Figure 36, A, this awkward arrangement is shown. It appears artificial because people normally don't leave one side of the crowd open. Everyone presses forward to get a better view.

In B, C, and D, the illusion of reality has been obtained without

destroying the sight lines. In B, the focal point has been moved
to a downstage area. Because of convention, the audience does not
expect the crowd characters to stand downstage of the curtain line;

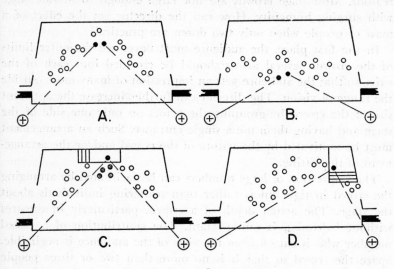

FIG. 36. CROWD COMPOSITIONS

therefore, the arrangement of the crowd appears real. Theatrical
convention in this case suggests that the crowd actually is standing
all about the dominant point, but the scene has been cut in half
and the audience is able to see only one part.

In the drawing C, the focal point has been moved upstage and
has been raised above the heads of the crowd. The dominant character need be raised a mere twelve to eighteen inches for everyone
in the audience to see. The sight lines can be further improved by
placing the smallest actors (shaded in the drawing) directly in
front of the focal point or by having the crowd members in the
central area kneel or sit.

In D, the focal point has been moved to one side of the stage
and raised. This arrangement is satisfactory because only one or
two actors need be placed stage left of the leading player to give
the impression that the crowd continues on that side.

Settings with levels to raise the focal point offer varied opportunities for creating striking compositions.

Filling the Stage

Stage crowds are almost always limited in size for practical reasons. Most stage crowds are not large enough to fill the stage with surging humanity. How can the director get the effect of a mass of people when only two dozen are practical?

In the first place, the audience must never see the outer limits of the crowd. Several actors should be crowded into each of the exits, so that the audience gets an impression of many more outside the range of vision. The director can further increase the apparent size of the crowd by grouping the actors on only one side of the stage and having them use a single entrance. Such an arrangement must be motivated by the nature of the crowd and/or the arrangement of the setting.

The impression of large numbers can be facilitated by arranging the crowd in tight knots rather than scattering individuals about the stage. The actual depth of a crowd, particularly in theatres without balconies, is unimportant. The contribution of a crowd member who is cut off from the view of the audience is negligible. Space the crowd so that it is no more than two or three people deep at any point. Never allow the crowd to form lines. Clusters of knots staggered in depth and distance from the focal point increase the appearance of size.

If real or psychological barriers can be constructed, fewer people will be needed. For example, if soldiers or guards can force the crowd to the sides of the setting, the crowd will seem larger and the focal point will be emphasized. Fear might be used as a psychological barrier to separate the crowd from a fight or struggle. The more stage area that can logically be cleared, the fewer people necessary to give the impression of a mass.

Light may also be used to increase the impression of crowd size. In general, a reduction of light which makes it more difficult to see and judge the crowd size increases the impression of large numbers. More specifically, if the stage can be lit with a high intensity at the central focal point and a gradual decrease in the illumination until the edges of the scene are in darkness, a tight concentration of people in the light and a scattered few in the darkness will give the impression of a large crowd.

Animation is a final factor affecting the impression of size. Violent activity will increase the feeling of size if it can be coupled with poor visibility and background sound. A very small group of players can give the impression of a tremendous mass if they are treated as the leader elements of a great unseen crowd represented in sound. A word of warning should be interposed. If the small group can be seen clearly, excessive animation may do more harm than good, as the audience will observe the actions of individual actors.

Casting and Costuming the Crowd

It may seem strange to couple casting and costuming under a single heading. However, the same principle influences both. The term, *crowd,* implies a mass without any easily identified individual characters. In both casting and costuming, this principle should be observed.

The crowd member who is atypical draws attention to himself. Extremes in physical stature, excessive animation, or any other differentiating characteristic should be avoided. If such a person can be the leader and thus a focal point, his individuality will be an asset; if not, he will weaken the mass effect.

For the same reason, the director must costume his crowd with care. Startlingly different costumes should be eliminated. This does not mean that crowd costumes cannot be colorful or bold. In the musical show, for example, the choruses may be dressed as vivid, colorful peasants or splendidly uniformed soldiers. However, only the leading characters should be set apart by contrasting colors or very elaborate costumes.

THE GROUP UNIT SYSTEM

This procedure is based upon the integral units or clusters found in the real crowd, two or three persons tied together by a common bond. The steps to be taken in directing a common type of crowd are suggested below. These steps are based on the assumption that the director has already decided upon the purpose, size, and characters of the crowd, the casting of the actors, and has written any dialogue necessary to sustain the crowd action.

Assigning the Units

A crowd of 25 actors could be broken down into five groups of
three actors, four groups of two actors, and two single players.
Each actor should be assigned a specific character, as suggested in
the section on acting, who fits logically within his cluster. The
most experienced and imaginative actors should play the individual
roles, for in the composition and movement of the crowd the individuals are given greater freedom than the units. In each group
the director should assign a dominant character or leader. This
leader should also be more experienced, if possible, because the
unit leader is responsible for his group's actions as well as its morale
and spirit.

The group unit serves several purposes. First, each actor has a
basis for developing a character. Second, the actor has two sets of
stimuli, the primary stimulus or focal point of the scene and the
secondary stimulus of his own group activity. This combination
helps provide the actor with things to do. Third, the member of a
unit has a feeling of belonging to an important segment of the
cast rather than being lumped in the mass called the crowd. This
division can help the director in another way. Fewer crowd members will lose their places or forget their movement if they belong
to a small unit in which each member helps the others. And finally, the director is able to handle the crowd in terms of groups
rather than individuals. This is extremely important in setting
crowd movement because nine groups will be much easier to direct
than 25 individuals.

The Basic Composition

Most crowd scenes can be built around a single composition.
The crowd enters. It reacts to the focal point in the scene. The
crowd exits. One ideal composition can be the basis of the scene.
The basic composition should be the starting point in directing
the crowd scene. Assuming a knowledge of focal point, sight lines,
and filling the stage, the director should build the composition.
The composition should represent an ideal arrangement of the
groups. It should also be the composition found at the climax of
the crowd scene. Using this composition as a starting point, the
director can work either backward to the entrance or forward to

the crowd's exit. The basic composition is simple to arrange and can be worked out in detail beforehand.

The Home Position

Next, the actors are assigned by groups to their exact positions in the basic composition. This is called the *home position.* Both the exact place on the stage and the exact body position of the actor should be assigned. It should be emphasized that irregularity in body position is essential to the crowd composition. If every actor takes a three-quarter-open body position the composition will appear artificial and dull. As a rule of thumb, it might be said that no two persons in any single group unit should have the same body position. After the players have found their home positions, each of the groups should be assigned an entrance and an exit. The group may both come and go through the same entrance, though a more varied effect can be achieved if each group exits through a different opening.

Crowd Movement

The direction of crowd movement is principally composed of moving the group units from the entrance to the home position and, in turn, from the home position to the exit. This movement must appear natural and not obscure the focal point in the scene. The actual movement should not be difficult because the director is working with groups which already have carefully defined their motivational patterns.

After the groups have reached their home positions in the scene, they obviously cannot stand statically at that point until it is time for them to exit. Complete changes in the basic composition can be made by moving the groups a step or so from their home positions. With the home position as the starting point, the director can easily experiment with all kinds of variations.

No mention has been made of the two individuals who were not assigned to group units. Since they are the most experienced members of the crowd, they may be moved frequently so that they join one group for a moment, then shift to another. This increases the possibilities for variations in the composition. They can be the crowd leaders if leaders are necessary. Their action should be blocked in as great detail as that of the leads.

The director may be tempted to break up the group units to form other units during the scene. This should be avoided because the success of the unit system depends upon the direction of the unit as an entity. The units may be combined to form larger groupings, but the identity of the unit should be maintained.

SPECIAL TYPES OF CROWD OR GROUP SCENES

Certain specialized group scenes have distinctive problems in composition and movement. Some of these scenes are encountered by the director again and again in the play production program.

Table Scenes

Prolonged eating or drinking scenes arranged about a table can create no end of difficulty for the director. The problem is to arrange the players at the table so that the illusion of reality is maintained without destroying the sight lines and the focal point. The problem is illustrated in Figure 37.

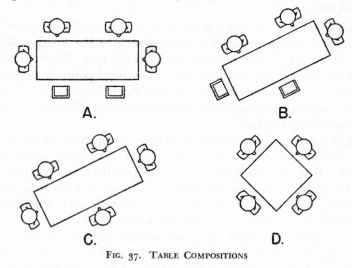

FIG. 37. TABLE COMPOSITIONS

In the drawing A, four characters are arranged about the upstage side of a large table. The sight lines are clear; however, such an arrangement is not very satisfactory for establishing a focal point. In a sense, the characters are arranged in a chorus circle; furthermore, the illusion of reality is destroyed. People seldom arrange themselves on only one side of a table.

By slanting the table slightly, as in B, the sight lines are maintained and the focal point may be more clearly established. The arrangement of the characters approximates a triangle with the apex the dominant point. The illusion of reality can be maintained if only three characters are involved, for it is conceivable that the characters might arrange themselves in this way.

The problems of sight lines and focal point are raised again in C, when five people sit at the table. If the person at the downstage edge of the table is small, the difficulty will be diminished. In *Life with Father,* for example, the two smallest Day children were always seated on the downstage edge of the table.

Actually, there is no way of arranging five or six people at a table without encountering some difficulty with sight lines and focal point. The solution to the problem depends upon the ingenuity of the director; however, several feasible solutions may be suggested. They are all based upon the premise that the logical arrangement need be held for only a few moments. For example, if the characters are arranged as in C, the person at the downstage position may be removed from the scene after the first few moments. The spectators will then accept the opening at the front as perfectly natural because they saw how the vacancy occurred. After the downstage character has been removed the composition will appear similar to that in B if the table is raked or like that in A if the table is set parallel to the footlights. Some characters are less important than others in any table scene. These characters should be seated downstage and later removed. Their removal may be motivated by giving them some task to perform such as going to the kitchen or removing dishes. In any case, the empty downstage chair has been explained. Many variations of this principle for opening the sight lines are possible.

Card Table Scenes

One of the most difficult scenes to compose effectively is the card table scene. If the card table is set parallel to the footlights, the downstage player covers the upstage player. In D, the table is set at an angle to the footlights. Note that in this arrangement the two downstage characters cover the upstage characters. However, using this placement as the basis, the characters can be jockeyed about the table so that the sight lines are reasonably clear. If the downstage characters sit somewhat out from the table and crowd the leg of the table upstage of them, the scene will be opened a little. By moving one of the upstage characters close to the upstage leg of the table, a focal point can be established. If one or more of the downstage characters can be removed, an arrangement approximating that in B can be obtained.

Tea Party and Cocktail Scenes

Party scenes are usually directed with the unit system. They are not crowd scenes in the sense of a large mass, but they do have some of the same problems: shifting the focal point from character to character, keeping the sight lines clear, and projecting a gay bustle of activity. The party scene can be directed by arranging two or three basic compositions for the scene and then working movement to and from them.

The Audience as a Crowd

A final type of crowd scene incorporates the theatre audience as part of the crowd. In Odets' *Waiting for Lefty,* the stage speakers actually harangue the audience. In Ibsen's *An Enemy of the People,* the heckling and jeering crowd is sometimes scattered throughout the audience. This novelty appeals to many directors who feel that the audience's participation and enjoyment are increased by having actors actually in the audience. The difficulties of this presentational style are numerous. Many members of the audience may not be able to follow the action, particularly if the theatre has a balcony. The aesthetic distance may be broken by thrusting the audience into the action of the play. This may or may not be desirable, depending upon the playwright's purpose. The desired crowd reactions may be hampered by the inertia of the theatre audience. The director should study the advantages and disadvantages carefully before introducing this innovation.

The animation and color of the crowd can seldom be matched by small groups of actors. More important, crowd scenes provide opportunities for eager beginners. And best of all, they are a challenge to direct. The next time a crowd scene looms in the play script, don't cut it, overlook it, or see how quickly it may be passed by; make it one of the high points of the production.

21

The Musical Show

SOONER OR LATER in the career of every director the opportunity to produce a musical show arises. The magnitude of the musical production with its actors, singers, dancers, and musicians is both exciting and frightening. The organizational problems are increased several fold. The production problems are doubled or tripled.

This chapter is written on the assumption that an analysis of the differences between the musical play and the regular play will be helpful. Basically, the musical show may be approached in the same manner as any other play; however, because of the magnitude of the musical production, problems in coordination arise. These problems are amplified because the play director seldom is skilled in all phases of musical production. He is not a singer or a choral master. He is not a dancer or a choreographer. He is not a musician or a conductor. Therefore, the stage director usually becomes a producer or coordinator of all the various elements which go into the production. The following sections trace the production of a musical comedy or operetta with special emphasis upon the part played by the stage director.

Cooperative Directing

Most musical productions involve at least three and usually four directors: the stage or general director, the musical director, the technical director, and the dance director. Some elaborate productions also have a fifth director, the orchestra director. With this much directing talent, a precise division of responsibility must be determined long before the show goes into rehearsal. The pattern of responsibility and authority is usually as follows.

The musical director is directly responsible for all music in the production. He helps cast the show. He trains the chorus and the leading singers. He usually rehearses the orchestra and conducts the show during the performances. Since most musical shows depend more upon the musical numbers than upon the acting, the musical director is of great importance to the success of the production.

The responsibilities of the dance director are the simplest to define. The dance director casts and directs the dancers. He is responsible for only those segments of the production which involve dance.

The technical director is responsible for scenery, lighting, costumes, make-up. In most musical productions he has to work extraordinarily closely with the general director, since multiple scene shifts are an integral part of the smoothness of the show.

The authority and responsibilities of the general director are more difficult to define. He works with the musical director in casting the show. He directs the acting or dialogue portions of the production. He usually controls all of the visual aspects of the production. In most productions the general director puts the entire show together and is ultimately responsible for the show as a whole. These last two responsibilities require the complete cooperation of the other directors. Many of the difficulties in directing a musical show arise during the assembly period.

Directing the musical involves problems in cooperative responsibility. The authority of the different directors will overlap no matter how carefully it has been divided; therefore, a directing team must work together for the good of the production. Above all, *one* director must act as final judge in settling controversies. There are bound to be differences of opinion about many things. Someone must have the authority to make final decisions, for the musical production requires a long series of compromises.

TRYOUTS AND CASTING

The tryouts for the musical are complicated by the search for three different talents—singing, acting, dancing. Because of the size

of the group usually involved, simultaneous open tryouts are necessary. The largest tryout group I ever encountered turned out for
a production of *Of Thee I Sing*. The number totaled 438.

The General Tryout

At the general tryouts, each director may work by himself.
Three rooms are needed: one each for singing, dancing, and acting. Each aspirant should be asked to show his abilities in each of
the three categories, regardless of his limitations in certain capaci-
ties. Production assistants can move the groups of candidates with
their tryout cards from one room to the next.

The acting tryouts should be conducted exactly as outlined in
the section on the screening tryout in Chapter 14. The director
should code the acting grades, since the card will move by student
messenger to the other tryout rooms.

The singing tryouts may be conducted in one of several ways.
The simplest procedure is to provide the group with the lyrics for
a typical song from the show. The melody can be taught to the
whole group by following community singing procedure. After the
song has been run over frequently enough so that everyone is
familiar with the tune, each individual should be asked to step
forward and sing it alone. At this time the musical director should
grade the voice in code. After each group has sung, the production
assistant should usher the groups to the third tryout room.

Most of the persons who try out for a musical show will have
had no dance training or experience; therefore, the dance director
should set up a series of dance steps of increasing difficulty. The
first may be nothing more than graceful hopping from one foot
to another in rhythm, but the third or fourth may be as complicated as a "shuffle off to Buffalo." An assistant can teach the steps
to small groups. Then each person is asked to dance each of the
steps by himself. The dance director can then record a coded
grade in dancing ability.

The Final Tryout

After everyone has completed the three types of tryouts, the
directors should meet to determine who is to be called back for
final tryouts. At this point, the dancers are frequently treated
separately, since they make only a few appearances in the show.

On the other hand, if the dancers must be regular chorus members—for example, in the show which troupes and must carry a small company—then the dancers' ability to sing becomes important, and they must be judged with the others. Specialty or solo dance tryouts should be conducted separately.

The most satisfactory procedure for setting up the call for final tryouts is to select two groups. The first group includes those who are to be considered for leading roles as well as chorus parts. The second group is called back for chorus parts only. This system saves time. Those who are not lead possibilities need not read a second time. Provision should be made for any player to withdraw his name from the "chorus only" list if he wants a lead in the show or no part at all.

The final tryouts should be conducted in two sections, first the chorus tryouts and then the lead tryouts. All of the directors should be present for the final tryouts. The final chorus tryouts should require that each person sing again. The musical director and the stage director can record a combined judgment after each performance.

The amount of weight placed upon such qualities as singing ability, physical attractiveness, size, and general enthusiasm depends a great deal upon the show to be cast. In an operetta such as The Vagabond King, physical appearance means little since the chorus represents townspeople. In a show like Of Thee I Sing, physical appearance is of major importance, for the chorus is made up of bathing beauties, White House secretaries, and the like. In the former case, the musical director should have virtual autonomy in selecting the chorus; in the latter, the stage director must ask that compromises be made between singing ability and physical attributes.

After the chorus tryouts have been completed, this group may be dismissed. Some directors conduct the two sections of final tryouts on succeeding evenings.

In the final lead tryouts, each person should be asked to sing and read in various combinations with other players. If the leading characters sing duets, it may be necessary to pair certain singers to ascertain the balance of voices.

The final casting decisions will represent the compromises mentioned earlier. The directors must, in each case, carefully weigh the role and determine whether singing or acting is more important to the show. Sometimes the choice between a superb singer who can't act and a fine actor who can't sing seems impossible.

There are several other methods for solving such a problem. In many cases the role in the show can be modified. Many of the songs in musical shows are not integral parts of the story, and their success does not depend upon a particular character singing them. Such tunes may be taken from the actor who doesn't sing well and assigned to the singer who doesn't need to be a particularly good actor. For example, the show can be rearranged so that in addition to the usual leading characters there are several singing leads who step out of the chorus. This procedure is doubly useful as it preserves top notch singing in both the solo and chorus work.

Another type of modification is to change the treatment given a song. Some songs, particularly those of the comic or novelty variety, can be successfully "sold" without good singing. Frequently, a good actor can get more out of such a song than a superior singer can. This treatment will probably worry the musical director who is naturally a music lover, but audience reaction must be given due consideration also.

PLANNING THE MUSICAL

The interpretation procedures employed in preparing the musical play are similar to those used in analyzing the regular play. The essential difference is in the definition of the working units. In the regular play, the motivational unit was used. In the musical play, a technical unit is used.

Plotting the Units

There are four types of units in the musical production: (1) dialogue units, (2) lead singing units, (3) chorus singing units, and (4) dance units. These units form the basis of the rehearsal plan, which will be discussed later. Each different type of unit is rehearsed separately. It is exceedingly important that the units be defined exactly; otherwise, when the general director tries to assemble the show, the pieces will not fit together.

The dialogue unit is defined as an acting scene that begins with the first spoken line after the preceding musical tag and concludes with the first bar of the orchestral introduction to the next tune.

A chorus singing unit begins with the musical introduction to chorus singing and ends with the last chord the chorus sings. A lead singing unit is similar to a chorus singing unit except that it covers only the solo work. A dance unit begins with the musical introduction to the dance and ends with the last chord of the music for the dance.

The exact beginning and ending of each unit must be set in advance. Each unit must be described in terms of: (1) personnel, (2) position on stage, (3) exact cue. If each director knows the personnel, position, and cue for each unit, the assembling process will be materially facilitated.

Analysis of a simple dance unit will illustrate the procedure.

1. End of dialogue unit.
   a. Actors leave stage on final gag line with laughter covering the exit.
   b. Gag line is orchestra cue.
2. Dance unit.
   a. Dancers off stage left and right.
   b. Orchestral introduction—four bars—brings dancers on.
   c. Thirty-two bars of dance—dancers remain on.
   d. Dancers hold position for applause.
   e. Orchestral tag—four bars—dancers dance off.
   f. Orchestral tag is dialogue cue.
3. Beginning of dialogue unit.

The dance director who has every dance unit sketched on paper before the first rehearsal knows exactly what his group must do. Each dance can be rehearsed with exact knowledge of position, personnel, and cue. When the assembling process begins and units that have been rehearsed in isolation are brought together, the sections will dovetail perfectly.

Framing the Music

The term, *frame*, may be new to many directors. It may be defined for theatrical purposes in its popular sense. A house is framed when the joists and studding are in place. They make up the skeleton to which is added the sheathing that encloses the structure. In the same sense, *to frame music* means to lay out the skeleton or outline of a musical number.

Most musical shows that have been presented upon Broadway and all original shows will need to have the music framed or re-framed. The rented score has an outline of the musical numbers and the accompanying orchestrations which are replicas, if not the battered originals, of some previous production. The music has been laid out to conform to the talents of the cast for whom it was written. Unfortunately, most amateur groups do not have the same distribution of talent as found in professional companies. For example, most Broadway or Hollywood musical leads are song and dance men. In many years of college production I have yet to find a good singer who can dance or, for that matter, a good dancer who can sing. This means that the musical numbers must be re-framed or at least patched to build a good production.

Every musical number must be set up with the same dramatic care as that given any dialogue unit. It is difficult, if not impossible, to select sections at random from the orchestration without weakening the number. Assuming that the director does not have an arranger available, what can be done? Obviously, the music can be played in its entirety as written. This procedure may not work with the available talent. Second, the music may be cut and patched. Cutting and patching is the process of omitting sections from the orchestration and joining the remaining sections together. It should be noted that all cutting and patching should be done by, or at least with the approval of, the musical director. It is impossible to cut an orchestration from one place to another if there is a key change without a key modulation written into the music. Even a few bars of key modulation require competent arranging and considerable work in copying for a sixteen- to twenty-piece orchestra.

The director who is fortunate enough to have an arranger available can frame his musical numbers to fit the talent. A few simple principles may help contain the enthusiasm most directors feel when building a number. First, avoid overdoing a tune. Many musical numbers are overly extended and lose the attention of the audience. Second, do not repeat any verse or refrain more than once in the same key. A raised key adds brilliance and excitement to a musical number. Third, start the number in a key low enough so that it may be raised and the chorus can still be sung. Fourth, avoid scoring a dance for more than 64 bars. Most dancers cannot sustain a dance for more than one 32-bar refrain. Fifth, avoid maintaining a single tempo throughout a musical number. Contrasts in time are more effective. Usually fast tempos are more exciting; therefore, save fast tempos for the latter part of the production number. Finally, let the end of a number notify the audience that it has been concluded.

It is essential to have all technical units plotted and the music framed before rehearsals begin. Only by having made all of the decisions beforehand can each of the directors work with maximum efficiency during the rehearsal period.

REHEARSING THE MUSICAL

The length of the rehearsal period for a musical is considerably longer than that for a regular stage play. The cast of the musical show is often less experienced in the ways of the theatre; therefore, the musical should be rehearsed at a slower pace than the regular play. Most musical productions are rehearsed from eight to ten weeks. The first six weeks are used for divided rehearsals. Approximately three weeks are set aside for assembling the production, and a week is used for mounting rehearsals.

The Divided Rehearsals

During the divided rehearsal period, five different types of rehearsals run simultaneously: (1) chorus rehearsals, (2) dialogue rehearsals, (3) lead singing rehearsals, (4) dance rehearsals, and (5) orchestra rehearsals. The early chorus rehearsals are devoted to learning the songs. After the songs have been memorized, the chorus movement and reactions should be rehearsed. The chorus should seldom be asked to rehearse more than two or at most three times a week during the first six weeks of rehearsal.

The dialogue in a musical show is much shorter than that found in the usual play. Acting rehearsals three or four times a week for six weeks should be more than enough to prepare the book.

Lead singing rehearsals should be conducted at the convenience of the singers and the musical director. The number of rehearsals will depend upon the experience and proficiency of the singers. Orchestra rehearsals should be scheduled by the musical director. The length and number will, as in the case of the lead singing rehearsals, depend upon the difficulty of the score and the ability of the orchestra members.

Dance rehearsals depend upon the skill of the dancers. It has been my experience that every moment that can be devoted to dance rehearsal is worth it. Six weeks is an unbelievably short period for teaching beginners to dance; however, with a superior dancing teacher it can be done. Some play production groups do not have a dance director available. In such a situation, configurated movement may be substituted for group dancing. Configurated movement is discussed under chorus movement. Specialty and solo dance rehearsals should be arranged at the convenience of the dance director.

During the divided rehearsal period, each segment of the production must be rehearsed to perfection. Once the assembling rehearsals begin there will be *no* opportunity to rehearse individual units.

The Assembly Rehearsals

Assuming that each of the individual units is ready, the assembling process is essentially one of building with blocks. These rehearsals will prove to be the most time consuming and trying periods of the producing process. The primary purpose of the assembly rehearsals is to establish a flow from unit to unit. No matter how carefully the individual units have been worked out, a great deal of work is required to make the transitions from one unit to the next appear effortless.

The assembly rehearsals should be built around the chorus work because the chorus is the largest and most unwieldy group. In addition, despite careful rehearsal, it is frequently the least prepared group. At all assembly rehearsals the chorus units should be rehearsed in full. Much of the time consumed during the assembly rehearsals will be spent on training the chorus to enter, visually sell its songs, and exit. This process is so complicated that it is discussed in detail in a later section as a special problem in musical production. Another reason for rehearsing all of each chorus unit is that the director dares not let a large chorus group sit around with nothing to do. Chorus members are seldom as intensely interested in the theatre as actors are. Idleness breeds restlessness and resentment in a chorus group. If the director cannot use the chorus members every minute that they are at rehearsal, he should dismiss them or re-plan his schedule.

The units of the show are usually assembled in the following sequence. First, the lead singing units are joined to the chorus units. In some cases this may be done prior to the assembly rehearsals. Next, the dance units are added, completing the production number. After the transitions have been cleaned up, the number should be run several times in order to crystallize what has been learned. During these run-throughs the timing, flow, and climactic build of the number should be analyzed. If the framing of the number is satisfactory, it may be set, and the next number can be assembled. If not, the number should be torn apart and corrected.

A word of warning. Most musical shows have from fifteen to twenty musical numbers. Rehearsal time must be carefully prorated among the numbers. It is easy to over-rehearse one number to the disadvantage of others. Rehearse the last numbers in the show first. Then if any number is under-rehearsed, it will be an early one and, hence, do less harm to the climactic build of the production.

After the musical numbers have been assembled, the dialogue units may be added. Time should not be taken at this point to run the entire unit of dialogue. The cast of the dialogue unit is usually three or four in number. It is unfair and unwise to make 50 to 100 players wait while these units are run. The process of joining the dialogue units to the musical numbers is reasonably simple. Take the last minute of dialogue and run through the transition into the musical number. At the end of the musical number continue into the first minute of dialogue. Work these transitions between the music and dialogue until they are smooth for each number in the show.

What about the orchestra? Some directors are eager to add the orchestra at the first possible opportunity. This is usually a mistake. For several reasons, it should not be added until the end of the rehearsal schedule. First, if the musical numbers are not completely ready, the orchestra's time will be wasted. Second, integrating the orchestra into the production is a full time rehearsal process by itself. Third, it takes time for an orchestra to start, stop, and start again in the middle of a tune. A single piano is a much more flexible tool to use during the early assembly rehearsals.

It is best to call the orchestra to one of the final assembly rehearsals. One full rehearsal in which complete attention is focused on fitting the orchestra to the production is probably sufficient. The orchestra need not be called back again until the dress rehearsals. Musicians' time is valuable and should not be wasted.

A psychological problem sometimes arises because of the peculiar position of the orchestra. The musicians frequently do not feel that they are an important part of the show. They feel a bit like hired help. This attitude can be avoided if the cast and chorus are encouraged to recognize with enthusiasm the orchestra's tremendous contribution to the production.

The assembly rehearsals will demand a great amount of imagination and quick thinking on the part of the director. If rehearsal time must be cut from the suggested schedule, let it be taken from the earlier divided rehearsals. Three weeks of rehearsal will be needed to assemble a production by all but the most experienced director.

The Mounting Rehearsals

The mounting rehearsals have the same purpose and follow the same procedures for the musical show as for the regular play except that a larger number of rehearsals will be needed because of the complexity of musical production.

ORGANIZING THE MUSICAL CAST

The company of the musical show, excluding the orchestra members and technicians, usually involves from 35 to 100 people. With a group of this size, a tight organizational pattern is an absolute necessity. The organizational procedure should fulfill two different purposes. In the first place, the organization should break the large chorus mass into several smaller groups capable of operating with some degree of autonomy. These smaller groups of players learn their specific tasks faster, and an *esprit de corps* arises in the group and strengthens the show. Another reason for breaking the large chorus into smaller groups is to facilitate the technical problems of direction.

A second advantage of a tight organizational pattern is that it permits a delegation of authority. An efficient set of controls can help in handling the chorus member who is slow to learn or not making a peak effort. The pressure arising from the student's own small group may be more effective than the remarks of the director. If strong and enthusiastic chorus members are given some authority, they can see to it that the group for which they are responsible functions smoothly.

Assuming a company of sixty (twelve leads and forty-eight chorus members) the organizational pattern might be developed in the following manner. The leads do not need specific procedure because they are a compact group in constant contact with all of the directors.

The chorus should be arranged into lines. The lines may be set up in terms of size, sex, vocal range, or special talent. Let us suppose that in a sample company the dancers are also singers and consistently work with the rest of the chorus. With such a setup the dancers would probably make up one of the lines. If the chorus is divided into three lines of sixteen per line, the first line might have sixteen men and women dancers. The second line might also have sixteen men and women selected by vocal range or perhaps size. The back line would have the same complement and perhaps be composed of the tallest members of the cast. The lines may be set up in almost any number of different ways.

Give each line a name. This helps in identification and also facilitates the group spirit. For example, in a production of Gershwin's *Girl Crazy* the lines were called "the Belles" (a girls' dancing line), "the Texans" (the second line of fellows and girls), and, finally, "the Oklahomans." By the time the show was performed each line was proud of its name and believed itself to be vastly superior to the other groups.

Next, split the lines into halves, stage right and stage left. This division is very useful in that all of the stage right halves of the lines will always enter and leave the stage from that side; in other words, each person is assigned a stage position at the outset. In addition, the exact entrance position can be set for each of the three lines, most musical sets having three entrances per side.

Finally, number each member of the chorus in terms of his place in the line. Usually the lines are numbered from the center out, since number one is the first person to enter the scene. A simple chorus layout is illustrated in Figure 38.

Reading from the organizational chart, any chorus member can be identified by: (1) line, (2) stage side, and (3) number. For example, Oklahoman-Left-Three is a specific person found in a definite position.

This organizational form helps in the delegation of authority. Six section captains should be chosen. The best position for them is number eight, for they will be the last to enter the scene and can be certain that all the members of their section are on. Select two side captains who are responsible for all of the chorus per-

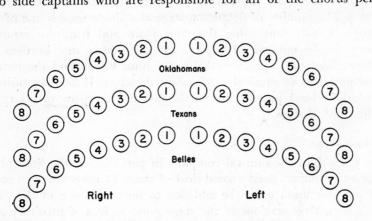

FIG. 38. CHORUS ORGANIZATION

sonnel on their respective sides of the stage. The side captains are usually production assistants rather than chorus members, and the section captains report to them. Finally, there should be a chorus manager who is to be responsible for the entire chorus.

How is the organizational pattern used? It facilitates roll call, for the members can count off. It aids in making the costume plot of the show, particularly if patterns of color are to be used. It is of great value in directing the movements and the compositions of the chorus. And perhaps the greatest use of all, it steadies inexperienced actors during the pressure of performance. A director who has seen college students panic to the extent that they don't know what musical number comes next will readily understand the need for organization.

Frequently directors (usually those who have never handled a large musical) feel that careful organization is unnecessary. Without a doubt, the chorus can be organized in any number of different ways. The important thing is to have some organizational framework to act as the backbone of the big show.

TECHNICAL ASPECTS OF MUSICAL PRODUCTION

Although technical production in the musical is similar to that in any other play, certain major differences create special problems. The number of people on stage at a single time is one of the major factors controlling the floor plans and furniture arrangement in the musical. Multiple scene shifts place new burdens on the technicians. The general director must understand the technical problems of musical production, therefore, if he is to build a colorful visual pattern and maintain the fast pace necessary to the musical show.

Floor Plans

The size of the musical company in part dictates the floor plan. Chorus numbers need a good deal of space. Dancers are even more dependent upon space. In addition to the actual size of the playing area, large sections of the stage must be free of furniture and properties to facilitate freedom of movement for both the dancers and the chorus.

Paradoxically, most dialogue scenes in musical shows are played with two or three characters. The difference in space requirements poses a real problem. A great void is opened up for the chorus unit; the dialogue units require practically no space. A compromise must be made.

In order to give the necessary expanse and still give an impression of some intimacy, most musical sets are very wide and comparatively shallow. The result is something akin to a pantry shelf. The width provides maximum opportunity to spread the chorus so that it may be seen and heard by the audience and so that the chorus, in turn, can see the director. On the other hand, the shallowness of the setting thrusts the dialogue scenes toward the audience where they may be adequately seen and heard. The size of the playing area may be reduced further for the dialogue scenes by area lighting. The playwright may also help stage the dialogue by placing some of these units in small settings or on the stage apron. It is obvious that if a specific stage lacks ideal width, the director will have to use depth instead to accommodate his chorus units.

Furniture Arrangement

Because of the need for open, uncluttered space, furniture and other heavy properties should be kept to a minimum. Heavy or cumbersome properties will also obstruct the fast scene shifts needed in many musicals. Use just enough furniture to create the atmosphere of the scene. For example, in *The Vagabond King*, one or two large tables and a couple of casks can give the impression of the tavern and at the same time leave enough space for the chorus.

In most cases, furniture should be placed somewhat upstage so that downstage areas are free for dancing. If any furniture is to be placed downstage, it should be set well to the side. Great care must be exercised to avoid blocking an entrance. Chorus entrances and exits are frequently hurried. A misplaced prop may spell catastrophe.

Platforms and Steps

The specifications of the stage on which the musical is to be produced will dictate the scene design. However, if any piece of scenery can be called "required," it is the platform or level. Any director who has handled large groups of people on stage realizes that interesting pictorial effects depend upon raising portions of the group. This is a prime consideration in the musical production.

Platforms and steps do create scenic problems. They are too bulky to shift either quickly or quietly. For this reason they should be set upstage so that they will have to be moved a minimum number of times or not at all. This principle is not antithetic to the idea of a shallow stage. If the deepest setting is shallow and wide, the levels may be set back and still be reasonably close to the audience.

Numerous Scenes

Some musicals appear to have been written with the producer in mind. They have no scene or costume changes. The beginning director should consider these factors in selecting his first musical, for his headaches can be reduced in number. Most good musicals, however, seem to go to the other extreme. They have numerous changes in locale and dress. Operettas usually have fewer changes of scene than musical comedies. The musical revue is replete with scenic problems, for some revues have as many as 25 different, totally unrelated scenes.

Scene shifts presumably lie within the province of the technical director, but the general director is vitally concerned. He must help in conceiving the floor plans and the shift plots. The general director's primary interest in scene shifting is his concern for time. Since he is responsible for the pacing of the show, he must determine the relationship between the length of the scene on stage and the time needed to shift to the next scene. A cardinal rule of musical production, broken again and again in the average non-professional production, is that from the rise of the act curtain to the fall of the same curtain at the end of an act, the show must never stop, regardless of the number of scenes involved. The audience must never be forced to sit in a darkened auditorium, listening to an orchestral reprise, waiting for a scene shift. Any stop in the action quickly destroys the mood of the production and breaks down the illusion of brilliance, excitement, and above all—SPEED.

In many cases, the preceding principle is difficult to apply. The playwright, who usually considers the director in arranging the scenes, frequently underestimates the time the non-professional company with limited technical facilities needs to shift scenery. The director must find a solution to this problem.

The Setting

Most musical shows use some variation of the wing and drop setting. The wings may be simple velour legs or complicated façades. The backdrop may be an actual canvas drop, a sky cyclorama, or a complicated arrangement of scenery. However simple or elaborate, the principle of space is comparable to that of the wing and drop setting illustrated in Figure 39.

In conventional theatrical terms, the apron is that portion of the stage which projects in front of the proscenium arch. For musical comedy purposes, the apron is defined as that portion of the stage which lies between the scene curtain and the footlights; therefore, there may be an apron entrance downstage of the tormentor. This area is used occasionally for specialty numbers.

In the wing and drop setting, a series of wings or legs are set parallel to the footlights on either side of the stage. They are placed at definite intervals and act as masking pieces. The back drop encloses the rear portion of the scene. As shown in Figure 39, the placement of the tormentors and wings establishes the entrances to the scene. Most shallow musical sets can be masked by two wings or legs. Thus, there are three entrances on each side

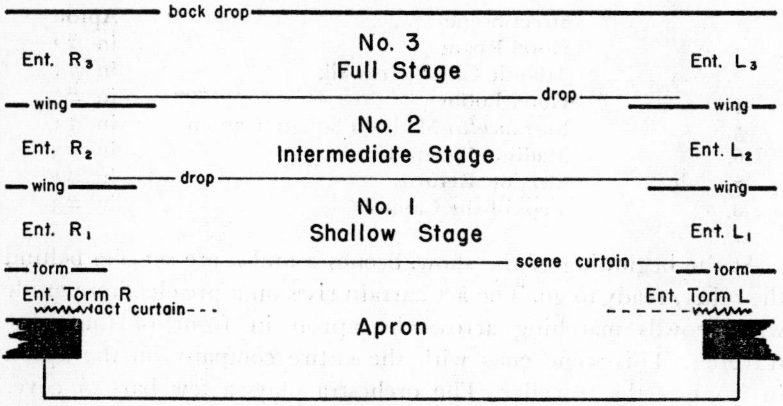

FIG. 39. SIMPLE WING AND DROP SETTING

above the apron or tormentor entrance. Since the wings are numbered from front to back, the entrances carry identical numbers. For example, Entrance Right 1 is in front of Wing Right 1, and so on.

The depth for setting and playing various scenes is likewise established by the placement of the wings. In theatrical parlance, "in #1" refers to a drop hung directly in front of wing #1. A scene "in #1" is played in front of this drop with very little depth. In a like manner, "in #2" establishes an intermediate depth and "in #3" is full stage. Remember, in the musical show the apron is used for many scenes. This differs from the regular play in which the playing line is not crossed. These different depths are basic to the flow of a show with many scenes.

Illustration of Scene Shifts

The use of different depths may be illustrated by plotting the scenes from a specific musical. One of America's finest musical comedies, *Of Thee I Sing*, by Gershwin, Kaufman, and Ryskind, has a total of thirteen scenes. The eight scenes of the first act are listed below with a separate column indicating how they may be set in depth. An analysis of the playing shows how the act may be played and shifted without breaks.

First Act Scene Plot for *Of Thee I Sing*

Scene Number	Locale	Depth
1.	Street Scene	Apron
2.	Hotel Room	in #2
3.	Atlantic City Boardwalk	in #1
4.	Hotel Lobby	in #3
5.	Entrance to Madison Square Garden	in #1
6.	Madison Square Garden	in #3
7.	Election Returns	in #1
8.	Steps of the Capitol	in #3

At the beginning of the show, Scenes 2 and 4 are set one behind the other, ready to go. The act curtain rises on a pre-election parade with crowds marching across the apron in front of the scene traveller. This scene ends with the entire company on the apron in front of the traveller. The orchestra plays a few bars of cover music while the crowd disperses with cheers and laughter. Then the traveller opens and the lights come up on the hotel room, set in #2. This scene is a dialogue unit and ends in a blackout. On the blackout and during the applause, a drop picturing a board-walk scene comes down in #1. The Atlantic City bathing beauties begin their parade number, entering left and right from the tormentor and #1 entrances. During this number, the hotel room set is struck from #2. Just prior to the end of the number the bathing beauties move onto the apron, the traveller closes in, and the boardwalk drop is raised. At the end of the number the bathing beauties are posed in front of the traveller for applause. After the applause the traveller opens, and the bathing beauties are found in the hotel lobby, Scene 4. Note that by using different depths, only one heavy scene shift, the removal of the hotel room scenery, has been necessary in the first four scenes. The scene shifts for the rest of the act are just as easily handled by changing the stage depth.

This rather involved illustration should emphasize the need for careful organization and precision in assembling the parts of a musical. The total dramatic effect is obtained by continuous action paced so that it reaches a climax at the end of the act. Any flaw in the organizational pattern may destroy the whole. The technical crews must be carefully organized and coordinated with the rest of the production. The director must lay out every shift long before the production goes into rehearsal.

Methods for Covering Shifts

In the first act of *Of Thee I Sing*, Scenes 3, 5, and 7 are cover scenes. They are written primarily to permit time for changing the full stage Scenes 4, 6, and 8. Sometimes the cover scene is inadequate in length to cover the shift. In these cases several other methods, some good, some bad, can be used to extend the time.

The orchestral reprise, the repetition of a previous number played by the orchestra, is the most used and the least satisfactory of the stalling devices. In poorly organized shows there is a wait for the shift at the end of almost every scene. Lights are played on the curtain, and the orchestra repeats a tune performed earlier. This procedure stops the progress of the show; it has no visual appeal whatsoever; it destroys all sense of pace; the break is often so severe that the audience becomes restless and turns away from the show to chat.

A second and slightly stronger method is the vocal reprise. A duet or trio steps onto the apron and sings the reprise. Its advantage lies in its appeal to the eye; otherwise, it has the same faults as the orchestral reprise.

The specialty, a third method of covering a shift, is superior to the vocal reprise. Audiences, for the most part, like specialties if they are well handled. They do, however, have the disadvantage of breaking the continuity of the production.

Another method of covering is the encore. If an encore can be worked on the apron, it can have color and excitement and maintain the continuity of the production. The problem with the encore is to make the audience really want it. After all, an encore is an extension of a musical number. If the audience has had enough of the tune as a regular part of the show, it may not be very enthusiastic about a repeat performance. The desirability of the encore can be increased by treating it in a manner totally different from the number itself.

The best method of covering a shift is the dissolve, a change in the playing depth during a musical number, permitting the traveller to be closed to cover the upstage shift. The full stage number at the end of a scene may be closed down or dissolved by closing the traveller part way through the number so that the latter part is played in #1. Or the musical number may begin on the apron or in #1 and later be opened up or dissolved by opening the traveller, exposing the full stage set.

In the Henderson–De Sylva show, *Good News*, the first three scenes are difficult to shift without dissolves.

Act I Scene Plot for *Good News*

Scene 1.	Campus Exterior	set in #3
Scene 2.	Dormitory Room	set in #2
Scene 3.	Administration Hall	set in #3

Scene 2 cannot be set until Scene 1 has been concluded. In this case, the authors have provided a dissolve for the change. In the first scene, the final tune, "The Best Things in Life Are Free," must be plotted to include the dissolve. The verse and the first refrain are sung as a duet between the leading man and the leading lady. The second refrain is sung by the chorus. At the end of this chorus refrain, the dissolve begins. Two specialty dancers step in front of the chorus and dance down to the apron. The scene traveller is closed behind them. The scene shift from the exterior to the dormitory room begins immediately. After the dancers have finished, they dance off left and right and lead the chorus onto the apron for a final refrain that completes the number. After the applause, eight bars of exit music cover the exit of the chorus left and right. Then the traveller opens on the dormitory scene.

Since almost every full stage scene in a musical show begins and ends with a musical number, the dissolve is usually the best method of providing covering time for shifts because the dissolve does not destroy the continuity of the show.

DIALOGUE IN THE MUSICAL

Few musical comedies have a good dramatic script. The plots and dialogue of most operettas are odious. It seems that excellent playwrights have seldom been stimulated to write book for the musical, a logical circumstance in that the primary emphasis is placed on the music. After the performance, audiences remember the songs and dances, the gaiety and color, which is the musical. In exceptional cases the comic lead may be remembered, but never the story.

The lack of good writing creates a major problem for the non-professional director. It is further complicated by the dated quality of many standard musical scripts. This is particularly true of operettas. The music with its universal appeal has lived on; the book is dead.

If eager writers are available, the director may do well to get permission to rewrite some musical books in their entirety. At the very least, extensive cutting will be necessary. The latter is the easier procedure for three reasons: the story is unimportant, the comedy scenes stand by themselves, and most musicals are too long, anyway.

Let us assume that the director has cut the script and added dialogue wherever necessary, what next? The show must be brought to life.

The technical treatment of music and dialogue in the musical show is somewhat different from that given a regular play. The give and take between the audience and the players is increased. The songs are sung quite frankly to the audience. The audience is expected to applaud the singers and dancers. The dialogue units are projected into the audience.

In Chapter 7, the "fourth wall" was defined as an invisible barrier between the actor and the audience. In the regular dramatic play, the actor must not break the fourth wall and make contact with the audience, or the illusion is broken.

In the musical show, the fourth wall is consciously broken during the musical numbers. The singing and dancing is directed to the audience. In the dialogue units, the fourth wall may be removed if the director desires. Note, however, that the dialogue units in some musical shows will be more effective if they are treated exactly as in the regular play. In *South Pacific,* the gentle love scenes between Liat and Lieutenant Cable should be set apart from the audience. In this case, preservation of the illusion of reality is essential. At the other extreme, the buffoonery of the leading comics in *The Desert Song* is more effective if played quite frankly for and to the audience.

Almost all comedy in the musical show is of the farce or burlesque variety. The techniques and responses desired for these types of comedy are detailed in Chapter 26, "Comedy."

COMPOSITION AND MOVEMENT

As stated in a general way earlier in the chapter, the desires of the general director and the musical director are at odds in setting composition and movement. The musical director wants his voices front, center, and motionless for best performance. The stage director wants colorful pictures with exciting movement to appeal to the eye. The compositional aspects of this conflict are, for the most part, settled by using levels and a shallow stage. If the musical director objects to excessive movement, a compromise must be reached on this score.

Chorus Arrangement

Three principles already discussed are basic to simple chorus arrangement: (1) division of the chorus into lines and sections, (2) assignment of a particular entrance to each chorus section, and (3) establishment of a "home position," discussed at length in the material on crowds, Chapter 21.

The chorus may be arranged by following each of the succeeding steps. Line up the chorus as shown in Figure 38. Place the front line of the chorus at floor level, the second line on steps or an intermediate level, and the third line on the highest platforms usable and available. Arrange a basic composition that creates an ideal pictorial effect, one that fulfills the demands of the script. In some shows this may be a straight line of military precision or irregular crowd formations in others.

Have each chorus member determine his exact position on the stage and assign this as his home position. Any number of different compositions can be arranged by moving the chorus members no more than two or three steps from their home positions. The home position should be used as the basis for all of the chorus compositions in the show.

If the choruses have been organized according to the suggested organizational pattern, there will be three chorus sections to each side of the stage. With the wing and drop setting there will also be three numbered entrances upstage of the apron on each side. Thus, each of the six chorus sections may be assigned a home entrance to be used throughout the production. The entrance letter and number is always the same as the chorus section number. For example, Line Right #3 always uses Entrance Right #3.

At first glance, this system of arranging the chorus with each section tied to a single entrance may seem inflexible and obvious. If the entrances, exits, and chorus groupings are handled with imagination, the members of the audience will not perceive the presence of an organizational pattern. Remember that the audience sees the production only once; the director, who is aware of the pattern at the start, sees the production dozens of times.

Chorus Movement

There are three distinct types of chorus movement: entrances and exits, crowd reactions to dialogue events, and movement during singing. Chorus entrances and exits are often difficult because the playwright has no real reason for bringing the chorus on stage except to have them sing. The script often reads "Chorus enters." Such an instruction is not very helpful to the director. Every entrance must be motivated. There must be a reason for it. An added hazard: most chorus people are not superior actors; they are unable to establish motivations for themselves. The director must find motivation in the script or create it from thin air.

If possible, stagger the entrances and exits of the chorus. Do not bring them on in a single rush, but build up the number of people on stage gradually through the last pages or so of dialogue. If this procedure won't work, let some chorus members motivate the entrance of the rest of the group. For example, add a line or so of dialogue, so that the first two or three chorus people who enter call back to the others and urge them to hurry. Numerous devices are possible. They must be selected by the director. The same principle applies to exits. Establish some kind of offstage motivation. Generally, it is much easier to supply reasons for leaving than it is to supply reasons for coming. Again, stagger the exit if possible so that the departure of the chorus does not resemble a stampede.

Crowd reaction to dialogue is also a problem in motivation. The musical chorus can be handled in exactly the same manner as any other crowd (see Chapter 21). Because of the lack of acting experience of most chorus people and the size of the group it will take considerable time to build the crowd reactions. These reactions should be rehearsed before the assembly rehearsals begin.

Songs must be sung and "sold" with activity and movement. Good singing is not enough. The audience must see as well as hear the vibrant enthusiasm of the number. Too much movement, however, lessens the chance for good singing, so a balance must be reached. The movement may be simple, spontaneous action arising from the situation. If so, be sure that the action is dynamic and imaginative. Every audience has seen enough of the drinking song interpreted with indolently waved, obviously empty beer mugs. Remember, weak voices singing enthusiastically will gain a greater audience response than fine voices lacking exuberance.

Another type of chorus activity with great audience appeal is configurated movement, simple precise chorus movement which helps to interpret the music. It may take the form of precision drills or merely graceful gestures and simple steps. The movements should stem from the music itself. They can project the mood of the song in a general way, or they can be a specific interpretation of the lyrics. The success of configurated movements depends upon absolute precision. They can be taught to any group with a good sense of rhythm.

Solo Movement

The principles controlling movement are the same for the soloist as for the chorus. The song must be projected physically as well as vocally. Most good singers have their own particular style. The director should incorporate this style in the movement pattern. Unfortunately, some lead singers have been trained in glee clubs and choirs, where physical activity is minimized. They must be taught to use the stage. Long before the assembly rehearsals, the general director should have the lead singers interpret their songs with action, then the director and the singer can work out the best method for selling the song.

The musical show is hard work, but the results are usually worth all of the energy expended. There are few greater thrills for the director or the players than the deafening applause that climaxes a successful musical production number. The color, excitement, and vibrance of the musical production have made it a favorite of playgoers throughout the centuries.

22

Central Staging

CENTRAL STAGING, the new vogue in theatrical production, is actually the oldest production procedure in the world. For centuries, the audience surrounded a central ring or playing area. A discussion of the resurgence of this oldest form is included here because it opens a new vista in production which can be used to advantage by many theatrical groups hampered by the lack of a modern stage and equipment. Central staging will not replace the present picture frame stage, but it can act as a substitute for, or complement to, present staging principles.

Definition of Central Staging

As the term implies, central staging involves a playing area located in the center with the audience seated on all sides. The earliest examples of this form are found in the tribal dances around the campfire. The Greek dancing ring was a refinement of the earliest form. The Roman arena, a further advancement in audience comfort, maintained the central playing area and has continued to the present day, still carrying its ancient name, *the circus.* The medieval platform stages—wagons rolled into the town square —were also central stages. The players performed on the top of the wagons with the audience clustered about. The Elizabethan stage shows a mixture of forms. The outer stage with the audience seated and standing on three sides was a modified central stage, while the inner stage took on some of the characteristics of the picture frame stage.

In the early 1600's, the bulk of the playing area was pushed behind the proscenium picture frame. The outer or fore stage gradually decreased in size until it became the narrow strip known as the apron in the contemporary theatre.

The prime reason for moving the stage behind the proscenium arch was to increase the possibilities of creating illusion. The constantly improving technical facilities were aimed at intensifying illusion. Richard Wagner, the famous German composer and originator of modern music-drama, insisted that a "mystic gulf" separated the audience from the stage. This physical distance was presumed to aid illusion. The remnants of Wagner's idea are found in the orchestra pit of the conventional theatre.

Today, the stage has again been wrested from behind its frame and set in the middle of the audience. The modern experimenters who have re-created the central stage believe that illusion can be preserved without a picture frame, mystic gulf, or elaborate technical production.

Central staging goes by many different names. The first of the modern central stages was constructed at the University of Washington. It is the Penthouse Theatre, the name having nothing to do with the placement of the stage. Margo Jones named the procedure Theatre-in-the-Round. An edifice for this style of production at the University of Miami, Florida, is called the Ring Theatre. Other titles which have been used are *arena staging, circus staging, circle staging.* In every case, the principle of placing the stage in the midst of the audience is observed.

The Physical Plan

The only absolute requirement for the central stage is a room of sufficient size to contain an audience and a playing area. The playing area is opened up in the center of the room, and the audience is arranged around the stage on every side with two or more aisles or entrances. In most arena theatres the audience is raised a step or two, so that everyone can see. In others, the stage is raised a foot or more, setting the players slightly above the audience.

The shape of the playing area depends upon the dimensions of the room. Every conceivable geometric arrangement has been tried. The playing area may be round, oval, elliptical, rectangular, or square. The circle, the oval, or the ellipse is usually the most satisfactory because the corners of the rectangler or square do not make very satisfactory playing areas.

The size of the playing area may vary, depending upon the requirements of the play and the space available. At the University of Washington, the auditorium is built in the shape of an ellipse, 42 feet by 48 feet at the largest dimensions.

The size of the audience is determined by the desired intimacy of the playing. The auditorium at the University of Washington seats 172 people. The Ring Theatre at the University of Miami seats 400 people in five rows around the stage but is planned ultimately to accommodate 900, only 100 or so less than the average New York legitimate house seats. Except for the demands of intimacy, there is no physical reason why the audience shouldn't run to thousands if the director desires.

Another physical requirement is that there be several entrances to the playing area. Usually from two to four aisles are used by the audience for entering or leaving the theatre and by the players as entrances and exits to and from the playing area.

The claim of the central staging enthusiasts that any room may be converted into a playing arena is probably somewhat exaggerated. It is important that the arena have a theatrical quality. If the room cannot provide a theatrical feeling, it should at least be neutral. Auditoriums built specifically for central staging are usually warm but neutral in color and texture. They exude a feeling of comfortable coziness which contributes to the intimacy of the playing style.

A final physical requirement is adequate lighting. The equipment may be simple and inexpensive, but it should provide a feeling of being in the theatre. It is difficult, if not impossible, to obtain a sense of the theatrical with the lighting normally provided in most classrooms. Theatrical illusion requires a darkened audience area and a lighted stage area.

In conclusion, the physical requirements of the central stage are few, for the style harks back to the day when a circle of earth or a wagon top was sufficient.

THE ADVANTAGES OF CENTRAL STAGING

New forms arise or old forms are revived because of a desire for progress. Some directors have felt seriously handicapped by picture frame staging. They feel that the audience should not be separated from the stage. Let us examine the advantages claimed for central staging.

Economy

Economy is an obvious advantage of central staging. Many small theatre groups have been unable to finance dramatic production because of the cost of elaborate technical equipment. With this new style, any group may enter the field of dramatic production without burdening costs.

Even the most lavish arena theatre is more economical than the picture frame theatre. The Wisconsin Union Theatre, one of the most elaborate college theatrical plants in the country, cost approximately $1,000,000 when it was built in 1939. Four or five superb ring theatres can be built for the same figure.

Simplicity

The harshest critics of the conventional picture frame production charge that modern drama is stifled by its own complexities. They feel that the emphasis on scenery, complicated lighting, technical and theatrical effects of all kinds have unduly subordinated the expression of the actor. The central stage, with its lack of frills and furbelows, can raise acting to the status it rightly deserves. Without question, the stark simplicity of central staging does emphasize the actor. It is the actor's theatre.

Imagination

Since central staging reduces scenic effects to a minimum, theatrical illusion depends upon the imaginative creation of the actor and the audience. The advocates of central staging claim, and rightly so, that imaginative flight can give the audience a fuller dramatic experience than can any attempt to reproduce the fantasy of drama upon the stage. Theatre is an imaginative form. The audience must be allowed to create its own illusions. Central staging encourages the audience to do so.

Intimacy

The fourth great advantage of central staging is intimacy. Since the audience is arranged on all sides of the playing area within three or four feet of the stage, the proximity of the spectator is assured. The advocates of central staging claim great advantages for this arrangement. They say that the audience is able to get closer to the play in mind and spirit as well as body. As Fred Koch, Jr., the director of the Ring Theatre at the University of Miami has said, "The audience no longer watches a play. It is enfolded by it and vibrates with it. The audience is the play." This may be true in part. Certainly the proximity greatly increases the power of the stimulus. Problems of hearing and seeing have vanished. The spectator can experience the most subtle changes in the actor's mood and demeanor.

It should be noted that intimacy, which was the basic premise of the first arena theatres, is gradually being decreased. For obvious commercial reasons, professional companies using central staging have increased the seating capacity to a thousand or more. Some of the spectators in these auditoriums are as far removed from the action as they would be in most conventional theatres.

The great advantage of intimate contact between the actor and the spectator may, in some instances, become a distinct disadvantage. This potentiality is discussed in the section concerning the problems of the central stage.

Subtlety and Reservation

The intimate contact of the actor and the auditor results in a fifth advantage for central staging. One of the great bugaboos of conventional staging is eliminated: problems of projection are nonexistent. The subtlety and reservation with which the actor may play is greatly increased, for lines, movement, and business must travel 30 to 40 feet in the arena rather than 100 to 200 feet.

The problem of projecting a simple and charming love scene when some spectators are 15 feet away and others are 100 feet from the action has always vexed directors. No actor can be very simple and charming when forced to project his voice 100 feet. This problem is compromised in the conventional theatre. The projection level is set for the midpoint in the house. As a result, the spectators in the first few rows of the conventional auditorium are treated to an artificial, forced performance, while those at the back of the house may have to strain to hear and see. The intimacy of central staging simplifies this problem.

Plasticity

The final advantage of the new-old form is derived from its added plasticity. By projecting the players into the audience, the third dimension is regained. No longer is the spectator treated to the largely two-dimensional view of the picture within a frame. In central staging, the opportunity to model in three-dimensional form is again possible. The realistic arrangements that appear in life can, with certain major alterations, be introduced upon the stage.

PROBLEMS OF CENTRAL STAGING

Although there are real advantages to the central stage, there are also some definite limitations. Some of these difficulties are inherent in the style, and others are merely the result of the seeming newness of the technique. Most audiences, actors, and directors have been trained in the conventions of the picture frame stage. The success of central staging is affected to some degree by these previous experiences. An even greater difficulty is the lack of good drama written for the central stage. The contemporary realistic drama is partially dependent upon the advantages of the picture frame, despite arguments to the contrary.

Problems of Illusion

What caused the development of the picture frame stage? Why was the central stage gradually shifted to a position behind the proscenium arch? Why was a physical space created between the audience and the stage? There must be some reason for a trend that began in the 1600's, was resolved in the 1800's, and continued to the present day. The trend was in a large measure based on the desire for greater illusion.

In Chapter 4, the need for aesthetic distance was emphasized. It was observed that detachment helps the spectator respond subjectively to the beauty of any work of art. Physical distance and aesthetic distance are essential to the necessary detachment.

Central staging, with its attendant proximity, hinders artistic detachment. Aesthetic distance is possible, but the problem of maintaining detachment is sharply increased. There is a much greater chance that the audience may objectify the scene and be-come aware of the techniques of the drama.

Koch has said of central staging that "the close-up, born in Hollywood, now emerges from its celluloid prison into the sunny world of flesh and blood actors. The theatre experience is electri-fied." Such may be the case. The possibility of increased empathic response is heightened. Empathy is as important to the theatre as aesthetic distance. The audience may, with greater intensity, identify themselves with the players. This greater intensity, how-ever, can create a problem, for complete identification destroys illusion.

The above are not criticisms of central staging. They are, rather, pleas for recognition of the differences in the style and the po-tential difficulties involved. The intimacy of the style requires greater subtlety of play. The balance between participation and detachment must be maintained.

Problems of the Audience

The novelty of theatre-in-the-round appeals to most spectators. Sitting so close to, and on any side of, the stage is an exciting experience. This novelty may account for an initial burst of audi-ence enthusiasm, but it cannot hold an audience for long. Arena theatres that have stood the test of time prove that there are other reasons for its success.

The physical arrangements of central staging may distress some spectators. Since some light usually spills from the stage into the audience, the spectator can see other playgoers across the stage. This may act as a distracting influence. It is difficult to suspend one's critical judgment when a restless youngster or an overdressed matron seated in full view across the stage is a constant reminder of the artificiality of the situation.

The individual auditor may be more aware of audience reac-tion in the arena situation. This should increase social facilitation, which is all to the good, providing the response is desirable. On the other hand, any undesirable reactions are facilitated accord-ingly. Thus the increased awareness can become a distinct disad-vantage. In other words, illusion may be more difficult to maintain because of the physical arrangement of the arena.

Some years ago, a comparative study was made of the effects of conventional and arena staging on the audience. It was found that many of the spectators were embarrassed by the intensity of the stimulation from the stage. When the characters in the play were embroiled in an intimate family argument, these spectators felt that they were intruders in the privacy of the home. This reaction corroborates the testimony concerning the increased intensity of the stimulus, but the result is undesirable. Perhaps this is the reason that the University of Washington usually limits its productions to comedies about which the audience can be comparatively objective.

Problems of the Actor

Central staging offers a great challenge to the actor. It removes many of the crutches upon which some actors lean, but, in turn, it raises the actor upon a pedestal to display his wares. The arena theatre is the actor's theatre. It must be remembered, however, that the arena plays no favorites. It emphasizes poor acting to the same degree that it does good acting.

Since the audience is able to examine at close range every flick of an eyelash, character portrayal must be complete to the last detail. Totality of characterization is imperative. The smallest gesture has meaning. In a like manner, the slightest misstep is distracting. Technique must be perfected.

The proximity of the central stage sharply limits the actor's range. Make-up and costume are less effective in covering disparities between the actor and the role. Type casting becomes more important. If the actor does not look or sound the part, there is no distance to help soften the discrepancy. Idiosyncrasies of the actor may pass unobserved on the conventional stage but are now seen and judged by the audience.

Problems of the Director and Designer

Each of the differences between conventional staging and central staging modifies the direction and staging of the play. The circular playing area, the surrounding audience, the scenic simplicity, the intimacy of the form create new problems.

Play selection procedures are limited by the new style. Most of the principles of direction discussed in Part Two must be modified. And finally, the problems of the designer and technician are different.

The rest of this chapter is devoted to a study of the techniques of play selection, the principles of direction, and the problems of staging the arena production.

PLAY SELECTION FOR THE CENTRAL STAGE

Play selection is a major problem in central staging, for the simple reason that most plays are not written for the arena. Most playwrights have written for the conventional stage with its scenic and illusory advantages. Even the medieval and classic plays which were written for central playing presuppose a very different kind of audience and playing style; therefore, almost every play must be adapted for central staging.

Although no blanket rules can be laid down defining the limitations in play selection for the central stage, certain guiding principles may be suggested. Imaginative directors may be able to overcome some or all of the difficulties. The beginner should ask the following questions before selecting a play for the central stage.

Is the Play Dependent upon Spectacle

The necessity for simplicity and intimacy in the arena production makes the extravaganza difficult if not impossible to produce. The arena production must not bog down in excessive scenery.

Does the Play Have Numerous Settings

The possibilities of changing scenery on the central stage are severely limited. Shows with multiple scenes will be hard to stage effectively. For example, Claire Boothe Luce's *The Women* has twelve scene changes. Such production is a major problem for the best-equipped conventional stage. Molnar's *Liliom,* Odets' *Golden Boy,* Coward's *Cavalcade,* and many of Shakespeare's plays have similar problems. If the show of many scenes can be produced with stylized fragments of settings it may be adapted to the arena. On the other hand, the play which requires complicated scene changes should be rejected.

Does the Play Require Complex Properties

The difficulties resulting from complicated or heavy property plots are similar to those created by multiple scenes. The mechanics of introducing the properties becomes a serious problem. The eight beds needed for *The Hasty Heart* would seriously hamper direction of the play for the central stage. The multiple scenes and properties of Wilder's *The Skin of Our Teeth* would make it a doubtful choice. Any play with a large dining room scene in which food must be set and dishes cleared is difficult; for example, *The Swan*. Complicated scenic and property novelties virtually eliminate some plays. The river in *Dead End* and the boat scene in *The Gentle People* are examples of such problems. In summary, any show dependent upon technical effects must be studied carefully to determine whether or not arena production is feasible.

Does the Play Depend upon Large Crowd Scenes

The large cast and the crowd are the bane of the central stage. The audience is so close to the stage that the illusion of a crowd is difficult to create. On the conventional stage, small groups may be directed so that they give the impression of a much larger crowd. This is not possible on the central stage.

Does the Play Have Scenes of Intense Emotion

The question of whether intensely emotional plays are advisable for arena production is debatable. Some directors feel that intensely emotional plays embarrass the audience. This is particularly true of contemporary plays in which the spectator can easily identify himself with the characters. Period plays have an advantage in that a mask of time softens the emotional identification of the spectator.

There is no doubt that a violent play or scene can be produced in-the-round providing it is handled with consummate skill and imagination, but the director must recognize the problems propounded by intense emotion.

What Types of Plays Can Be Produced

Much of the preceding discussion has imposed limitations upon the selection of plays for the central stage. It may appear that the

possibilities for arena staging are too limited to make it worthwhile. Such an assumption is foolish. The vast bulk of drama can
be successfully produced on the central stage.

Reversing the limiting characteristics indicates the best choices
for this style of production. If scenic spectacle will not work, plays
that depend primarily on acting will. Although naturalistic settings
are difficult, plays that can be treated in a simple, suggestive, or
symbolic style lend themselves to the central stage. Shows with
multiple settings may be hard to produce, but hundreds of plays
do maintain the unities of time and place. Complex properties can
be eliminated from many plays and render such drama satisfactory
for arena production. Shows with large casts and crowds increase
the directing problems, but imaginative cutting may make them
acceptable. If not, there is a great quantity of fine drama not dependent upon large numbers of players.

The one-act play is in many ways ideal for the central stage.
It usually has continuous action; it is simple in structure; it has
a small cast; it is seldom dependent upon complex scenic effects. The
central stage may open up new vistas of drama, untouched because
of the complexities of conventional production.

PRINCIPLES OF DIRECTION

Each of the principles of play directing discussed in Part Two
will be modified to some extent by the removal of the picture
frame and the projection of the stage into the audience. The
composition, movement, emotional key, and tempo will all undergo
changes.

The purpose of the production remains the same. The interpretation of the story, the moods, and the meanings do not change.
The change in the stage should merely facilitate the laughter and
the tears of drama. The following discussion considers the differences in the principles of direction.

Floor Plans and Furniture Arrangement

Some directors maintain that the central stage is "just like life."
This is a mistaken concept. The central stage is as highly artificial
as the conventional stage. You cannot line the edges of the stage
with furniture as you line the walls of the average living room

without curtailing the possibilities for imaginative action. Furniture placed in such a manner acts as a fence that screens the actors from the audience and tends to destroy the feeling of intimacy. A more satisfactory method of arranging furniture is a modification of the usual placement. The major pieces of furniture are placed near the center of the room, and a few smaller pieces are placed near the edges. The two types of floor plans are shown in Figure 40.

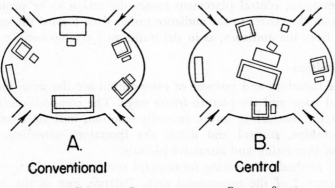

A.
Conventional

B.
Central

FIG. 40. FURNITURE PLACEMENT ON THE CENTRAL STAGE

The advantages of central placement can be seen by comparing the two drawings, though either plan can be used. In each plan, exactly the same pieces of furniture have been used. With the traditional arrangement, it is more difficult to use the furniture effectively. Whenever a player sits on a piece of furniture, his back is turned to that part of the audience nearest him, and the other pieces of furniture block the view of the spectators on the opposite side of the stage. Most action on a stage tends to center about furniture clusters. With a traditional arrangement, furniture cannot serve its normal and usual purposes. Furthermore, if the players stand in groups in the center of the room, their backs are to the audience.

If some furniture is placed at the center, action can be handled in a more logical manner. The major piece or pieces of furniture can act as motivating forces which encourage the players to use them. The smaller pieces of furniture at the edges of the stage help to motivate the actor to the outer portions of the stage. A motivated movement pattern is thus established. Such a pattern utilizes the entire stage area and provides maximum variety in movement.

Central placement can be easily adapted to every kind of room. In the tea scene, the tea table may be centered. In the bedroom scene, the bed and perhaps the vanity may be placed center. In the living room scene, the sofa and a desk might be centered, as in Figure 40.

Remember, central placement causes the action to be projected out from the center to the audience rather than toward the center, away from the audience, as in the traditional arrangement.

Composition

The functions and purpose of composition are the same for the central stage and the picture frame stage. The compositions must reflect the motivating forces, intensify emotion, indicate character relationships, control and direct the spectator's attention, and present interesting and attractive pictures.

The methods of creating meaningful compositions change with the removal of the proscenium arch. Balance, one of the major considerations on the conventional stage, does not exist on the central stage. Coherence is seldom a problem because the central stage is usually so small that it is difficult to get a scattered effect.

The problems of controlling and directing attention are greatly increased. Most of the key factors, which direct attention when the audience can see from only one side, are meaningless when the audience is placed on all sides.

Body position, probably the most important single compositional means of controlling attention on the picture frame stage, is worthless. On the central stage, an open body position for one side of the house is a completely closed body position for the opposite side of the house. In a similar way, area has lost much of its effectiveness as a means of controlling attention. Downstage or nearer one section of the audience is upstage or away from the audience on the opposite side of the stage. Space relationships also have lost some of their value. A character who is separated from the group as seen from one angle will be covered by the group for the spectator who is seated ninety degrees farther around the circle.

With the loss of body position, area, and space, some of the other compositional factors take on a greater importance.

Level and focus are very important in controlling attention. Emphasis can be maintained by placing the dominant character at a higher level than the less dominant characters. Unfortunately, level gained by the use of steps and platforms is seldom used. Most differences in level come from the standing, sitting, and prone positions. Direct visual focus will lead the attention of any part of the audience to the focal point of the composition.

As the compositional factors have lost their power, the non-compositional factors have gained in strength. The speaking character is dominant; the moving character is dominant; and such factors as amount of light, brilliance of color, and energy of portrayal will direct attention.

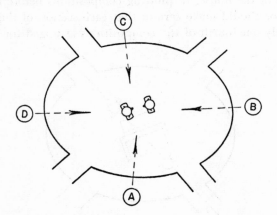

FIG. 41. SIGHT LINES ON THE CENTRAL STAGE

No composition on a central stage can be ideal from all points in the house. Any picture set to be meaningful and attractive from one point of observation loses at least a part of its value when viewed from the side or back. The conventional stage has the advantage of placing all of the spectators on one side. Each composition may be tailored for the restricted sight lines of the audience. In the arena, all sight lines are of equal importance.

On the conventional stage, compositions are arranged for the entire audience. The spectator sitting in the best seat in the house and the spectator sitting in the worst seat can see clearly if the sight lines are observed (see Figure 27).

The more complex problem of sight lines on the central stage is illustrated in Figure 41. If a composition is ideal for spectator A and satisfactory for C, it is bound to be weak for spectators B and D, who are looking at the same scene from different angles. What can be done to make central compositions satisfactory for all spectators?

The first solution is rotation. Since any composition can be ideal from only one direction, this view of the composition should be continually turned. As many compositions must be arranged for spectators B, C, and D as are set for spectator A. This does not imply that an observable pattern of rotation need be used. It merely means that the director must conscientiously direct from every side of the house. In plotting compositions before rehearsals, the director should make certain that each section of the audience has roughly one-fourth of the compositions arranged for it.

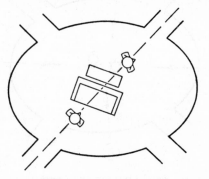

FIG. 42. COMPOSITION

A second solution is to open the compositions. The furniture placement discussed earlier influences this procedure. If the furniture is arranged around the sides of the room, much of the action will take place at the edges of the stage and be focused toward the center of the room. With central placement, the actors are more frequently found at the center of the stage and the action more often focused toward the audience. This is illustrated in Figure 42.

Composition on the central stage can also be strengthened by loosening the arrangements and using the aisles. In the conventional stage picture compositions are usually arranged with characters rather close together. This must be done so that the audience with its two-dimensional view can see the interrelationship of the characters. In central staging, the reverse is true. The audience has a three-dimensional view, and thus the compositions may be loosened, the characters set farther apart. Compare Figures 41 and 42; note that the closely placed actors cover each other from more sight lines than do the separated characters.

The aisles also may be used to advantage to reduce covering and eliminate some of the weakest body positions. In Figure 42, the closed body position of one of the characters is in line with the aisle. Notice, also, that the characters cover each other completely only at the sight line from the aisles. The aisle sight line is indicated by the line of dashes in Figure 42.

Movement

The preceding discussion should indicate that composition is less effective and more difficult on the central stage. The opposite is true of movement. The central stage is a "stage of action." Since static compositions cannot be of equal artistry for all of the audience, increased movement which changes compositions rapidly supplants static composition in maintaining the dramatic effect. This is the greatest reason why static plays that do not call for generous activity are difficult to produce in-the-round.

The principles and purposes of movement are the same on the central stage as on the conventional stage, though the technical application differs somewhat.

Since balance is not important in central staging, the dress or counter is unnecessary although it can be used to loosen the composition. Movement for position is no longer related to upstage and downstage or left and right. Most positional movement is related to the aisles and to arranging compositions which are reasonably satisfactory from all sides.

Movement should be used to rotate the compositions; thus, curved movement is practical. If the stage has central furniture placement, blocking will stem from the central furniture cluster as from the hub of a wheel. Any movement that rotates the action should improve the view for different portions of the audience. Curved movement is illustrated in Figure 43.

Notice that as each character moves in a curve, his body position changes in relation to various parts of the audience. In addition, the movement appears logically motivated because of the central furniture placement. Obviously, curved movement must be inter-

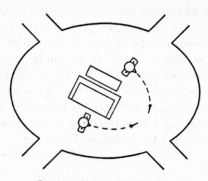

Fig. 43. Curved Movement

spersed with straight line movements, so that the audience does not get the artificial impression of a wheel that is turning before their eyes.

The only entrances to the playing area are the aisles, usually from two to four in number. They are also used to seat the audience. The use of the aisle for character entrances and exits creates a definite problem. Usually, no furniture may block an entrance or exit. If some of the aisles are not used for entrances or exits in the play, however, they are good locations for furniture because the actor who has his back to an aisle is not completely closed to any member of the audience.

Despite the difficulties in entering and exiting, the central stage offers great opportunity for imaginative movement impossible on the conventional stage. Action assumes a new and more vital place in the drama.

Business

The close-up provided by the central stage magnifies the importance of stage business. The subtlety of the acting style makes detailed visual elaboration of character necessary. The audience is able to see every movement, no matter how small.

The principles of stage business outlined in Chapter 9 will operate, for the most part, on the arena stage. The only real change is in the principle of opening business to the audience. Business opened for one section is closed for another.

The need for precision and timing is increased. On the conventional stage, some business can be telescoped or condensed. Condensation is more difficult on the central stage. For example, eating and drinking are usually at least partially faked on the conventional stage. Faking must be very carefully handled in the arena because the audience can see what is happening.

In many ways, business is easier to execute because it can be more natural. It need not be intensified, and compositional problems are frequently fewer. Embraces, telephoning, and kneeling, may be handled with complete naturalness, but some business is much more difficult. Occasionally, a particular object must be emphasized for the audience. The emphasis is simple when the audience is on only one side, but such stress is more complex when the audience surrounds the actor and playing area.

In conclusion, stage business is increased both in amount and complexity. It must be more elaborate and carried out in greater detail with greater precision. Characters must be more fully developed visually as every visual cue helps the imaginative flight of the audience.

Emotional Key

The basic principles of expressing emotion are the same, regardless of the method of staging. Any modification comes in the projection of the emotion.

Simplicity is the keynote in central staging. Subtlety and reserve are necessary to the expression of emotion. The intimacy of the form reduces the need for violent vocal or physical projection. In the motion picture, the tense closing of a fist can express anger as vividly as a flailing gesture used on the conventional stage. In this sense, central staging is similar to the motion picture. Carefully selected vocal and visual patterns can convey the feeling without excessive activity. The audience is able to see and sense the muscular tension of the actor without broad display. One of the great advantages of the arena is the possibility, hitherto withheld, of portraying the most subtle nuances of emotion.

Tempo and Timing

Since central staging lacks the attention-getting technical devices of the conventional stage, the actors and the play must provide the excitement by themselves. Thus, tempo is frequently increased. In Chapter 11 it was observed that vitality and broad visual and vocal projection contribute directly to the impression of high speed in playing. Since arena playing does not require broad projection, this aspect of tempo has to be supplanted by an increase in the actual speed. This is one of the important reasons why static plays are difficult to produce. The vitality of the dialogue contributes greatly to the feeling of swiftly paced action. On the other hand, the intimacy of the arena makes a feeling of vibrance and enthusiasm easier to produce with less effort.

The physical arrangement of the central stage increases the problems of timing, particularly for entrances and exits. The elimination of doors makes entering the playing area through one of the aisles an extended process. The impact that can be the effect of the abrupt entrance or exit is difficult to achieve on the central stage, for the actor can be seen while he traverses the length of the aisle. The entering actor must assume the character before he enters the aisle. The timing of the entrances so that the actor arrives in the acting area at the precise moment that he should join the action requires extended rehearsal.

TECHNICAL PROBLEMS IN CENTRAL STAGING

Technical production in the arena is very different from conventional staging. Some aspects of technical production are greatly simplified by the starkness of the style. At the same time, the proximity of the audience to the stage creates new problems. The essential modifications in technical production are briefly summarized below.

Lighting

The equipment required for lighting the central stage is nominal. The placement and control of the light sources are more complex. The problem is clear-cut. How can the stage area be lit adequately without lighting the audience at the same time? On the conventional stage, lighting instruments can be masked and directed away from the audience. On the central stage, any light focused to shine on the actors from one side tends to spill into the audience on the opposite side. For this reason, most lighting in the arena theatre must come from above. This is called *top lighting*. Unfortunately, top lighting casts shadows on the actors' faces. These shadows can be softened somewhat by using table and floor lamps on the stage. Of course, the light from on stage sources should not be so bright that it distracts the audience. The placement of table and floor lamps must be studied carefully so that the lamps do not obstruct the sight lines between the actors and the audience. Lighting is very important in separating the stage and audience areas. Avoid letting light spill into the audience.

Costumes

Costume bills mount in central staging as a result of the proximity of the audience. The advantage of distance is gone. The makeshifts, satisfactory on the conventional stage, are impossible on the central stage. The arena may be thought of as a dress salon. The actors are the models or mannequins. Every detail of costuming can be seen by the audience. Any flaw in the material, the workmanship, the cleanliness, or the pressing is immediately noted by the spectator. Costumes must be exact. Such problems discourage the production of costume shows.

Make-up

It has been said that stage make-up is a craft; motion picture make-up is an art. The motion picture close-up shows every detail of the make-up, and the camera is a harsh critic of subterfuge. The striking similarity between the motion picture and the central stage is apparent. Make-up for the arena production must appear real at close range. In actuality, make-up is de-emphasized. For the women of the cast, street make-up, subtly heightened, will frequently suffice. Obviously, complex character make-ups are extremely difficult to reproduce. Beards, wigs, lines, and shadows appear false unless created with great artistry. This limitation in the use of make-up is one of the factors which necessitate close type casting.

Properties

Just as costumes and make-up must bear close scrutiny, so must properties. Dime store dishes look like dime store dishes. The battered chest with a fresh coat of paint looks like a battered chest with a fresh coat of paint. *The New York Times* looks like *The New York Times*. Properties, therefore, must be exact and of high quality. Faking is virtually impossible.

Property changes take place in front of the audience during the intermissions between the scenes. The simpler these changes can be, the less distraction will accrue when the change is made. These are the reasons for choosing shows in which the property plot is not burdensome.

Scene Changes

The problems of scenery are identical to those of properties. The scenery must be complete and appear real. Two-dimensional, painted scenery seldom gives the impression of three dimensions at close range. Thus, scenery must be simple or, better yet, non-existent. Scene changes also must be made in front of the audience. Some theatres dress the stage and property hands in simple uniforms such as neutral smocks or jackets, so that the individuality of the crew member does not distract. Scene and property changes must be accepted by the audience as conventions of the arena.

The Light Curtain

The curtain of the central stage is made of light. When the play is ready to begin, the house lights are dimmed out, the actors feel their way to their places either by counting steps or by following a trail of phosphorescent dots, and the stage lights are brought up. If the curtain is to be effective, the blackout of the house must be complete. At the end of the scene, the process is reversed. The actors must wait several seconds for the incandescence or afterglow of the lights to subside. The light curtain must be very carefully rehearsed and timed, so that actors are not caught in incongruous positions.

There is considerable truth in the statement that the central stage is similar to the motion picture. Every element of the production is brought sharply into focus. This new contact between the actor and the audience is the central stage's greatest advantage. With the greater intimacy, the actor, director, and technician will be judged anew. To succeed, they must be masters of the dramatic arts.

23

Styles of Production

STYLE MAY BE DEFINED as the kind of treatment given a production. Most plays may be produced in various ways, depending upon the point of view of the director or the particular mood or message he desires to stress. In some plays, the style is determined by the playwright. It is not so much that the playwright tells the director how to produce the play, but rather the fact that the play is written in a manner which demands a particular mode of presentation or production.

The treatment to be given a play is a decision that lies within the director's province. During his analysis of the script, he must determine the playwright's purpose and how it may best be communicated to the audience. The director is, first of all, an interpreting agent. The production is certainly a creative endeavor, but the production should give power to the playwright's message. The director who selects the style of production because he desires to experiment, rather than because he sincerely believes that it will strengthen the meanings of the play, does both the playwright and the audience a disservice.

PRESENTATION AND REPRESENTATION

Though there are infinite variations, two basic styles of dramatic production are readily discernible, though not so readily separable. They are representational or illusory staging and presentational or conventional staging.

Representational or Illusory Staging

Representational or illusory staging, with which this book has dealt almost exclusively, accounts for most play production. It is the attempt to represent life, to create the illusion for the audience that life of a particular time, place, or kind is actually occurring. The director of the representational production is pleased when the spectator at the end of an act has to shake himself to realize that he is in a theatre rather than in Amanda Prynne's apartment, or on Chris Christopherson's coal barge, or in the Elysian Fields. It is said with validity that representational staging is anti-theatrical; that is, it wholeheartedly rejects the existence of the stage platform and, indeed, the theatre itself.

The illusion created in representational staging may be real, partly real and partly unreal, or completely unreal, but in every case an illusion is created.

Presentational or Conventional Staging

Presentational or conventional production procedures are characterized by the frank recognition that the stage is merely a platform. The stage does not represent a kitchen, or a boxing ring, or a room in Hades. It is a platform where the drama is acted out or presented. It is theatrical in the sense that the production is, admittedly, in a theatre, on a stage. It is conventional in that the production's acceptance by an audience depends upon a series of conventions or rules of procedure, as in reality all theatrical production does. The prime difference is the amount and purpose of the convention.

The oriental drama and the classic Greek drama were essentially presentational. The oriental property man who changed the setting before the eyes of the audience was obviously a property man. The audience accepted this theatrical rule or convention and joined in the spirit of the production. The chorus, the formal architectural backgrounds, the grotesque masks worn by the actors in Attic drama were theatrical conventions.

Whether or not an illusion is created in presentational staging is a matter of controversy, the debating of which lies outside the province of this volume. Leading theatrical writers such as Sheldon

Cheney and Lee Simonson maintain that even the most conventional staging does aim at creating illusion. Mordecai Gorelik, on the other hand, devotes almost 500 pages to proving that conventional or presentational staging is non-illusory. The student who is interested in a detailed study of this controversy is referred to Sheldon Cheney's *The Theatre,* Lee Simonson's *The Stage Is Set,* and Mordecai Gorelik's *New Theatres for Old.*

In all fairness, one experimental theatrical form, highly presentational in nature, should be mentioned. It is the Epic theatre of Bertolt Brecht and Erwin Piscator. The Epic theatre is frankly anti-illusory. It is a propaganda theatre aimed at substituting thought for emotion. It wishes to make the stage a "play machine." It desires the elimination of the proscenium frame and the box setting. Decidedly experimental in style, Epic production offers new possibilities for the advanced director who is encouraged to study the style elsewhere.

At the outset, it was mentioned that presentation and representation are often difficult to separate. All productions have certain elements of each. Even the most representational production is based upon the theatrical conventions of excessive vocal projection, a three-walled room, painted scenery, and other equipment.

Some contemporary productions employ a mixture of the two styles. The open stage platform of *Our Town,* the masks of *The Great God Brown,* the "inner thoughts" of *Strange Interlude*—all are highly conventional elements in otherwise largely representational plays.

Even the presentational Epic drama occasionally employs representational elements such as scenes with distinct locale and fully developed characters.

Since most contemporary drama is primarily illusory and representational, a discussion of style fruitful, at least, for the beginning director may be an analysis of the degrees of reality employed in dramatic production.

The styles of dramatic production may be classified in two basic categories: styles which create reality in varying degrees and styles which are departures from reality.

REALISTIC STYLES

It was pointed out in Part One that no dramatic production is an actual representation of life. The process of transferring life to the stage automatically implies modification, change, selection, arrangement. Realistic styles strive for an illusion of reality. The scene depicts real places and things; the characters are real humans who respond to psychological stimuli much as they would in life. The setting, the actors, the lighting, the properties—all attempt to create the feeling of reality. This illusion may be accomplished in one of several ways. The differences depend upon the amount of selection and arrangement.

Naturalism

Naturalism is the most intensely realistic style. It aims at a reproduction of life upon the stage with a minimum of selection and arrangement. It has been called "slice of life" drama. Naturalism originated in the last half of the nineteenth century as a revolt against the artifice and sentimentality of the Romantic stages. As is true of most revolts, it went to the opposite extreme. Naturalism was based upon the concept that the theatre is life. Antoine, the father of naturalism, shocked the theatrical world with his reproductions of life. The naturalists rejected the "well-made" play. Their scenes were largely tableaux of life. In revolt against the ornate and beautiful, though meaningless, baroque scenery, the naturalists reproduced replicas of life. In revolt against the declamatory style of acting, the naturalistic actors "lived" their parts and played their roles with absolute verisimilitude, ignoring the audience even to the point of playing entire scenes with their backs to the audience.

The dominant factor in naturalism is the lack of selection and arrangement. Contemporary naturalistic productions do not carry this factor to the extremes mentioned above, but they are replete with all of the accessories of life. The professional production of *Tobacco Road* is a good example. The play by Erskine Caldwell presents a ruthless picture of life in the Georgia cracker country. Its episodes, while showing some evidence of selection and arrangement, faithfully portrayed the simple, harsh, indolent life of the natives. The setting, with great concern for the literal, reproduced the hut and surroundings of the Lester family. The walls of the house were not painted scenery; they were actual clapboard. The ground upon which the actor stood was not a floor cloth painted to simulate earth; it was real dirt in which the character could root, dig, and spit. The costumes were filthy rags. The pump produced water. The language and actions of the characters were as passionate and crude as they might be expected to be in life. In the original production, prior to its turn to crude burlesque which traded upon smut, *Tobacco Road* was a literal representation of a particular segment of American life.

Despite the apparent literalness of the production, many examples of theatrical selectivity can be found. The characters were lighted so that they could be seen. The compositions were arranged so that the dominant actors were emphasized. The actors projected their lines so that they could be heard. The story of the play telescoped and intensified the action into a series of crises and a climax. The sound effects were recorded. The back drop was cloth. Indeed, selection played a dominant role in the choice of the particular characters, the particular situation, this particular prototype of a cracker family.

Almost any realistic play can be produced in a naturalistic manner. The director must decide how literally the play should reproduce life. His decision should be based upon whether or not the play will be strengthened by such a production.

Simplified Realism

Sometimes called *selective realism,* simplified realism is, as the label suggests, a simplification or selection of the means used by the playwright, the designer, and the actor to create the illusion of reality.

Most contemporary theatrical productions exemplify simplified realism. The playwright, designer, and actor choose only those elements necessary to the illusion. The most clear-cut difference between naturalism and simplified realism is found in the area of design.

In designing the setting for Lillian Hellman's *The Little Foxes,* the naturalist would reproduce the 1900 drawing room in its entirety. The clutter of furniture, the antimacassars, the myriad pictures on the wall and on top of the piano, the maze of mementos on the table tops, the numerous lamps, fussy doilies and scarves, everything Grandma had in her drawing room would be included. In a simplified setting for the same play, only those items which actually contributed to the illusion of reality would remain. By careful selection, the designer could create the impression of a cluttered drawing room without impeding the play's action or distracting the audience's attention. Reproduction for the sake of reproduction would be discarded.

In a similar way, the writing in most modern plays represents a selection from life rather than a duplication of life. In Sidney Kingsley's *Dead End*, sometimes produced in a naturalistic manner, the impression of activity on New York's East Side is created. In actuality, the language and conduct of the young East Side hoodlums would more often than not be violent and obscene. In the play, the illusion of reality is captured by an occasional introduction of violence and obscenity.

Acting is more selective in the simplified realistic production than in the naturalistic production. The characters are based upon natural qualities and mannerisms, but they are stripped of all nonessentials. As pointed out in the discussion of human conduct, real human activity is confused and random. The process of characterization is one of selecting and coordinating the particular mannerisms, qualities, and traits that heighten the effectiveness of the character in contributing meaning to the play.

Most productions in the high school and community theatre follow the pattern of simplified realism. It may be said that this is the basic contemporary pattern. The introduction of any other style represents a departure from the norm.

Suggestivism

Suggestivism is an extremely simplified realistic style. It is easier to reproduce in design than in playwriting or acting. In a suggestivistic production the settings are stripped to the minimal suggestions necessary to maintaining an illusion of reality. It may be differentiated from symbolism in that it is still concerned with portraying outer rather than inner reality.

In a suggestivistic setting for Andreyev's *He Who Gets Slapped*, the backstage area of the circus might well be represented by a few key circus properties placed within a drapery setting. The purpose is still to create the realistic illusion of a circus, but the selectivity in the design is so great that only a suggestion of the real remains. The rest must be filled in by the imagination of the spectator. Probably the most important principle in governing suggestivistic design relates to the selection of the symbols. If the design is to serve its purpose, the symbols must be sufficiently universal to communicate readily the desired suggestion to the audience.

Most productions on the central stage are good examples of suggestivism. The central stage, surrounded by the audience, is ill-adapted to the complexities of the more realistic forms. Simple realistic symbols—a massive chair to suggest a throne room—create the illusion of reality.

Dialogue is seldom written in a suggestivistic style. The writing is simplified realism; the intense selection occurs in the production. Also, there is probably no such thing as suggestivistic acting. The relationship of the actor to the scene does change, however, in the suggestivistic production. In naturalistic and simplified realistic productions, the actor is surrounded by scenery. The setting shares the limelight with and provides the environment for the actor. The elimination of most of the elements of scenery in suggestivistic staging catapults the actor into greater prominence. Indeed, this may be one of the primary reasons for a suggestivistic production. The director may feel that the force and meaning of the play will be more dynamic if the acting is given greater significance, one of the major advantages claimed for the central stage.

The Realistic Continuum

The director should discover upon looking back at the discussions of naturalism, simplified realism and suggestivism, that they represent points upon a continuum. A continuum may be defined as a line upon which there may be an infinite number of gradations between the end points. So it is with realism. At one end of the continuum is naturalism, demanding an almost fanatic reproduction of life in writing, design, and acting. At the opposite extreme, suggestivism has eliminated all of the realistic qualities, at least in design, except those absolutely essential to maintaining the illusion of reality. Between these two extremes there lie an infinite number

⌄f production possibilities. Simplified realism is merely a point on the line.

Considerable advantage is to be gained in recognizing the possibility of degrees of reality. An entire new vista should open to the director. He need not aim at any particular point or for any specific type of realistic production but may feel free to include or exclude any element, depending upon its contribution to the meaning and unity of the whole play. In other words, the director is a free agent.

DEPARTURES FROM REALISM

The styles of production that depart from reality are much more difficult to classify than the realistic styles. For the most part, they result from the director's desire to expand the dramatic horizon beyond the confines of mere representation. Departures are many in number and divergent in type. Some have distinct practical value for the contemporary producer. Others are less useful, though some helpful ideas may be derived from even the most extreme forms. Each of these forms involves an increase in abstraction as it decreases objective reality. These attempts to produce impressions different from or greater than those represented by the exterior aspects of life increase the problems of communication.

Abstraction and Communication

Throughout this text, we have dealt with the principles of communicating to an audience the meanings and emotions resulting from human conflict. The communication is based on the spectator's recognition of similar experiences in his own background. The sound symbols are in the form of language which communicates the thought patterns and actions of real people responding to real stimuli. The visual backgrounds are understandable in that they express locale and atmosphere in a way that is readily recognizable. In this representative drama, the process of communication is reasonably straightforward.

Even in the most extreme examples of suggestivism, the symbols are still representative. They stand for readily recognizable external realities. For example, a Gothic arch may suggest the locale of a church; a judge's bench represents a courtroom; a single tree denotes a forest.

In the departures from realism, the symbols cease to be representative and become conventional. A Gothic arch no longer suggests a church but may symbolize the power of religion. A judge's bench no longer stands for a courtroom; it may represent the scales of justice. The single tree may become the symbol for Mother Earth, or the genealogy of a family, or even the power of evil. Further modifications of the symbols may aim to communicate still other meanings. Distortion of line and form, changes in color and texture, all may convey meanings.

A similar comparison can be made between realistic and nonrealistic writing and playing. The characters of realism are representative. They are real people in real situations motivated by psychological forces, responding in a real manner. In the departures from realism, the characters may take on allegorical qualities. Their actions and speech may have meanings that are no longer representative. The story of *Peer Gynt* is more than the narrative of the travels of an egotistical young man. *The Time of Your Life* has meaning beyond that of the story of diverse people in a barroom. *Hotel Universe* by Philip Barry, *The Dream Plays* of Strindberg, *The Sunken Bell* by Hauptmann signify more than is represented. Of still a different genre, Ernst Toller's *Man and the Masses (Masse Mensch)*, Kaiser's *Gas,* Gogol's *The Inspector General,* Brecht's *Three Penny Opera,* and numerous other plays try to reach beyond the mere representation of life.

The problem which the director faces in any departure from realism is the communication of desired meanings. If the nonreal play is to expand the horizon of drama, if it is to turn its thought inward toward the beliefs and dreams of man, if it is to move an audience to the acceptance of great social ideals, these qualities must be transferred to the audience.

Frequently, the beginning director and actor produce scenes which are meaningless to the audience. When challenged as to its import, the director says, "To me, the scene means this.... I have used these visual and auditory means to symbolize these qualities." The clue to the failure of the scene lies in the first two words: "To me!" It may mean this or that to the director, but unfortu-

nately the meanings have been communicated to no one else. He
has felt that the symbols should give expression to his ideas, but
they are not concrete enough to arouse the desired response in
the audience. Drama, more than any other art form, depends upon
direct communication. The message of the playwright must be
transferred with some degree of uniformity to the audience.

Abstraction and Motivation

Both real and nonreal drama are based on the human being.
In realistic drama, the human beings are motivated by basic drives,
by physical, social, and psychological situations, and by their own
individual complexes. Many of the departures from realism are
sufficiently subtle so that there is no noticeable change in the
motivation of the characters. In other more violently nonrealistic
forms of drama, the human motivational pattern may seem to
break down. In other words, the actions of the characters cannot
be explained in simple human terms. There is no question that
the characters are motivated, but the source of the motivation
seems obscure. This change in or distortion of the motivational
pattern can usually be traced to a change in the kinds of forces
motivating the character, to motivation arising from the actual
style of the production, or to distortions in motivation stemming
from the playwright's point of view.

In seeking out greater truths, the playwright may drive his
characters by symbolic motivational forces. In Eugene O'Neill's
Strange Interlude, with its nonreal device of the "stream of con-
sciousness," the motivational pattern is completely logical and
clear. On the surface, the characters are motivated by the pressures
and conventions of the society. The "inner thoughts" are merely
expressions of the secret reactions every human experiences in the
privacy of his own mind. Once the audience accepts the convention of "inner thought," no further difficulty in communication should arise.

The reactions of Joe in William Saroyan's *The Time of Your
Life* are harder to explain in terms of normal human behavior.
His reactions are continually motivated by a fundamental good-
ness which is not part of the average human reaction pattern.
The play supposedly proves that love has greater power than
malevolence. It is noteworthy that many playgoers were confused

by Saroyan's play. They were unable to divine his "inner meanings."

This modification of the normal human motivational pattern reaches one kind of extreme in the allegorical play. In *Everyman*, for instance, the characters are not human, at all, but the embodiment of the virtues and vices. The thoughts and actions of the characters are motivated by the quality they symbolize.

The specific style of the play may also influence the motivational pattern. In producing Capek's *R.U.R.*, the mechanistic elements of man's behavior may be stressed by blocking the actors in geometric patterns and emphasizing in speech and gesture the mechanical elements of the robot. Barrie's *Peter Pan* might be produced in the style of a children's storybook, with the actions of the characters drawn in the crude, bold, elementary strokes of children's painting.

The motivational pattern may also be modified by the point of view of the production. In the search for greater truth and beauty, the director may make characters symbolize emotions, social concepts, even propagandistic slogans. In such cases, the characters' motivational patterns are distorted by the point of view they present.

The purpose of the preceding discussion is to emphasize that all humans respond because of motivation. The kind of motivation may change, but the heart of the character's action and thought and speech lies in motivation. The director must search for these basic forces.

NONREAL STYLES OF PRODUCTION

A brief survey of some of the different production techniques, most of which represent a turn from naturalism, may suggest new concepts of production to the director. Some of these styles stray very little from realistic production, others are radically different.

Stylization

Previously when we have used the term style, we have referred to the techniques of any type of production. Stylization is more than general production technique. It is the specific or exact manner of production which the play demands. Every play is a specific entity and may require a specific style to communicate its meaning. To stylize a play implies that the director must create an individual mode or fashion in the production.

The possibilities of stylization are limitless, both within the confines of realism and without. A particular production style may reach beyond the possibilities of realism, but it need not destroy it. The romantic play—romantic in the sense of love and affection— may be styled to include light, color, texture, settings, action, and even speech that symbolizes the romantic characteristics of the play. Examples of stylization were suggested in the preceding mention of *Peter Pan* and *R.U.R.*

It should be clear that even in these examples the realism of the play is sacrificed. It is impossible for *both* the external reproduction of life and a particular style to dominate a production at the same time; for if the production is stylized, style becomes one of the important factors motivating the production of the play.

Symbolism

Symbolism, like stylization, results from the desire to project more than the external elements of reality. Symbolism may be differentiated from suggestivism in that the symbols used are conventional rather than representative. For example, the symbol of "dat ol' davil sea" in O'Neill's *Anna Christie* stands for classic fate which explains the problems of the stage characters far better than any worldly difficulties.

The symbolists are interested in production procedures that express the inner meaning of the play. They make great use of the technical advances in lighting by using light to suggest specific qualities rather than employing it solely for illumination. In eliminating the purely representational background, they strive to create a unity of design, lighting, acting, and script. They feel that every element of the production should contribute to the expression of the greater, more sweeping and philosophical meanings of the play. When we realize that symbolism had its inception in the time of Gordon Craig and Adolph Appia, it is clear that many of the ideas of the symbolists are taken for granted today. Unity of production, atmosphere in design and playing, suggestion of greater values, simplification of technical means—all bases of symbolism—are inherent in most modern productions. After all, the symbolists are concerned with creating an illusion. They merely use more imaginatively powerful means to accomplish their purpose.

Expressionism

Expressionism, which arose as an art form after World War I, seems almost impossible to define. According to Gorelik, "The distinguishing feature of Expressionism would seem to lie ... in a symbolism noted for the vehemence of its symbols." The disillusionment and frustration of the Germans after the war provided fertile ground for this violent form of expression.

The desire to create an illusion of reality was discarded. Theatrical effect, ofttimes an illusion of unreality took its place. Any symbolic device was used if it would jar or shock the audience into accepting the playwright's social message.

Probably the most famous expressionistic plays are Kaiser's *Gas I* and *Gas II*, written in 1918 and 1920, a treatise on the evils of industrialism. This fiery form of expressing an idea with its terse, cryptic speeches, its energetic style of action, its violent scenic distortions, soon wore itself out. American expressionistic plays such as Kaufman and Connolly's *Beggar on Horseback* and Elmer Rice's *The Adding Machine* reduced the vehemence of the expression considerably.

As several experts have suggested, the only real value derived from the Expressionistic movement is a recognition of the worth of distortion in creating emotional effect. Particularly in the area of design, the emotional effects of distorted perspective and violent unreality in color, line, and mass are particularly useful.

Other Dramatic Styles

Numerous other dramatic styles can be mentioned: formalism with its neutral nonrepresentative settings; constructivism, emphasizing the machine-like quality of the man and society with its ramps, stairs, framework of platforms, and its energetic, non-psychological, machine-like acting; epic drama with its completely presentational staging. The student who is interested in any of these styles as possibilities for staging the nonreal play is referred to the bibliography.

The purpose of this chapter has been to suggest some of the

ways of producing a play. It has not attempted to tell the director how to apply the techniques because the specific production style will depend upon the interpretation given the play by the director. If the director is more aware of the possibilities, better able to recognize the characteristics of differing styles, and can perceive some of the problems of staging the play, the preceding discussion will have served its purpose.

24

Period Drama

MANY DIRECTORS are torn between a desire to produce the very best in drama and the fear that such may not please the audience. Both the desire and the fear are perfectly natural. The desire arises from a recognition on the director's part that plays which have stood the test of time must be good plays. Furthermore, the director is stimulated by the challenges they offer. The fear arises from the unknown. The language, the customs, the dramatic form, the poetry seem strange to the director who is steeped in contemporary fare. He frequently does not know where to begin; and, therefore, he often does not begin at all. But perhaps the fear can be allayed and the challenge made even more exciting.

Definition of Period Drama

Period drama is written in an historical period for an audience other than a contemporary one. Time being relative, it may be wise to draw an arbitrary line of demarcation. We may say with some justification that any drama written prior to 1900 may be classified as period drama. Without a doubt, some plays written a good deal later than 1900 will fall into the period classification; but prior to that time the style of writing, the style of playing, the subject or theme, and the audience differ so completely from their modern counterparts that recognition is immediate.

Note that "costume" plays written today are not period plays. The costume plays may be laid in a different historical period, but they are essentially modern plays in that they are written for consumption by a modern audience. Costumes may be added, some minor changes in language may be made, but they are still thoroughly contemporary in concept and style.

Employing our definition, Pinero's *The Thunderbolt,* written in 1908 and dealing with a social code quite different from our own, is a period play. Sidney Kingley's *The Patriots,* laid in 1790 but written in 1942, is not. In the former play, the subject matter, the style of writing, even the basic conflict is alien to the contemporary audience. The latter is written for the modern audience.

SELECTING THE PERIOD PLAY

In the chapter concerning play selection, the "good" play was defined. Each of the criteria of the good play should be applied to the period drama. Since the period drama has stood up under critical evaluation over a great period of time, there can be little doubt of its literary worth. Its present day dramatic value may be somewhat harder to determine. Since it was written for an audience with certain characteristics, habit patterns, backgrounds, and codes of conduct different from those of today, the greatest test will be to determine if it can be adapted to a modern audience. The universality of its appeal must be studied carefully.

Universality of Conflict

One of the factors which has made most standard and classic drama stand out through the ages is the universality of the conflict. Much of the appeal of Shakespeare's tragedies lies in the fact that greed, jealousy, ambition, and love are universal characteristics, understandable to people of any age or time. The drives of ancient kings or modern dictators are basically much the same.

Universality of Subject

The subject matter must have an appeal for the modern audience. Ibsen's *An Enemy of the People* has lost much of its appeal because it deals with a controversy over sanitation. Today, we take sewage disposal for granted. The modern audience is not much interested in a discussion of such a subject. If the play can be produced with the emphasis placed on some more universal characteristic, such as the freedom of speech and thought, as in the case of the adaptation starring Fredric March, then it may still have universal appeal.

Universality of Character

Do the characters have meaning in the contemporary world? In Chapter 4, the need for sympathy and participation of the audience with the characters of the play was emphasized. In selecting the period play, the director ought to make certain that the characters can be understood and appreciated. The basic human qualities of an Antigone or a Medea can be understood and appreciated by anyone. The highly artificial quality of the characters molded by the social code of the late nineteenth century makes some of these characters hard for the modern audience to accept.

Universality of Comedy

In Chapter 25, it is explained that humor is based on incongruity. In the period play, appreciation of the incongruity frequently depends upon a knowledge of the manners, customs, and language of the times. Such incongruities have little appeal for the modern audience because they are not understood. On the other hand, Molière's comedies treat universal human foibles which can be exceedingly funny to the modern audience. The director should evaluate the humor before selecting the period play.

ADAPTING AND PRODUCING THE PERIOD PLAY

Almost every period play needs to be adapted for a modern audience. Some directors try occasionally to reproduce period plays in the image of the original production. They re-create elaborate classic stages, and maintain the period style of the production. Although they may have value academically, these reproductions frequently become so burdened with their period trappings that they lose the spirit and theatrical excitement of the original.

Some of the pitfalls of period production can be avoided if the inexperienced director will determine in advance how he plans to handle the following characteristics peculiar to most period pieces.

Language

Period plays are written in the language of their time. Language difficulties arise from two sources, archaic language and stilted, formal, or elaborate language. In adapting archaic language, the director may either substitute words familiar to the audience, depend upon the inflection of the line to carry the meaning, or cut the line. If a substitution is made, it must maintain the rhythm and flavor of the line. Substitutions of or within well-known lines are impossible.

Length

The inordinate length of many period plays acts as both an advantage and a disadvantage. Contemporary theatrical convention dictates that two and one-half to three hours is long enough to hold an audience. There are, of course, exceptions, such as Maurice Evans' "full length" *Hamlet,* which prove that audiences may be held for a greater length of time. Time passes quickly if the performance is superb. Most non-professional performances are bound to have some weaknesses, and the shorter time limit should probably be observed. The advantage of inordinate length lies in the opportunity to cut out needless or difficult sections without shortening the play too much.

Scenes and Settings

Numerous scenes and settings introduce a third problem to the production of a period play. The classic Greek dramas present no difficulty, for they maintain the unities of time, place, and action. In Shakespearean drama, the changes in scene and setting are endless. The costs and problems of technical production may seem insurmountable, but the difficulties can be handled in several ways.

First, some scenes may be cut entirely; others can be joined together by choosing a locale suitable to the scenes involved in the merger. A second method is to use a unit setting in which the basic framework of the setting remains stationary throughout the production. The third and simplest solution is to stage the play in drapes with simple changes in properties and light suggesting changes in place and time.

Many older plays are divided into a traditional five acts. The modern director will find it to his advantage to make the production conform to the contemporary divisions of no more than three acts. Intermissions jar the audience and destroy the mood of the production. The fewer intermissions the better, providing the spectator does not have to sit through an act lasting more than ninety minutes at the very longest. In some cases, plays will logically halve. This is probably ideal if the divisions are not too long.

Complicated Plots

Complicated plot structure is one of the major problems of many period plays. Judicious elimination of sub-plots will simplify and may materially strengthen the total effect of the production. Cutting out extraneous sub-plots will remove large blocks from the play and should not be done without careful deliberation on the part of the director. He must be certain that the continuity of the production is not damaged. What the director chooses to cut is determined by the particular interpretation given the play.

Cutting the Period Play

Indiscriminate cutting without previous research is inexcusable; however, the director should realize that he is a creative artist and has a right to create his own production in his own way. He should not disregard the work of other, perhaps greater, artists. At the same time, he need not and should not feel bound to produce a replica of some previous production.

Translations

The director should take care in selecting the translation of a foreign play. Though it may seem the height of naïveté, many beginning directors are unaware that there is frequently more than one translation available. Any translation is, at best, an interpretation of the play by the translator. It is impossible for a writer to change a play from one language to another without leaving his imprint. A translation which may have been ideal at the time of its accomplishment, say fifty years ago, may be quite unsatisfactory for the contemporary audience.

The famous Gilbert Murray translations of the Greek classics, thought to be vibrant in their time, seem stilted and formal to most modern audiences. Similarly, the William Archer translations of Ibsen reflect the artificiality, formality, and attitudes of Archer's own period.

In many cases, there is, of course, only a single translation available. The director should, then, acquaint himself with the translator's background and characteristics to determine, if possible, the affect which he may have had upon the play.

Differences in Expressing Thought and Emotion

One of the major problems of the period play lies distinctly within the control of the director. The difficulty arises from changes in the manner and mode of expressing thought and emotion from one period to another. Contemporary society is, in many ways, a casual, informal society. Manners which were the backbone of previous social structures have been discarded. Actions which would have horrified our grandmothers are taken for granted today. Subjects which were discussed in whispers or not at all in other times are now common parlance.

The particular problem and its solution depend upon the specific play and audience, but some pitfalls are obvious. First, period love scenes must be treated gingerly. The artificial, highly romantic style of the love scenes may embarrass the modern playgoer. The verbosity of the hero sounds ridiculous to the modern ear. The scene may be softened, however, by underplaying, reducing the intensity of the playing. In addition, some of the superfluous dialogue may be cut, and the movement in the scene may be modified. Broad, lavish gestures and business such as kneeling, which may be called for in the script, should be eliminated.

In a similar way, scenes involving elaborate expression of emotion should be underplayed. Above all, it is necessary to supply the motivational justification for the speech and movement. If the spectator can be made to accept the action or speech as conceivable, he will not laugh at a serious scene. The problem is similar to overplaying in any intense scene. Any scene can be burlesqued by pushing it too far, playing it so that the actions are not substantially motivated.

Dealing with subjects which were taboo in the period of the play but common knowledge today requires subtlety in direction. Underplay the violence of the character's reaction to such subjects. If the characters are played sympathetically and with sufficient integrity, the spectator will respect the sincerity of the character's actions even though he is unable to understand the reason for them.

Many of the problems stemming from differences in customs can be solved by fine and sincere acting. We may feel that our neighbor is a bore, but if we recognize that he is a sincere person we do not laugh at him. Characters from period plays will also be well treated by the modern audience if they appear to deserve it.

Period Comedy

The universality of period comedy was mentioned as one of the criteria in play selection. Comedy arising from word play, puns, or clever witticisms is humorous only if it has the same meaning for the contemporary auditors that it had for the period spectator. Comedy derived from character and situation can be transferred intact from period to period. The ugly, aging spinster preening herself before a mirror while awaiting an introduction to a smart young man is universally comic. This scene was as funny in Congreve's *The Way of the World*, written in 1700, as it is today. The thrashing given the unsuspecting *Doctor in Spite of Himself* appeals to both Molière's audience and our own. The clever mistaken identity in *She Stoops to Conquer* transfers directly to the modern audience because it arises from situation and character rather than line. The comic characters of period drama will be humorous today if they have an integrity and a reality the modern audience can respect.

Soliloquies and Asides

The soliloquy and the aside were frankly directed to the spectators in period acting. This theatrical convention has been discarded by the illusory directors and writers of illusory drama; however, asides need not be cut in producing period drama. Rather, they should be handled within the framework of the illusion. The soliloquy and, frequently, the aside can be treated as the subjective thought of the character. In period comedy, the aside may be retained in its natural form and deliberately used for the fun of it.

Another period convention is found in the conversation which is not overheard by someone in the same room. If you stop to think about it, this convention is no more ridiculous than many others accepted by the modern audience. However, since the modern spectator is accustomed to the strict maintenance of the illusion of reality, the director is advised to strain his ingenuity to provide some psychological justification for the situation. Either justify the relationship or remove the character who is not supposed to hear the conversation.

Poetry

The modern actor, particularly the non-professional actor, has been trained in a theatre devoted to realism. Realism presupposes prose. Indeed, the more monosyllabic, terse, and choppy, the better. With such a background, it is little wonder that most actors approach poetic drama with trepidation.

Probably the most important thing to remember about poetry in drama is that the drama rather than the poetry is the key element. The playwright has employed the poetic form because he feels that it will add to the magic of the play. He desires an elevation of expression, a grandeur of style offered by the rhythms of poetry.

One of the first questions asked by the inexperienced actor is, "Shall I read the lines so that the poetry is emphasized or should the sense of the line be stressed even though the poetry is lost?" The question is almost always stated so that it assumes a dilemma. It implies a need for *either* this *or* that. Would that the answer might be so simple. Instead, the answer must involve a happy middle point which is gained by stressing both the poetry and the sense.

It must be remembered that although all dramatic dialogue is somewhat artificial, poetic dialogue is more so. To ignore the rhythms of the poetry merely makes it seem more labored and complicated. If, however, the actor is carried away by the rhythms of the poetry (and unfortunately many inexperienced actors are carried away) sound also supplants meaning for the listener, and that, in turn, destroys the dramatic qualities of the line.

The problem of handling choruses of voices is somewhat different from individual reading. It has been my experience that choral groups frequently tend to become so involved in the sound and rhythms that meanings are totally lost. In this situation, it would appear that the stress should be laid heavily on the meaning.

Interpreting the Period Play

Should the period play be produced authentically? Should it be produced in a streamlined modern version? Should the message of the author be allowed to stand on its own merits? Should the play be interpreted to convey a particular modern message? These decisions on interpretation rest with the director. How much leeway he has in changing the play is a moot question.

The inexperienced director would probably be advised to avoid extreme interpretative changes. Some experts suggest that after the director has proved that he can produce a period play effectively without altering the fundamental message, then, and only then, may he begin to experiment.

The breadth of the possible changes in interpretation may be suggested by noting some outstanding contemporary productions which radically re-interpreted the original meanings. The Orson Welles' Mercury Theatre production of *Julius Caesar* was produced in modern dress as an anti-fascist play, and the same group's production of Thomas Dekker's *The Shoemaker's Holiday* was interpreted as a farce about democracy. A more recent innovation was the Arthur Miller adaptation of Ibsen's *An Enemy of the People,* which stressed the freedom of the individual.

Staging the Period Play

Some educational theatres are admirably equipped to produce certain of the classics in their original form. At the University of California, a specially constructed Greek amphitheatre encourages authentic production of the classics. At the University of Illinois, Shakespeare's stage has been reproduced in detail. The advantages of such stages are obvious, providing they do not limit the imagination applied to period productions. Most theatres, however, are limited to the modern picture frame stages. Here, too, the classics can be produced, but the staging requires greater imagination. A brief survey of the key periods of drama, with simple suggestions for staging and playing, may be helpful.

Greek drama should be reasonably simple to stage because it usually maintains the unities of time and place. Thus, it is readily adaptable to the picture frame stage. Robinson Jeffers' modern adaptation of *Medea* is an excellent example of modern staging. The play was staged in a simple exterior setting that observed classic lines. The chorus may be reduced to three or four people if desired, and its speeches may be given to the individual members. In the Jeffers' adaptation, the chorus was composed of three women of Corinth. The grandeur of the speech may be attained by using greater force, dynamics, sustention of sound, and projection. The static aspects of the drama may be relieved by the introduction of movement. Variety in composition may be gained through the use of steps, ramps, and platforms.

The medieval mystery and morality plays are also readily played in the picture frame stage. Simple suggestive units of scenery may be employed. In a recent and delightful college production, a simple medieval wagon was rolled onto the stage by the actors, and the scenes were played at the sides and in front of the wagon. The unit setting with minor changes in properties and lighting may also be used. An open air production of *Everyman* was produced imaginatively on the exterior steps of a local theatre.

The medieval play, like the Greek drama, is more conventional than representational in style. Illusion may be enhanced by treating the speeches as the subjective thoughts of the characters. As in the Greek drama, the static quality can be removed by the addition of action.

The primary problem in producing Shakespearean drama on the contemporary stage is that of maintaining a rapid and fluid production. The Elizabethan stage, with its forestage, inner stage, and upper stage, made for instantaneous changes in scene. Unit settings with minor changes in properties or shifts in the acting areas from one part of the stage to another will help maintain the necessary speed and flow. Light may be used to change the locale. The playing spaces can be differentiated through the use of steps and levels.

The acting in Shakespearean drama should be full and broad, though not declamatory. The use of asides and soliloquies has been discussed in an earlier section. The heart of Shakespearean drama lies in the beauty of the lines. The actor must maintain the poetry and still express the meaning.

The comedies of Molière were originally played within the confines of a picture frame. As such, they are readily adapted to the modern stage. The acting is characterized by the boisterous enthusiasm of modern farce which is discussed in Chapter 25.

Restoration comedy, as opposed to the comedy of Molière, is a comedy of manners. With simple suggestions of change in scene, the staging can easily be adapted to the modern theatre. The key to its style of play lies in the retention of customs and manners of the time and clever reading of the witty dialogue. The comedy of manners is also considered in Chapter 25.

From 1700 to the present, most plays were written for the picture frame stage and thus are fitted to contemporary staging.

Costuming the Play

The subject of costume is an interesting one. A recent study indicates that authenticity of costume is of little importance. The average spectator seems to be unable to recognize changes in style unless there is some distinct identifying feature. He may recognize costumes with which he has had some direct contact, such as American Civil War or Colonial costumes. On the other hand, the subjects in the study were unable to differentiate the costumes of the fifteenth to the eighteenth centuries, a span of 300 years! Notably, even graduate students studying the history of the theatre were unable to define period costumes accurately. Therefore, complete authenticity seems to be of little significance except to satisfy the desires of the producer.

Should the play be costumed in the period in which it was written? Again there is little regularity of practice. Shakespeare dressed his characters in the Elizabethan period, regardless of the historical setting of the play. Modern producers of Shakespeare have dressed his plays in many different periods. *Hamlet* has been played in medieval costume, Elizabethan costume, nineteenth century costume, and even modern dress. In a recent motion picture production of *Macbeth,* Orson Welles costumed the play in medieval dress, representing the actual period of the play. This move toward authenticity received more adverse criticism than applause.

MODERN DRESS

What about modern dress productions of period plays? The decision involves more than merely changing the costume plot. It is not necessarily a simple solution, and the novelty of the procedure alone is not enough to recommend it. A modern dress production is the final test of the universality of the play. If the play is not based upon universals, contemporary costume may merely make it appear more artificial.

The advantage of the modern dress production lies in its ability to bring the play closer to the audience. By removing the barrier of time, the audience may more readily empathize with the characters. Since the time between the writing and the producing of the play is bridged by costume, the modern dress production should emphasive the modern aspects of the play.

The greatest potential disadvantage of the modern dress production is that the updating of costume may further strain the audience's imagination. The incongruous formality of the characters' actions, language, and conduct may appear ludicrous to the contemporary audience. Modern dress can also bring any melodramatic elements of the play so close to the audience that the action and ideas no longer are conceivable. The audience may lose the perspective which laying the play in its own period provides.

Some of the problems of producing the period play have been considered in a cursory analysis. At first glance, they may appear to be so complex that the inexperienced director will shy away from period production, but it is hoped that they will have the opposite effect. The sensitivity and imagination of the director can be brought to bear in period production. The adaptation, the interpretation, and the staging all present challenges. The need for production of the fine dramas of the world is great. The gauntlet is down.

25

Comedy

MAN LOVES TO LAUGH. He is differentiated from other forms of animal life by his ability to appreciate and respond to the comic. Based on a desire for laughter to relieve the tensions of living, a comic form has developed through the centuries. The style of performance changes from time to time, and the level of appreciation varies. Even the things at which we laugh are not always the same, but laughter has always been an important force in man's existence. The comedian, jester, or society wit is accorded recognition. As a result of this craving for the comic, the study of humor has been undertaken by great philosophers and street corner buffoons.

The purpose of this analysis of comedy is to attempt to lay down the bases, the types, the styles, and the methods of playing comedy in the modern theatre. Comedy is more difficult to direct than serious drama because it is more technical. Direction depends upon a clear understanding of what is comic, why it is comic, and how the non-comic can be made comic. Some directors have a natural feeling for humor. Others do not. It is hoped that the following material will add to the knowledge of those who can feel it and increase the understanding, sensitivity, and capabilities of those who cannot.

Definition of Comedy

Much of the discussion of comedy has been obscured by a confusion in definition. A classic concept laid down by Dante differentiated comedy from tragedy by the manner in which the play ended. If the play ended in catastrophe, it was called a tragedy;

comedy ended happily. The definition is confusing, for many plays have violent, deadly serious conflicts and crises but end happily, with the hero triumphant. They may have little or no lightness, frivolity, or laughter, yet, by definition, they are comedies.

For the purposes of this study, a comedy is defined as any play in which enjoyment of laughter supersedes the serious qualities. This more popular definition does not imply that a comedy may not have a serious message, for laughter can be pointed. The definition is broad in scope, for it includes all kinds of laughter from the guffaw in response to broad buffoonery to the refined chuckle reserved for the delicate witticism.

WHAT PROVOKES LAUGHTER?

Incongruity

Many theories concerning the comic have been asserted through the ages. The greatest acclaim has been awarded the theory, posited by the philosopher Kant and his followers, that *incongruity* is the basis of the comic. Any inappropriate or inconsistent relationship has the potential of provoking laughter. It may be incongruity in words, ideas, or associations. We laugh at the incongruity of the fat man and the skinny man. We laugh at the incongruity of Mrs. Malaprop's misuse of language. We laugh at the incongruity of the little Androcles who fears his massive wife but not the mighty lion. The list could be extended indefinitely. Gross incongruities appeal to the small child. Strange noises or unique sights will often cause the child to laugh. The more subtle incongruities of the witticism evokes response from the highly trained intellectual. Incongruity can be safely considered the major basis of most laughter.

Universals of Comedy

Incongruity is a broad term. The comic player or writer must recognize the types of incongruity which are universally comic when placed in the right frame of reference. These may be called the universals of humor. They are elements that exploit or intensify the basic incongruity.

Exaggeration. Exaggeration is the comedian's strongest weapon. The incongruity in the situation can be intensified by exaggeration.

It is the process of expanding a relationship or idea beyond its
natural form. Exaggeration is basic to all of the cruder forms of
humor. The brutal slapstick of pie-throwing comedy intensifies the
inconsistencies by exaggerating them.

Superiority. Superiority over our fellow man, particularly over
those who stand in high places, helps to aggrandize the individual
ego. Thus, when the audience is able to perceive a mighty individual
making a mistake which the spectator knows he, himself, would not
make, the onlooker is pleased and laughs. The incongruity of the
situation is intensified because the ego is expanded. There is the
story of the company executive who was so formal and precise that
he was heartily disliked by his fellow workers. When he went to
lunch one day with a coat hanger still sticking out of his coat, his
colleagues roared with laughter. The incongruity lies in the thought
of a man wearing a coat hanger with his coat. The intensification
comes from the healthy feeling of superiority each of us experiences.

Escape. The humor in escape arises from a release of tension. If
the movie hero toward whom we are sympathetically inclined is
caught on the top of a flagpole, we may empathically try to help
him down. We become tense with worry. When the camera angle
changes and shows us that the flagpole is less than six feet high,
we are convulsed with laughter. Why? The incongruity of a six-foot
flagpole is enough. When this is coupled with our escape from
the tensions of worrying about the hero, the response is greatly
intensified.

Surprise. Surprise is similar to escape in its power to facilitate
laughter. In a recent production of an old-time melodrama, the
heroine was tied to the tracks in the conventional fashion. An
onrushing express of magnificent proportions was created in the
imaginations of the audience by sound effects and light. At the
propitious moment, a toy train chugged its way into sight. The incongruity of the little train alone would provoke laughter. The
surprise of it, after the audience had imaginatively conjured a
mighty express, greatly increased the laughter.

THE COMIC ATTITUDE

Comedy, to be appreciated, requires a special frame of reference.
The spectator must know that something is supposed to be funny,

or the situation must be one in which laughter is socially acceptable, or the humor will be destroyed. In each of the illustrations in the preceding section, the laughter depends upon the preparation for laughter.

One of the funniest scenes in motion picture history was that of Harold Lloyd clinging to a slippery flagpole suspended high above a city street. Examine a similar situation, not humorous in the least. Suppose you respond to the calls of your neighbor and find him hanging from the eaves of his house with a concrete drive directly beneath him. You will not laugh. The situations are virtually identical; each man is hanging from a roof top; yet one is funny, and the other is not. What is the difference between the two? The difference lies in the attitude with which the situation is viewed. The spectator's comic frame of reference or attitude toward Harold Lloyd is lacking in the case of the neighbor. The comic attitude depends in a large measure on two factors: recognition and objectivity.

Recognition. The theatre spectator must be informed that he is to witness a comedy. The playwright usually makes his comic intentions obvious from the beginning. The name of the play, the exaggeration of the characters, the extreme situation, the obviously incongruous speeches signal the audience at the outset that they are to take the play lightly. If the playwright does not clearly indicate his comic intent at the beginning, such notification becomes the director's responsibility. Bits of incongruous business can be inserted and incongruous characters may be played more broadly at the early stages of the play to advise the audience that a comedy is forthcoming.

Objectivity. Once the spectator knows that he is to witness a comedy, he assumes an objective attitude toward the play. This attitude is quite different from that necessary to the appreciation of serious drama. In the serious drama, the director wants the spectator to empathize with the protagonist and the play. The spectator must identify himself with the characters, join in the conflict, and, at the same time, maintain an artistic detachment. The audience should assume a more objective attitude to appreciate comedy. The spectator should not identify himself strongly with the characters. The spirit of fun is recognized in comedy. The spectator knows that no real harm can come to the hero; he senses that there is nothing serious in the conflict; he knows that everything will come out all right, that the hero will win and the villain will be vanquished. The recognition of the comic spirit and resulting objective attitude explains why Harold Lloyd's plight is funny although your neighbor's is not.

CRITERIA FOR CLASSIFYING COMEDY

Classification of the various types of comedy can be helpful to the director. An understanding of the techniques and aims of the playwright helps determine the style in which the comedy should be played. If direction fails to recognize the quality the playwright has given his work, it can ruin an excellent play.

Emphasis in the Writing

The emphasis in comedy may be placed on the situations, the characters, or the lines. While a mixture of all three elements is found in most comic drama, special emphasis is usually placed on one or more of the three elements. This emphasis may be used to differentiate comic styles.

Level of Appreciation

A second method of differentiating the kinds of comedy is to determine the level of appreciation necessary to enjoyment. Some comedies require a great deal of intellectual acuity to appreciate them. Others require no training whatsoever. For example, the witticisms of Oscar Wilde or William Congreve demand a highly refined sense of humor if they are to be understood, let alone enjoyed. At the opposite extreme, it takes little or no training or intellectual appreciation to understand and enjoy the antics of Olsen and Johnson or Abbott and Costello. This range of appreciation can be used to differentiate high and low comedy styles.

Desired Response

Just as the need for training in appreciation varies for different styles of comedy, the type of response to be elicited also varies. Not all comedy is aimed at getting roars of laughter. The more refined and intellectual styles aim at gentle chuckles and smiles; the lower and broader types of comedy point for the belly-laugh. The director must realize what kind of response is desirable. Some directors are prone to think of any comedy in terms of great bursts of laughter. They are displeased and frightened when the response is modest. Appreciation of comedy line, character, and situation may be expressed in a quiet as well as a boisterous way. If the director does not realize this difference between comedies, he may broaden the style of play and thereby spoil the subtle pleasantries of high comedy styles.

Style of Playing

As a result of the differences in emphasis in the writing and in the levels of appreciation and response, the style of play varies with different types of comedy. Highly refined comedy is played with a detail and grace in acting which is unnecessary in the broader comic forms. A knowledge of comic type helps the director determine the acting style to be applied.

TYPES OF COMEDY

Many methods of classifying comedy have been used. The following categories are set up on the basis of the criteria suggested above. Obviously, there is a mixture of styles in most comedies, but the basic differences in emphasis, appreciation, and response stand out with considerable consistency.

Comedy of Manners

The term *comedy of manners* defines a style that frequently lampoons the manners and customs of a particular segment of society, usually the upper classes or aristocracy. The term *drawing room comedy* is also frequently applied although it is in some ways a misnomer. The term arises from the fact that most of these comedies are laid in a drawing room, but so are many other kinds of comedy that cannot be considered comedies of manners. A third term used to describe the comedy of manners is *high comedy,* a refined comedy, as opposed to the crude low comedy. Regardless of the term used to describe it, the characteristics of the comedy of manners are fairly simple to isolate, though it must be stressed again that different comic styles are to be found mixed together in almost any comic play.

The primary emphasis in the writing of the comedy of manners is placed on the line or speech. The humor depends more upon the wit of the lines, the clever turning of a phrase, than upon either the characters or the situations. The beauty, vividness, and cleverness of the language is one of the keys to recognition of the drawing room comedy.

Examine a classic example from Oscar Wilde's *The Importance of Being Earnest*. Lady Bracknell is interviewing Jack Worthing to determine his suitability as a spouse for Gwendolen.

> LADY BRACKNELL: ... How old are you?
> JACK: Twenty-nine.
> LADY BRACKNELL: A very good age to be married at. I have always been of the opinion that a man who desires to get married should know either everything or nothing. Which do you know?
> JACK: I know nothing, Lady Bracknell.
> LADY BRACKNELL: I am pleased to hear it. I do not approve of anything that tampers with natural ignorance. Ignorance is like a delicate exotic fruit; touch it and the bloom is gone ...

Note that the humor in the last speech arises from the clever turning of the phrase. The incongruity of the thought is obvious. The character and the situation are unimportant except that they provide a logical opportunity to develop the line.

The characters found in the comedy of manners are usually over-refined. They are the aristocratic bluebloods, the fops, the dudes, the dilettanti. They are usually so refined that they are pretentious and thus open to ridicule. The playwright acts as critic and lampoons the characters' silly actions, thoughts, and manners. The fun is derived from the way the characters act and think rather than from their individual characteristics. Most high comedy characters are much alike. The lords and ladies of the drawing room are cast from a similar mold. The women are usually silly, gossiping snobs; the men are pompous, stilted fools.

Situation in the comedy of manners is relatively unimportant. It is used as a background against which the characters parade their idiosyncrasies and expound their foolish notions. This is one of the reasons that these plays are laid almost exclusively in drawing rooms, the ideal background for societal intrigue and gossip.

The preceding discussion of the balance of qualities in the comedy of manners indicates the levels of appreciation and response. Both are extremely high. The training and acuity necessary to appreciation is great. Since the comedy appeals largely to a highly intellectual person, the response usually reflects the refinement of the audience. The chuckle rather than the guffaw is the order of the day.

The comedy of manners requires a very special style of play. In the first place, the aristocratic atmosphere of the drawing room dictates that the acting must have the refinement and charm that will reflect the "good taste" of the situation. Ladies and gentlemen do not romp in the drawing room. They react in terms of the elegance of their backgrounds and the period. Manners and refinement, regardless of how ridiculous they may seem, determine the speech, the gestures, the compositions, and the movement of the characters.

In the second place, the characters have the high veneer of the finishing school. The polish must be preserved. The outward display of decorum, tradition, and manners must be maintained, regardless of the crudities beneath. The characters come from the reserved upper classes. As such, grace and precision in movement will help convey the meanings.

The characters of the drawing room pride themselves on their sharp tongues, their casual wit, their worthy birthright. They prattle and gossip. The tempo of playing is quick. Lines are telescoped between the important bits of humor (see "Technique in Comedy," p. 435). These characters do not punch home the humor, rather they point it delicately or toss it away.

Do not misunderstand. Drawing room comedy should not be static. The quickness of pace, the emphasis upon charm and grace, the use of mannered action should keep the production moving briskly. As Alderdyce Nicoll, one of the great dramatic critics, has said, "Laughter does not arise from incident or situation, but from graceful playing." Several examples of the comedy of manners from different periods which will bear careful study are William Congreve's *The Way of the World,* Richard Sheridan's *The School for Scandal,* Oscar Wilde's *The Importance of Being Earnest,* Somerset Maugham's *The Circle,* and Noel Coward's *Private Lives.*

Romantic and Sentimental Comedy

Romance and sentiment are keystones of most contemporary American comedy. These plays picture life as it might be or should be, seldom as it is. They are filled with the oft-told tale of romance, tears, and final happiness. The audience's enthusiastic reception of these sentimental comedies is based in wish fulfillment. Romantic and sentimental comedy have a great deal in common but really rest at opposite ends of a scale of sentimentality. *Cyrano de Bergerac* is probably the prototype of romantic comedy. It is the picture of an extravagant idealism. It involves some sentimentality but does not primarily depend upon it. At the opposite extreme on the scale are the crassly sentimental, saccharine radio soap operas swimming in excessive emotionalism. Plays such as *Junior Miss, Kiss and Tell, Dear Ruth,* and most Hollywood pictures are based on appeals to sentiment. Sometimes these plays are called domestic comedies since they concern the simple victories and defeats of family life.

The emphasis in the writing of romantic and sentimental comedy is different from that of the comedy of manners. In the romantic comedy, primary emphasis is laid on character and situation rather than on line. The story follows the life and loves of Mary Jones. The character of Mary is fully developed.

The romantic comedy mixes the objectivity of the comic attitude with the subjectivity of the serious play. The audience is expected to sympathize and empathize with Mary Jones to some degree at least.

Plot and story are tremendously important in romantic comedy. Much of the humor is derived from observing Mary Jones face and overcome the problems of life. The situations tend to be extravagant and often fanciful, just as the characters are extravagantly ideal. On the other hand, the situations are usually close enough to life so that the spectator can identify himself with the characters.

The importance of line decreases in sentimental comedy. The witty line and clever wordplay are discarded. Instead, the warm humor of the lines is usually related to the characters' reactions to the situations. Sentimental and romantic comedy, more than any other type, stress equal emphasis upon character, situation, and line. Most sentimental comedies follow the traditional pattern of boy meets girl, boy loses girl, boy gets girl.

The amount of training and intellect necessary for appreciation is less than that required for the comedy of manners. Since the play concerns characters and situations within the experience and background of the audience and wordplay is eliminated, no special training is required for enjoyment. The desired response is broader than that in the drawing room comedy. Warm, sympathetic, and hearty laughter is the anticipated audience reaction.

Little need be said about the problems of playing this type of comedy because it is very realistic. The characters are complete. Certain incongruous characteristics may be emphasized, but essentially they are recognizable people. Since this kind of comedy follows a completely normal motivational pattern, it is the easiest type to produce.

Farce Comedy

The term *farce* comes from the Latin word *farcire,* meaning *to stuff.* The derivation clearly illustrates the meaning of *farce,* a play which has been stuffed with comic characters, situations, and lines. Farce has little inward appeal. In fact, some of the most hilarious incidents are basically brutal or pitiful, such as Sheridan Whiteside's broken leg in *The Man Who Came to Dinner,* Susie's delicate condition in *Boy Meets Girl,* or the kidnapping of Irwin in *Three Men on a Horse,* or the beatings of Sganarelle in Molière's *A Doctor in Spite of Himself.* These incidents are treated so completely within the comic frame of reference that the audience never for a moment stops to sympathize or empathize with the character involved.

In writing the farce, emphasis is placed upon situation and incident. The humor arises from the comic characters plunging into and emerging from outlandish situations. Examine the incidents noted above. Each of them, to quote the judges in *Caponsacchi,* is "Quite possible but highly improbable."

The characters of farce comedy are frequently just as extreme as the situations and incidents. They are quite different from the complete three-dimensional characters of the romantic comedy. Farce characters are highly selective. They are built on a few, simple, incongruous comic characteristics. The element of caricature enters the character development. Certain specialized characteristics are blown out of all proportion to their natural form.

The bully is the prototype of a bully. The nincompoop is the complete nincompoop. The scholar is ponderously scholarly.

In the farce, a new kind of line takes on importance. The "gag" line or the smart crack reaches it clearest form. The humor in the line does not depend upon wit. There is usually nothing distinctive about its language. The humor comes from the incongruous twist put upon some aspect of the character or the situation. A classic gag line comes from the farce *Born Yesterday*. In complete disgust, Billie Dawn says to her junk-dealer boy friend, Harry Brock, "Do me a favor, Harry,—Drop dead!" The laughter stems from the incongruity of the situation plus the fact that all of us have felt that way about someone at some time. A discussion of the playing of the gag line is found in the section on comedy techniques.

The level of appreciation in farce comedy is very low. Farce has many of the qualities of the comic cartoon which even the child can understand and enjoy. Since the level of appreciation is elementary and the characters are very broad and highly selective, farce is considered low comedy. In farce, many of the aspects of slapstick are used. The desired response is rousing laughter. The characters are extreme; the situations and incidents are ridiculous; the gag lines are obvious; all are aimed at getting the fullest laughter response possible.

The playing style in farce is highly technical and extremely broad. Exaggeration of the incongruities of character and situation is the keynote. Farce characters are vibrant and enthusiastic characters. Even the slowly moving imbecile is violently imbecilic. The selected aspects of character are played to the hilt; but most important of all, farce characters are sincere. One of the great, dangerous mistakes in playing farce lies in the tendency to play the characters with a tongue-in-cheek attitude because they are so ridiculous. Farce characters must be played with utter sincerity, for the comedy lies in the ridiculous attempts of a ridiculous character to meet a ridiculous situation with tremendous sincerity. The farce character is not the least bit funny if the audience detects any *strain* to be funny on the part of the actor playing the role. The tantrums of Sheridan Whiteside in *The Man Who Came to Dinner* are humorous only so long as they are conceivable. They are conceivable just as long as the character is a sincere picture of the world's greatest egomaniac. More farces have been rendered ineffective by losing sight of the motivational forces driving the skewed characters to respond than through any other single factor.

The specific technical procedures for handling the farce are discussed in a later section. Every bit of humor must be wrung from every comic character, every absurd situation, every gag line, every bit of stage business. Farce is indeed a broad style "stuffed" with every imaginable kind of fun.

Burlesque

The term *burlesque* is used here to suggest the lowest form of comedy, a ridiculous, caricatured, overdrawn representation. The term should not be confused with the present day burlesque theatre which has substituted the peep show for the brilliant horseplay of the burlesque in the days of Eddie Cantor, Joe Penner, Bert Lahr, and Bobby Clark. The humor in burlesque arises from an overdrawn, tongue-in-cheek treatment of a serious subject or from the heavy, overly serious handling of a trivial subject. In either case, any dependence upon reality and a logical motivational pattern has been eliminated. The audience knows that the characters are not serious. Deliberate and obvious incongruities are exaggerated far beyond the limits of reality. The antics of Charlie Chaplin in his early pictures are burlesques of serious situations. Most contemporary melodramas such as *Gold in the Hills,* or *He Ain't Done Right by Nell* are burlesqued versions of the nineteenth century form.

The emphasis in the writing is difficult to determine. The characters, situations, and lines are overdrawn. Characters, in any real sense, cease to exist. The personality of the performer stands clearly before the character. Abbott and Costello, for example, in one of their movies, played the parts of colonial characters. Costello was a tinsmith. He was dressed in a colonial costume, and that was as deep as the character development went. In every other way—speech, posture, movement, thought, and attitude—he was still Costello. In other words, the burlesque lay in the ridiculous thought of Costello's being a colonial tinsmith.

As mentioned above, situation is sharply overdrawn. One of the best examples of the parody on situation is Bert Lahr's hilarious woodman sketch. Lahr, dressed as a wood cutter, recites George Morris's sentimental poem, "Woodman, Spare That Tree." Ax in hand, he chops on an obviously papier-mâché tree as tears flow down his cheeks. At the end of each stanza he strikes another blow at the tree, and from offstage a handful of clothespins is tossed in his face. The scene is intensely humorous, but neither the character nor the situation is real.

The burlesque speech has the same hyperbolic quality as the situation and character. The farce line is funny because it is a conceivable statement of a foolish but possible relationship. The burlesque gag line is merely a farce line exaggerated to a point where there is no longer any hint of reality. The broadest incongruous twists and turns are used to make fun of the burlesqued situation or character.

The level of appreciation is obviously not very high. Burlesque is the crudest form of buffoonery. The level of response is likewise broad and crude. The only real purpose of the burlesque is to evoke loud guffaws. Note that the spectator's point of view has changed in burlesque. In all other styles of comedy the spectator enjoyed the characters in the play. In burlesque, the audience enjoys watching actors make fun of the characters, situations, and lines.

The style of acting is just as overdrawn as any of the other elements. The playing becomes slapstick and violent. The naïve fun of the Three Stooges consists of their hitting each other over the head and poking each other in the eye. The humor arises from a series of physical and vocal absurdities. Burlesque play is characterized by the rubber billy club, custard pies, and seltzer bottles. As such, projection, movement, business, and tempo are all greatly exaggerated.

Very few burlesque scenes will be presented by the average director. The reason for differentiating the form is to point out the dangers of allowing farce to slip into the realm of burlesque. Some directors feel that if a scene is funny when played in a broad style, it can be funnier in a still broader style. This is frequently untrue, for as the scene is pushed beyond the point of conceivability, the audience becomes confused about the director's and playwright's purpose. The spectator does not know whether to laugh at the actors or at the characters. An uneasy response is the result. One final reason for treating burlesque with care: It needs a master comedian to play it effectively.

MIXTURES OF COMIC STYLES

Any attempt to categorize must result in classes which are all inclusive and mutually exclusive. Upon reading the preceding sections, the beginning director may infer that a play written as a comedy of manners will have no other elements present. Even a cursory examination of comic drama shows that nothing could be farther from the truth. Undoubtedly, classic examples of drama in each of the categories will have an amazing consistency, but most comedies have a mixture of different styles.

This blending of styles can occur in one of several different ways. The styles may be deliberately mixed by the playwright in his writing. He may insert some farce situations or romantic characters in a comedy of manners; or the play may be written rather consistently in one style and deliberately produced in a totally different one by the director. The trend is generally downward. The comedy is lowered or broadened: a drawing room comedy played as a farce. And finally, though the writing may be perfectly consistent, the style may be mixed in the playing. Different characters are played in different styles. If handled with discretion, mixtures can be perfectly satisfactory. If not, the resultant production may be badly confused and the unity necessary to successful dramatic production lost.

Mixtures in the Style of Writing

Occasionally, the playwright hands the director a comedy which is a potpourri of styles. Such a play usually indicates the writer's lack of skill and is extremely difficult to produce. More frequently the playwright mixes the comic styles for a particular reason.

In George Kelly's *The Torchbearers,* the characters who make up the little theatre group are farce characters, warm and human, but farce, nevertheless. The situations are priceless farce. One character, Mr. Ritter, at first glance does not seem to fit into the play at all. The husband of a dramatically inclined wife, he literally stands apart from the rest of the cast. Kelly has set Mr. Ritter apart deliberately, for Ritter is the one normal person on the stage. He is the audience projected behind the footlights. The ludicrous activities of the drama group are made more entertaining by noting the responses of the one non-dramatic fellow. The director who tries to make a farce character out of Mr. Ritter seriously injures the play.

Mixtures between Style of Writing and Playing

Some plays are written in one style and produced in a different style with gratifying results. Certain problems do arise, however, when a director tampers with the style. Throughout this text, emphasis has been laid on the director's responsibility to the playwright. If a change in style perverts the author's intent, the change should not be introduced. It is obvious that the commercial director will seldom be deterred from changing the author's style if the result can be made to produce clanging turnstiles.

Changes in style from high forms of comedy to lower forms are easily accomplished, but low comedy can seldom be successfully raised in its style of play. Almost all successful changes are examples of the former.

The Lindsay and Crouse play *Life with Father* was originally produced on Broadway as a nostalgic, heart warming, romantic costume comedy. By the time it had circled through the provinces, the style of play had been broadened until it was pure farce. The New York actor has little respect for the "provincial" audience. He mistakenly believes that any subtlety would be lost on the middle-westerner.

A classic example of how high comedy may be changed into farce was the Tallulah Bankhead production of Noel Coward's *Private Lives*. Coward's play was listed earlier as one of the examples of drawing room comedy. The hilarious production mounted for Miss Bankhead was played in a rather broad farce style with only the slightest homage paid to the comedy of manners genre.

As a final example, most contemporary productions of *The Importance of Being Earnest* are treated in a farce style. In fact, it should be admitted that some scholars classify this play as farce. The situations and the characters are amenable to very broad play.

Mixtures in the Style of Playing

Mixtures in style of play not dictated by the playwright are usually a mistake. Again and again directors let a production slip out of hand because they happen to have a particularly amusing actor who turns the play into a tour de force. When the reviewers say "he stole the show," there is an implication that a lack of balance exists in the production. Audiences generally like broad low comedy play. Therefore, the clever actor may well become a focal point by playing in a broader style that sets him off from the rest of the characters.

In summary, the broader the style in which a comedy is played, the greater will be the number and the volume of the laughs. Temptation is great, but remember: Most comedies above the level of farce have other values which must not be neglected.

TECHNIQUE IN COMEDY

Successful comedy is based upon a meaningful blend of logical motivation and imaginative and intelligent use of specific technique. This rather largely objective application of technique makes comedy more difficult to produce than serious drama; not that serious drama has no technique, but rather that the amount of technique needed for successful projection of comedy is much greater. The steps in developing the blend of comic technique and motivation may be laid down as follows.

Find the Incongruity

Since comedy is based upon inconsistencies in the relationships of ideas, words, associations, or events, the first step in creating the comic is to find the incongruity. In most instances it will be found in the situations, the characters, or the lines, or in the interrelationships of any combination of the three. The humor derived from the presentation of the village washerwoman at the country club reception comes from the inconsistencies of character and situation. The humor of a timid young man who, convinced of his indestructibility, punches the world's champion boxer arises from an inconsistency in character. The humor of the uneducated clod's using the language of the intelligentsia arises from the combination of line and character.

Once the incongruity has been recognized, and it requires imagination to find the more subtle inconsistencies, the director must find ways of making the incongruity plausible and ways of projecting it.

Determine the Motivation

With the exception of burlesque, the spectator is observing a character, not an actor, who has ideas, attitudes, and actions, reacting in a situation. Regardless of how thin the motivation may be—and in farce it is sometimes quite illogical—the spectator must be able to ascertain a plausible reason for the character's reactions. Let us assume that a little man is expected to push a big man. The incongruity is based in the temerity of the small man; however, there is little humor in the process of pushing, itself. The comedy stems from the motivation or the reason behind the action. There must be some thread of logic in the little man's action. Perhaps the little man has been driven to desperation; perhaps he is drunk and has always wanted to push a big man; perhaps he is proving to his wife that he is a man. The action becomes funny as the motivation becomes clear. The motivational pattern is also important in establishing the comic frame of reference for the spectator. Preparation for the laughter is laid in the motivation of the character. Incongruity can be apparent only when there is a basis for comparison. The pseudo-intellectual who makes a mistake in grammar is funny only after we have decided definitely that he is a pseudo-intellectual.

Project the Comedy

After the incongruity has been found and the motivational base established, the means for making the comic inconsistency apparent to the audience must be chosen. The basis for projection is found in the universals of comedy. For instance, if surprise is to be the basis for the laughter, the director should use all of the techniques at his disposal to make the situation a real surprise.

One of the oldest comedy bits is a window polishing routine in which the actor industriously polishes a window pane, then surprises the audience by reaching through it. The question the director must consider is, "How can the surprise be made more complete?" One method might be through suspense. As the actor polishes the window, he may stop to pick small bits of dirt off the pane, he may lengthen the polishing process (but never to the point wherein the audience loses interest), he may breathe on the pane to get a higher gloss. The resulting surprise and laughter will be increased because the preparation has increased the tension in the audience. In each comic instance, the director must determine the universal upon which he is going to build his projection of the inconsistency.

Intensify the Incongruity

Part of the preceding illustration has shown how a director may increase the laughter by intensifying the incongruous twist in the material. A prerequisite for comedy direction is the ability to intensify the comic elements.

The director has at his disposal three types of techniques: the visual, the auditory, and, perhaps most important of all, the use of time. The director must be able to use each of these with authority if he is to succeed in creating laughter.

Visual techniques. Intensification of the comic line or situation can be brought about by the use of either movement or business. The impact of the line is strengthened because the audience can see as well as hear. In the musical comedy *Good News,* the sorority girls are wondering what to serve the boys at a luncheon before the game. One of the girls suggests some leftover potato salad. The potato salad is brought on and one of the girls says, "No one would touch it Wednesday night; perhaps the rest did it good." She smells it and says, "No." The line itself has a humorous twist, but the business accompanying the line creates the real laughter. If the girl winces slightly when she smells the potato salad, the line is more pointed. In a recent very low comedy production of the show, three girls simultaneously crowded in to smell the salad. Instead of wincing, they were practically knocked down by the odor. The audience roared its approval. Coupling physical and vocal reaction intensifies the comedy.

Vocal techniques. The incongruity in comedy lines can be pointed up by vocal change. Sometimes this is accomplished by exaggerated emphasis upon the humorous part of the line. Occasionally, it is handled by dropping the humorous part casually. In each case the stress upon the comic is intensified by establishing a contrast to the material preceding the line. There are two principal types of comedy lines. One is called a *gag line,* the other a *throwaway line.*

The gag line usually consists of three parts. The preparation for the gag communicates all necessary information to the audience; the pause sharply points up the gag to follow; and finally, the punch, the gag itself, is trust home to the audience, frequently visually as well as vocally.

The line quoted earlier from *Born Yesterday* is a gag line. The three parts can readily be examined.

BILLIE: Do me a favor, Harry .... Drop dead!

<u>   Preparation   </u>   <u>Pause</u>   <u>Punch</u>

In many cases, the preparation is supplied by one character and the gag is thrown by another, as in the following lines from *You Can't Take It with You*. Grandpa is arguing with Mr. Henderson, the local Internal Revenue agent.

GRANDPA: What is interstate commerce anyhow?
HENDERSON: There are forty-eight states—see? And if there weren't interstate commerce, nothing could go from one state to another. See?
GRANDPA: Why not?—They got fences?

In this illustration, all the discussion prior to the last dash, which indicates the pause, is preparation. The gag is, "They got fences?"

The throwaway line is almost the exact reverse of the gag line. Instead of punching the humorous turn, it is either gently laid in the laps of the audience or seemingly tossed away. It apparently is given no emphasis whatsoever. Actually, it is pointed but not by raising the projection. The emphasis may be made by dropping the projection of the humorous quip in contrast to the rest of the line, or it may be pointed by opening a slight pause before delivery. In any case, the throwaway line is as clearly emphasized as the gag line. The methods are different.

In Somerset Maugham's *The Circle*, Lady Kitty, a middle-aged woman who uses every conceivable means including "touching up" her hair to recapture her youth is talking to Arnold about another lady.

ARNOLD: Her hair is very pretty.
LADY KITTY: It's not touched up, is it?
ARNOLD: Oh, no.
LADY KITTY: I just wondered. It's rather a coincidence that her hair should be the same colour as mine...

The subtle implication found in this delightful line would be ruined if the latter part of the line were to be punched as a gag.

Yet the humor must be pointed if the audience is to perceive it. It may be accomplished by a slight pause after the preparation; it can be done by dropping the projection of the last part of the line so that it stands apart in contrast with the rest of the speech. In other words the humorous part of the line may be flipped, tossed, thrown away.

Another device for setting the wit apart in the throwaway line is telescoping, hurrying a line so that the gist or feeling of the line is clear though some of the words may not be understood. If the preparation is telescoped, then a slowing of the pace on the quip points it up in clear relief.

Obviously, many lines may be read in any number of ways with comparable results. If the play has sufficient performances, the director may suggest altering the treatment of a line that does not receive the anticipated response. In non-professional productions, changes should be made at the discretion of the director, not the actor.

Timing. Throughout the preceding discussion, the factor of time has been unavoidably introduced. Timing is one of the foundation stones of comedy. The technical use of time is simple to discuss but difficult to execute. Time is used to point up lines and action. It can create suspense or anticipation on the part of the spectator, making the comic revelation more amusing. The dramatic pause grips the audience and focuses its attention. The great comedians are all masters of timing. Some say that a sense of timing is a natural faculty not to be taught. Try to answer the following question. Should the dramatic pause between the preparation and the gag be a fraction of a second, one count, three counts? There can be no perfect answer until the instant of playing. Change any factor in the situation, the character, the preparation of the line, and the timing must be changed. Even the attitude of the audience at that particular moment will affect the timing. The actor and the director should be able to feel the correct moment for release after a moderate amount of experience.

The preceding discussion of timing is not very helpful. But experience with laugh-provoking lines and lines that do not bring laughter will quickly show the director the essentials of timing. Careful observation of master comedians at work on the stage, screen, radio or television will also be helpful.

Overplayed Comedy

Nothing is quite as painful for the actor and the director as care-fully worked out comedy business that does not get a laugh. Even the audience is aware that something has gone wrong. Sometimes with untried material the line or the situation just is not funny, or the business may get no response because of visual, vocal, or timing faults, but frequently failure results because the intensification or exaggeration of the business has been carried too far. The moment comedy technique becomes obvious to the audience, humor is lost. Many times actors and directors are carried away by their own amusement during rehearsals. The inserted business seems ex-tremely funny because of the hilarious mood of the occasion. When the same piece of business is presented before an audience it falls flat. How can the overplaying of business be avoided? The simplest solution is never to intensify anything. Some directors follow this philosophy. They never take a chance; thus, they never miss—nor do they get the most out of the material. As in the case of timing, the breaking point in intensification is something to be learned through experience. The imaginative director will increase the breadth and intensity of his comedy as his experience grows. One day his comedy will misfire; then he will have found the breaking point.

A word of advice to the beginning director. Warn your actors that gags may fail and encourage them to continue playing in the style in which the play was rehearsed. Never let them work harder at being funny. Whole scenes can be destroyed because actors try harder to recover a lost cause—the gag that failed. Comedy depends on relaxation and poise, not on labored attempts to be funny.

Handling Laughter

One of the major problems in directing comedy is the handling of laughter. After all, the audience has come to the theatre to laugh. The players must let the audience have its fun. If all laughter came like a thunderclap and lasted for four seconds, the problem of direction would be simple. The director would merely fill the four seconds with business and sustain the action through the laughter. Unfortunately, audiences seldom laugh in the same way at the same line any two nights in a row. The director, therefore, should teach his actors to handle the laughs as they come.

The term *riding a laugh* means to hold up the action and lines until the laughter has abated. If the actor reads his next line during a laugh, either the line is lost in the uproar or the laugh is cut short as the spectator strains to hear. Neither is desirable. On the other hand, if the actor waits until the audience has completely finished laughing, a gap is opened in the play. It is the same as if a cue were not picked up. The audience is confused.

Laughter in the theatre usually comes in a wave of sound. The spectators who are quick to perceive the humor begin laughing. Their laughter emphasizes the humor for others in the audience who begin to laugh as they perceive the humor. Some laughs start very quickly; some start extremely slowly and then build to magnificent proportions. Regardless of the start, the wavelike action is present. The next line must be held until the laughter has passed its crest and is well on the down swing, but the line should never

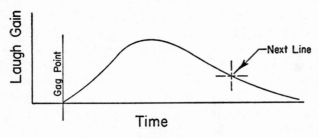

FIG. 44. RIDING LAUGHTER

be held until all laughter has stopped The wave of laughter and the timing of the next line is illustrated in Figure 44.

If the actor starts his line too soon, on the rise in laughter, he should stop and start again at the correct time, providing he hasn't already killed the laugh. In rehearsal, the play should be directed as though there were no laughs expected; then if the laugh does come, the actor can ride it. If the gag misses, nothing will be lost, for the play moves ahead. After a series of performances, covering business may be set for large, regularly occurring laughs.

Comedy is more difficult to produce successfully than serious drama because it depends less upon emotion and more upon technique. Thus, comedy is the testing ground for any director. Most comedies are reasonably funny because of the playwright's magic. The perfectly timed, perfectly executed, perfectly hilarious comic production is proof of the director's genius.

Appendix

Selected Bibliography

The following bibliography is intended for the student rather than the scholar. As such, it does not pretend to be exhaustive. Many of the volumes included, however, have extensive bibliographies which can provide the student with an almost unlimited horizon if he wishes to explore any of the areas with greater thoroughness.

At the end of the bibliography, a list of the major dramatic publishers and some of the leading theatrical suppliers is included to help the director who does not have access to this type of information. All of the publishers and many of the suppliers have useful catalogues.

GENERAL PSYCHOLOGICAL BACKGROUNDS

Allport, F. H. *Social Psychology*, Boston: Houghton Mifflin, 1924. Includes a brief but careful analysis of audience psychology.
Asch, S. E. *Social Psychology*, New York: Prentice-Hall, Inc., 1952.
Dewey, Richard, and Humber, W. J. *The Development of Human Behavior*, New York: Macmillan, 1951. A recent and thorough study of human conduct.
Dockeray, Floyd C., and Lane, G. Gorham. *Psychology*, New York: Prentice-Hall, Inc., 1950. Contains a superior analysis of motivation and emotion.
Hollingworth, H. L. *The Psychology of the Audience*, New York: American Book Co., 1935. One of the clearest analyses of audience behavior.
Young, Kimball. *Social Psychology*, New York: Crofts, 1930. An early but excellent survey of man's relationship to society.

Also:

Cannon, W. B. "The James Lange Theory of Emotions," *American Journal of Psychology*, XXXIX (1927) 106-124.
Lebon, Gustave. *The Crowd, A Study of the Popular Mind*, New York: Macmillan, 1900.
Lippmann, Walter. *Public Opinion*, New York: Harcourt, Brace, 1922.

Martin, Everett Dean. *The Behavior of Crowds,* New York: Harper, 1920.
Shaffer, L. F. *Psychology of Adjustment,* Boston: Houghton Mifflin, 1936.
Thonssen, Lester, and Fatherson, Elizabeth. *Bibliography of Speech Education,* New York: H. W. Wilson, 1939.

GENERAL THEATRICAL BACKGROUNDS

Cheney, Sheldon. *The Theatre,* New York: Longmans, Green, 1929. A popular and comprehensive history of theatrical art.
Freedley, George, and Reeves, John A. *A History of the Theatre,* New York: Crown, 1941. A good history of the theatre. Many different illustrations. Excellent bibliography.
Gassner, John. *Masters of the Drama,* New York: Random House, 1940. A comprehensive history of plays, playwrights and production styles. One of the most useful of all dramatic works.
Gorelik, Mordecai. *New Theatres for Old,* New York: Samuel French, 1940. A penetrating study of the history of changing production styles with emphasis upon presentational staging.
Hughes, Glenn. *The Story of the Theatre,* New York: Samuel French, 1928. An extremely simple and brief survey of theatre history.
Langfeld, Herbert Sidney. *The Aesthetic Attitude,* New York: Harcourt, Brace, 1920. A clear, helpful discussion of aesthetics.
Nicoll, Alderdyce. *The Development of the Theatre,* (rev. ed.), New York: Harcourt, Brace, 1937. One of the most scholarly of the theatre histories with interesting illustrations and an extensive bibliography.
Simonson, Lee. *The Stage Is Set,* New York: Harcourt, Brace, 1932. A history of stage design, emphasizing illusory staging with a worthwhile discussion of the place of theatre in modern society.

Also:

Gagey, Edmund. *Revolution in American Drama,* New York: Columbia University Press, 1947.
Geddes, Norman Bel. *Horizons,* New York: Little, Brown, 1937.
Jones, Robert Edmond. *Dramatic Imagination,* New York: Duell, Sloan & Pearce, 1941.
Macgowan, Kenneth. *The Theatre of Tomorrow,* New York: Boni & Liveright, 1921.
Mantzius, Karl. *A History of Theatrical Art,* 6 vols. Translated by Louise von Cossel. London: Duckworth, 1903-1921.
Millett, Fred B., and Bentley, Gerald Eames. *The Art of the Drama,* New York: Appleton-Century, 1935.
Mitchell, Roy. *Creative Theatre,* New York: John Day, 1929.
Sobel, Bernard. *Theatre Handbook and Digest of Plays,* New York: Crown, 1940.
Stanislavski, Constantin. *My Life in Art,* New York: Little, Brown, 1924.
Stuart, Donald Clive. *The Development of Dramatic Art,* New York: Appleton, 1928.

DRAMATIC THEORY AND PLAYWRITING

Archer, William. *Playmaking,* New York: Dodd, Mead, 1912. The first modern text in playwriting.

Baker, George Pierce. *Dramatic Technique*, Boston: Houghton Mifflin, 1919. Mr. Baker's famous course published in book form.

Clark, Barrett H. *European Theories of the Drama*, (rev. ed.), New York: Crown, 1947. A comprehensive anthology of critical writings beginning with Aristotle. An extremely valuable source book.

Gallaway, Marian. *Constructing a Play*, New York: Prentice-Hall, Inc., 1950. A new book with an interesting approach to play construction.

Krows, Arthur Edwin. *Playwriting for Profit*, New York: Longmans, Green, 1928. A comprehensive and detailed study of playwriting.

Lawson, John Howard. *Theory and Technique of Playwriting*, New York: Putnam, 1949. A meaningful dissertation on playwriting.

Matthews, Brander. *A Study of the Drama*, Boston: Houghton, Mifflin, 1910. An early book, still one of the best introductions to the problems of the theatre.

Potts, L. J. *Comedy*, London: Hutchinson's University Library, 1948. An interesting analysis of comedy.

Rowe, Kenneth T. *Write That Play*, New York: Funk & Wagnalls, 1939. A recent and popular text.

Also:

Anderson, Maxwell. *The Essence of Tragedy and Other Footnotes and Papers*, Washington, D.C.: Anderson House, 1939.

Bentley, Eric. *The Playwright as Thinker*, New York: Reynal and Hitchcock, 1946.

Bergson, Henri. *Laughter*, Translated by C. Brereton and F. Rothwell, New York: Macmillan, 1911.

Brunetière, Ferdinand. *The Law of the Drama*, New York: Dramatic Museum of Columbia University, 1914.

Eastman, Max. *Enjoyment of Laughter*, New York: Simon and Schuster, 1936.

Freytag, Gustav. *The Technique of the Drama*, Translated by E. J. MacEwan, Chicago: Scott, Foresman, 1894.

Hamilton, Clayton. *So You're Writing a Play*, New York: Little, Brown, 1935.

———. *The Theory of the Theatre*, New York: Henry Holt, 1939.

Hardwicke, Sir Cedric. *The Drama Tomorrow*, New York: Cambridge University Press, 1936.

Kozlenko, William, (ed.). *The One-Act Play Today*, New York: Harcourt, Brace, 1938.

O'Hara, Frank Hurbert, and Bro, Marguerite. *A Handbook of Drama*, Chicago: Willett, Clark, 1938.

Seyler, Athene, and Haggard, Stephen. *The Craft of Comedy* (4th ed.), New York: Theatre Arts, 1945.

Thompson, Alan Reynolds. *The Anatomy of Drama*, Berkeley: University of California Press, 1942.

Wilde, Percival. *The Craftsmanship of the One-Act Play*, New York: Little, Brown, 1932.

PLAY PRODUCTION AND DIRECTION

Dean, Alexander. *Fundamentals of Play Directing*, New York: Farrar & Rinehart, 1941. An expansion of Mr. Dean's directing course at Yale.

Dolman, John. *The Art of Play Production*, New York: Harpers, 1946. An aesthetic approach to the problems of direction and production.

Gassner, John, (ed.). *Producing the Play,* New York: Dryden, 1941. A compendium of production advice with articles by leading professionals.

Granville-Barker, Harley. *Prefaces to Shakespeare,* 2 vols. Princeton: Princeton University Press, 1947. Good advice on period production.

Heffner, Hubert C., Selden, Samuel, and Sellman, Hunton D., *Modern Theatre Practice,* (3rd ed.), New York: Crofts, 1946. A simple, thorough, and comprehensive survey of the practice of play production.

Hughes, Glenn. *The Penthouse Theatre,* New York: Samuel French, 1942. The first discussion of the arena stage.

Jones, Margo. *Theatre in the Round,* New York: Rinehart, 1951. An interesting discussion of a famous arena theatre.

Ommanney, Katherine Anne, and Pierce, G. *The Stage and the School,* (rev. ed.), New York: Harpers, 1950. A simple and comprehensive survey of dramatic appreciation and production for the high school.

Selden, Samuel. *The Stage in Action,* New York: Crofts, 1941. A highly stimulating if somewhat abstract study of play directing.

Smith, Milton. *Play Production,* (rev. ed..), New York: Appleton-Century-Crofts, 1948. A revision of one of the most popular general surveys of play production.

Also:

Brown, Gilmor and Garwood, Alice. *General Principles of Play Direction,* New York: Samuel French, 1937.

Clark, Barrett H. *How to Produce Amateur Plays,* (rev. ed.), New York: Little, Brown, 1925.

————, and Royer, Jessica. *The Complete Acted Play,* New York: F. S. Crofts, 1943.

Drummond, A. M. *A Manual of Play Production,* Ithaca, N. Y., published by the author, 1939.

Hewitt, Barnard. *Art and Craft of Play Production,* Philadelphia: Lippincott, 1940.

Lees, C. Lowell. *Play Production and Direction,* New York: Prentice-Hall, Inc., 1948.

Shaw, George Bernard. *The Art of Rehearsal.* New York: Samuel French, 1928.

THEORY AND TECHNIQUE OF ACTING

Albright, H. D. *Working Up a Part,* Boston: Houghton Mifflin, 1947. A simple text for the beginning actor. Excellent drill selections.

Archer, William. *Masks or Faces?* New York: Longmans, Green, 1888. An old but still valuable digest of many opinions on the art of acting.

Boleslavsky, Richard. *Acting: The First Six Lessons,* New York: Theatre Arts, 1933. Stimulating essays, in dialogue form, on acting.

Calvert, Louis. *Problems of the Actor,* New York: Henry Holt, 1918. A helpful analysis by a successful actor.

Cole, Toby and Chinoy, Helen, (eds.). *Actors on Acting,* New York: Crown, 1949. A comprehensive anthology of writings on acting. Basic to any thorough study of the theory of acting.

D'Angelo, Aristide. *The Actor Creates,* New York: Samuel French, 1939. Acting as taught at the American Academy of Dramatic Art.

Eustis, Morton. *Players at Work,* New York: Theatre Arts, 1937. Discussions of technique by contemporary actors.

Franklin, Miriam. *Rehearsal,* (3rd ed.), New York: Prentice-Hall, Inc., 1950. The principles of acting discussed simply with plentiful exercises.
Lees, C. Lowell. *A Primer of Acting,* New York: Prentice-Hall, Inc., 1940. A popular elementary text. Excellent bibliography.
Stanislavski, Constantin. *An Actor Prepares.* Translated by Elizabeth Reynolds Hapgood. New York: Theatre Arts, 1936. A complete system of acting by the great Russian actor and director.

Also:

Alberti, Eva. *A Handbook of Acting,* New York: Samuel French, 1932.
Bosworth, Halliam. *Technique in Dramatic Art.* New York: Macmillan, 1934.
Coquelin, Constant. *The Actor and His Art.* Translated by Elsie Fogerty, London: George Allen and Unwin, 1932.
Gillette, William. *The Illusion of the First Time in Acting.* New York: Dramatic Museum of Columbia University, 1915.
Kjerbühl-Peterson, Lorenz. *Psychology of Acting,* Boston: Expression, 1935.
Komisarjevsky, Theodore. *Myself and the Theatre,* London: Wm. Heinemann, 1929.
Rosenstein, Sophie, Haydon, Larrae A., and Sparrow, Wilbur. *Modern Acting: A Manual.* New York: Samuel French, 1936.
Selden, Samuel. *A Player's Handbook.* New York: Crofts, 1934.
Strasberg, Lee. "Acting and the Training of the Actor," *Producing the Play.* ed. John Gassner, New York: Dryden Press, 1941.
Young, Stark. *Theatre Practice,* New York: Scribner's, 1926.

STAGECRAFT

Barber, Phillip. "The New Scene Technician's Handbook," *Producing the Play,* ed. John Gassner, New York: Dryden Press, 1941. A comprehensive survey of the problems in stagecraft set forth in easy-to-use handbook form.
Buerki, F. A. *Stagecraft for Non-Professionals,* F. A. Buerki, Wisconsin Union Theatre, 1945. An extremely clear and simple survey of scenic problems.
Burris-Meyer, Harold and Cole, Edward C. *Scenery for the Theatre,* New York: Little, Brown, 1938. Probably the most complete and detailed discussion of scenery. For advanced students.
McCandless, Stanley. *A Method of Lighting the Stage,* New York: Theatre Arts, 1939. The lighting techniques of one of America's foremost lighting experts.
Selden, Samuel and Sellman, Hunton D. *Stage Scenery and Lighting,* New York: Crofts, 1936. A widely used textbook.

There are also good discussions of stagecraft in several of the books listed under Play Production and Direction.

Also:

Aronson, Joseph. *The Encyclopaedia of Furniture,* New York: Crown, 1938.
Cornberg, S. and Gebauer, E. L. *A Stage Crew Handbook,* New York: Harper, 1941.
Fuchs, Theodore. *Stage Lighting,* New York: Little, Brown, 1929.
Fuerst, Walter Rene, and Hume, Samuel. *Twentieth-Century Stage Decoration,* 2 vols. New York: Knopf, 1928.

Gould, G. G. *The Period Furniture Handbook,* New York: Dodd, Mead, 1928.
———. *Period Lighting Fixtures,* New York: Dodd, Mead, 1928.
Krows, Arthur. *Equipment for Stage Production,* New York: Appleton-Century. 1928.
Meyer, Franz Sales. *A Handbook of Ornament,* (rev. ed.), Chicago: Wilcox and Follett, 1946.
Napier, Frank. *Noises Off, A Handbook of Sound Effects,* London: Frederick Muller, 1936.
Nelms, Henning. *Lighting the Amateur Stage,* New York: Putnam, 1932.
Smith, Milton. *Equipment in the School Theatre,* New York: Bureau of Publications, Teachers College, Columbia University.

COSTUME AND MAKE-UP

Barton, Lucy. *Historic Costume for the Stage,* Boston: Baker, 1935. Perhaps the best known study of costume.
Chalmers, Helena. *The Art of Make-up,* New York, Appleton, 1935. A popular elementary text.
Corson, Richard. *Stage Make-up,* New York: Crofts, 1937. A very popular general survey of make-up problems.
Factor, Max. *Hints on the Art of Make-up,* Hollywood: Max Factor Make-up Studios, 1936. Good advice on stage make-up from the movie capital.
Grimball, Elizabeth, and Wells, Rhea. *Costuming a Play,* New York: Century, 1925. A brief but well selected survey of the principal periods.
Strenkovsky, Serge. *The Art of Make-up,* New York: Dutton, 1937. An elaborate and thorough discussion.

Also:

Dabney, Edith, and Wise, Carl W. *A Book of Dramatic Costume,* New York: Crofts, 1935.
Kohler, Carl, and Von Sichart, Emma. *History of Costume,* London: Watt, 1928. Republished, Philadelphia: David McKay, 1937.
Sage, Elizabeth. *A Study of Costume,* New York: Scribner, 1926.
Walkup, Fairfax Proudfit. *Dressing the Part,* New York: Crofts, 1938.

ORGANIZATION AND MANAGEMENT

Much of the writing in the areas of theatre organization and business management is either inadequate or badly dated. However, some helpful suggestions may be found in the following.

Selden, Samuel, (ed.). *Organizing a Community Theatre,* New York: Theatre Arts, 1945. A National Theatre Conference survey.

Also:

Bernheim, Alfred L. *The Business of the Theatre,* New York: Little, Brown, 1929.
Dean, Alexander. *Little Theatre Organization and Management,* New York: Appleton, 1926.
Halstead, William P. *Stage Management for the Amateur Theatre,* New York: Crofts, 1937.

Krows, Arthur Edwin. *Play Production in America,* New York: Henry Holt, 1916.
Stanton, Sanford E. *Theatre Management,* New York: Appleton-Century, 1929.
Whorf, Richard B., and Wheeler, Roger. *Runnin' the Show,* Boston: Baker, 1930.

BIBLIOGRAPHIES OF PLAYS

Baker, Blanch M. *Dramatic Bibliography,* New York: H. W. Wilson, 1933.
Bates, Mary E., and Sutherland, Anne C. (Eds.). *Dramatic Index,* Boston: F. W. Faxon, 1915 ff.
Firkins, Ina Ten Eyck. *Index to Plays, 1800-1926.* New York: H. W. Wilson, 1927.
———. *Index to Plays Supplement.* New York: H. W. Wilson, 1935.
Gilder, Rosamond. *A Theatre Library.* New York: Theatre Arts, 1932.
Logasa, Hannah and Ver Nooy, Winifred. *An Index to One-Act Plays, 1900-1924.* Boston: F. W. Faxon, 1924.
———. *An Index to One-Act Plays. Supplement, 1924-1932.* Boston: F. W. Faxon, 1932.
———. *Index to One-Act Plays. Second Supplement, 1932-1940.* Boston: F. W. Faxon, 1941.
Olgebay, Kate. *Plays for Children.* New York: H. W. Wilson, 1928.
Ottemiller, John H. *Index to Play Collections.* New York: H. W. Wilson, 1943.
Seligman, Marjorie, and Frankenstein, Louise N. *Plays for Junior and Senior High Schools.* New York: H. W. Wilson, 1932.
Shay, Frank. *Thousand and One Plays for Little Theatres.* New York: Appleton-Century, 1923.
Smith, Milton. *Guide to Play Selection.* New York: Appleton-Century, 1934.

ANTHOLOGIES

Bentley, Eric. *The Play,* New York: Prentice-Hall, Inc., 1951.
Buck, Philo; Gassner, John; and Alberson, H. S. *A Treasury of the Theatre,* 2 vols. New York: Dryden Press, 1940.
Carpenter, Bruce. *A Book of Dramas,* New York: Prentice-Hall, Inc., 1949.
Chandler, Frank W., and Cordell, Richard A., *Twentieth Century Plays,* New York: Nelson, 1934.
Clark, Barrett H. *World Drama,* 2 vols. New York: Appleton, 1933.
Cordell, Kathryn Coe and William H. *Pulitzer Prize Plays,* New York: Random House, 1937-1940.
Dunn, Ester C. *Eighteen Famous Elizabethan Plays,* New York: Modern Library, 1932.
Gassner, John (ed.). *A Treasury of the Theatre: From Ghosts to Death of a Salesman* (rev. ed.), New York: Crown, 1950.
———. (ed.). *Twenty Best Plays of the Modern American Theatre,* New York: Crown, 1939.
———. (ed.). *Best Plays of the Modern American Theatre,* Second Series, New York: Crown, 1947.
———. (ed.). *Twenty-Five Best Plays of the Modern American Theatre,* Early Series, New York: Crown, 1949.
Hartley, Lodwick, and Ladu, Arthur. *Patterns in Modern Drama,* New York: Prentice-Hall, Inc., 1948.
Kozlenko, William. *One Hundred Non-Royalty One-Act Plays,* New York: Greenberg, 1941.

Mantle, Burns, and Gassner, John. *A Treasury of the Theatre*, New York: Simon and Schuster, 1935.
Mayorga, Margaret, (ed.). *Best One-Act Plays*, 13 vols. New York: Dodd, Mead, 1937-1951.
———. (ed.). *Twenty Non-Royalty One-Act Popular Classics*, New York: Greenberg, 1946.
———. (ed.). *Twenty Short Plays on a Royalty Holiday*, 3 vols. New York: Samuel French, 1938, 1940, 1947.
Moore, Cecil A. *Twelve Plays of the Restoration and Eighteenth Century*, New York: Modern Library, 1933.
Oates, Whitney J., and O'Neill, Eugene, Jr. *The Complete Greek Drama*, New York: Random House, 1938.
Quinn, Arthur Hobson. *Representative American Plays*. New York: Appleton-Century, 1938.
Shay, Frank, and Loving, Pierre. *Fifty Contemporary One-Act Plays*, New York: Stewart Kidd, 1920.
Shay, Frank. *Fifty More Contemporary One-Act Plays*. New York: Appleton, 1928.
Theatre Guild Anthology. New York: Random House, 1936.
Tucker, S. Marion. *Twenty-Five Modern Plays*, New York: Harper, 1931.
Tupper, Frederick, and James W. *Representative Dramas from Dryden to Sheridan*, New York: Oxford University Press, 1934.

PRINCIPAL PLAY PUBLISHERS

Walter H. Baker, 178 Tremont Street, Boston, Massachusetts.
Dramatic Publishing Company, 59 East Van Buren St., Chicago, Illinois.
Dramatists Play Service, Inc., 6 East 39th St., New York, New York.
Samuel French, Inc., 25 West 45th St., New York, New York.
Longmans, Green & Co., 55 Fifth Avenue, New York, New York.
Rowe, Peterson & Co., 131 East 23rd St., New York, New York.
Tams-Witmark Music Library, 115 West 45th St., New York, New York. (*Operettas and Musical Comedies*)

Manuscript Services:

American Educational Theatre Association, Manuscript Play Project, c/o Executive Secretary, American Educational Theatre Association, see Educational Theatre Journal for address.
American National Theatre and Academy, Script Service, 139 West 44th Street, New York, New York.

THEATRICAL SUPPLIERS

General Theatre Suppliers:

Theatre Production Service, 1430 Broadway, New York, New York.

Stage Hardware and Rigging:

American Stage Equipment Company, Inc., 525 West 45th Street, New York, New York.
J. H. Channon, Inc., 1447-1455 West Hubbard Street, Chicago, Illinois.
J. R. Clancy, Inc., Syracuse, New York.

Stage Lighting:

Century Lighting, Inc., 521 West 43rd Street, New York, New York.
Duwico Theatrical Electrical Equipment, 250 West 54th St., New York, New York.
Display Stage Lighting Company, 254 West 47th St., New York, New York.
Kliegl Bros., 321 West 50th Street, New York, New York.
Major Equipment Company, 4603 West Fullerton Avenue, Chicago, Illinois.
Midwest Stage Lighting, 55 West Wacker Drive, Chicago, Illinois.

Scene Paint:

Gothic Color Company, 90 Ninth Avenue, New York, New York.
A. Leiser and Company, 48 Horatio Street, New York, New York.
Stroblite Company, 35 West 52nd Street, New York, New York. Luminous fluorescent paints and fabrics.

Theatrical Fabrics:

Dazians, Inc., 142 West 44th Street, New York, New York. *Also,* 125 No. Wabash, Chicago, Illinois.
Maharam Fabric Corp., 130 West 45th Street, New York, New York. *Also,* 115 South Wabash, Chicago, Illinois.

Sound Effects:

Gennett Records, 1600 Broadway, New York, New York.
Major Sound Effect Records, distributed by Thomas J. Valentino, Inc., 150 West 46th Street, New York, New York.
Standard Radio Transcription Service, 360 North Michigan Boulevard, Chicago, Illinois.

Make-up:

Max Factor's Make-up Studios, Hollywood, California.
M. Stein Cosmetic Company, 430 Broome Street, New York, New York.

Costumes:

Brooks Costume Company, Inc., 1150 Sixth Avenue, New York, New York.
Eaves Costume Company, Inc., 151 West 46th Street, New York, New York.
Lester Costumes Ltd., 14 West Lake Street, Chicago, Illinois.
Van Horn & Son, 811 Chestnut Street, Philadelphia, Pennsylvania.
Western Costume Company, 5335 Melrose Ave., Hollywood, California. *Also some properties.*

Draperies and Drops:

J. C. Hansen, 423 West 43rd Street, New York, New York.
Albert F. Runnel Scenery Studios, 1904 Putnam Street, Detroit, Michigan.
Kaj Velden Studios, Inc., 1589-1597 John Street, Fort Lee, New Jersey.

Miscellaneous:

Encore Studio, Inc., 410 West 47th Street, New York, New York. *Property, Sale and Rental.*
E. Vernon Hall, 6828 West Highland Avenue, Chicago, Illinois. *Smoke effects.*

Director's Glossary

Above—A movement or position farther upstage or away from the foot-lights.

Act Curtain—The main curtain of the theatre. Usually placed directly behind the grand drapery.

Acting—The creation of an intellectual and emotional dramatic characterization projected by means of voice and action to an audience.

Action—The events of the play as expressed in movement and dialogue. The movement and business of an actor.

Ad-lib (ad libitum; at pleasure.)—Lines or business not specified by the script. Occasionally spontaneous additions made during performance.

Antagonist—The character in a play who most prominently opposes the wishes or actions of the protagonist or principal character.

Apron (also "Forestage")—The section of the stage between the front curtain or the proscenium and the audience.

Apron Scene—A scene played on the apron. In vaudeville and musical productions, apron scenes alternate with full stage scenes to allow time for changing scenery.

Arc Lamp—A lighting instrument which derives its light from a flame (arc) between two carbon electrodes, differentiated from an incandescent lamp, a typical electric light bulb.

Area, Acting *or* Playing Area—An arbitrarily defined section of the stage having attention value. The areas within the sight lines of the audience.

Area, Stage—An arbitrarily defined section of the stage; e.g., *Down Right,* meaning that section near the footlights and to the actor's right as he faces the audience.

Asbestos—A fire curtain usually made of asbestos or some other fireproof material hung immediately behind the proscenium arch. Usually held by a fused link which will separate automatically in case of fire and lower the curtain.

Aside—A speech directed to the audience. May be treated as vocalized thought, depending upon the kind of production.

Assembly Rehearsal—A rehearsal in which various parts of a production are put together; e.g., the singing and dialogue units of a musical production.

Atmosphere—*See* Mood.

Attic Theatre—The theatre of ancient Athens and of Attica, approximately the fourth century B.C.

455

Backdrop—A large canvas or velour hanging at the back of a stage setting. If canvas, it is usually painted to depict a scene such as a sky.

Backing—A drop or flat placed behind an opening in the set, such as an arch or a window, which masks the backstage area from the view of the audience (*see* Masking).

Backstage—Behind the scenes.

Balance—An equilibrium of forces. Used in drama to imply either a physical equilibrium as in a composition or an aesthetic equilibrium as a balance in mood, characters, conflicting forces.

Basic Drives—The forces which affect all human thought and action; e.g., "drive for security" (*see* Chapter 2).

Batten—A long pipe or strip of wood upon which scenery or drops are hung. Most theatres are equipped with a series of battens hung at different depths parallel to the proscenium.

Below—A position farther downstage or nearer the footlights. The opposite of "above."

Blackout—The sudden elimination of all the stage lights. Sometimes used to label brief playlets or sketches usually of a humorous nature characterized by a blackout at the end of the scene.

Blocking Action—The process of setting the movement pattern of the play either on paper or with the actors at rehearsal.

Body Position—A term signifying the degree to which the actor's body is facing the audience (*see* Chapter 7).

Border—A drop or curtain hung parallel to the proscenium, upstage of the teaser, which conceals the rigging and loft of the stage house.

Borderlight—A pan or strip of low wattage lamps usually circuited in different colors, hung directly behind the borders.

Box Set—A setting in which the walls are completed on three sides with flats, usually with a framed ceiling completing the "box."

Build—To increase the tension or emotional key of a scene, usually until a climax is reached.

Burlesque—A broad, low-comedy style of writing or playing.

Business, Stage—Detailed pantomimic action exclusive of movement.

Call—Announcement of the time at which the actors are required to be in the theatre, usually one to one and one-half hours before a performance.

Call Board—A bulletin board, conveniently located in the backstage area, on which all notices of importance to the company are posted.

Casting—The process of matching the actor to the role.

Character Roles—Parts which are largely dependent upon special individual characteristics.

Characterization—The process of portraying the individual complex of qualities in a role. Accomplished through appearance, action, response to motivation, etc.

Chorus—A group of readers acting as a unit used to interpret the meanings of a play. Also, a term used to distinguish the group of singers and dancers who do not have lines or solos in a musical production.

Chorus Circle—An arrangement of characters in a semicircle. Usually undesirable in the realistic production (*see* Chapter 7).

Claque—A person or group of persons paid to applaud or laugh during a performance.

Clear Stage—A command to leave the stage, given to all actors and crews not involved in the opening moments of the scene.

Climax—The point of highest dramatic tension in a play. Usually the turning point at which the major conflict can proceed no further without beginning the process of resolution. Also any high point in a scene or action.

Closed Turn—A stage turn executed so that the actor turns his back to the audience. Opposite of "open turn."

Comedy—Writing or playing which provokes laughter based upon the audience's recognition of incongruities in the characters, situations, or lines (*see* Comedy of Manners, Romantic and Sentimental Comedy, Farce Comedy, Burlesque).

Comedy of Manners (also "Drawing Room Comedy")—Writing or playing which presents aristocratic or sophisticated characters in drawing room situations, lampooning the manners and attitudes of a period or class with emphasis upon customs, manners, and witty lines.

Comic Relief—The inclusion of comic scenes in an otherwise serious play, intended to provide relief from the tension of the serious drama.

Company—A group of performers and technicians permanently attached to a show. Frequently, the group working on a play.

Constructivism—Abstract stage settings based on structural principles. Usually characterized by steps, ramps, platforms arranged in a skeletal framework.

Convention—A principal theatrical style which stresses the existence of the stage platform. Also any accepted rule or principle.

Costume Play—*See* Period Drama.

Counter—*See* Dress.

Counter Focus—*See* Delayed Focus.

Counter Movement—Any movement in opposition to the general movement of a group.

Cover—To obscure or hide an actor or piece of business from the audience. May be intentional, as in a stabbing scene. The sight lines are broken when unintentional covering takes place.

Cross—To move about the stage in any direction or to pass in front of another character.

Cue—Any pre-determined signal to an actor or crewman to perform the next action related to the performance. It may be a word, movement, sound, or gesture.

Cue Sheet—A listing of all the signals for entrances, sounds, changes in light, etc. It may be included in a prompt book to be used by the stage manager.

Curtain Call—The raising of the curtain after the conclusion of the play, during which the actors acknowledge the applause of the audience.

Curtain Line (also "Playing Line")—An imaginary line at which the act curtain meets the floor. Sometimes a line drawn between the downstage edges of the setting. Also, the final dialogue line prior to the lowering of the curtain.

Cyclorama (Abb. *cyc*)—Any set of curtains or draperies enclosing a scene on three sides. Also a taut canvas drop or plaster dome representing the sky and taking the place of a backdrop.

Delayed Focus (also "Counter Focus")—Secondary emphasis placed upon a minor character to soften the emphasis on the major focal point.

Denouement—The unraveling of the plot of the play. It follows the climax and concludes the play.

Development—The second structural unit of a play, usually the period from the exposition to the climax.

Dialogue—The exchange of speeches by the actors.

Dimmer—An electrical device used to control the intensity of light. Lights may be "dimmed up" as well as "dimmed down." To "dim out" is to remove gradually all of the light.

Dissolve—The transition from one scene to another in which one scene fades into or out of another. In motion pictures and television a process in which one picture fades out as the second fades in.

Down Stage—A position on the stage near the footlights or audience. The opposite of "up stage."

Dramaturgy—The art of writing plays.

Drawing Room Comedy—*See* Comedy of Manners.

Dress (also "Counter")—To make a compensatory movement in opposition to a major movement. Used to balance the composition.

Dress Rehearsal—One of the final rehearsals of a production which is handled as if it were a performance.

Dress the Setting—The addition of details such as pictures, flowers, ornaments, etc., to complete the setting.

Drop—A piece of scenery usually made of painted canvas, battened at the top and bottom, which may be raised (flown) or lowered (dropped). Frequently, any drapery which can be raised and lowered.

Dropping—The process of decreasing the emotional tension or the vocal projection in a scene. The opposite of "topping."

Emotional Key—The amount and kind of emotional tension in a scene or character.

Emphasis—The process of intensifying or stressing any aspect of the production.

Entr'acte—*See* Interlude.

Entrance—The process of coming on stage. Also, the arch or doorway in the setting through which the actors enter.

Epic Theatre—A non-illusory theatrical style which began after World War I, its principal proponents being Bertolt Brecht and Erwin Piscator.

Epilogue—A scene or speech appearing after the play has been concluded. Usually included to interpret the action or meaning of the play.

Episode—A self-contained incident. Thus an episodic play is one with many loosely connected incidents.

Exciting Moment—*See* Inciting Moment.

Exit—The process of leaving the stage, or the opening in the setting through which an actor may leave the stage.

Exit Line—The final line read by an actor before leaving the stage.

Exposition—The play's first structural unit in which the playwright supplies the antecedent information necessary to the understanding of the play as it develops.

Expressionism—In art, a movement principally in Germany before and after World War I, in which the subjective is represented by the objective. In drama, characterized by the creation of violent subjective images.

Extras—Characters in a play who have no lines. They are never important as individuals. Also called "supers" or "walk-ons."

False Proscenium—*See* Inner Proscenium.

Fantasy—A representation of the unreal, usually romantic in nature.

Farce Comedy—A low comedy style of writing or playing in which ludicrous situations and exaggerated characters provoke boisterous laughter.

Flat—The principal component of most settings. It is a wooden frame covered with canvas and painted to represent any desired texture.

Flies—The overhead area of the stage. Pieces of scenery are "flown" or raised into the flies by ropes and pulleys.

Floodlight—A lighting instrument composed of a metal pan or hood with several small bulbs or one large one. It cannot be focused, and it is used to flood an area or object with light.

Floor Cloth (also "Ground Cloth")—A piece of canvas used to cover the stage floor. Its purpose is to soften sound and decrease the reflection of light.

Floor Plan (also "Ground Plan")—A line drawing of the stage setting and major properties as they would appear from directly above.

Focal Point—The major point of interest in any picture or scene to which the viewer's eye is directed first.

Focus—The process of directing the attention of the viewer toward the focal point (*see* Delayed Focus).

Follow Spot—A spotlight, usually in the front of the house, which may be focused on an actor moving about the stage. Principally used in musical productions.

Footlights—A row of low-wattage lamps placed at the front edge of the stage, providing general illumination and usually circuited in several colors.

Foreshadowing—A suggestion or indication of some action which will occur later in the play.

Forestage—*See* Apron.

Formalism—A conventional, non-representational type of setting. May range from a bare stage to an architectural façade.

Fourth Wall—An imaginary wall completing the box setting. The audience peeps through this wall into the room. Occasionally defined in naturalistic settings by placing properties on the playing line.

Frame (as music)—The process of outlining or laying out the framework of a musical number (*see* Chapter 21).

Framed Picture—A concept defining the stage scene as a picture, framed by the proscenium arch of the theatre.

French Scene—A division used by the French indicating the entrance or the exit of a character in the play.

Front—The auditorium and lobby, as opposed to the stage. *Front of the house* activities include business, ticket sales, ushering, etc. *Front lights* are spotlights located at some point in front of the proscenium arch.

Gauze (also "Scrim")—A large net curtain usually stretched taut. A scene lighted from behind the curtain appears soft and iridescent. When light is played on the front of the curtain, the curtain appears opaque.

Gelatin—A thin sheet of transparent material dyed in color. Used to add color to light emanating from lighting instruments.

Gesture—Movement of any part of the body, such as hands, arms, shoulders, head, as opposed to movement of the entire body.

Give Stage—In acting, to assume a less dominant position in relationship to another actor, usually by moving slightly downstage and closing the body position. The opposite of "take stage."

Grand Drapery—A painted canvas or velour piece, often festooned, usually hung directly behind the proscenium arch and in front of the act curtain. In older theatres, it fills in the upper portion of the proscenium arch.

Green Room—A backstage lounge room for actors and their friends.

Gridiron—A framework of steel affixed to the stage ceiling, used to support rigging necessary to flying scenery.

Ground Cloth—*See* Floor Cloth.

Ground Plan—*See* Floor Plan.

Group Unit System—A system for directing crowd scenes, based upon the smallest segment in a crowd, the *integral unit* (*see* Chapter 20).

Heads Up—A warning command to signify that an object is either falling or being lowered.

Hold—To suspend dialogue and action for laughter or applause. In the case of laughter, "Ride." Frequently, to delay; e.g., "Hold the curtain."

Home Position—An arbitrarily assigned position in a basic composition. The basis of the arrangement of crowds in the *group unit system*.

Hood—The large metal container of a lighting instrument which houses the bulb. Occasionally, a floodlight.

House—All parts of the theatre in front of the footlights, as opposed to the *stage*, all parts of the theatre behind the footlights.

House Lights—All of the lights in the auditorium except the "exit" lights. House lights are controlled from the stage.

Illusion of Reality—The acceptance by the audience of the setting, characters, and story as being a real place with real people, undergoing real experiences.

DIRECTOR'S GLOSSARY

Improvisation—The creation and performance of a role without rehearsal or pre-determined dialogue.

In One, in Two, in Three—A method of defining the depth of the playing space in a wing and drop setting. *In one* is in the shallow space downstage of the first set of wings and border or drop; *in two,* playing space in front of second set; *in three,* full stage.

Inciting Moment (also "Exciting Moment," "Overt Act")—The moment in the play when the equilibrium of forces is destroyed by some visible act and the conflict is joined.

Inevitability—The unavoidable sequence of events resulting from the particular combination of drives, situation, and character complexes found in the play.

Inner Proscenium (also "False Proscenium")—A framework of neutral color draperies or flats used to cut down the size of the proscenium arch. Sometimes composed of the teaser and the tormentors.

Integral Unit—The smallest unit in a crowd, usually composed of two or three people who have some common bond and attend the event together.

Interlude (also "entr'acte")—In the Elizabethan theatre, a short farce played between the acts of a longer play. In general, light dramatic fare played between the acts of a longer play.

Key—*See* Emotional Key.

Kill—In acting, the loss of the desired effect of a line or piece of business; e.g., "to kill a laugh" means *to lose a laugh.* Also a production term meaning to remove or eliminate; e.g., "To kill a light" means *to turn it off.*

Left *or* Right Stage—The actor's left or right as he faces the auditorium.

Leg (also "Leg Drop")—A relatively narrow drop, usually hung in pairs, in place of wings on the sides of the stage.

Level—The vertical relationship of the actor to the stage floor, such as prone, sitting, standing. Also platforms, steps, or ramps which raise the actor above the stage floor.

Light Plot—A chart of the lighting instruments, placement, cues, and changes for the entire production.

Lines—In acting, the speeches of the actors. In production, a set of ropes usually three or four in number attached to battens, running up to the gridiron and back down to the fly gallery, used to raise and lower scenery.

Linnebach Projector—A large lantern for projecting images from a slide onto a backdrop. The image becomes part of the setting.

Masking—The process of concealing from the view of the audience any part of the stage or action not meant to be seen. Usually accomplished with a piece of scenery or a drop. In acting, also "covering."

Melodrama—A play stressing excitement, suspense, external situation, and plot involvement. The characters are frequently overdrawn and lack plausible motivation. A play in which theatrical thrills are more important than the revelation of truth.

Miracle Play—A medieval dramatic representation of events related in the Bible.

Mise en Scene—The completed work of the stage director.

Mood (also "Atmosphere")—The dominant emotional spirit or quality of a play.

Morality Play—Medieval plays with characters personifying vices and virtues, death, joy, friendship, etc.

Motivation—The sum total of forces or reasons behind a speech or action.

Motivational Unit—A small scenic unit in which all of the motivational forces remain unchanged (*see* Chapter 6).

Mounting Rehearsal—The final rehearsals before production, the technical rehearsals and the dress rehearsals.

Move On—A movement toward the center of the stage from either side. "Move off" means to move away from the center toward the sides of the stage. Also "move up," toward the back of the stage and "move down," toward the front edge of the stage.

Movement, Stage—The process of moving about the stage, differentiated from "business."

Musical Comedy—Light comedy set to music, usually containing a singing and dancing chorus, in which the songs and dances are more important than the dramatic elements.

Mystery Play—In the later Middle Ages, liturgical drama performed by the laity. The dramatic representation of scriptural events performed by the trade guilds.

Naturalism—In drama, a production form concerned with an exact reproduction of life. An extreme form of realism.

Objectivity—That which deals with outer reality, as opposed to *subjectivity*, which concerns inward thoughts or feelings.

Open (also "open up")—The process of turning and playing more directly toward the audience. Occasionally, the process of separating characters in a composition.

Open Turn—In acting, the process of turning toward the audience. The opposite of "closed turn."

Opera, Grand—A drama in which music is the most conspicuous feature and all of the text is sung.

Operetta—Literally, *little opera*. Technically, a one-act opera. Popular meaning: any light opera which often involves spoken as well as musical dialogue.

Overlap—*See* Telescope.

Overplay—To give undue exaggeration to lines or action. In burlesque, overplaying is often deliberate.

Overt Act—*See* Inciting Moment.

Overt Action—Any action which can be seen.

Pace—The control and change of tempo.

Pantomime—A general term used to describe action which tells a story without words.

Parallel—A production term denoting a base for a platform which may be folded up when not in use.

Parallel Movement—Simultaneous movement in which two or more characters move in the same direction and at the same speed, across the stage.

Passion Play—A dramatization of the martyrdom of Christ.

Period Drama—A play written before the turn of the century, as opposed to the "costume play," which may be laid in any period but is written for the contemporary audience by a contemporary author.

Permanent Setting—A setting which is unchanged, or largely unchanged, during the performance despite any changes in locale demanded by the play.

Pick Up—To accelerate. Frequently refers to cues, meaning a shortening of the interval between the cue and the succeeding action or speech.

Pin Rail—A fixed beam of steel or wood, placed in the fly gallery or on the stage floor at one side of the stage, to which are attached the lines that are used to raise and lower scenery or drops.

Places—A command used by the director or stage manager to call all actors and technicians to their "places" of work. It tells them that an act or scene is about to begin.

Plant—The process of inserting an idea which will be of greater significance later in the play.

Play Script (also "Script")—The play in its written form.

Play Up (also "Point Up")—To make a particular line, action, or scene more emphatic.

Playing Line—The imaginary line between the downstage edges of the setting (*see* Curtain Line).

Playing Space (also "Playing Area," "Acting Area")—Those portions of the onstage space which are within the sight lines and may be used for playing.

Plot—In playwriting, the story of the play revealed through a series of situations which are unfolded in a pre-arranged manner. In production, a detailed layout of items and procedures; e.g., scene plot, prop plot, light plot, etc.

Plug—In acting, the process of giving added stress or emphasis to a line or bit of business. In production, a small canvas-covered piece of scenery used to "plug" up a hole; e.g., the space under a staircase.

Pointing—*See* Play Up.

Polishing Rehearsal—Rehearsals during which all of the details of action and speech are perfected.

Portal—A false proscenium set or hung directly behind the permanent proscenium. Occasionally, a small doorway in the thickness of the permanent proscenium.

Pre-casting—The process of casting actors before the tryouts have been held.

Presentational Staging—Staging which is non-realistic, emphasizes the presence of the stage platform, and avoids the representation of external reality (*see* Representational Staging, Convention).

Producer—The owner of the production. In contemporary American theatre, there are frequently dozens of owners, each of whom holds a small share. In this situation, the producer is the person or persons actually controlling the production of the play.

Production—All the elements involved in putting a play on the stage.

Profile (of role)—A statement of the vocal, physical, emotional, and tonal qualities which are required to play a particular role.

Project—The process of intensifying either speech or action so that it will carry to the audience.

Prologue—An introductory scene performed prior to the actual beginning of the play.

Prompt Book—A copy of the play script in which all information necessary to the production of the play is recorded.

Prompter—A production assistant who helps the actor recall forgotten lines.

Properties (also "Props")—All pieces of furniture and set dressings plus all objects needed for the action of the play. Large objects or fixed objects such as furniture or draperies are called "stage props." Small objects are called "hand props." Hand props used by a single character—fans, cigaret cases, etc.—are "personal props."

Proscenium—The wall which contains the permanent arch separating the auditorium from the stage.

Protagonist—Literally, *first character*. The hero or central figure of the play who usually carries the main thought of the play.

Rake—A production term meaning *slanted, sloped,* or *set at an angle.* "Raked stage," a stage floor which is inclined from the apron to the back. "Raked set," a setting which is set at an angle not parallel or perpendicular to the footlights.

Ramp—A sloped or inclined platform which takes the place of steps.

Realism (*see* Naturalism, Suggestivism, Representational Staging)—The approach to production which searches out the facts and principles of external reality and uses them with varying degrees of selectivity to reproduce life on the stage (*see* Chapter 23).

Rehearsal—The process of preparing the play for production (*see* Blocking Action, Mounting Rehearsal, Polishing Rehearsal, Dress Rehearsal, Assembly Rehearsal).

Representational Staging—Any stage form which attempts to reproduce life (*see* Realism).

Resolution—In playwriting, the structural unit in which the conflict of the play is resolved, following the climax.

Return—A flat, placed parallel to the footlights and attached to the downstage edge of the setting, which carries off into the wings behind the tormentor.

Revolving Stage—A circular disc which pivots at the center. It may be either portable or permanent. An aid to quick changes of scenery. Settings may be placed on the stage like wedges of pie.

Revue—A stage show containing musical, dance, and vaudeville sketches.

Often satirizes or parodies current topics. May or may not be unified around a central theme. Plot is usually unimportant.

Rhythm—The regular recurrence of emphasis or beat.

Riding a Laugh—Withholding the next line until the laughter has subsided enough for the line to be heard.

Rigging—The ropes and pulleys attached to the gridiron and run from the pin rail to the battens. Used to fly scenery or lighting instruments.

Romantic *or* **Sentimental Comedy**—Comic representation of life as it might or should be, rather than as it is (*see* Romanticism).

Romanticism—The representation of the chivalrous and adventurous. The art of making the remote and improbable seem immediate and plausible; e.g., the average Hollywood film.

Routine—A pre-arranged and rehearsed series of actions; e.g., a *dance routine,* a specially prepared dance.

Royalty—A fee paid to the playwright or publisher for production rights to the play script.

Run—A production term meaning to carry or slide a flat. Also the shortened form of the rehearsal term, *run-through.*

Run-through—A rehearsal term meaning to play or perform an entire scene or act without interruption.

Satire—A production which calls attention to social abuses by ridiculing them.

Scenario—The outline of a play.

Scene—In common usage, a division of an act, usually denoting a change in time or place. Occasionally, a synonym for "setting." Also, the locale of a play.

Screening Tryout—A high speed tryout procedure in which the aspirants who are conceivable for any role in the play are separated from those who are not.

Scrim—*See* Gauze.

Sentimental Comedy—A comedy of accepted standards. A romantic story which emphasizes sentiments or feelings and ends happily.

Set—To make permanent after rehearsal, as lines or business. Also an abbreviation of "setting."

Setting—The place in which the action occurs. In production, the complete arrangement of scenery, properties, and lighting which establishes the place of the action.

Share—A directing term meaning to assume a position on stage with reference to another actor, so that equal dramatic emphasis is placed on each character.

Shift—The process of striking and/or setting up properties, scenery, and lighting equipment.

Sides—Typed copies of actors' roles in which only the actor's own lines and cues are given.

Sight Line—A line of vision from any seat in the auditorium to the stage. In common usage, the line of vision from the worst seats in the house which are usually at the sides and the top of the balcony.

Situation—The total complex of physical, social, and psychological circumstances.

Skit (also Sketch)—A short dramatic episode usually satirical or humorous.

Sliding Stage—A low platform upon which settings may be mounted, which is as wide as the playing opening and operates on casters or tracks. Two or three such stages are frequently used. While one stage is in use, the others may be shifted (*see* Wagon Stage).

Social Interaction—The pattern of action and reaction experienced whenever two human beings come into social contact (*see* Chapter 2).

Soliloquy—Similar to the aside, except that the actor is alone on stage and the speech is usually longer. May be treated as subjective thought or directed to the audience, depending upon the kind of production.

Spotlight—A lighting instrument which can be focused upon a limited area.

Stage Brace—A wooden brace of adjustable length which may be attached to the back of the scenery by a hook and cleat and to the floor of the stage by a stage screw or peg.

Stage Depth—The distance from the footlights to the back wall of the stage.

Stage Directions—Instructions given in the play script for business, movement, sound effects, etc.

Stage Manager—The person responsible for all stage activities during performance. In the commercial theatre, the chief assistant to the director during rehearsals.

Stagecraft—The art and craft of stage production.

Static Scene—A scene in which there is little or no action.

Steal—In acting, the process of taking attention from the actor upon whom it rightly belongs.

Stock Company—A permanent company which usually produces a different play every week or two.

Strike—In production, to remove from the playing area; e.g., a property, a light, or a whole setting.

Striplight—A strip of low-wattage lights in a trough which may or may not be separated into compartments. Used for lighting backings. Occasionally, any strip of lights such as borderlights or footlights.

Strong *or* **Weak**—A speech or action which is strong or weak in dramatic value.

Style—The techniques and manner of producing any play (*see* Chapter 24).

Stylization—The highly individual, often mannered treatment of a specific production in which the mode or manner of producing the play becomes one of the key elements in production.

Subjectivity—Concerned with inner thoughts and feelings. The opposite of "objectivity."

Suggestivism—A production style involving radically simplified realism and employing simple representative symbols.

Suspense—A continued and increasing uncertainty, one of the fundamentals of dramatic excitement.

Switchboard—A master electrical control panel through which various combinations of light can be regulated.

Symbolism—A theatrical style originating at the beginning of the twentieth century, which deals with symbols of life and inner meaning rather than with objects of external reality.

Tableau—A striking pictorial representation or scene in which silent and motionless living models pose in picturesque attitudes.

Tag Line—The final line in a scene or act or the line prior to an exit or curtain (*see* Exit Line and Curtain Line).

Take Stage—To assume a more dominant position in relationship to another actor, usually achieved by moving slightly upstage which gives a more open body position. The opposite of "Give Stage" (*see* Share).

Teaser—A neutral-colored border placed just upstage of the house curtain and downstage of the tormentors. Used to mask the flies and adjust the height of the stage opening.

Technique—The established procedure for the execution of any art. Also, the details of such procedure.

Telescope—In acting, to condense lines so that only the most important meanings are projected. Also, to overlap speeches at the cue.

Tempo—The impression of speed of playing. Dependent upon rate of reading, cue-pickup, projection, etc.

Theme—The central thought of the play as differentiated from plot, mood, or tone.

Throw Away—In acting, to underplay or underemphasize a line, piece of business, etc. May be deliberately used to gain effect in contrast to pointing or plugging.

Timing—The precise use of time to gain the greatest theatrical effect from a line or piece of business. The process of determining the time pattern for lines or business.

Tonality—The particular feeling tone, mood, quality, or timbre projected by a scene or an actor.

Topping—To emphasize a line or an action so that it is more climactic than the preceding line or action. The opposite of "dropping."

Tormentors—A pair of neutral-colored flats placed on either side of the stage just upstage of the teaser. They serve to mask the wings and vary the width of the playing opening.

Tragedy—One of two principal classic types of drama. A dramatic form in which the principal person or persons, through passion or some limitation of character, are brought to catastrophe.

Tragi-comedy—A play in which the implications of tragedy are averted by comic incidents and a happy ending.

Trim—In production, to adjust or tie off a drop to a specific height or position.

Tryout—A procedure for auditioning actors for a play or season of plays.

Uncover—To move out from behind another actor or piece of furniture, or to open up or turn a piece of business so that the audience may see it. The opposite of "cover."

Understudy—An actor who rehearses a major role so that he can be ready to play it if the actor who usually plays the role is unable to perform.

Unities—A classic concept maintaining that the *time* represented as elapsing during the action of a play is the same as that required by the acting, the *place* of action is unchanged, and all *action* is relevant to a single plot.

Upstage—That part of the playing area farthest from the audience. Upstage areas are said to be "above" downstage areas.

Vaudeville—A variety show composed of unrelated acts loosely connected by a master of ceremonies or musical interludes.

Wagon Stage—In medieval theatre, a booth built on a wagon. The booth frequently had a playing area on top. Several wagons were drawn through a town, and different scenes were performed in sequence in designated streets. In modern usage, *see* Sliding Stage.

Weak—Lacking in force or attention value. The opposite of "strong."

Well-made Play—In dramaturgy, a play which is constructed to a precise pattern with exposition, complication, climax, resolution, and conclusion skillfully handled in accordance with the laws of play structure.

Wings—The offstage areas to the left and right of the playing space. In production, hinged flats usually set in pairs on either sides of the stage to mask the offstage areas.

Wing and Drop Setting—A setting which encloses the stage area with several pairs of wings and a backdrop (*see* Chapter 21).

Index

A

Abbott and Costello, 424, 431
Above, 455
Abstract staging (see Departures from realism, Nonrealism)
Abstraction and motivation, 403-404
Abstraction in style, 401-402
Accident to performer, 280-281
Act curtain, 306, 455
Acting, 287-304 (see also Actor)
  burlesque, 432
  comedy of manners, 427
  comedy of Molière, 418
  common faults, 296-302
  criticism, 302-304
  crowd scenes, 335-336
  definition, 455
  director's qualification, 66
  farce comedy, 429-430
  mixed styles of play, 434-435
  naturalistic, 397-398
  problem in ensemble play, 300-301
  role, 227-230
  romantic comedy, 428-429
  Shakespearean drama, 417-418
  simplified realism, 399
  style in comedy, 425
Action, 8, 455
  center of, furniture, 319
  covert, 8
  dramatic, 11
  lack of, 8
  motivation, 9-22
  overt, 8
  playwright's tool, 26
  resulting from emotional tension, 168
Actors: (see also Acting)
  amount of emotion, 293
  central staging, 379
  creative ideas, 288-289

  determining range, 233-235
  difference between, 288
  directing, 292-293
  director's responsibility, 58
  experience, 217
  handling, 287-304
  judging, 231-232
  kinds of, 289-296
  play selection, 192-193
  qualities, 288
  range of, 233-235
  relationship to director, 287-289
  run-away, 266
  strengths and weaknesses, 289
  time at rehearsal, 247
  at tryouts, 214-216
Ad lib, 455
Adapting script, 206
Adding Machine, The (Rice), 406
Aesthetic Attitude, The (Langfeld), 50
Aesthetic distance (see Artistic detachment)
All My Sons (Miller), 82, 83
Amount of movement, 128-129
Anderson, Maxwell, 310
Andreyev, Leonid, 399
Angel Street (Hamilton), 243
Anger, portrayal of, 163
Anna Christie (O'Neill), 145, 228, 405
Antagonist, 7, 455
  in formula, 11 (Illus.)
Anthologies, 198
Antigone (Sophocles), 240
Anti-type casting, 236-237
Antoine, 55
Appia, Adolph, 405
Approach and withdrawal, 168
Apron, 306-307, 363, 455
Apron scene, 455
Arc lamp, 455
Archer, William, 412

Architectural logic in setting, 312
Area, playing (*see* Playing area)
Area, stage, 455
Arena staging, 306 (*see also* **Central Staging**)
Aristotle, 29-31, 33
Arms and the Man (Shaw), 57
Arrangement in composition, 113-116
Articulation and projection, 300
Artist, director as, 64-65
Artistic detachment, 49-53
  balance with participation, 52-53
  breakdown in, 52
  central staging, 377
Asbestos, 455
Asides, 414-415, 455
Asymmetrical balance, 101-102 (*Illus.*)
Atmosphere (*see* Mood)
Attack, definition, 177
Attention:
  central staging, 384
  control of, 103-113
    body position, 105-108
    contrast, 112-113
    focus, 111-112
    level, 109-110
    other factors, 116-117
    playing area, 108-109
    relative strength, 117-118
    space, 110-111
  definition, 103
  directed by tempo, 174-175
  during performance, 268-269
  focal point, 104
  and movement, 121
Attic drama, 395, 455
Attitude of actor, 232
Audience:
  attention at performance, 268-269
  in central staging, 378-379
  for comedy, 46
  coughing, 269
  as crowd, 346
  differences, 276
  director's responsibility, 59
  factors in building, 45-48
  make-up of, 41-43
  in play selection, 192
  as psychological crowd, 42-45
  psychological influences, 43-45
  restlessness, 269
  test, 262-263

Audience attendance, reasons, 38-41
Audience detachment (*see* Artistic detachment)
Audience participation, 49-53
  balance with detachment, 52-53
  in performance, 272
Audience response, 48-53
  in script analysis, 203
Auditions (*see* Tryouts)
Auditorium, 306-307
Author (*see* Playwright)
Awake and Sing (Odets), 7

B

Back cross (*see* Crossing)
Backdrop, 456
Backing, 456
Backstage, 456
Balance:
  in acting styles, 301
  in central staging, 384, 387
  between characters in acting, 301
  in composition, 99-102
  definition, 456
  other aesthetic factors, 103
  participation and detachment, 52-53
  in performance, 272-273
  physical, 100-103
  in play selection, 197
  psychological, 102
  in setting, 319
  in stage business, 150
Balanced actor, 295-296
Balancing stage (*see* Dressing stage)
Barrie, J. M., 404-405
Barry, Philip, 402
Bases of play direction, 4
Basic drives, 10, 12, 456
  affecting character, 41
  in audience attendance, 38-41
  in emotional key, 166
  and motivational unit, 82-83
Batten, 456
Beggar on Horseback (Kaufman, Connelly), 406
Behrman, S. N., 258
Below, 456
Bibliography, dramatic, 198
Blackout, 456
Blocking action, 206-208, 456
Blocking rehearsals, 254-257

Body position, 105-108, 456
  attention value, 117
  central staging, 384
  eight basic positions, 105 (*Illus.*)
  symbols for, 212
Border, 456
Borderlight, 456
Born Yesterday (Kanin), 438
Box office, 280
Box setting, 306-307, 456
Boy Meets Girl (Spewack), 429
Brecht, Bertolt, 396, 402
Brunetière, Ferdinand, 6
Build, 456
Burlesque, 431-432, 456
Bury the Dead (I. Shaw), 247
Business, stage:
  central staging, 388-389
  creating and projecting, 146-150
  definition, 119, 143
  purposes, 143-144
  technical problems, 150-157
  types of, 144-146

C

Caldwell, Erskine, 397
California, University of, 416
Call, 456
Call board, 456
Call, curtain, 281-282, 457
Cantor, Eddie, 431
Capek, Karl, 404
Card table scenes, 344-346 (*Illus.*)
Casting:
  actor's range, 233-235
  changes, 238
  crowd scenes, 341
  defining the role, 227-230
  definition, 227, 456
  double, 239
  educational, 236-237
  ensemble, 237-238
  family, 238
  individual actor, 235-237
  judging the actor, 231-232
  musical show, 348-351
  obligation, 238
  in play selection, 193-194
  precasting, 240-241
  psychology, 236-237
  special problems, 238-239
    tentative, 238
    type, 235-236
    unity, 238
    variety, 237-238
Catalogues of publishers, 198
Cavalcade (Coward), 380
Center door fancy, 313
Central staging:
  advantages, 374-377
  business, stage, 388-389
  composition, 384-387 (*Illus.*)
  costumes, 391
  definition, 372-373
  direction of, 382-390
  emotional key, 389
  floor plans, 382-384
  furniture arrangement, 382-384 (*Illus.*)
  light curtain, 392
  lighting, 390-391
  make-up, 391
  movement, 387-388 (*Illus.*)
  play selection, 380-382
  problems, general, 377-379
  properties, 392
  scenes, changes, 392
  sight lines, 385-386 (*Illus.*)
  size and shape, 374-375
  suggestivistic staging, 400
  technical problems, 390-393
  tempo, 390
Character:
  burlesque, 431-432
  business, 144-145
  comedy of manners, 426
  complex, 10, 16-18
    emotional key, 166
    motivational unit, 77, 83-84
  dropping, 297
  farce comedy, 429-430
  and movement, 121-122
  playwright's material, 25
  portrayal, 252
  romantic comedy, 429
  type, 219
  universality in period drama, 410
Character relationship, composition,
  94-95
Character roles, 456
Characteristics of role, 228-230
Characterization, definition, 456
  script analysis, 204
Cheney, Sheldon, 396

Children's Hour, The (Hellman), 81, 191
Chorus: *(see also* Musical Show)
  arrangement, 368-369
  circle in composition, 115 *(Illus.)*
  definition, 456
  movement, 369-370
  rehearsal, 355
  tryouts, 349-350
  units, 351-352
Cigarettes, lighting, 152
Circle, chorus *(see* Chorus, circle)
Circle dress *(see* Dressing stage)
Circle in composition, 115
Circle staging, 373 *(see also* Central staging)
Circle, The (Maugham), 427, 438
Circular response, 15
Circus, 372
  staging *(see* Central staging)
Claque, 48, 457
Clark, Bobby, 431
Clear stage, 457
Climax, 30-31, 33
Closed tryouts, 221-223
Closed turn, 457 *(see* Turning)
Closing doors, 151-152
Closing performance, 276
Cocktail party scenes, 346
Cohan, George M., 38
Coherence:
  central staging, 384
  composition, 99
Comedy:
  ability to hear, 270-271
  classification criteria, 424-425
  definition, 420-421, 457
  incongruity, 421
  laughter, 421-422
  mixture of style, 433-435
  period drama, 414
  projection, 436-439
  techniques, 435-442
  types, 425-432
  universality in period drama, 410 *(see also* Comedy of manners, Romantic comedy, Farce comedy, Burlesque)
  universals, 421-422
Comedy of manners:
  acting style, 427
  characters, 426

definition, 425
  emphasis in writing, 426
  situation, 426-427
Comic attitude, 422-424
Comic relief, 457
Commercial theatre:
  crowd scenes, 333
  polishing, 258
  understudy, 279
Company, 457
Company curtain call, 282
Complex, character *(see* Character, complex)
Complication, 30-32
Composition:
  attention in *(see* Attention)
  basic crowd, 342-343
  body position, 105-108 *(see* Body position)
  central staging, 384-387
  contrast, 112-113
  crowd scenes, 337-341
  definition, 92
  focus, 111-112 *(see* Focus)
  geometric arrangement, 113-116
  Greek drama, 417
  home position, 343
  level, 109-110, 461
  motivational aspects, 93-95
  musical show, 368-369
  pictorial aspects, 98-105
  playing area, 95-97 *(see also* Playing area)
  principles, 92
  space, 110-111 *(Illus.)*
  symbols, 212
  technical aspects, 95-97
Conclusion, 30-31, 34
Conduct of rehearsals, 245-246
Conflict:
  dramatic formula, 11
  human, 6-22
  intensified by tempo, 175
  motivational unit, 78
  script analysis, 203-204
  universality in period drama, 409
Congreve, William, 414, 424, 427
Connelly, Marc, 243, 406
Constructive criticism, 303-304
Constructivism, 406-457
Contrast, 112-113
  in composition, 103

Convention, 457
Conventional staging, 395-396
Cooperative attitude, 232
Copying model in acting, 293
Copyrights, 195
Costs in play selection, 194-195
Costume drama (*see* Period drama)
Costume plot, 208-209
Costumes:
  central staging, 391
  costs of, 195
  crowd scene, 341
  identifying period, 418
  polishing rehearsals, 259
  technical rehearsals, 262
Coughing, 269
Counter focus, 457
Counter movement, 140, 457
Cover, 457
Coward, Noel, 122, 183-184, 427, 434
Craig, Gordon, 405
Criteria for tryouts, 214-216
Critic, director's qualification as, 65
Critical comment, script analysis, 202
Criticism, 302-304
Crossing, 132-135, 142, 457
  back, 134-135 (*Illus.*)
  definition, 132
Crowd: (*see also* Crowd scenes, Group
  scenes)
  basis of, 329-330
  level of response, 332
  make-up of, 330-333
  psychological, 42-45
Crowd scenes:
  acting in, 335-336
  audience as crowd, 346
  basic composition, 342-343
  casting, 341
  central staging, 381
  costuming, 341
  directing, 341-344
  general problems, 333-336
  group unit system, 341-344
  levels of response, 334
  movement, 343
  problems in staging, 336-341
    changing focal point, 337-338
    filling stage, 340-341
    sight lines, 338-339 (*Illus.*)
  settings, 339
  size, 334, 340-341

  stereotyped, 335
  when to use, 333
  writing, 334-335
Crystallizing blocking, 255
  play, 259
Cue, definition, 177, 457
Cue-pickup, 177-178
  definition, 177
  kinds of, 177-178, 184
Cue sheet, 457
Cul-de-sac, 313
Curtain:
  act, 306
  guillotine, 306
  light, 392
  traveller, 306
Curtain calls, 281-282, 457
Curtain line, 458
Cutting period drama, 412
Cutting script, 206
Cuttings for tryouts, 217
Cyclorama, 458
Cyrano de Bergerac (Rostand), 156, 193,
  240, 428

D

Daggers, business with, 155
Dance: (*see also* Musical show)
  director's duties, 348
  rehearsal, 355
  tryouts, 349-350
  units, 351-352
Dante, 420
Dead End (Kingsley), 381, 399
Dear Ruth (Krasna), 252, 428
Death of a Salesman (Miller), 7
Death scenes, 156-157
Definition in stage business, 147
Dekker, Thomas, 416
Delayed focus, 112, 458
Denouement, 458
Desert Song, The (Harbach, Hammer-
  stein II), 368
Design, director's qualification, 66-67
Design of setting, 308-309
Designer, director's responsibility, 58
Development, 458
Dialogue, 26, 458
Dietrich, John E., 198
Dimmer, 458
Direct focus, 111-112

Direction:
actor in crowd scene, 336
amount, 60-63
central staging, 382-390
motivational unit, 84-86
musical, 347-348
overdirection, 60-62
underdirection, 62-63
Direction of movement, 123-125 (*Illus.*), 130
Director: (*see also* Direction)
as creative artist, 56
during performance, 262, 264-267
as interpretative artist, 56
knowledge of actor, 289
model for actor, 293
place of, 56 (*Illus.*)
play selection, 193
play structure, 34-35
qualifications, 64-67
relationship to actor, 287-289
responsibilities, 57-60
rise of, 54-56
and technical actor, 291-293
Dissolve, 366-367, 458
Distortion, 7
Dockeray, Floyd C., 160
Doctor in Spite of Himself, A (Molière), 414, 429
Doll's House, A (Ibsen), 73, 80, 83, 85-90, 137
Dominance (*see* Attention)
Doorways (*see* Entrances)
Double casting, 239
Down stage, 458
Dracula (Balderston), 149, 263
Drama:
and audience, 37-53
definition, 3, 4
and director, 54-67
formula, 11
and human conflict, 6-22
law, 6
and life, 23
non-real, 7, 404-407
and playwright, 23-36
Dramatic action, pyramid, 31 (*Illus.*)
Dramatic key (*see* Key, emotional)
Dramatic pause, 180
Dramatic personality of actor, 231
Dramatic qualities in play selection, 190

Dramaturgy, 458
Drapery setting, 306
Drawing room comedy, 458 (*see also* Comedy of manners)
Dream Play, The (Strindberg), 402
Dress rehearsal, 260-263
Dress setting, 458
Dressing stage, 133-134 (*Illus.*), 142, 458
circle, 134-135 (*Illus.*)
definition, 133
Drinking business, 152
Drives, basic (*see* Basic drives)
Drop, 458
Dropping:
emotional key, 171-172, 458
time factor in, 172
Dropping out of character, 297
Duke of Saxe-Meiningen, 55
Dull performance, 176
Duration of movement, 127, 130

E

Eating and drinking business, 152
Educational casting, 236-237
Effects plot, 209
Eligibility, 217
Elizabethan costume, 418
Elizabethan drama, 411 (*see also* Shakespearean drama)
stage, 372
Embraces and kisses, 152-154
Emotion: (*see also* Key, emotional)
actor's control, 234-235
amount of, 293
bases for naming, 160
central staging, 381
and composition, 94
conventionalized, 162-165
conveyed by tempo, 175
definition, 158-159
inducing in actor, 292
James-Lange theory, 290
and movement, 121
in period drama, 413-414
recognition, 159-161
stereotype, 160-161
summary, 161
Emotional actor, 293-295
Emotional characteristics of role, 229
Emotional control, 294
Emotional identification, 50-51

INDEX 475

Emotional key (*see* Key, emotional)
Emotional tension (*see* Key, emotional)
Empathic response, 49-50
  central staging, 378
  embraces and kisses, 153
Emperor Jones (O'Neill), 84
Emphasis:
  business for, 145
  shared, 106 (*Illus.*)
  single, 107-108 (*Illus.*)
Encore, 365-366
Enemy of the People, An (Ibsen), 7,
  346, 409, 416
Ensemble, casting of, 237-238
Entering and exiting, 136-138, 142
  central staging, 388
Entr'acte, 458
Entrances, 314 (*Illus.*), 458
  defining, 313
  floor plan, 327
  hinging doors, 313
  wing and drop, 363
Epic theatre, 396, 406, 458
Epilogue, 458
Episode, 459
Escape, in comedy, 422
Eustis, Morton, 295
Evaluating performance, 267-274
Evans, Maurice, 411
Everyman, 417
Exaggeration, 7, 437
Exciting moment (*see* Inciting action or
  moment)
Exit line, 459
Exciting (*see* Entering and exciting)
Experience, actor's, 231-232
Exposition, 30-32, 459 (*see also* Story-
  telling)
Expressionism, 7, 406, 459
Extra, 459

F

Fantasy, 7, 196, 459
Farce comedy:
  acting style, 429-430
  definition, 429, 459
  emphasis in writing, 429
Fast tempo (*see* Tempo, characteristics)
Faults in furniture arrangement, 321-
  323
Ferrer, José, 229
Fighting business, 154-155

Final tryouts, 223-224
Fireplace, 318-319
  floor plan, 327
Five readings, The, 202-205
Flat, 459
Flexibility of actor, 233-235
Flies, 459
Floodlight, 459
Floor cloth, 459
Floor plan, 324-328, 382-384, 459
  laying out, 326-327 (*Illus.*)
  musical show, 360-361
  use of scale, 324-326
  uses, 324
  workable, 309
Flowers at performance, 282-283
Focal point, 47, 48, 104, 459
  crowd scenes, 337-338
Focus, 111-112
  attention value of, 117
  central staging, 385
  dominance through, 112 (*Illus.*)
Follow spot, 459
Fontanne, Lynn, 258, 295
Footlights, 306-307, 363, 459
Foreshadowing, 459
Forestage, 459
Form of setting, 310
Formalism, 406, 459
"Fourth wall," 51, 96, 459
  in musical show, 367-368
Framed picture, 96-97, 460
French scene, 35, 460
Freytag, Gustav, 30-31, 33
Front, 460
Furniture:
  arrangement, 309, 319-324
  central staging, 382-384
  common faults, 322 (*Illus.*)
  floor plan, 327
  motivation from, 109, 319
  musical show, 361
  problem pieces, 323-324

G

Gag line, 438
Gap versus pause, 180
Gas I, Gas II (Kaiser), 402, 406
Gauze, 460
Gee, Ronald G., 198
Gelatin, 460
Gentle People, The (I. Shaw), 381

Geometric arrangement, 113-116
Gershwin, George, 358, 364
Gesturing, 150-151, 460
Girl Crazy (Gershwin), 358
Giving stage, 131 (*Illus.*), 140, 460
Gogol, Nikolai, 402
Golden Boy (Odets), 77, 138, 380
Good News (DeSylva-Henderson), 437
Good play, 189-190
Gorelik, Mordecai, 396, 406
Grand drapery, 306, 460
Great God Brown, The (O'Neill), 396
Greek drama, 395, 411, 412
   dancing ring, 372
   staging, 417
Green Pastures, The (Connelly), 243
Green room, 460
Gridiron, 460
"Group mind" theory, 42
Group scenes, 344-346 (*see also* Crowd scenes)
   table scenes, 344 (*Illus.*)
Group Theatre, 55
Group unit system, 341-344, 460
Guillotine curtain, 306
Guns, business, 155-156

H

Hamilton, Patrick, 243
Hamlet (Shakespeare), 58, 78, 157, 240, 252, 411, 418
Hampden, Walter, 229
Hasty Heart, The (Patrick), 381
Hauptmann, Gerhart, 402
Hayes, Helen, 295
He Who Gets Slapped (Andreyev), 399
"Heads up," 460
Hedda Gabler (Ibsen), 123, 240
Hellman, Lillian, 81, 191, 398
Home position, 368, 460
Hotel Universe (Barry), 402
House, 460
Howard, Sidney, 81, 292
Human conduct in drama, 6-22

I

I Know My Love (Behrman), 258
Ibsen, Henrik, 73, 80, 87-90, 123, 202, 346, 409, 412, 416
Illinois, University of, 416
Illness of performer, 280-281

Illusion:
   central staging, 376-377
   definition, 48-49
   participation in, 49-51
   reality, 23
   symbolistic staging, 406
Illusory staging, 396
Imagination:
   director's qualification, 64
   lack of, 292
Importance of Being Earnest, The (Wilde), 145, 426-427, 434
Improvisations, 224, 461
In One, In Two, In Three, 461
Inciting action or moment, 31-32, 461
Incongruity, 421
   comic technique, 435
   intensification, 437-439
   timing, 439
Individuality in play selection, 190-191
Inner feeling, 290-291, 293
Inner proscenium, 461
"Inner thought," 403
Innocents, The (Archibald), 316
Inspector General, The (Gogol), 402
Integral business, 144
Integral unit, 331-332, 461
Intensification:
   comedy, 437-439
   creating role, 295
   playwright's process, 29
   stage business, 148
Interaction: (*see also* Social interaction)
   acting, 300-301
   controlling emotional key, 166, 169-170 (*Illus.*)
   motivational unit, 83
Interpretation rehearsals, 251-253
Interpreting the script, 200-213
   backgrounds, 201-202
   characterization, 204-205
   five readings, 202-205
   period drama, 416
   production planning, 205-209
   production problems, 205
   prompt book, 209-213

J

James-Lange theory of emotion, 290
Jeffers, Robinson, 417
Jones, Margo, 373

Julius Caesar (Shakespeare), 144, 416
Junior Miss (Chodorov, Fields), 428

K

Kaiser, Georg, 402, 406
Kaufman, George S., 364, 406
Kelly, George, 433
Key, emotional:
  central staging, 389
  characteristics of tempo, 179
  definition, 165
  dropping, 171-172
  opposite, 172
  principle for controlling, 168-172
  sources of, 165-167
  sustaining, 171
  symbols for, 213
  topping, 170-171
Kingsley, Sidney, 399, 409
Kiss and Tell (Herbert), 428
Kisses, business of, 152-154
Koch, Fred, Jr., 376

L

Lahr, Bert, 431
Lane, G. Gorham, 160
Langfeld, Herbert S., 50-51
Laughter, 421-422
  technique for handling, 440-441
Law of the Drama, 6
Lebon, Gustave, 42
Legs, 363
Length of rehearsals, 244-245
Level, 109-110, 461
  attention value of, 117
  central staging, 385
Life With Father (Lindsay and Crouse), 282, 345, 434
Light curtain, 392
Light plot, 209, 461
Lighting:
  beginning of play, 46
  central staging, 390-391
Lighting cigarettes, 152
Liliom (Molnar), 337, 380
Line in composition, 113-114 *(Illus.)*
Lines (rigging), 461
Lines:
  gag, 437-438
  reading, 299
  throwaway, 438-439

Little Foxes, The (Hellman), 398
Lloyd, Harold, 423-424
Longfellow, William Wadsworth, 191
Luce, Claire Boothe, 380
Lunt, Alfred, 258, 295

M

Macbeth (Shakespeare), 7, 83, 240, 418
Make-up for central staging, 391
Man and the Masses (Masse Mensch) (Toller), 402
Man Who Came to Dinner, The (Kaufman, Hart), 429
Mannerisms in acting, 298
Manuscript play service, 198
Matthews, Brander, 30, 33
Maugham, Somerset, 427, 438
Medea (Euripides), 240
Medea (Jeffers), 417
Medieval drama, 417
Melodrama, 196, 461
Mencken, H. L., 90
Mercury Theatre, 416
Meredith, Burgess, 295
Midsummer Night's Dream (Shakespeare), 144
Miller, Arthur, 82, 416
Model, scale, 327-328
Modern dress, 419
Molière, 414, 418
Molnar, Ferenc, 337, 380
Mood:
  definition, 462
  motivational unit, 78, 84
  setting, 308
Monkey's Paw, The (Jacobs), 145
Monotony, 182-186
Moscow Art Theatre, 55
Motivation:
  abstract staging, 403-404
  comic technique, 436
  complex, 12-22
  crowd, 330-331
  definition, 10, 462
  dramatic formula, 11
  fireplace, 318
  from furniture, 109, 319
  illustration of, 10-11
  movement, 130
  sources, 10

Motivation (*cont.*)
  stage business, 146-147
  summary, 20-22
Motivational unit:
  analysis, 79-84
  blocking, 256
  characteristics, 73-77
  dangers in method, 86
  definition, 36, 73, 462
  determining tempo, 180-181
  direction, 84-86
  emotional key, 167
  importance of recognition, 76
  interpretation rehearsals, 253
  sample analysis, 87-90
  types, 77-79
Mounting rehearsals, 260-263
Movement, stage:
  central staging, 387-388
  characteristics, 123-129
  configurated, 370
  crowd scenes, 337-341, 343
  definition, 462
  differentiated from business, 119
  Greek drama, 417
  musical, 368-370
  principles, 120-122
  summary, 129-130
  symbols, 213
  techniques, 130-141
  and tempo, 179
  when to move, 122-123
Murray, Gilbert, 412
Muscular tension, 158-159, 163
Music: (*see also* Musical show)
  cutting, 353
  rented scores, 353
Musical director, duties, 348
Musical show:
  casting chorus, 350
  composition and movement, 368-370
    (*see also* Crowd scene)
  cooperative directing, 347-348
  covering shifts, 365-367
  definition, 462
  dialogue, 367-368
  directors, 347-348
  floor plans, 360-361
  "fourth wall," 367-368
  framing music, 352-354
  furniture arrangement, 361
  numerous scenes, 362

  organizing cast, 357-360
  planning, 351, 352, 353 (*Illus.*)
  rehearsing, 354-357
  scene shifts, 364-365
  settings, 362-364
    wing and drop, 363 (*Illus.*)
  technical aspects, 360-367
  tryouts and castings, 348-351
Mystery play, 462

N

Nathan, George Jean, 279
Naturalism, 7, 462
  in play selection, 196
  staging, 397-398
Negative criticism, 304
New Theatres for Old (Gorelik), 394
Nicoll, Alderdyce, 427
Night Must Fall (Williams), 78, 145
Non-real drama, 7, 404-407 (*see also*
  Style of production)
Number of rehearsals, 242-244
Numerous settings, 311
  central staging, 387

O

Objective criticism, 302-304
Objectivity, definition, 462
  in comedy, 423-424
Odets, Clifford, 77, 138, 346
Of Mice and Men (Steinbeck), 18, 84
Of Thee I Sing (Gershwin, Kaufman,
  Ryskind), 350, 364-365
Olsen and Johnson, 424
Once in a Lifetime (Kaufman, Hart),
  145
O'Neill, Eugene, 84, 145, 228, 403
Open cue, 178
Open tryouts, 220
Open turn (*see* Turning)
Opening and closing doors, 151-152
Operetta, definition, 462
Opposite keys, 172
Orchestral reprise, 365
Our Town (Wilder), 396
Overacting, 297-298, 462
Overdirected play, 60-62
Over-rehearsed blocking, 255
Overt act, 32, 462
Overt action, 462

P

Pacing (see Tempo)
Pantomime, 143, 462
at tryouts, 224
Parallel movement, 140, 463
Participation, audience (see Audience participation)
in play selection, 195
Patriots, The (Kingsley), 409
Pause, dramatic, 180, 439
"Peep hole" stage, 305
Peer Gynt (Ibsen), 240, 402
Penthouse Theatre (Univ. of Washington), 373-374, 379
Performance:
audience differences, 276
closing, 276-277
controlling excitement, 265-266
curtain calls, 281-282
director's demeanor, 266
director's place at, 266-267
dress rehearsal, 262
evaluating, 267-275
excessive excitement, 265
flowers, 282-283
high school director, 267
illness and accident, 280-281
making changes, 274-277
need for excitement, 265
played as rehearsed, 266
pranks, 276
projection levels, 270-271
prompter, 277-278
recording, 275
responsibilities of director, 264-267
reviews, 278-279
run-away actor, 266
second night letdown, 276
seeing and hearing, 270-271
special problems, 277-283
stage manager, 267
understudy, 279-280
Period drama:
adapting and producing, 410-418
comedy, 414
complicated plots, 412
cost, 411-412
costuming, 418-419
cutting, 412
definition, 408-409, 463
interpretation, 416

poetry, 415-416
scenes and settings, 411-412
soliloquies and asides, 414-415
stages, 417
translations, 412-413
Permanent setting, 463
Personal interview tryouts, 221-223
Personal tonality, tryouts, 219
Personality of actor, 231
Peter Pan (Barrie), 404-405
Petrified Forest, The (Sherwood), 273
Philadelphia Story, The (Barry), 145
Physical and vocal control, 219
Physical appearance and flexibility, 233
Physical characteristics of role, 228-229
Physical situation, 10-11, 14
Picture frame stage, 305
Pinero, Arthur Wing, 409
Piscator, Erwin, 396
Pitch in portraying emotion, 164
Place for rehearsal, 246-247
Places, 463
Plan, floor (see Floor plan)
Planning production, 205-209
Planning rehearsals, 242-250
Planning setting, 309-312
Plant, 463
Play:
backgrounds, 201-202
beginning the, 46-47
parts, 32-34
structure, 29
Play selection:
balance in season, 197
central staging, 380-382
choosing season, 195-197
good play, 189-190
kinds of variety, 196-197
period play, 409-410
practical problems, 193-195
sources of plays, 197-198
theatrical worth, 190-193
Player at Work (Eustis), 295
Playing area:
attention values, 117
central staging, 384
divisions, 97 (Illus.)
dominance, 108 (Illus.)
nomenclature, 97
principle of attention, 108
sight lines, 96
Playing line, 463

Playwright:
  director's responsibility, 57
  lines of development, 72
  materials, 24-25
  process, 27-29
  script analysis, 201-202
Playwriting:
  burlesque, 431
  comedy of manners, 426
  farce comedy, 429
  naturalistic, 397
  romantic comedy, 428-429
  simplified realism, 399
  suggestivism, 400
Plot, 463
Poetic drama (see Period drama, poetry)
Pointing, 463
Polarization, 43
  beginning of play, 47
Polishing rehearsals, 257-260
Pranks in performance, 276
Precasting, 240-241
Presentational staging, 395-396, 463
Private Lives (Coward), 122, 183-184,
    427, 434
Producer, 464
Production assistant, 219
Production costs, 194-195
Production planning, 205-209
Production style, 394-407 (see also Style
    of production)
Profile of role, 228-230, 464
Professional theatre (see Commercial
    theatre)
Projection:
  in casting, 231
  comedy, 436-439
  conventionalized emotion, 162-165
  definition, 178, 464
  during performance, 270-271
  lack, in acting, 299
  means of, 299-300
  musical, 370-371
  tempo, 178-179
  tryouts, 219
Prologue, 464
Prompt book, 209-213 (Illus.), 464
  making, 212
Prompter, 277-278
Properties:
  blocking rehearsals, 256-257
  central staging, 392

  definition, 464
  plot, 209
  polishing rehearsals, 259
  technical rehearsals, 261
Proscenium arch, 306-307, 464
Protagonist, 7, 11, 464
Provincetown Players, 55
Psychological balance, 102
Psychological crowd (see Crowd, psy-
    chological)
Publisher's catalogues, 198
Purpose of movement, 120-121, 129
Pygmalion (Shaw), 20

Q

Qualifications of director, 64-67
Quality, vocal, 165

R

Radio production, 253
Rake, 464
Rate in portaying emotion, 165
Rate in projection, 300
Reading ability, tryouts, 219
Realism, 7, 397-400, 464
  illusion of, 23
  play selection, 196
Realistic continuum, 400-401
Realistic staging, 398-399
Realistic style, 397-401 (see also Style
    of production)
Rearrangement, 28
Recognition in comedy, 423
Recording the performance, 275
Rectangular setting, 310
Regimentation, 45
Rehearsal:
  assembly (musical), 355-357
  atmosphere at, 247
  attendance at, 247
  attitude, 291
  blocking, 254-257
  conduct of, 245-246
  divided (musical), 354-355
  dividing play, 247
  fatigue, 245
  growth of play, 244
  interpretation, 251-253
  length, 244-245
  mounting, 260-263

musical show, 354-357
number, 242-244
place, 246-247
plan, 250-263
polishing, 257-260
practical units, 247
preliminary preparation, 250-251
schedule, 248-249
time, 245
time for crowd, 334
units, 247-248
Representational staging, 395-464
Reprise, orchestral, 365
Resolution, 30-31, 33, 464
Response:
  audience *(see* Audience response)
  circular, 15
  comedy, 424-425
  levels of crowd, 332
  serial, 15
Responsibilities of director, 57-60
Restlessness, 269
Restoration comedy, staging, 418
Return, 306-307, 464
Reviews, 278-279
Revolving stage, 464
Revue, 464
Rhythm, 465 *(see also* Tempo)
  in composition, 103
Rice, Elmer, 406
Riding laughter, 441, 465
Rigging, 465
Ring staging, 306, 373 *(see also* Central
  staging)
Ring Theatre (University of Miami),
  374
Rising and sitting, 151
Road companies, 280
Role, acting, 227-230
Romantic comedy, 196, 428-429, 465
Routine, 465
Routine movement, 141
Royalty, 194-195, 465
R.U.R. ("Rossum's Universal Robots"),
  (Capek), 404-405
Run-through, 259, 263, 465
Ryskind, Morris, 364

S

Saroyan, William, 403
Satire, 196, 465

Scale, use of, 324-326 *(Illus.)*
Scale model, 327-328
Scenario, 465
Scene: *(see also* Setting)
  French, 35
  shifts, 364-365 *(see also* Shifting scen-
    ery)
Schedule for rehearsals, 248-249
School for Scandal (Sheridan), 427
Screening tryouts, 220-221, 465
Script analysis, 200-213
Scripts for tryouts, 217
Seasonal auditions, 225-226
Second Mrs. Tanqueray, The (Pinero),
  77, 80, 138, 144
Selection:
  creating role, 295
  playwright's process, 27
  stage business, 147
Selection of play *(see* Play selection)
Selective realism, 398-399
Sensitivity:
  director's qualification, 64
  lack of, in acting, 291-292
Sentimental comedy *(see* Romantic comedy)
Serial response, 15
Setting:
  architectural logic, 312
  balance in, 319
  box, 306, 307
  color, 308
  cost, 195
  crowd scenes, 339
  design, 308-309
  drapery, 306
  floor plan, 324-328 *(see also* Floor
    plan)
  form, 310
  furniture arrangement, 319-324 *(see
    also* Furniture)
  mood, 308
  musical show, 362-364
  number of, 311
  period drama, 411-412
  planning, 309-312
  requirements, 308-309
  scale model, 327-328
  shape, 310
  shifting *(see* Shifting scenery)
  sight lines, 311-312 *(see also* Sight
    lines)

Setting (*cont.*)
  size, 310
  style, 311 (*see also* Style)
  wing and drop, 306
Seventh Heaven (Strong), 52
Shakespeare, William, 78, 380
Shakespearean drama, 417-418
Share, 465
Shaw, George Bernard, 20, 57, 201
Shaw, Irwin, 247
She Stoops to Conquer (Goldsmith), 414
Shifting scenery, 311, 364-365, 465
  central staging, 392
  covering, 365-367
Shoemaker's Holiday, The (Dekker), 416
Shooting, business of, 155-156
"Show must go on," 280
Sides, 465
Sight lines, 96, 312 (*Illus.*), 465
  central staging, 385-386
  crowd scenes, 338-339
  furniture, 320
  setting, 311-312
  staircase, 316
  table scenes, 344-345
Silver Cord, The (Howard), 81, 292
Simonson, Lee, 396
Simplified realism, 398-399
Simultaneous movement, 139-140 (*Illus.*), 142
Simultaneous speech, 184
Situation, 10, 14, 466
  analysis motivational unit, 82
  burlesque, 431-432
  comedy of manners, 426-427
  emotional key, 166
  farce comedy, 429
  physical, 10-11, 14
  playwright's material, 25
  romantic comedy, 429
  script analysis, 203
  social, 14
Skin of Our Teeth, The (Wilder), 381
"Slice of life," 24, 397
Social anonymity, 44
Social drama, 196
Social facilitation, 44
  central staging, 379
Social interaction, 10, 15-16 (*Illus.*), 466
Social situation, 14
Soliloquies and asides, 414-415, 466

Sound effects plot, 209
Sources of plays, 197-198
South Pacific (Rodgers, Hammerstein II), 368
Space, 110-111 (*Illus.*)
  attention value, 117
  central staging, 384
Specialty, 365
Speed and tempo, 176-177, 185
Speed of movement, 126-127
Spotlight, 466
Square in composition, 114-115
Stabbing and shooting business, 155-156
Stage, 305-308 (*Illus.*)
  musical show, 362-364
  size for crowd, 334
  technical rehearsals, 262
Stage brace, 466
Stage business (*see* Business, stage)
Stage directions, 466
Stage falls, 156
Stage Is Set, The (Simonson), 396
Stage manager, 262, 466
  responsibilities, 267
Stage movement (*see* Movement, stage)
Staircase, 316-318 (*Illus.*)
  floor plan, 327
Stalled cue, 177-178
Stanislavski, Constantin, 55
Stealing stage, 131-132, 466
Steinbeck, John, 18, 84
Stereotype:
  acting, 302
  emotional, 160-161
  stock, 301-302
Stimulus, 15
  crowd reaction, 43
Stock company, 466
Stock stereotype, 301-302
Storytelling: (*see also* Exposition)
  aspect of composition, 93-94
  business, 145
  motivational unit, 77
  movement, 121
Strange Interlude (O'Neill), 396, 403
Strike, 466
Strindberg, August, 402
Striplight, 466
Structure of play, 29
Struggling and fighting business, 154-155
Study of the Drama (Matthews), 30

Style:
   balance in acting, 301
   mixtures in comedy, 433-435
   in planning production, 205
   setting, 311
Style of production:
   abstraction and communication, 401-403
   abstraction and motivation, 403-404
   conventional staging defined, 395-396
   definition, 394
   departures from realism, 401
   expressionism, 406
   failure of abstraction, 402-403
   illusory staging defined, 395
   play selection, 196-197
   realism, 397-401
   symbolism, 405-406
Stylization, 466
Subject:
   playwright's material, 25
   universality in period drama, 409-410
Subjectivity, 466
Suggestivism, 399-400, 466
Sunken Bell, The (Hauptmann), 402
Superiority in comedy, 422
Surprise in comedy, 422
Suspense, 466
Sustaining emotional key, 171
Swan, The (Molnar), 381
Symbolism, 405-406, 467
Symbols, stage, 212-213
   conventional, 402-403
   representative, 401-402
Symmetrical balance, 100-101 *(Illus.)*

T

Table scenes, 344-346
Taking stage, 130-131 *(Illus.)*, 140, 467
Tea scenes, 346
   furniture, 324
Teaser, 306-307, 467
Technical actor, 289-293 *(see also* Actor)
Technical aspects of composition, 95-97
Technical director, duties, 348
Technical effects, 272
Technical rehearsals *(see* Mounting rehearsals)
Technique, 467
Technique of the Drama (Freytag), 30

Telescoping, 427, 439, 467
   in crowd scenes, 335
   cues, 184
Tempo:
   attention directed by, 174
   central staging, 390
   characteristics of, 177-180
   comedy of manners, 427
   definition, 176, 467
   determining, 180-182
   gaining variety, 182-186
   life, 173-174
   rule for, 181
   stage use, 174-175
   summary, 185-186
   symbols, 213
Tension, dramatic, 30-31 *(Illus.)*, 35
      (see also Key, emotional)
   muscular, 158-159, 163
   vocal, 299
Tentative casting, 238
Test audience, 262-263
Theatre, The (Cheney), 396
Theme, 467 *(see also* Subject)
   motivational unit, 76, 81
   script analysis, 203
There's Always Juliet (Van Druten), 263
Thomas, W. I., 12
Three Men on a Horse (Holm, Abbott), 429
Three Penny Opera (Brecht), 402
Throwaway line, 438-439, 467
Thunderbolt, The (Pinero), 409
Time for rehearsal, 246-247
Time of Your Life, The (Saroyan), 402-403
Timing, 467
   movement, 128
   stage business, 149
Tobacco Road (Caldwell), 397-398
Toller, Ernst, 402
Tonality, actor's, 235, 467
Topping, emotional key, 170-171, 467
Torchbearers, The (Kelly), 433
Tormentor, 206, 307, 363, 467
Tragedy, 196, 467
Tragi-comedy, 467
Translations, 412-413
Traveller, curtain, 306
Triangle in composition, 115 *(Illus.)*
Triangular setting, 310
Trim, 467

Tryouts:
 criteria, 214-216
 definition, 467
 forms, 217-218 *(Illus.)*
 information, 217
 invitations, 241
 musical show, 348-351
 organization, 217-219
 picture of aspirant, 218
 procedures, 224
 production assistant, 219
 record of commitments, 217
 recording system, 219
 seasonal auditions, 225-226
 special techniques, 224-225
Turning, 135-136 *(Illus.)*, 142
Type casting, 235-236

U

Unadjusted Girl, The (Thomas), 12
Uncover, 467
Underacting, 298
Underdirected play, 62-63
Underprojection, 178-179
Under-rehearsed blocking, 255
Understudy, 279, 468
Unit, motivational *(see* Motivational Unit)
Unities, 468
Unity:
 in casting, 237
 in composition, 98
 in performance, 272-273
Universality in play selection, 191-192
 in period drama, 409-410
Universals of comedy, 421-422
Upstage, 468

V

Van Druten, John, 263
Variety:
 casting, 237
 composition, 99
 definition, 181-182
 lack, in acting, 300
 performance, 273-274

play selection, 196-197
 tempo, 181-186, 175
Vaudeville, 468
Visibility, 149-150, 319, 340
Visual aspects of acting, 296-298
Visual projection *(see* Business, stage)
 emotion, 162-165
Visualization, director's qualification, 64
Vitality, director's qualification, 65
Vocal characteristics, 229
 control, 233-234
 pattern, 300
 projection of emotion, 162-165
 quality, 300
Voice of the Turtle, The (Van Druten), 147
Volume in projection, 300
Vowel sustension, 300

W

Wagner, Richard, 373
Waiting for Lefty (Odets), 346
Way of the World, The (Congreve), 414, 427
Welles, Orson, 416, 418
"Well-made play," 397, 468
Wilde, Oscar, 424, 426-427
Wilder, Thornton, 381
Windows, placement, 315 *(Illus.)*
 floor plan, 327
Wing, 363
Wing and drop setting, 306 *(Illus.)*, 363, 468
Wings, 468
Winterset (Anderson), 145, 310, 331, 334-335
Wisconsin Union Theatre, 258, 375
Woollcott, Alexander, 279
Women, The (Boothe), 380
Work, William, 198

Y

Yellow Jack (Howard), 7
You Can't Take It With You (Kaufman, Hart), 438